100 WALKS IN

Scotland

100 WALKS OF 2–10 MILES

First published 2003
Researched and written by Kate Barrett, Rebecca Ford, Ronald Turnbull, Hugh Taylor
and Moira McCrossan
Field checked and updated in 2007 by Dave McFadzean, Rosey Priestman, Hamish Scott,
Ronald Turnbull, Hugh Taylor and Moira McCrossan

Series Management: Bookwork Creative Associates
Series Editors: Sandy Draper and Marilynne Lanng
Designers: Elizabeth Baldin and Andrew Milne
Picture Research: Michelle Aylott
Proofreaders: Suzanne Juby and Pamela Stagg
Cartography provided by the Mapping Services Department of AA Publishing

Produced by AA Publishing
© Automobile Association Developments Limited 2008

Published by AA Publishing (a trading name of Automobile Association Developments Limited,
whose registered office is Fanum House, Basing View, Basingstoke, Hampshire RG21 4EA;
registered number 1878835)

This product includes mapping data licensed from the Ordnance
Survey® with the permission of the Controller of Her Majesty's
Stationery Office. © Crown Copyright 2008. All rights reserved. Licence number 100021153.

A03370

ISBN-13: 978-0-7495-5602-0

A CIP catalogue record for this book is available from the British Library.

The contents of this book are believed correct at the time of printing. Nevertheless, the
publishers cannot be held responsible for any errors or omissions or for changes in the
details given in this book or for the consequences of any reliance on the information it
provides. This does not affect your statutory rights. We have tried to ensure accuracy in this
book, but things do change and we would be grateful if readers would advise us of any
inaccuracies they may encounter.

We have taken all reasonable steps to ensure that these walks are safe and achievable by
walkers with a realistic level of fitness. However, all outdoor activities involve a degree of risk
and the publishers accept no responsibility for any injuries caused to readers whilst following
these walks. For more advice on walking safely see page 13. The mileage range shown on the
front cover is for guidance only – some walks may be less than or exceed these distances.

Visit AA Publishing's website www.theAA.com/travel

Colour reproduction by Keenes Group, Andover
Printed by Printer Trento Srl, Italy

Acknowledgements
The Automobile Association would like to thank the following photographers, companies and
picture libraries for their assistance in the preparation of this book.

3 AA/J Henderson; 18/9 AA/P Sharpe; 41 AA/D Hardley; 42 AA/M Alexander; 58/9 AA/S
Anderson, 74/5 AA/S Anderson; 116/7 AA/D Forss; 133 AA; 134 AA/S Gibson; 153 AA/R Elliot;
154 AA/J Smith; 167 AA/J Smith; 168 AA/J Smith; 187 AA/D Hardley; 188 AA/S Anderson; 204/5
AA/S Anderson; 218/9 AA/D Forss; 241 AA/R Weir; 242 AA/S Day; 270/1 AA/E Ellington; 293
AA/R Weir; 294 AA/J Smith; 306/7 AA/S Whitehorne; 328/9 AA/J Beazley; 346/7 AA/J Smith

Right: Looking down Glen Coe from the pass (Walks 69 and 70)

AA

100 WALKS IN

Scotland

100 WALKS OF 2–10 MILES

Contents

Contents

Contents

Contents

Rating

Each walk is rated for its relative difficulty compared to the other walks in this book. Walks marked ✦✦✦ are likely to be shorter and easier with little total ascent. The hardest walks are marked ✦✦✦.

Walking in Safety

For advice and safety tips see page 13.

Locator Map

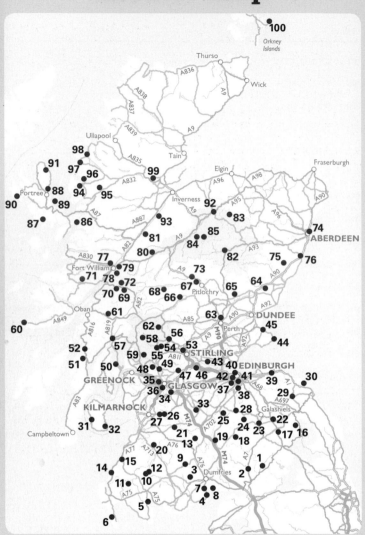

Legend

→	Walk Route		Built-up Area
1	Route Waypoint		Woodland Area
– – –	Adjoining Path	👫	Toilet
🔆	Viewpoint	P	Car Park
•	Place of Interest	🔲	Picnic Area
⌂	Steep Section	)(	Bridge

Introducing Scotland

Almost half the size of England, yet with barely one-fifth of its population, Scotland is a country of huge spaces and mountains on a grand scale not found anywhere else in Britain. It is also a nation steeped in history, the violent conflicts with its southern neighbour only one strand in a fascinating story.

Walking in Scotland

Scotland's western seaboard is littered with islands – some great, some tiny – and with vast fjord-like sea lochs which penetrate to the heart of the highest mountains. This is the crucible of what we now think of as the Scottish identity, and yet it is only a part of the story. In the south-east the borderlands have their own unique identity, their rounded sheep-shaven hilltops and deep valleys producing many tales and a character and people very different from the swirling Celtic kilts of the west. The south-west too has it's own stories, with its Celtic origins mixed up with Britons, Irish and Viking traditions.

Southern Uplands

The Southern Uplands stretch across the British mainland, forming a barrier between the Scots and the English, and in doing so hosting some of the most colourful and bloody chapters in Scotland's history. To the east, the high, rounded sheep walks of the Borders have always harboured proud families. In late medieval times they were the reivers, striking across into England at any time to take cattle and pillage their impoverished neighbours. The Union of the Crowns put an end to this lawlessness, but their balladry lived on and was immortalised by Robert Burns, Sir Walter Scott, and later, in the stirring words of Hugh MacDiarmid.

South-West Scotland

The south-west was relatively peaceful, by comparison, until religious conflict in the 17th century tore families apart and culminated in the atrocities of the 'Killing Times', when troops loyal to the Crown were set against Presbyterian worshippers who refused to accept the Episcopalian church. Many hundreds died for the cause and their haunting memorials still stand in remote valleys and on dramatic shorelines.

The Central Belt

The central belt – the incisions of the Forth and the Clyde – is where most people actually live. This is where Scotland's own Industrial Revolution set the country on course to become the engine at the heart of the British Empire. From the Clydeside yards came the ships that kept a maritime kingdom playing on a world stage. The two great rival cities of Edinburgh and Glasgow vie for supremacy. Glasgow has the people, the football teams and the exceptional architecture of Charles Rennie Mackintosh and Alexander 'Greek' Thomson. Edinburgh has the political capital, the royal capital, the festival and the tourists.

Highlands

But it is the Highlands that have come to define the myth of Scotland. Barely have you left Glasgow's northern suburbs and their breathtaking panoramas

Using this book

INFORMATION PANELS

An information panel for each walk shows its relative difficulty rating (see page 7), the distance and total amount of ascent (that is how much ascent you will accumulate throughout the walk). An indication of the gradients you will encounter is shown by the rating ▲▲▲ (fairly flat ground with no steep slopes) to ▲▲▲ (undulating terrain with several very steep slopes).

MINIMUM TIME

The minimum time suggested is for approximate guidance only. It assumes reasonably fit walkers and doesn't allow for stops.

SUGGESTED MAPS

Each walk has a suggested map. This will usually be a 1:25,000 scale Ordnance Survey Explorer map.

START POINTS

The start of each walk is given as a six-figure grid reference prefixed by two letters indicating which 100km square of the National Grid it refers to. You'll find more information on grid references on most Ordnance Survey maps.

DOGS

We have tried to give dog owners useful advice about how dog friendly each walk is. Please respect other countryside users. Keep your dog under control at all times, especially around livestock, and obey local bylaws and other dog control notices. Remember it is against the law to let your dog foul in many public areas, especially in villages and towns.

CAR PARKING

Many of the car parks suggested are public, but occasionally you may find you have to park on the roadside or in a lay-by. Please be considerate when you leave your car, ensuring that access roads or gates are not blocked and that other vehicles can pass safely. Remember that pub car parks are private and should not be used unless you have the owner's permission.

MAPS

Each walk is accompanied by a sketch map drawn from the Ordnance Survey map and appended with the authors' local observations. The scale of these maps varies from walk to walk. Some routes have a suggested option in the same area with a brief outline of the possible route. You will need a current Ordnance Survey map to make the most of these suggestions.

come into view. It is no coincidence that Loch Lomond is at the heart of Scotland's first National Park. This long freshwater lake, edged by silver birch and Scots pine, almost captures something of everything you will see as you travel further north – the highest mountains, the red deer lurking shyly waiting for the traffic to pass, the capercaillie shrieking its presence above the heather.

There are many differences in the Highland scene as you travel from west to east. The western mountains are jagged and rise up fiercely from the glens. In the east they are less spiky, but no less massive. On both sides of the A9, which serves as a convenient divider, you'll find deep valleys, sparkling lochs and remote beauty. The Spey Valley winds its way east and its crystal waters have long been famous for salmon fishing and as an ingredient in whisky, Scotland's national drink, which had its origins in these distant straths and glens.

Flora and Fauna

The red deer is truly the monarch of the Highland glens, and you will often glimpse their herds grazing on the lower braes. The best season is autumn, when the stags become territorial and the hills echo with their eerie roars. The Highlands are home to the wild cat too, a shy solitary creature, similar, but not to be confused with, a feral tabby. The golden eagle patrols the Highland skies, but the crowds flock to watch the handful of ospreys that return to the Rothiemurchus pine forests every year to nest. On Skye you may be lucky enough to identify the monstrous wings of a sea eagle. These enormous birds have been re-introduced to the Inner Hebrides, but are still extremely rare.

The wilder reaches of the Southern Uplands match the Highlands for their habitat diversity, but the feral goat is the animal you will most likely see, skulking away in a grassy hollow. On the Solway coast, the Caerlaverock salt marshes host over 12,000 barnacle geese in winter, as well as the most northerly colony of natterjack toads. Roe deer can often be seen in the woods and upland pasture, and red squirrels retain this bastion against the invasive grey.

Through the Seasons

This far north you can expect snow on the higher peaks well into May (see page 16, Scotland's Weather). Unless you have experience or training in dealing with the different hazards posed by winter walking, it is advisable to stay out of the mountains at this time of year. At low level, particularly in the west, you will find it can be very wet and windy at any time of the year – hill fog shrouds the mountains and you may wonder whether even the most expensive waterproofs will suffice. Walking is a very popular pastime throughout Scotland, but you will find the paths and tracks tend to be rougher than in England. A sturdy pair of modern walking boots will repay your investment quickly in terms of comfortable walking.

To avoid the midges, which can make walking very uncomfortable in the north and the west throughout the summer, get yourself a good insect repellent. Choose windier days and, if you are planning a trip, aim for the first few weeks in May or the middle of September. At these time you'll find the weather is often more settled, and you may be rewarded by clear skies, light winds and plenty of sunshine. Don't forget that daylight is relatively short at this latitude in the winter, so make sure you get an early start and carry a torch in your rucksack.

The Walks

There are few better places to start walking in Scotland than just over the border from England. In Newcastleton you will be barely a stone's throw from both Cumbria and Northumberland, and yet the accents will be Scottish (though the local newspaper may come from Carlisle). The Borders is a wild country, untamed in history and now only softened by the presence of millions of trees.

Shepherds and Poets

In Kirk Yetholm you will see the countless hordes who wearily traipse in from the south, completing the last section of England's Pennine Way in a different country. But you can steal a highlight by cutting into the Cheviots from here, to enjoy their airy heights from the back door.

This is a land of shepherds and poets and occasionally of men who embodied both. The remote Etterick Valley was the home of James Hogg, who combined his knowledge and love of the fells where he kept his sheep, with a sublime mastery of the Scots language. Hugh MacDiarmid is remembered on the hills above Langholm for his passionate words and his love for his homeland, while Dryburgh celebrates a view once favoured by Sir Walter Scott. John Buchan, creator of Richard Hannay, hero of *The Thirty-Nine Steps,* also trod these hills, as you'll discover if you visit the heights above Broughton.

The size of the Southern Uplands always comes as a surprise to walkers. The scale of the Devil's Beef Tub, near Moffat will cause you to catch your breath, and feel grateful the car park is relatively elevated in its position. You will understand why the Tweed Valley commands so great a place in history when you follow this great river as it winds away from Peebles or Dryburgh. Other border towns have their own stories. Selkirk was the birthplace of the explorer Mungo Park. Mary, Queen of Scots, came close to death from a fever while staying in a house near Jedburgh Abbey. At Traquair you'll discover the oldest continually inhabited residence in Scotland.

Bracing Peaks

The Uplands continue into the south-west and you will not be able to escape history here either, though a bracing climb of their highest peak, the Merrick, will force you to concentrate on your route finding and fitness rather than the origins of the landscape. You could restrict your explorations to the lowlands, but even these can be rough, as an English army discovered when they encountered a Scottish force led by Robert the Bruce in Glentrool. Hunting for the Wells of the Rees in bad weather might be equally tasking.

The summit of Criffel to the south of Dumfries, is perhaps an easier target for lovers of high places and grand views. Below you the marshes of the Nith Estuary and the Solway are guarded by the astonishing three-cornered stronghold of Caerlaverock Castle. Down the coast at Arbigland, apprentice seaman John Paul grew up to become Admiral John Paul Jones, first hero of the US Navy and scourge of British waters during the American War of Independence. Further west, Wigtown's maritime notoriety stems from the execution by drowning of two Covenanter women in 1685.

Walking in Safety

All these walks are suitable for any reasonably fit person, but less experienced walkers should try the easier walks first. Route finding is usually straightforward, but in many cases you will find that an Ordnance Survey map is an essential addition to the route maps and descriptions. In open country we have tried to select routes wherever possible that are clearly visible on the ground. However, in some of the more remote places, this is not always practical. Use common sense when approaching this kind of terrain. If the visibility is poor and you are not confident of your ability to find your way, do not be afraid of abandoning your plans and coming back another day, when the weather is fine. One of the joys of exploring Scotland on foot is the enormous scope of its countryside. The harder walks will still be there when you return.

RISKS

Although each walk here has been researched with a view to minimising the risks to the walkers who follow its route, no walk in the countryside can be considered to be completely free from risk. Walking in the outdoors will always require a degree of common sense and judgement to ensure that it is as safe as possible.

- Be particularly careful on cliff paths and in upland terrain, where the consequences of a slip can be very serious.

- Remember to check tidal conditions before walking on the seashore. You can be cut off by the incoming tide even in places where the risk appears slight, for instance on a well-populated beach front. In more remote areas, there will be little chance that anyone will be able to see you in distress.

- Some sections of route are by, or cross, busy roads. Take care and remember traffic is a danger even on minor country lanes.

- Be careful around farmyard machinery and livestock, especially if you have children with you. Keep your dog under tight control so as to avoid alarming farm animals. In shooting and stalking areas, seek local advice about access arrangements and cause as little disturbance to game as you can.

- Be aware of the consequences of changes in the weather and check the forecast before you set out. Carry spare clothing and a torch if you are walking in the winter months. Remember the weather can change very quickly at any time of the year, and in moorland and heathland areas, mist and fog can make route finding much harder. Don't set out in these conditions unless you are confident of your navigation skills in poor visibility. In summer remember to take account of the heat and sun; wear a hat and carry spare water.

- In remoter country, carry a whistle and a survival bag or tent too – if you have an accident you may have to wait several hours before help arrives. If you do have an accident requiring the emergency services, make a note of your position as accurately as possible and dial 999. Remember you cannot rely on getting a signal on a mobile phone in many mountain valleys, even if they are populated.

COUNTRYSIDE CODE

- Be safe, plan ahead and follow any signs.

- Leave gates and property as you find them.

- Protect plants and animals and take your litter home.

- Keep dogs under close control.

- Consider other people.

For more information about the Countryside Code visit
www.countrysideaccess.gov.uk/things_to_know/countryside_code

Industrial Origins

Looking back up the Nith Valley and its various tributaries, there are several places to attract the curious walker. The pretty village of Moniaive has long been a magnet to artists, but in nearby Glenkiln you'll find a whole valley dedicated to sculpture, particularly the work of Henry Moore. Wanlockhead, deep in the Lowther Hills, is not only Scotland's highest village but also boasts the country's second oldest subscription library. The oldest can be found in Leadhills, a mile (1.6km) or so over the hill into South Lanarkshire. It was industry which created these remote settlements, in this case lead mining. Two more walks in this book owe their origins to industrial colonisation of the hills. The immense iron foundries at Dunaskin were created because of the abundance of raw materials in the area, never mind that the area in question was 1,000ft (305m) up in the bleak uninhabited hills of South Ayrshire. Today you can visit a fascinating visitor centre on the site and walk among the ruins of the now deserted workers' village built on the hill above. Muirkirk is also an industrial settlement, built on the Ayrshire bogs and wastes. In 1787 an ironworks was founded here to exploit the locally mined coal and iron ore. A town with over 5,000 inhabitants grew up, then gradually slipped away as economic changes kicked in. Walk among the evocative buildings and see how the community has fought to survive. Similar tales can be told all over south-west Scotland, and now you can walk on disused railways and see the remains of former industry in the Irvine and Clyde valleys. One industrial site that has seen a renaissance in its fortunes is New Lanark, where Robert Owen's pioneering planned mill town is now a World Heritage Site.

Heart of the Nation

Several places claim to be the true heart of Scotland's story. Perhaps Edinburgh is among the most worthy. This truly great city commands several fine walks, not least those up to Arthur's Seat or around its breathtaking Georgian New Town. Edinburgh's backcloth is formed by the Pentland Hills, an odd corner of mountain rising from an upland plateau. Hidden on its northern flank is mysterious Rosslyn Glen, with its chapel and castle. Before you are done with the south, visit St Abb's Head, to see how wild the sea can be, then head across the Forth to visit Culross and Crail and then St Andrews.

Amazing Connection

With so much great walking to the south and the north, it seems a shame

---

PUBLIC TRANSPORT

Despite its size, and the remoteness of some of its communities, Scotland has an enviable public transport network which can deliver you to the start of a walk in some remarkably obscure places. The best place to start is on the internet with the Traveline Scotland website (www.traveline. org.uk, then select Scotland from the regional maps). This will give you timetable information covering the whole country and covers all forms of transport including some domestic flights. You can also access this service by phone on 0870 608 2 608. Trains in Scotland are run mostly by Scotrail (08457 48 49 50 for national rail inquiries). A national network of long distance coaches is run by Citylink, which will take you all the way to Skye and the west coast as well as principal stops on the A9 (www. citylink.co.uk). In central western Scotland transport is overseen by Strathclyde Passenger Transport, a local government body which ensures the various elements of the network are properly integrated. Most of the ferries you may encounter will be run by Caledonian Macbrayne (www.calmac.co.uk). Because of the size of the country and because getting to the outlying islands can be quite challenging, there is also a reasonable network of domestic flights, connecting Edinburgh, Glasgow and Aberdeen airports with much smaller local airfields.

to waste your time in the central belt of Scotland. But make sure you find time to visit the amazing Falkirk Wheel, joining the Forth and Clyde Canal with the Union Canal, and making east–west navigation possible again. And if you're in the mood for canal walking, the Kilsyth tow path on the Forth and Clyde can be combined with a return trip along the Antonine Wall, the last great frontier defence in the Roman Empire. A much later empire was created by the industrial might of Clydeside. Today, Glasgow can hold its own culturally with its rival in the east, and is worthy of a thorough exploration on foot.

DON'T MISS
Now the Skye Bridge has taken the thrill out of the journey across the Kyle of Lochalsh, the Caledonian Macbrayne crossing from Ardrossan to Brodick on Arran is probably the last great ferry trip for the walker. The island's profile stands out across the waters of the Firth of Clyde, with Goatfell and shapely Cir Mhor inviting the mountain lover, and the south end offering the promise of excellent walking at a lower level. 'Scotland in miniature' claim the tourist brochures, and they don't lie.

Highland Vision

From the Byne Hill in Ayrshire, Ailsa Craig stands prominently in the Firth of Clyde. Across these same waters to the north you can catch your first glimpse of the Highlands as the peaks of Arran rise from the sea. Another ferry will take you to the Cowal Peninsula, where Puck's Glen is a lovely corner of the former Benmore Estate, which includes a nationally important botanic garden. Glasgow folk flocked to these semi-wild sites in search of escape. You can see other targets of their enthusiasm – Carbeth, Loch Ard, Aberfoyle, Loch Katrine – the Highland boundary fault is lined by resorts and places of retreat. Climbers found their feet in the strange formations of the Whangie, and many a romance has blossomed on the shores of Loch Lomond.

Highlands Proper

The Highlands proper offer some of the best walking in Britain, but a lot of it is on the mountain tops and outside the remit of this collection. That isn't to say you won't be among the mountains though. Here you will find walks to the Lost Valley of Glen Coe, beneath the slopes of Ben Nevis, Britain's highest peak, and in the Coire Lagan on Skye, where the awesome Cuillin Hills rise straight up out of the sea. Skye is a good place to visit at any time of the year for the range of walking it offers. The weirdly shaped Quiraing is fascinating to explore, little Raasay will give an island experience all by itself.

In Search of Monsters

Mull too, is worth crossing to, even if it's just to hop over to Iona, the magical far-off isle where Scottish Kings were laid to rest. It rivals Kilmartin Glen in importance in Scottish history, but cannot claim the crowning stones of Dunadd.

In the far north-west, Flowerdale and Torridon will offer you glimpses of a truly vast and mostly uninhabited wilderness, though you might prefer the gentle seashore around Shieldaig. The shores of Loch Ness were once home to Aleisteir Crowley, though the notorious diabolist never saw the famous monster.

To the East

Crossing over to the east, you will find more high mountains and deep glens. This is the home of the Scots pine and the lovely Rothiemurchus woodlands. You'll also find plenty of royal stories and whisky to pursue at Braemar and Glenlivet. At the mouth of Glen Tilt stands Blair Athol, where the duke is allowed to raise his own army. Fortingall bizarrely claims to have been the birthplace of Pontius Pilate. Lovely Glen Prosen opens out to Kirriemuir, which definitely was the birthplace of J M Barrie, creator of Peter Pan.

But for all the places that claim to be the crucible in which Scotland was made, perhaps the true honour should go to Stirling. Much fought over, in virtually every war that was ever fought for Scotland, it spans the gap between Highland and Lowland, with views to both.

Scotland's Weather

Scots will tell you that Scotland does not have a climate: it only has weather. This is by far the most mountainous area of Britain, and the only part to reach over 4,000ft (1,220m), so weather conditions can be extreme. Its position on the edge of the continental landmass of Europe, surrounded on three sides by sea, means that the weather is always varied. And it's by no means all bad – plenty of east coast towns have less rain than Rome, and remember that conditions can vary dramatically in just a short distance.

In general terms, the eastern side of Scotland tends to be cool and dry, the western side milder and wetter. The occasional outbreak of haar (summer sea mist) along the coast is often a sign of bright sunshine only a little way inland. At any time of year you are likely to meet some form of rain, but with Scotland's ever-changing weather patterns, the chances are that it will not last for long.

Best of Times

The best times of the year for sunny weather are in the spring and early summer (April and June), when the countryside also looks its best. In high summer (July and August) the weather is changeable – it may be hot and sunny, but it can also be cloudy and wet. Generally late summer and early autumn (September and October) are more settled and there's a better chance of good weather, but nothing is guaranteed, and mist can settle in the glens for days at a time. Late autumn and winter (November to March) can be cold, dark, wet and dreich (dreary), but you can also have sparkling, clear, sunny days of frost, when the light is brilliant. Winter can bring severe conditions of wind and snow to the Highlands and high ground, and these should not be underestimated. The cities are great to visit any time regardless of the weather.

Extremes

Scottish weather centres have recorded Britain's lowest temperatures:-17°F (-27°C) at Braemar in January 1982, and again at Altnaharra in 1995. They also claim Britain's strongest gust of wind – a massive 173mph (278kph), recorded on the top of Cairn Gorm in March 1986. Sun-lovers should avoid Cape Wrath in January – it recorded just half an hour of sunshine during the whole of that month in 1983. And Fort William regularly tops the list of the wettest towns in the UK. Scotland's highest temperature was recorded in Dumfries in 1908 – 91°F (33°C), and was almost matched in more recent years at Kelso in 1990.

Daylight

The amount of daylight varies significantly in Scotland throughout the year, and because of its latitude, may vary considerably from the rest of Britain. So, at the time of the summer solstice or 'longest day', around 21 June, the sun will be above the horizon for 17 hours 35 minutes in Glasgow and more than 19 hours in Shetland (the 'simmer dim'), but only 16 hours 39 minutes in London. At the winter solstice, around 21 December, the sun appears above the horizon for 7 hours and 49 minutes in London, but only just scrapes over the horizon in Shetland for 6 hours.

There are two days of the year when day and night are of equal length, and they are associated with high tides and sometimes extreme weather conditions. The spring equinox falls around 21 March and the autumn equinox around 22 September.

Note that, by the rules of British Summer Time (BST), clocks go forward by 1 hour towards the end of March (Greenwich Mean Time or GMT +1), and revert to GMT at the end of October.

www.metoffice.com

The official government body in charge of weather forecasting across the whole of the United Kingdom, offers a daily forecast plus an overall view of the weather in forthcoming weeks. It is the source of the UK's shipping forecast, a much-loved national institution, broadcast daily on BBC Radio 4.

www.accuweather.com

A comprehensive and user-friendly site offering weather forecasts for the day and forthcoming week, a sailing forecast, a climate guide for selected Scottish cities, and in summer, a grass pollen count for the whole United Kingdom. There is also an online weather service aimed specifically at outdoor users.

Mountaincall
www.metoffice.gov.uk

Weathercall
www.weathercall.co.uk

Overleaf: The Pass of Glencoe (Walks 69 and 70)

Remembering the Reivers at Newcastleton

A quiet walk through borderlands where cattle raiding was once a part of everyday life for the local inhabitants.

1

DISTANCE 5.75 miles (9.3km)   **MINIMUM TIME** 2hrs 45min

ASCENT/GRADIENT 689ft (210m) ▲▲▲   **LEVEL OF DIFFICULTY** ✦✦✦

PATHS Quiet byroads and farm tracks, one grassy climb

LANDSCAPE Rolling borderlands and moors

SUGGESTED MAP OS Explorer 324 Liddesdale & Kershope Forest

START/FINISH Grid reference: NY 483875

DOG FRIENDLINESS Dogs on lead; sheep, cows and ponies graze on route

PARKING Douglas Square

PUBLIC TOILETS Langholm Street, next to fire station

It might seem quiet today, but the area around Newcastleton was once what tabloid newspapers would now describe as 'war-torn'. Ownership of these borderlands was hotly disputed between England and Scotland for hundreds of years and there were frequent battles and skirmishes. You'll pass a reminder of those turbulent days on this walk.

Raids and Revenge

Because places like Newcastleton were so remote from the centres of power in both London and Edinburgh, they were difficult to defend and had a reputation for lawlessness. Feuds often developed between powerful local families, and violent raids and cases of cattle rustling (reiving) were common – cattle were a valuable asset. These were ruthless people who could probably have shown the Vikings a thing or two.

A raid would commonly be followed by an illegal revenge attack (which of course was better fun, being illegal) or sometimes a legal 'Hot Trod'. This was a pursuit mounted immediately after a raid and had strict rules – including one stating that a lighted turf had to be carried if the trod crossed the border. When reivers were caught they were often taken hostage (the ransom money was very handy), taken prisoner, or even killed. Not surprisingly the countryside became studded with sturdy castles and fortified 'pele' towers, so that people could better defend themselves.

The most powerful family in this area were the Armstrongs, the principal reiving clan in the Borders. They were extremely influential and held large tracts of land. Their main seat was Mangerton Tower, the rather pitiful remains of which you can see on this walk. The Armstrongs were said to be able to muster 3,000 mounted men whenever they wished to launch a raid into England. They were ruthless and violent, running a rather successful protection racket as one of their money-making ventures. Imagine the mafia with cows and you'll get the picture.

It wasn't until the Union of the Crowns took place in 1603, following the death of Queen Elizabeth I, that the Border wars ceased and the power of the reiving clans was finally dispersed. Keen to gain control and make his mark as an effective ruler of the new united kingdom, James VI of Scotland (James I of England) banned weapons and established mounted forces to police the area. Reiving families – often identified with the help of local informers – were scattered and members transported or even executed.

After Archibald Armstrong of Mangerton was executed in 1610, the Armstrongs lost their lands to the Scotts, another powerful local family. However, the family didn't disappear and members of this once fearsome tribe have continued to make their mark on the world. Most famous of all must be Neil Armstrong, who carried a fragment of Armstrong tartan when he stepped on to the surface of the moon, in 1969.

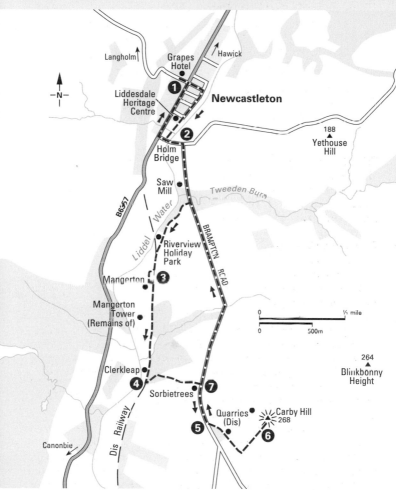

WALK 1 DIRECTIONS

❶ From Douglas Square in the centre of Newcastleton, with your back to the Grapes Hotel, walk along Whitchester Street (or any of the other streets opposite) and go down to the river, the Liddel Water. Turn right, then walk along the river bank and join the footpath downstream to reach Holm Bridge. Here, turn left at the top of the steps and then cross over the bridge.

❷ After about 100yds (91m), turn right and follow the Brampton Road, passing static caravans on either side. You'll eventually pass an old saw mill with a corrugated iron roof and will then reach the Tweeden Burn Bridge. Cross the bridge and walk uphill, then turn right and join the metalled track signed for Riverview Holiday Park. Continue on this road until you near the farm buildings.

❸ At farm entrance, fork left on to the bed of the old railway line, which has joined you from the right. This line once linked Carlisle to Edinburgh but was closed following the Beeching cuts of 1963. Follow the line as it leads past the remains of Mangerton Tower, in a field to your right, and continue ahead until you reach Clerkleap cottage.

❹ Walk 50yds (45m) beyond the cottage and turn left over a

rotting gate. A rough path leads up left then turns right to join a rough track. This leads through woodland and on, uphill, to join the road by Sorbietrees farm. Turn right now and walk along the road, past the farm, to a small stand of conifers on the left. Turn left through the gate.

❺ Bear right now and head up the left-hand side of the trees. Walk past the top of the wood following a dry-stone wall up below a former quarry to the field's top corner. Climb over the field gate ahead. Now open grassy slopes lead up left, to the cairn and fallen walls on the summit of Carby Hill. The views are truly great from here. Known locally as Caerba Hill, this was the site of a prehistoric settlement.

❻ Retrace your steps to reach the road again, then turn right and walk back past Sorbietrees farm.

❼ At the farm, continue on the main road as it bears right and follow it back over the Tweeden Burn Bridge and up to the Holm Bridge. Cross the bridge and walk straight on for 100yds (91m), then turn right on to the B6357 and walk back to the village square via the little heritage centre.

A Poet's Passions at Langholm

An exhilarating climb is followed by a more gentle stroll past Hugh MacDiarmid's memorial.

> **DISTANCE** 3.75 miles (6km)   **MINIMUM TIME** 2hrs
>
> **ASCENT/GRADIENT** 919ft (280m) ▲▲▲   **LEVEL OF DIFFICULTY** ✚✚✚
>
> **PATHS** Firm hill paths and tarmac roads
>
> **LANDSCAPE** Lush green borderlands and fine views
>
> **SUGGESTED MAP** OS Explorer 323 Eskdale & Castle O'er Forest
>
> **START/FINISH** Grid reference: NY 364849
>
> **DOG FRIENDLINESS** Keep on lead as there are plenty of sheep
>
> **PARKING** Riverside car park (free)
>
> **PUBLIC TOILETS** At car park and off main street of Langholm

The Scots have long been passionate about their independence and take great pride in their rich culture. On this walk you'll pass a memorial to one of the founding fathers of the modern Scottish nationalist movement – the poet Hugh MacDiarmid.

A Cultural Giant

MacDiarmid, whose real name was Christopher Murray Grieve, was born in Langholm in 1892 and is considered one of Scotland's leading 20th-century poets, and deserves to rank alongside Robert Burns in cultural importance. His early working life was spent in journalism, working in Montrose and London, and he then turned to writing poetry. A man of passionate views – he was a communist and nationalist – his verses were written in local dialect, mixed with words taken from the older Scottish tongue. His volumes of poetry included *Sangschaw*, his first book which was published in 1925, *Penny Wheep* (1926) and *A Drunk Man Looks at the Thistle* (1926). His works sparked a renewed interest in Scottish language and culture and he became a central figure in the country's literary revival.

Championing Home Rule

During the 1930s he moved to Shetland, where he continued to write. He made a great impression on those who met him there and was once described as: 'Unmistakably the genius, with tensely thoughtful features and smouldering, deep-set eyes… (he is) almost rustically Scots… wearing a kilt and a plaid, both of bright tartan.' Years later another writer was to describe him as 'a magnificent mouse of a man'. He was by this time involved in the early nationalist movement, which had started in Scotland after the First World War and grew in strength during the 1920s. Together with other writers, such as Lewis Spence and Neil Gunn, MacDiarmid voiced a desire for Home Rule for Scotland. The movement grew into the Scottish National Party which was formed in 1934.

After the Second World War, MacDiarmid moved back to the Borders, living with his wife in a two-room labourer's cottage near Biggar. It was simple in the extreme and had no water or electricity, but it was from here that he embarked on lecture tours all over the world. He would often travel to Edinburgh, where he would drink with other Scottish writers like Norman MacCaig and Sorley MacLean.

MacDiarmid died in 1978, his love of Scotland as strong and passionate as ever. He was buried in Langholm, against the wishes of the local 'gentry' who disliked his radical views. Above the door of his old home are inscribed the telling words:

> The rose of all the world is not for me
> I want for my part
> Only the little white rose of Scotland
> That smells sharp and sweet and breaks the heart

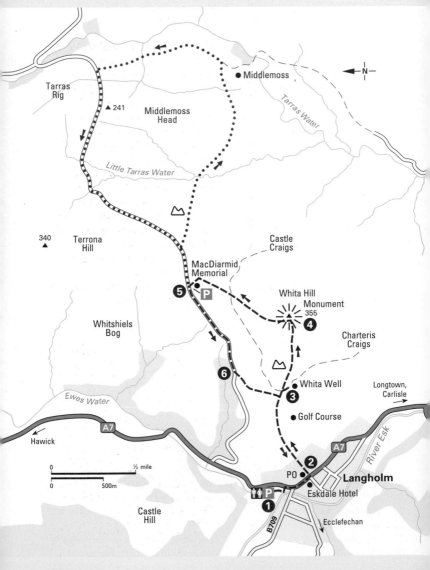

WALK 2 DIRECTIONS

1 Cross grass downstream, then go through a hedge gap on the left to pass through a small garden to the A7 above. Head into Langholm along the High Street to the post office on the left.

WHERE TO EAT AND DRINK

The Eskdale Hotel serves a good selection of bar food. Next door is the Flo'er O' Eskdale coffee shop that serves scones and sandwiches (closed on Sundays).

2 Immediately past the post office, turn left up Kirk Wynd. It becomes a tarred path, then a rough track running up to the left of the golf course to a gate. Follow the grassy path up and slightly right to reach a green seat beside Whita Well, a natural spring.

3 Now take the path to the left of the seat, running steeply up the hill. Follow it under a line of pylons and up to the top of Whita Hill. There are stone steps up to the monument, a 100ft (30m) high obelisk commemorating Sir John Malcolm, a famous soldier, diplomat and scholar.

4 From St John Malcolm's monument, walk back a few paces to join the wide gravel track that runs in front of it, then turn right. It's easy walking now, following this clear track downhill. Eventually you'll reach a metal sculpture on the left-hand side. The sculpture, which resembles an open book, was created by Jake Harvey and is a memorial to Hugh MacDiarmid.

5 Bear left past the sculpture to a small car park, and turn left. You now simply follow the road as it winds downhill – it's quite a long stretch but it's fairly quiet. Go back under the line of pylons then, just after a copse on your right-hand side, take the path on the left, signposted 'Langholm Walks 10'.

6 Follow this footpath, slightly uphill and then above a wall, where it runs through a small boggy patch. After this you shortly return to the gate you reached on your outward journey. Turn right, through the gate, and retrace your outward route.

EXTENDING THE WALK

You can extend this walk to take in a remote section of moorland, by heading right at Point **5**, the MacDiarmid memorial. Follow the road over a cattle grid and a short distance downhill to a waymarker on the right. A small path runs down towards the distant Middlemoss farm. After a footbridge over Little Tarras Water, it bends slightly right, following the reedy hollow of an older trackway. Bear left alongside a field wall, on a rough track then a path through two kissing gates, to Middlemoss's access track. Follow it left to the road, and turn left back to Point **5**.

WHILE YOU'RE THERE

Near by is Ecclefechan, the birthplace of Thomas Carlyle (1795–1881). An historian, critic and essayist, Carlyle was one of the most influential thinkers of the 19th century. His house is now a small museum. Just 8 miles (12.9km) north of Langholm, where the White Esk meets the Black Esk, was the location of a Handfasting Fair. This was held every August from the 16th to 18th centuries. Couples would pair off for a year's trial marriage and return the following year to declare whether they would be married or not.

The Glenkiln Outdoor Sculptures

Discover the works of Henry Moore, Epstein and Rodin in a unique countryside setting.

DISTANCE *4 miles (6.4km)*   **MINIMUM TIME** *2hrs 30min*

ASCENT/GRADIENT *312ft (95m)* ▲▲▲   **LEVEL OF DIFFICULTY** +++

PATHS *Country roads, farm tracks, open hillside*

LANDSCAPE *Sculptures, hills, woodland and reservoir*

SUGGESTED MAP *OS Explorer 321 Nithsdale & Dumfries*

START/FINISH *Grid reference: NX 839784*

DOG FRIENDLINESS *Keep on lead on farmland, particularly at lambing time*

PARKING *Car park in front of statue of John the Baptist*

PUBLIC TOILETS *None on route or near by*

During the mid-1950s Tony Keswick, a Dumfriesshire landowner with a penchant for sculpture, acquired a copy of August Rodin's *John the Baptist* from the Musée Rodin in Paris. Keswick did not hide it away in a darkened vault or even in a gallery. It stands today, as it always has, in open countryside, atop a hillock, its outstretched arm beckoning across the water of Glenkiln Reservoir.

An Amazing Collection

Keswick was given the hill farm of Glenkiln by his father in 1924 as a 21st birthday present but he rarely visited it until the 1950s. That first Rodin was the start of an amazing collection of art. On a visit to the studio of Henry Moore, he immediately recognised that Moore's *Standing Figure* would be ideal placed on a large flat boulder that stood by the roadside near the farm. This was followed by Moore's *King and Queen*. Of the six casts made, the Glenkiln piece is the only one in a private collection. Keswick tried a number of sites around his land before placing it on a hillside overlooking the reservoir. The sculptures look out serenely over their domain, separate from, yet part of the landscape that surrounds them.

Hard Times

Epstein's *Visitation* is in the collection of the Tate Gallery in London. Keswick obtained Epstein's own copy purely by chance. He was with the artist when a group of workmen arrived to cart the work off to melt it down. Epstein, although famous, was so hard up that he was selling some of his work for scrap to pay the foundry bill for a bust of Winston Churchill he was working on. Keswick was appalled and promptly bought the statue. It depicts the Virgin Mary with folded hands, head slightly bowed and an expression of utmost serenity on her face. She's located a bit off the beaten track and surrounded by Scots pine within the tumbledown walls of a long abandoned sheep fold. To stumble, seemingly almost by accident, on this figure, particularly on a slightly dark and misty winter's day, when the sheep have gathered around her, is one of the magical moments of Glenkiln.

GLENKILN

Glenkiln has been a popular attraction since Tony Keswick placed his first sculpture out of doors. He positively encouraged people to come and see the collection and today it remains as a tribute not just to the work of the artists but to the memory of a remarkable man who saw sculpture as a complement to nature.

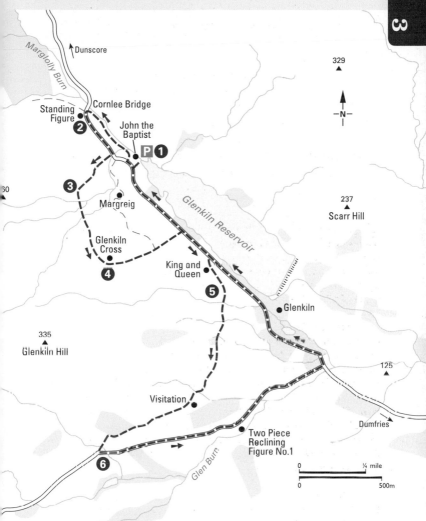

WALK 3 DIRECTIONS

❶ From the car park in front of the statue *John the Baptist*, return to the main road and turn right. Cross a cattle grid then turn right and go past the statue to the Marglolly Burn. Turn left and walk along the bank towards Cornlee Bridge. Just before the bridge turn left and head back to the road. Henry Moore's *Standing Figure* is before you at the junction with a farm road.

❷ Turn left and head back along the main road. Just before the entrance to Margreig farm

27

on the right is a muddy track running across the field to a gate in the dry-stone wall. Head up and through the gate then keep straight ahead, uphill and towards a telephone pole. At the pole veer left and follow the track uphill. The Glenkiln Cross should now be visible in front of you.

WHILE YOU'RE THERE

Enjoy a visit to Ellisland, the Dumfriesshire farm where Robert Burns wrote 'Tam O' Shanter'. Situated on the A76, a few miles north of Dumfries, this is where Burns came with his bride, Jean Armour, to start a new life here as a farmer. Unfortunately the land was poor, the venture failed and the poet moved to Dumfries and life as an exciseman.

❸ There are several footpaths and tracks available here. Take the one that is closest to a large tree in front of you. Cross over a burn at the tree and then take the path that skirts to the left of it. Veer right and then head for the high ground. Once the cross comes into view again head directly towards it.

❹ From the cross turn to face Glenkiln Reservoir and then head downhill towards a telephone pole. Go through a gate in the fence at the bottom of the hill and then turn right on to the road. After a short distance along here a farm track leads uphill to the

WHERE TO EAT AND DRINK

This is a fairly remote spot and ideal on warm days for a peaceful picnic. Alternatives include the George Hotel in the picturesque village of Dunscore about 6 miles (9.7km) away or the Craigdarroch Arms in the even more picturesque village of Moniaive beyond that. Both are friendly family-run establishments providing good wholesome food in a traditional country bar setting.

right. Go through a gate and on to it. To your right on the hillside is Henry Moore's *King and Queen*.

❺ Continue on this track. Go through a gate, pass a small wooded area on your right and then bare hillside until you spot a small stand of Scots pine on the left. Leave the road at this point and continue to the trees and Epstein's *Visitation*. Return to the road and then continue to the end where you go through a gate, cross over a bridge then turn left on to the road.

❻ Go downhill on this road for 0.5 mile (800m), crossing a cattle grid. Just before the end of the conifer plantation on the left, look out for Moore's *Two Piece Reclining Figure No. 1* on your right. Follow the road all the way downhill from here, turn left at the junction and continue on this road until you reach the car park.

WHAT TO LOOK OUT FOR

It's easy to miss, but just after going through the gate on the farm track past *King and Queen*, look out for a small block of Dumfriesshire sandstone on the right. It's weathered and a bit faded but you can still make out the inscription. On one side is 'Glenkiln' and on the other 'Henry Moore 1898–1986'. This was Tony Keswick's personal memorial to his favourite sculptor.

The Solway Shore from Carsethorn to Arbigland

Visit the birthplace of John Paul Jones,
the 'father of the American Navy'.

DISTANCE 5.5 miles (8.8km)	MINIMUM TIME 2hrs 30min
ASCENT/GRADIENT 82ft (25m) ▲▲▲	LEVEL OF DIFFICULTY +++
PATHS Rocky seashore, woodland tracks and country road	
LANDSCAPE Seashore, woodland and pasture	
SUGGESTED MAP OS Explorer 313 Dumfries & Dalbeattie, New Abbey	
START/FINISH Grid reference: NX 993598	
DOG FRIENDLINESS Good walk for dogs	
PARKING Car park by beach at Carsethorn	
PUBLIC TOILETS At John Paul Jones Museum	

The man hailed in the USA as the 'father of the American Navy' was born John Paul in a poor gardener's cottage at Arbigland, on the Solway coast in 1745.

Young Seaman

At the age of 13 John signed up as an apprentice seaman journeying to Virginia on the *Friendship of Whitehaven*. He later signed on as third mate on a slave ship, the *King George of Whitehaven*. He lasted two years and advanced to first mate before he quit in disgust with the slave trade. On his passage home he acquired his first command when the captain and mate of his vessel died of fever. As the only qualified man left, John took control and brought the ship safely home. The owners rewarded him with permanent command. He had a reputation for a fiery temper and was once charged with murder but found not guilty. In 1773 he fled the West Indies, after killing the ringleader of a mutiny, and went to Virginia. It was around this time that he changed his name to John Paul Jones.

American Naval Officer

In the lead up to the American Revolution (War of American Independence) when Congress was forming a 'Continental Navy', Jones offered his services and was commissioned as a first lieutenant on the *Alfred* in 1775. Later, as captain of the *Providence*, he advised Congress on naval regulations. In 1778, after a daring hit-and-run raid on Whitehaven, he sailed across the Solway to Kirkcudbright Bay to kidnap the Earl of Selkirk and ransom him for American captives. However the earl was not at home and the raiding party had to be content with looting the family silver.

Famous Battle

In September 1779, as commodore of a small squadron of French ships, John Paul Jones engaged his ship the *Bonhomme Richard* with the superior HMS *Serapis* and HMS *Countess of Scarborough* off Flamborough Head. After a dreadful four-hour fight, in which Jones was injured and his ship sunk, he eventually won the battle, transferred his crew to the *Serapis* and sailed for Holland with his prisoners and booty.

John Paul Jones died in France in 1792 and his body lay in an unmarked grave for over a century. His remains were eventually taken back to the USA amid great ceremony and he was finally laid to rest in the chapel crypt of the Annapolis Naval Academy in 1913.

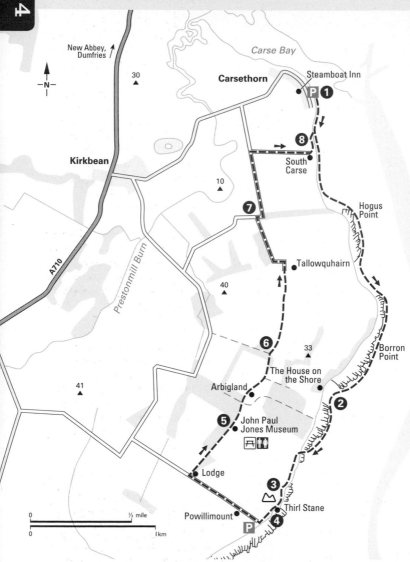

WALK 4 DIRECTIONS

1 From the car park at Carsethorn head down on to the beach and turn right. Continue walking along the

shore for approximately 2 miles (3.2km). The beach at this point is sandy and may be strewn with driftwood, but if the tide has come in you will be walking over more rocky ground.

2 After you reach The House on the Shore, which is beside the beach on your right, continue around the small headland and along the beach to the next one, then look for a faint path heading uphill to join a well-defined track that heads alongside a stone wall.

3 Continue along this track and then descend steeply to arrive at the beach beside an impressive natural rock arch called the Thirl Stane. You can go through the arch to the sea if the tide is in, although if the tide is out on this part of the coast, the sea will be far off in the distance.

WHERE TO EAT AND DRINK

The Steamboat Inn, just opposite the car park at Carsethorn, has been trading since 1813 and, while offering up-to-the-minute comforts, still retains the atmosphere of those bygone days when immigrants left here to take the steamer to Liverpool for onward transport to the colonies. A real fire, real ales and a reputation for the best food in the district makes this a natural choice for walkers and families.

4 Continue from here along the rocks on the pebble shore and up a grassy bank until you reach a car park. Exit the car park on to a lane. Continue on the lane past Powillimount. Turn right when you get to a lodge house on the right-hand side and walk along the estate road to reach the cottage birthplace of John Paul Jones.

5 There is a fascinating small museum here. Continue along the road past the gates to Arbigland, on to the road signed 'No vehicular traffic'. Follow the road as it turns right and along the side of some of the Arbigland Estate buildings.

WHAT TO LOOK OUT FOR

The rocks between Hogus Point and Arbigland date from the Carboniferous era some 345 million years ago. Fossils in this area are well exposed and those of coral, cuttlefish, fish vertebrae, shells and tooth plates can be found. Near the beach at Powillimount look for fossilised tree ferns.

6 When the road turns left at a cottage, go right on to a dirt track. Follow the dirt track until it emerges on to a surfaced road next to Tallowquhairn to your right. Take the road away from the farm, turning sharply left around some houses, then right and continue to a T-junction.

7 Turn right and follow this road round to the left. Follow the long straight road as far as the right turn to South Carse. Go along the farm road and straight through the farm steading as far as you can go, then turn left.

8 To return to the shore again, walk along a footpath passing a brightly coloured caravan and the rear of some cottages. Look out for a narrow track heading downhill to the right, giving access to the beach. Turn left along the beach to the car park.

WHILE YOU'RE THERE

The Victorian Shambellie House, just outside New Abbey, contains a unique collection of costumes and is part of the National Museums of Scotland. The clothes are displayed in a series of tableaux. In the dining room is an after-dinner game of carpet bowls c1905 while two women in 1920s evening dress are playing the gramophone in the library and a 1930s bride is getting dressed in the bedroom.

On the Trail of the Wigtown Martyrs

*Visit the memorial to two women drowned
at the stake for their religion.*

DISTANCE 4 miles (6.4km)	**MINIMUM TIME** 3hrs
ASCENT/GRADIENT 98ft (30m) ▲▲▲	**LEVEL OF DIFFICULTY** ✦✦✦

PATHS Roads, old railway tracks and pavements

LANDSCAPE River estuary, pasture and woodland

SUGGESTED MAP OS Explorer 311 Wigtown, Whithorn & The Machars

START/FINISH Grid reference: NX 439547

DOG FRIENDLINESS Keep on lead near livestock

PARKING At Wigtown harbour

PUBLIC TOILETS None on walk

On 11 May, 1685, two Wigtown women were dragged out on to the salt marshes near the town and tied to stakes. Eighteen-year-old Margaret Wilson and her companion, Margaret McLaughlan, aged 63, had been sentenced to death for their religious beliefs.

The Killing Times

This was during that period in Scots history known as the 'Killing Times' when the Covenanters were persecuted for their beliefs. They were called Covenanters after a petition signed in Greyfriars churchyard in Edinburgh, in 1638, and thereafter in churches throughout the country. The Covenant reaffirmed the belief of Scottish Presbyterians that there was a special relationship between God, as head of the Church, and the people. This ran contrary to the belief of the Stuart monarchy in the divine right of kings. Charles II sought to control the Church by appointing Episcopalian bishops and ministers. Presbyterian ministers were ousted from their churches, but simply took to the hills with their congregations and held open-air services called conventicles. Troops patrolled the hills and moors and if they came across these illegal meetings, broke them up by taking some worshippers prisoner and killing others on the spot.

Sentenced to Death

Margaret Wilson and Margaret McLaughlan were two Wigtownshire Covenanters who were tried in the tollbooth at Wigtown for rebellion and taking part in several battles against the Crown. Found guilty, they were sentenced to death by drowning and taken to the tidal Bladnoch River. When they reached the execution site, the soldiers placed the older woman's stake further out in the estuary so that she would die first and thus terrify her younger companion to the point where she would yield and swear an oath to the King. But this was to no avail. While Margaret McLaughlan drowned the younger woman sang the 25th Psalm and then, as the water started to rise around her, began to pray out loud. The water covered her but after a while the soldiers pulled her up, revived her and asked her if she would pray for the King. A friend cried out to her urging her to say 'God save the King', but all she uttered was 'God save him if he will, for it is his salvation I desire'. On hearing this some of her relatives urged the commanding officer to release her. He asked her to swear the oath or be returned to the water. She refused saying 'I will not, I am one of Christ's children, let me go'. But they would not let her go and she was again thrust under the water until she died.

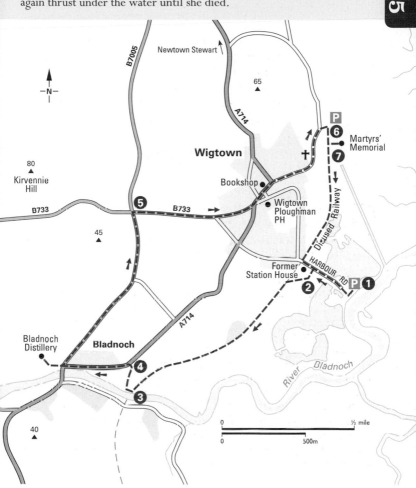

WALK 5 DIRECTIONS

1 Leave the car park, turn right and head uphill on a narrow country lane called Harbour Road. The house on the left near the top of the road was the former station house for Wigtown. Just before it you will see a farm gate on the left. Go through it and on to a farm track.

2 Follow the track to the point where it goes through another gate then veer right and climb up the old railway embankment. This has a good grassy surface along its entire length. Proceed along the length of the embankment.

3 A wall across the track will stop you at the point where the former railway bridge carried the track across the River Bladnoch. Turn right and go down the side of the embankment and cross a gate into a field. Veer right and head across the field to the far corner then go through a gate on to the main road.

WHERE TO EAT AND DRINK

Café Rendezvous is a walker-friendly place that serves first-class food, including home-made soup, salads, sandwiches and a small but tasty selection of main dishes. After a long walk refuel on a massive portion of mouthwatering Irish stew or the Wigtown Bay chowder made from freshly caught local fish. Fresh, high-quality local ingredients, a top chef and friendly staff are the key elements in the success of this family-run establishment. Children are welcome in the dining room.

4 Turn left and walk through the hamlet of Bladnoch. At the junction by a roundabout, cross the road to enter the Bladnoch Distillery car park. After visiting the distillery head back out of the car park and turn left at the roundabout. Continue along this road (the B7005) for approximately 1 mile (1.6km) until you get to a crossroads.

5 Turn right on to the B733 and walk along it to reach Wigtown. When you reach the centre of the town bear left round the square and head towards the large and impressive former county buildings. Pass them on your right, then the church and war memorial on your left and continue downhill. Eventually turn right into the car park for the Martyrs' Memorial.

6 Walk through the car park and then turn right and head along the path leading to the Martyrs' Memorial. Turn left and walk out over the sands on a specially constructed wooden causeway to reach the poignant memorial erected on the spot where the two women were drowned.

7 Return to the path and turn left. Go through a kissing gate then another gate, slightly below the level you are walking on and to the left. At the end of the path go through another gate in front of the station house, turn left on to Harbour Road and return to the car park.

WHILE YOU'RE THERE

Don't miss a visit to the Bookshop in North Mains Street. It has the largest stock of second-hand books in Scotland, displayed in a Georgian building that is a labyrinth of rooms crammed with floor-to-ceiling bookshelves. Comfortable seats can be found in odd corners and by the fire where browsers can sit and, well, browse. The coffee is always on and always fresh. And it's free.

WHAT TO LOOK OUT FOR

The salt marshes along the last section of the walk are rich in plant and animal life. Look for eel grass, the only flowering plant that can grow under the sea, and glasswort which used to be burned and its ashes used in glass production. You may spot curlews wading in the marshes using their long curved beaks to probe the mud for the tiny invertebrates that inhabit the creeks and pools.

Port Logan or Fictional Ronansay?

*A linear coastal route to a fishing village
where everything is not as it seems.*

DISTANCE 2.5 miles (4km) **MINIMUM TIME** 2hrs

ASCENT/GRADIENT 492ft (150m) ▲▲▲ **LEVEL OF DIFFICULTY** +++

PATHS Shoreline, country lanes and hill tracks, 1 stile

LANDSCAPE Hill, pasture and shoreline

SUGGESTED MAP OS Explorer 309 Stranraer & The Rhins

START/FINISH Grid reference: NX 097411

DOG FRIENDLINESS Keep on lead near livestock

PARKING Public car park on road to Logan Fish Pond

PUBLIC TOILETS At car park

The couple standing by a building beside the harbour at Port Logan were perplexed. Pointing to a ferry timetable on a notice board on the wall they asked a passing villager, 'Can you really get a ferry from here to Skye?' The local just smiled and pointed to the sign on the building, which declared it to be Ronansay Primary School. 'It's just a set for the television people,' he told them.

Film Location

Like other visitors to this picturesque village, they could be excused for feeling a wee bit confused. If they walked west along the main street and down some steps to the McPhee Stores, they would have seen a thriving village shop, the walls lined with racks of fresh vegetables, crates of lemonade bottles, plastic buckets and spades and the fishing nets beloved of small children on holiday at the seaside. However, the shop was just a façade. Small clues gave the game away like the advert for the *Oban Times* beside the door and window stickers advertising the *West Highland Free Press*. Port Logan was the television double for the fictional island of Ronansay in the series *Two Thousand Acres of Sky*.

Fictional Ronansay

In the BBC television series Ronansay is just off the coast of Skye and its islanders are trying to attract new blood into their community. To save the village school from closure, they need two new children. Michelle Collins stars as a young mother, desperate to escape from a seedy, inner city housing estate, who sees the Ronansay advert and decides it's just what she needs. The only problem is that the islanders are looking for a family and Abby, Michelle's character, is a single mother. She talks her best pal, Kenny, played by comedian Paul Kaye, into pretending to be her husband and going to live in Ronansay with her and the kids. The series has now ended but popular repeats on satellite television ensure a steady stream of visitors in search of the well-known Ronansay locations.

Glorious Scenery

In the outdoor scenes, shot in and around Port Logan, the glorious Galloway scenery takes over as the main star. Nearby Portpatrick masqueraded as Skye and other locations include Dunskey Castle, Drummore and Stranraer.

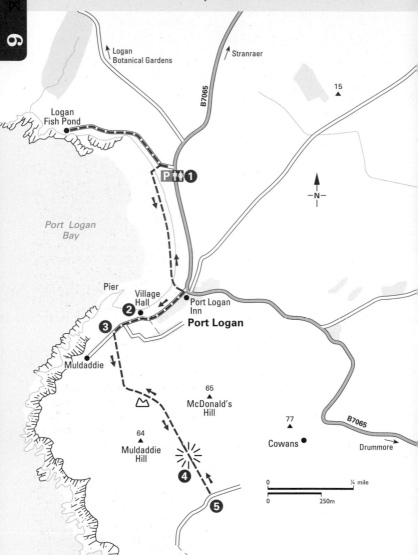

WALK 6 DIRECTIONS

❶ From the car park go across a wooden walkway, down some steps on to the sand and turn left to walk along the beach. When you reach the start of the village, climb on to the road in front of the Port Logan Inn. Turn right and then continue walking along the main street, passing the war memorial to reach the village hall. In *Two Thousand Acres of Sky* the village hall featured as the village school, and had a school sign fixed to the front.

There was also a timetable for Caledonian MacBrayne ferries displayed on a notice board on the wall. Opposite the village hall is a small but picturesque harbour with a rather unusual lighthouse. Nowadays, Port Logan harbour is used only by a few pleasure craft.

2 Port Logan was a thriving fishing port in the past and during the filming of the television series, the pier was festooned with fishing gear, gas bottles and sacks of coal, but they were just props. Move away from the harbour area and continue along the road to the farm of Muldaddie.

3 Just before the farm turn left on to an old hill track and head uphill. Near the top look back downhill for a magnificent view

back to the village and across Port Logan Bay to the Mull of Logan. The track is heavily overgrown here, and is blocked by a barrier made from gates, but this can easily be crossed by a going over a stile at the side.

4 Continue along the track to a T-junction, following the public footpath sign.

5 Retrace your steps to Port Logan then go back on to the beach, turn right and retrace your steps to the car park. From here you can continue along a rough road to the Logan Fish Pond. It's right at the end on the left and is by the only building there.

Criffel and New Abbey

A 13th-century love story of the Lady Devorgilla, set forever in stone.

DISTANCE 3.75 miles (6km)	**MINIMUM TIME** 3hrs
ASCENT/GRADIENT 1,686ft (514m) ▲▲▲	**LEVEL OF DIFFICULTY** +++

PATHS Forest road, rough hill and wood tracks, 1 stile

LANDSCAPE Hills, tidal estuary, woods and pasture

SUGGESTED MAP OS Explorer 313 Dumfries & Dalbeattie

START/FINISH Grid reference: NX 971634

DOG FRIENDLINESS Keep on lead near livestock

PARKING Car park at Ardwall farm

PUBLIC TOILETS None on route

The majestic ruins of Sweetheart Abbey dominate the village of New Abbey. Set against the backdrop of Criffel, Dumfries's highest hill, they stand as testimony to one woman's love, devotion and determination.

A Lasting Memorial

Sweetheart Abbey was founded in 1273 by Devorgilla, Lady of Galloway, as a memorial to her late husband, John Balliol, and as a last resting place for them both. When Balliol died at Barnard Castle in 1269, Devorgilla had his heart removed from his corpse, embalmed and placed in a silver-mounted ivory casket which she carried everywhere with her.

Devorgilla lived long enough to see the abbey rise beside the River Nith. She died in 1289 at Barnard Castle, Durham, and her body was carried to Dumfries, her last journey following that of her husband through the north of England into Scotland. She was interred at Sweetheart Abbey, next to her husband near the high altar, and the cask containing his heart was placed on her breast. Her devotion and attachment to her husband led the monks to give the abbey the name *dulce cor* or sweet heart. Within the abbey there can still be seen a, now headless, effigy of her holding the casket.

Originally the abbey was called New Abbey, to distinguish it from the nearby mother house of Dundrennan, and so the village that subsequently grew up around it took its name. At the Reformation, supported by the local population and the powerful Maxwell family, the abbot, Gilbert Brown, refused to give up the abbey. Eventually, in 1610, after two evictions and arrests, he was finally sent into exile.

The villagers had considerable affection for the abbey and, in 1779, started a fund to ensure its preservation. Now under the care of Historic Scotland, it remains one of the most impressive abbey ruins in Scotland. Although the roof has gone, the cruciform church and massive central tower, built from red Dumfriesshire sandstone, still stand.

The monks of Dundrennan, Glenluce and New Abbey were members of the Order of the Cistercians founded in 1098 at Cîteaux in Burgundy. Directed by the rule of St Benedict they observed a life of poverty, chastity and obedience. In 1136, some white monks of this order travelled north from Rievaulx, in Yorkshire, to found the abbey at Melrose and six years later came to Dundrennan. Although they lived an austere life the Cistercians played an important part in the trading network. They were the largest producers of wool in the country, at their peak accounting for around 5 per cent of Scotland's total wool production. They provided employment and helped establish towns and burghs throughout the country.

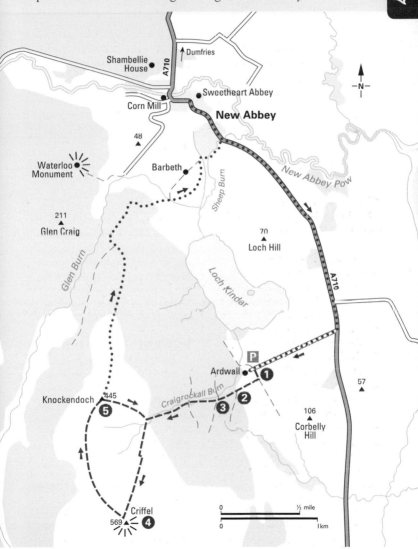

WALK 7 DIRECTIONS

❶ Exit the car park via a kissing gate, cross a farm road and then go through another kissing gate and continue along a track. Turn

right after 70yds (64m) then head towards the hill on a track between dry-stone walls. When the road starts to curve left, in front of the wood, take the rough track off to the right.

WALK 7

② Follow a track uphill through the trees following by the Craigrockall Burn. It narrows in places and the ground is very uneven with several large boulders to climb over or around.

③ When you reach a T-junction with a forest road, keep straight ahead to pick up the trail on the other side and continue uphill. Cross another forest road and eventually reach a fence. Cross the fence and veer to the left, heading towards the summit of Criffel.

WHILE YOU'RE THERE

There's an opportunity to see how oatmeal and flour were produced at New Abbey Corn Mill. This classic example of a Galloway country mill is the last survivor of a once common-place industry. The fully restored, working, 18th-century mill is powered by a waterwheel and offers regular demonstrations of the miller's trade.

④ From the trig point you'll have a superb view. Across the Solway to the south is England and the hills of the Lake District. A little to the right of that is the Isle of Man, while the coast of Ireland is visible to the west. The ancient Scotti tribe came from Ireland and founded Scotland. On a good day the summit of Criffel is the best restaurant in town, provided you have remembered to pack the food. When you've eaten your picnic and enjoyed the view (see What To Look Out For) head roughly north-west from the cairn, following a faint path that leads towards the broad ridge that runs from Criffel to the neighbouring hill of Knockendoch. Head downhill, then continue, ascending again, to the summit of Knockendoch.

WHERE TO EAT AND DRINK

Conveniently situated right at the entrance to Sweetheart Abbey is the Abbey Cottage tea room where visitors can enjoy anything from a cup of tea and a scone to snacks and light meals. Elsewhere in New Abbey its worth taking the time to check out the 19th-century, Tudor-style Criffel Inn with its superb selection of cask beers and over 120 malt whiskies. The atmospheric bar is also the best place to sample their excellent meals, freshly prepared using local produce.

⑤ From the summit cairn head east and go downhill. In the summer, when the heather is particularly thick, the going can be fairly tough and you'll have to proceed slowly and with caution. Make for the fence that runs across the hill in front of you. Turn right here and follow it back to the point you crossed on the way up, then and retrace your steps to the bottom of the hill.

EXTENDING THE WALK

To avoid repeating the first section of the walk, why not continue along the heathery ridge from Point **⑤**, then descend through the forest into New Abbey. You can return to the start by following the A710, then turning right.

WHAT TO LOOK OUT FOR

From the summit of Criffel look east towards Caerlaverock Castle on the opposite bank of the River Nith. Beyond that you will be able to see a nature reserve among the Solway Merses and beyond that a patchwork of lush, rolling pastures, marked out by ancient dry-stone walls.

Right: Amongst the ruins of Sweetheart Abbey (Walk 7)

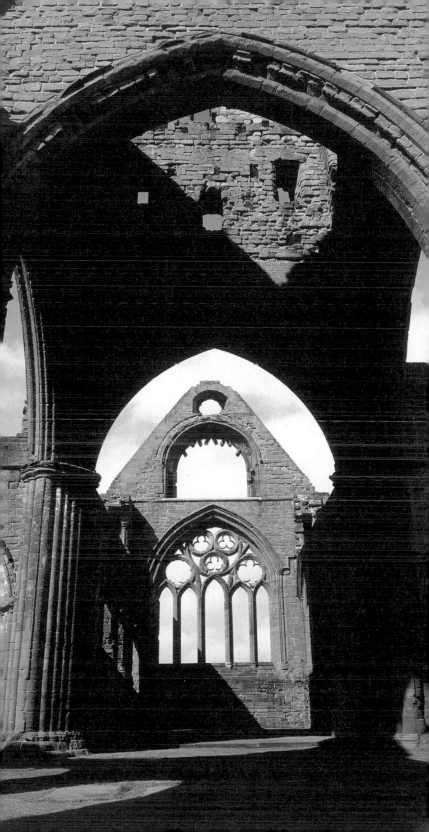

Caerlaverock Castle and the Solway Merses

A ramble taking in an ancient fortress and a
National Nature Reserve.

DISTANCE 5.25 miles (8.4km)	**MINIMUM TIME** 2hrs 30min
ASCENT/GRADIENT 82ft (25m) ▲▲▲	**LEVEL OF DIFFICULTY** ✦✦✦

PATHS Country lanes, farm tracks and salt marsh, 1 stile

LANDSCAPE Pastures, salt marsh, riverside and hills

SUGGESTED MAP OS Explorer 314 Solway Firth

START/FINISH Grid reference: NY 051656

DOG FRIENDLINESS Keep on lead while on reserve

PARKING Car park at Wildfowl and Wetlands Trust Reserve

PUBLIC TOILETS At Wildfowl and Wetlands Trust Reserve

Against the impressive backdrop of Criffel, guarded by the wide waters of the Solway Firth, the salt marshes and the impressive medieval castle of Caerlaverock, this out-of-the-way corner of Scotland is a haven for wildlife and a treasure trove of history.

A Castle Under Siege

Caerlaverock, the Castle of the Lark, was once the main gatekeeper to south-west Scotland. Protected by mudflats and the shifting channels of the sea, it was vulnerable only from the landward side. During the Scottish Wars of Independence (1286–1370) it was attacked frequently. From the siege of Caerlaverock by Edward I in 1300 through to the 17th century it was continually besieged, levelled and rebuilt. Its garrison last surrendered in 1640. Partially demolished, it crumbled to an ivy-covered ruin until restoration in the mid-20th century. Within the ruined walls of this triangular fortress, conservators continue their work on one of the finest Renaissance residences in Scotland.

Preserving the Balance

Conservation work of a different kind takes place on the merse (salt marsh) that bounds the Solway coast. Here Scottish Natural Heritage (SNH), the Wildfowl and Wetlands Trust (WWT) and the Caerlaverock Estate work at preserving the delicate balance that allows farming and wild fowling to exist alongside a National Nature Reserve.

The desolate open spaces, unchanged for centuries, echo to the cry of the wild geese in winter, the oystercatcher and heron in summer and the mating chorus of the natterjack toad in spring. But it wasn't always so. Wildfowling had seriously reduced the goose population to a few hundred in 1957, when the local landowner, the Duke of Norfolk, agreed to divide the merse into an area for controlled shooting and a wildlife sanctuary, now the National Nature Reserve. This is also one of the last places in Britain where scientists can study the important natural processes of growth and erosion of salt marshes.

Left: Two sides of Caerlaverock Castle's triangular moat (Walk 8)

CAERLAVEROCK

Sir Peter Scott

In 1970 the Duke offered the naturalist, Sir Peter Scott, the lease of Eastpark Farm for the WWT. Here, every October, the Spitsbergen population of barnacle geese fly in from Norway to their winter quarters along the merse. The birds can be seen from specially constructed hides along roads shielded with high hedges to minimise disturbance to wildlife.

Whooper swans overwinter here too, along with the pink-footed goose, pintail, scaup, oystercatcher, knot, bar-tailed godwit, curlew and redshank. Staff at Eastpark organise a variety of events to help visitors appreciate the reserve, including birding, natterjack toad and bat spotting, and pond dipping. As part of the conservation process, wildfowling is permitted in winter. Barnacle geese are protected but other species are fair game. The wildfowlers are experts at recognition and SNH wardens ensure fair play.

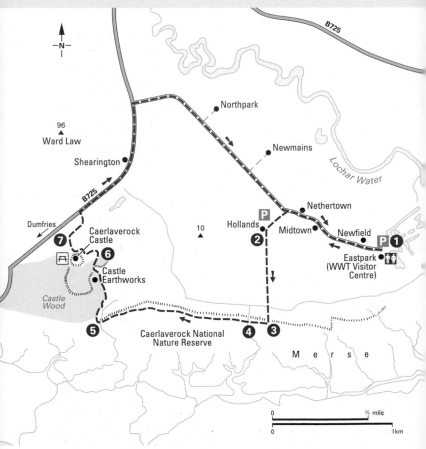

WALK 8 DIRECTIONS

❶ Exit the car park and turn right on to a farm road. Follow this past the farms of Newfield and Midtown then turn left and go past a bungalow and some houses. Just before the farm of Hollands there is a waymarker pointing to a car park, on the right, and straight ahead for walks. Go straight ahead and continue to the farm steading, then turn left.

2 Go through a gate and on to a farm track. This stretches away into the distance and has high hedges on both sides. Continue along this track between the hedges and on, over an overgrown section, until you reach the end then turn right at the signpost indicating Caerlaverock.

3 A sign here informs visitors that regulated wildfowling (shooting) takes place between 1 September to 20 February. Follow the rough track through the grass along the edge of the merse in the direction of the arrow on the footpath waymarker post. The path can be very boggy at all times and the grass will be high in the summer.

4 The path through the nature reserve varies from faint to non-existent; Wellington boots are recommended. It splits at several points and then meanders back and forth, but all the lines of the path rejoin and you'll end up at the same place whichever one you decide to take.

5 Eventually some cottages can be seen in the field to the right. Bear right, through a gate and into the field. Walk to the left around the field perimeter, past some

cottages, then turn left through a gate to emerge on to a farm track, passing a sign for Caerlaverock Castle and into the castle grounds.

6 Follow the road past the old castle, which has been excavated and has information boards to explain the ruins, and go through a wood with nature trail information boards to Caerlaverock Castle. There is a children's playground, a siege machine and picnic tables around the ramparts of the castle.

7 At the far end go through an arch and continue to the T-junction with a country lane. Turn right and continue for about a mile (1.6km), then turn right on to another lane signposted 'Wildfowl and Wetlands Reserve'. Continue on this road past the farms of Northpark, Newmains and Nethertown and then back to the car park at Eastpark.

The Last Turning in Moniaive

The village that inspired the 19th-century school of artists known as the Glasgow Boys.

DISTANCE 5 miles (8km)   **MINIMUM TIME** 3hrs

ASCENT/GRADIENT 295ft (90m) ▲▲▲   **LEVEL OF DIFFICULTY** ✦✦✦

PATHS Dirt roads, hill tracks, forest road and country lane

LANDSCAPE Hills and woodland

SUGGESTED MAP OS Explorers 321 Nithsdale & Dumfries, Thornhill; 328 Sanquhar & New Cumnock, Muirkirk

START/FINISH Grid reference: NX 780910 (on Explorer 328)

DOG FRIENDLINESS Keep on lead near livestock

PARKING Moniaive village car park

PUBLIC TOILETS Ayr Street, passed on walk

Moniaive is one of Scotland's most picturesque villages. Situated at a crossroads where the waters of three glens meet, it has a natural attraction for artists. James Paterson came here in the summer of 1879, the first of several summer painting visits. When he married, in 1884, he decided to settle in Moniaive and moved into Kilneis on the outskirts of the village. Originally a small stone cottage, Paterson's father commissioned the architect John James Burnet to enlarge it as a wedding present to his son and his bride.

A Rebellious Bunch

Paterson was born in Glasgow in 1854 to a prosperous middle-class family of cotton and muslin manufacturers. He persuaded his father to give him a small allowance to enable him to study art in Paris. Courting controversy, he became part of the group of painters known as the Glasgow Boys, which included W Y Macgregor, E A Walton and James Guthrie, who would meet at life classes in Macgregor's Glasgow studio. They were a rebellious bunch and detested the moribund traditions of the Royal Scottish Academy (RSA). Influenced by the realism of contemporary French painters, they successfully exhibited in London and throughout Europe while being ignored by the Scottish establishment. In later life their painting became more conservative and Paterson was finally elected to the RSA and became its librarian and secretary.

Landscape Painter

Much of Paterson's finest work was completed in Moniaive. A landscape painter, he had a wooden studio built on the banks of Craigdarroch Water. Today his watercolours and oils can be found in galleries throughout the world but his most famous work hangs in Glasgow's Kelvingrove Museum and Art Gallery. *The Last Turning* shows a woman in black walking along a country lane. To her left is the water of a mill pond and across it the spire of the clock tower on the schoolmaster's house. The pond is long gone, replaced by a century's growth of trees, but everything else remains the same and in winter it's possible to glimpse the tower through the trees.

From 1897 Paterson had a studio in Edinburgh and lived for only part of the year in Moniaive. By 1906 he had moved his family permanently to the capital. He died in Edinburgh in 1932 but his son, Hamish Constable Paterson, himself an artist, returned to live in Moniaive in 1953. Another Paterson artist, Ann Paterson Wallace opened the James Paterson Museum in the village in the 1990s. With her collection of Paterson memorabilia and Paterson's own photographs, she has created a memorial to her grandfather and a valuable resource for anyone wanting to study the Glasgow Boys.

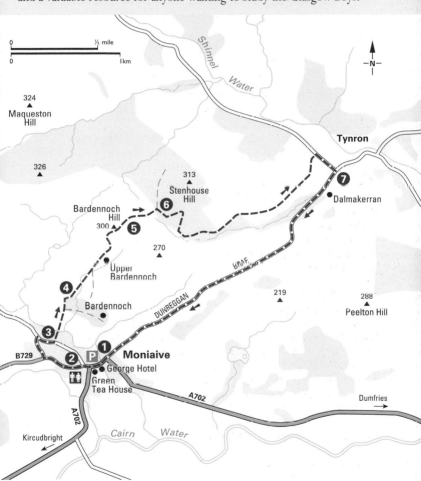

WALK 9 DIRECTIONS

❶ Exit the car park and turn right. At a nearby T-junction turn right and go over the pedestrian bridge, beside a garage, to enter Moniaive High Street at the George Hotel. Walk along the High Street to the Market Cross of Moniaive, pass it and then turn left and cross the road. Turn right at the other side and head up Ayr Street, passing the public toilets.

MONIAIVE

WALK

9

WHILE YOU'RE THERE

Visit Kircudbright, an ancient town on the Solway coast west of Dumfries. The light in this part of the world is unique and has always attracted artists. E A Hornel, another of the Glasgow Boys, painted here and eventually set up home in the Broughton House. It is now a museum (National Trust for Scotland) and is much as Hornel left it.

2 The imposing building on the right with the clock tower is the former village schoolmaster's house. Continue up Ayr Street passing a park on the right and some wooden garages on the left. Take the next right on to a narrow lane. Continue to the end of the lane and, at a T-junction turn right.

3 Pass a modern bungalow on the left, then a field, then turn left on to a dirt road at the end of the field. Cross a bridge and continue up the road to Bardennoch. When the road curves right to enter the grounds of the house, go straight on and follow the road, which goes up the side of the wood and uphill.

4 At the end of the woodland section go through a gate and continue uphill on the road. Cross a fence and then at the top, near the ruin of Upper Bardennoch, go through another gate. From here continue to climb towards a stand of Scots pine, circle them keeping them on your right and continue to the summit of Bardennoch Hill.

5 From the summit keep going in the same direction towards some woodland. A wall should be running beside you to the right. Head slightly downhill to come to the corner where this wall meets one running in front of the woodland. Cross the wall and go on to a forest road.

6 Turn right and follow this road downhill through several gates until it goes through a final gate, at a T-junction with a country lane, where you turn right. At the next T-junction the left turn will soon take you to the hamlet of Tynron which is worth visiting. Otherwise turn right again.

7 Follow this road past Dalmakerran farm, then uphill and through a hazel wood. Continue uphill passing a stone cottage on the right then, further along, another house. The road starts to go downhill again on to Dunreggan Brae. At the bottom of the hill re-enter Moniaive and turn right into the car park.

WHAT TO LOOK OUT FOR

The lane that runs between Ayr Street and North Street is where James Paterson painted his best-known work *The Last Turning*. When you reach the stone garage turn around and look back the way you came. To the right, 100 years ago, there was a mill pond instead of trees when the unknown 'woman in black', seen in the painting, was walking along the lane.

WHERE TO EAT AND DRINK

The Green Tea House in Chapel Street welcomes children and serves a wonderful selection of hot meals and snacks, all made from organic ingredients by Catherine Braid – the Organic Country Cook. Try the delicious soups with freshly baked bread, bacon baps with brie, pasta dishes or some of the awesome sweet and sticky things washed down with tea or coffee from a cup the size of a soup bowl.

The Battle of Glentrool – Road to Independence

Forest trails lead to the site of Robert the Bruce's turning point during the bitter Wars of Independence.

> **DISTANCE** 5 miles (8km)   **MINIMUM TIME** 2hrs
> **ASCENT/GRADIENT** 300ft (91m) ▲▲▲   **LEVEL OF DIFFICULTY** ✦✦✦
> **PATHS** Forest trails, metalled roads, 1 stile
> **LANDSCAPE** Hillside, loch and woodland
> **SUGGESTED MAP** OS Explorer 318 Galloway Forest Park North
> **START/FINISH** Grid reference: NX 396791
> **DOG FRIENDLINESS** Great walk for dogs
> **PARKING** Caldons
> **PUBLIC TOILETS** Caldons Campsite

The year 1314 is etched deep in the Scottish consciousness with Robert the Bruce's famous victory over the English forces at Bannockburn regarded as the culmination of the Wars of Independence. But Bannockburn was not the end of the conflict and it could be argued that an earlier skirmish, when the two nations clashed at Glentrool, was a far more important step on the road to independence.

Scotland was an independent country long before these wars, but had been left without a monarch following the death of Alexander II in 1286 and that of his only heir, Margaret of Norway, on her journey to Scotland. The Guardians of Scotland asked Edward I of England to adjudicate on the various claimants to the succession. He agreed but also used it as an excuse to re-assert his claim as overlord of Scotland. Edward chose John Balliol as King but made him swear an oath of fealty. His reign was a somewhat rocky affair. Known to his subjects as 'Toom Tabbard' or empty jacket, Balliol, the puppet king, was frequently humiliated by Edward and eventually removed by him, leaving Scotland to be run by English officials. He retired to his estates in Normandy where he died in 1315.

Braveheart and Bruce

Armed resistance to English occupation was led by Sir William Wallace, a shadowy figure about whom little is really known prior to his uprising. He was in turn appointed Guardian of Scotland by the nobility and then betrayed by them in 1305, taken to London and executed there.

Meanwhile Robert the Bruce was advancing his claim to the Scottish throne. He murdered his rival claimant, John, the Red Comyn, in Greyfriars church, in Dumfries and launched a series of attacks on the English in the south-west. He was crowned King of Scots at Scone on 25 March, 1306, but following a series of defeats he fled to Rathlin Island, off the Antrim coast, where he regrouped before returning to Scotland early in 1307. After attacking English forces in Galloway, an army was dispatched to capture him. But this wild and inhospitable part of Scotland was Bruce's home territory and he set up an ambush. Using a small part of his force to lure the English on to the southern shores of Loch Trool, he concealed the bulk of his men on the slopes above the loch. The English were forced to dismount and follow in single file and, when they were at their most vulnerable, the Scots blocked the path and hurled a barrage of heavy boulders down on them. This was the turning point in Bruce's fortunes and he went from here to further victories against the enemy, culminating in the Battle of Bannockburn.

Edward I counterattacked between 1317 and 1319, seizing Berwick, a town of great strategic importance on the border. In 1322 the Scottish nobility appealed to the Pope to support independence in the Declaration of Arbroath. Support was granted in 1324 and in 1328 England finally recognised Scotland as an independent nation in the Treaty of Edinburgh.

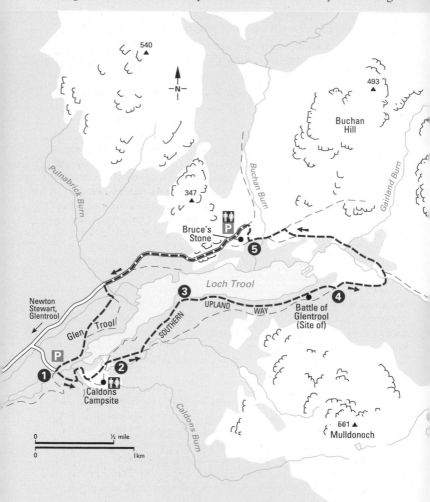

WALK 10 DIRECTIONS

❶ Leave the car park and follow the Southern Upland Way

markers. Cross the bridge over the Water of Trool. Cross another bridge over the Caldons Burn. Next, take a left turn on to a footpath that runs along the banks of the river. Cross over a bridge.

2 Follow this well waymarked trail and at a fork by a waymarker turn right, and then head uphill and into the forest.

WHERE TO EAT AND DRINK

Eating places are few and far between, but there is no place better for a picnic and you'll find lots of suitable spots on the walk. The nearest tea room is a few miles back on the road to Glentrool at the Stroan Bridge visitor centre. With friendly staff serving a variety of snacks, light meals and delicious hot soup, it's a popular place to stop.

3 Keep on the path uphill and through a clearing, then go through a kissing gate and re-enter the woodland. Continue along the southern side of Loch Trool until you reach an interpretation board near the loch end. This marks the spot where Robert the Bruce and his army cleverly lured the superior English forces into a well-planned ambush and routed them.

4 Follow the path from here, leaving the woodland and heading downhill and to the left, before leaving the Southern Upland Way. Turn left, go through two gates and over a wooden bridge. Cross the bridge over Gairland Burn and continue. Eventually reaching the bridge over the Buchan Burn, cross over and take the path to the left, branching off uphill.

5 Follow this to the top and Bruce's Stone, which was raised to commemorate the victory at the Battle of Glentrool, the first victory in the Independence Wars.

WHAT TO LOOK OUT FOR

From the south side of Loch Trool look across the water to see the famous Bruce's Stone on it's vantage point on the far bank. Behind that is the massive backdrop of Merrick, at 2,765ft (843m) the highest hill in the Southern Uplands with the lower Benyellary in front and to the left, connected by the narrow ridge of the Neive of the Spit. A path to the summit of both starts from near Bruce's Stone (see Walk 12).

From here, looking across the clear waters of the loch to the tree-clad hills opposite, is one of the finest views in Scotland. Follow the track past the stone then turn left on to the narrow road. Head through the car park and keep going until you reach a waymarker on the left which leads to a forest trail, and take this to return to the start of the walk.

The Wells
of the Rees

*Take this strenuous walk along the Southern
Upland Way in search of the past.*

WALK 11

DISTANCE *6.25 miles (10.1km)*   **MINIMUM TIME** *3hrs 30min*

ASCENT/GRADIENT *558ft (170m)* ▲▲▲   **LEVEL OF DIFFICULTY** +++

PATHS *Forest roads, forest track, very rough ground*

LANDSCAPE *Hills, forest and loch*

SUGGESTED MAP *OS Explorer 310 Glenluce & Kirkcowan*

START/FINISH *Grid reference: NX 260735*

DOG FRIENDLINESS *Keep on lead near livestock*

PARKING *Near Derry farm*

PUBLIC TOILETS *None on route*

Sitting 'on the hillside at the back of the sheiling called Kilgallioch' wrote Davie Bell, 'are three dome-shaped structures of great antiquity'. These were the Wells o' the Rees, the rees in question being sheep pens surrounding the wells.

A Determined Effort

Davie Bell, popularly known as 'The Highwayman', rode his bicycle all over the roughest parts of south-west Scotland in the 1930s and '40s and chronicled his exploits in a weekly column in the *Ayrshire Post* (see Walk 12). He was intrigued by the Wells o' the Rees and mounted several expeditions in search of them. Although he came close, time and again he was defeated by thick bracken and an almost featureless landscape. Today, the waymarked Southern Upland Way (SUW) takes walkers to within 100yds (91m) of the wells and a signpost points them out. But when Davie Bell was roaming these moors, often on his bicycle, but sometimes on foot, there were no long distance footpaths or signposts. Many paths and tracks would have criss-crossed the moor but they were the tracks used by herdsmen and farmers to their remote steadings.

Davie eventually found the wells after getting directions from the farmer's wife at Kilgallioch. He described them as 'three piles of stones... skilfully constructed, with each well having a canopy and the shape of the whole like that of a beehive'. Made of flat stones and oval in shape they were 'streamlined into the hillside, with a recess over the well for a utensil'. Sixty years later the people are gone but the wells remain.

This part of Galloway was sparsely populated before the forestry came, but when trees replaced sheep, shepherds and their families abandoned their lonely sheilings to ruin and decay. With the opening of the SUW, walkers trudge this wild landscape once again. These latter-day pilgrims, follow in the footsteps of early Christians on their way to Whithorn.

Although locals told Davie Bell the wells were built by the Romans, it seems more likely that they were made for the pilgrims. According to the Revd C H Dick in his *Highways and Byways of Galloway and Carrick,* the wells

WELLS OF THE REES

may have been part of the ancient church and graveyard of Kilgallioch, which was near by, although he walked across the moors from New Luce in 1916 and saw nothing in the way of ruins. The pilgrims' route to Whithorn was also the path followed by lepers on their way from Glenluce Abbey to the leper colony 1.5 miles (2.4km) north of Loch Derry at Libberland.

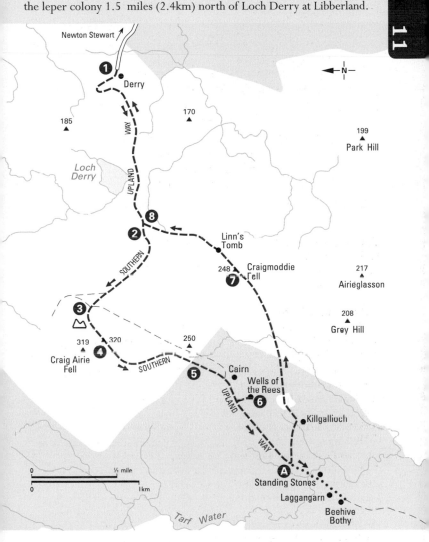

WALK 11 DIRECTIONS

1 Cross a cattle grid and head west along the Southern Upland Way (SUW) on a well-surfaced forest road. Pass Loch Derry, on your right in just under a mile (1.6km) and then continue on the forest road, passing a signpost on the left to Linn's Tomb.

2 Follow the road as it curves to the right, then, following the SUW markerpost, turn left, leave the road and head uphill. It's a steep climb from here, on a well-trodden path with waymarkers.

3 Cross over a forest road and then continue on the uphill path heading towards the summit of

53

WELLS OF THE REES

Craig Airie Fell. Reach the summit at a trig point.

❹ From the OS triangulation pillar, continue on a well-marked path towards a waymarker on the horizon. Turn left at the waymarker and head downhill on a footpath that twists and turns to another waymarker near the bottom. Turn right here and keep going until you reach the edge of the forest.

❺ The SUW now follows a forest ride. Shortly you'll come to a clearing with a cairn on your left. Keep straight ahead following the waymarkers to the next clearing where a sign points left to the Wells of the Rees. Turn left and head downhill, across a dry-stone wall and then a gap in another wall. In winter will find the

wells easily but in summer, when the bracken is thick, you'll have to poke about a bit. The first two wells are on your right as you come through the gap and the other is off to the left.

❻ Retrace your steps from here to the signpost and turn left. Continue along the Southern Upland Way to reach a junction with a forest road. Turn left and follow it to the end, then continue along a faint path, cross a wall and continue east towards Craigmoddie Fell.

❼ Climb to the highest point then look to your left to Loch Derry then, to the right of it, Derry farm. Head in a straight line for Derry farm then drop down off the fell and pick up a path heading towards Loch Derry.

❽ Follow this to go through a gate and on to the forest road. Turn right and return to Derry farm and the start.

EXTENDING THE WALK

You can extend this walk by carrying on along the SUW from Point ❹ to find the Standing Stones of Laggangarn and beyond that to the beehive bothy, then return to Point ❹.

Cycling on the Merrick

*Follow in the cycle tracks of Davie Bell,
the original mountain biker.*

DISTANCE 9 miles (14.5km) **MINIMUM TIME** 5hrs	
ASCENT/GRADIENT 2,339ft (713m) ▲▲▲ **LEVEL OF DIFFICULTY** +++	
PATHS Hill tracks, section to Loch Enoch can be very boggy, 1 stile	
LANDSCAPE Hills, lochs and trees	
SUGGESTED MAP OS Explorer 318 Galloway Forest North	
START/FINISH Grid reference: NX 415804	
DOG FRIENDLINESS Keep on lead at lambing time and near livestock	
PARKING Bruce's Stone car park	
PUBLIC TOILETS At car park	

A 1940s photograph shows a group of young men gathered round the cairn at the summit of the Merrick, south-west Scotland's highest mountain. Nothing unusual there, except for the fact that they all have bicycles. It's a record of the successful outcome of a challenge from a newspaper editor and a tribute to one of Ayrshire's cycling pioneers.

The Highwayman

David E T Bell (1907–65) was born and educated in Dumfries, then moved to Ayr where he worked as a gardener. Health and fitness were his passions and when he was introduced to cycling he saw it as a means to achieve both. But Davie Bell was much more than a sportsman. He was a local historian and an outdoor man with an eye for nature. He had a wonderfully descriptive writing style, which ensured that thousands followed his adventures as 'The Highwayman' in his weekly column in the *Ayrshire Post*.

One week the *Post* published a letter from a reader who had gone to the summit of Merrick on a pony. He closed his correspondence with the challenge, 'It only remains for someone to make the ascent on a bicycle'. The Highwayman rose to the bait and, with four friends, set off through the mist-covered Minnoch Valley heading for Merrick. Riding and walking, sometimes using a sling to carry their bikes, they progressed slowly up the hill, some of them collapsing and gasping for breath, while Davie's pal, Harry Fairbairn kept up a constant monologue, 'Jings this is smashing. I never saw anything like this'. Eventually they reached the summit. Then followed the descent of the sloping ridge of the Neive of the Spit to Benyellary. From Benyellary they covered another 2,000ft (610m) at a slower pace to finally descend through granite boulders to Loch Trool.

Davie Bell's passion for 'rough stuff' continued for the rest of his life, making journeys to remote bothies like Back Hill of Bush or hauling his bike to the summit of Ailsa Craig. On each journey he took his readers with him, producing a weekly column for 30 years. When he died in 1965 subscriptions poured in from friends and admirers and a memorial cairn was erected at Rowantree Toll on the Straiton–Newton Stewart road.

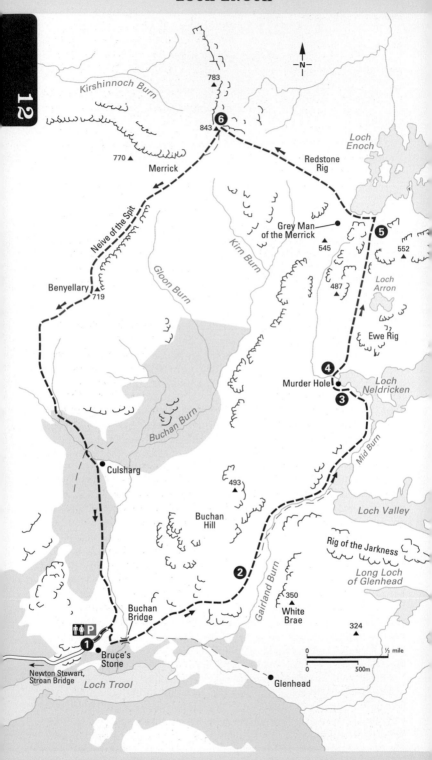

783 ▲

6

Loch
Enoch

843 ▲

770 ▲

Merrick

Redstone
Rig

Kirshinnoch Burn

Neive of the Spit

Grey Man
of the Merrick

545 ▲

552 ▲

5

Benyellary ▲
719

487 ▲

Loch
Arron

Kirn Burn

Ewe Rig

Gloon Burn

4

Murder Hole

3

Loch
Neldricken

Culsharg

Buchan Burn

Mid Burn

493 ▲

Buchan
Hill

Loch Valley

Rig of the Jarkness

2

Gairland Burn

Long Loch
of Glenhead

350 ▲
White
Brae

324 ▲

Buchan
Bridge

1

Bruce's
Stone

Newton Stewart,
Stroan Bridge

Loch Trool

Glenhead

0   ½ mile
0   500m

WALK 12 DIRECTIONS

1 From the car park at Bruce's Stone head east along the narrow road, across the Buchan Bridge. Continue a short distance then turn left and go uphill to cross a stile. Follow the path along the wall, then veer right and head uphill to rejoin the wall. Go through a gate and turn right on to a path. Follow this up the valley of the Gairland Burn with Buchan Hill on your left.

WHAT TO LOOK OUT FOR

From the corner of Loch Enoch come back a little way to the south-west, heading towards the summit of Buchan Hill and look for a large outcrop called the Grey Man of the Merrick. It's a well-known landmark and resembles the face of a man.

2 To your left is the ridge of Buchan Hill and to the right is White Brae, and to the farside of that the Rig of the Jarkness. Do not cross the Gairland but keep going on the path to reach Loch Valley, skirting it to the west and then continue beside the Mid Burn to reach Loch Neldricken.

3 Head for the far west corner of the loch to find the infamous Murder Hole featured by S R Crockett in his novel *The Raiders* (1894). The story is based on a local legend that unwary travellers were robbed on these hills and their bodies disposed of in the loch.

WHERE TO EAT AND DRINK

The Galloway Hills is a pretty remote area. Not only is a picnic a good idea but by the time you've conquered Merrick you will feel in need of sustenance. The other options include a visit to the Stroan Bridge tea room (see Walk 10) and The House O' Hill at Bargrennan (see Walk 11).

4 From the Murder Hole head north, crossing a burn and then a wall. Pass to the west of Ewe Rig and tiny Loch Arron and eventually reach the south side of Loch Enoch. Don't worry if the track vanishes or becomes indistinct, just keep heading north and you'll eventually reach the loch.

5 As you approach Loch Enoch you will see the outline of Mullwarchar beyond it and to the right. When you reach the loch go left and cross another wall. The slope in front of you is the Redstone Rig and although you have 1,000ft (305m) to climb it is not particularly taxing.

6 From the summit cairn of Merrick head downhill towards a narrow ridge called the Neive of the Spit to reach the summit of Benyellary, the Hill of the Eagle. From here follow the footpath downhill beside a dry-stone wall then turn left and keep going downhill, into the forest, to reach the bothy at Culsharg. From there continue downhill to return to the car park.

WHILE YOU'RE THERE

Take a trip to Whithorn where St Ninian founded his early church, Candida Casa, the White House, towards the end of the 4th century. Once a popular place of pilgrimage, and a thriving community until pilgrimages were banned under pain of death after the Reformation, it is once again receiving attention because of recent archaeological discoveries. You can visit the interpretation centre, the dig and the old priory.

Overleaf: Looking over the trees to Loch Trool (Walk 12)

Wanlockhead: Scotland's Highest Village

Discover the secrets of lead and gold mining in 'God's Treasure House'.

WALK 13

DISTANCE 3.75 miles (6km)	**MINIMUM TIME** 3hrs
ASCENT/GRADIENT 525ft (160m) ▲▲▲	**LEVEL OF DIFFICULTY** +++

PATHS Footpaths, hill tracks, hillside and old railway lines, 1 stile

LANDSCAPE Hills, mining relics and village

SUGGESTED MAP OS Explorer 329 Lowther Hills, Sanquhar & Leadhills

START/FINISH Grid reference: NX 873129

DOG FRIENDLINESS Keep on lead near livestock

PARKING Museum of Lead Mining car park

PUBLIC TOILETS At car park

A unique combination of changing pressures within the earth's crust several million years ago, led to the formation of rich mineral veins in this part of the Southern Uplands. Everything from gold to zinc and copper has been found locally, but it was the rich deposits of lead that resulted in the establishment of Scotland's highest village. By the 17th century a permanent, if primitive, settlement was established. Accommodation consisted of one-room cottages with often as many as eight people living in them. They cooked over the open fire in the middle of the room and smoke was vented through a hole in the roof.

By the late 19th century, when lead mining was at its peak, some 850 people lived here in much improved cottages. These cottages were bigger, with an attic room and a proper cooking range. In 1871 the miners founded a co-operative society, bought all their supplies there and received a share of the profits. Amazingly this continued until 1971.

A Thriving Community

The miners valued the little leisure time they had and were very active in forming local clubs and societies. There were curling, bowling and quoiting clubs, a drama group and even a silver band. The Library, the second oldest subscription library in Europe, was founded in 1756 by the minister and a small group of villagers. Wanlockhead fared better than most libraries with a donation of books from the local landowner the Duke of Buccleuch. He also funded the building of a new school and the salary of the teacher.

The miners' children learned to read, write and count and could also take lessons in Latin and Greek. A government inspector visiting in 1842 was so impressed by the standard of learning he concluded that 'the children of the poor labourers of Wanlockhead are under as good, or perhaps better system of intellectual culture than even the middle class children of South Britain generally'.

As the price of lead slumped, and mines became exhausted, the miners gradually drifted away. The last of the mines, Glencrieff, closed in 1934 and the village went into decline until only 30 people remained. In the 1960s

WANLOCKHEAD

the local authority offered to re-house them elsewhere but they resolutely refused to leave. Thanks to their determination, an influx of new blood, renovation of houses and the opening of the Museum of Lead Mining, Wanlockhead has survived as a community into the 21st century. But it almost vanished, like countless other mining villages, which are now just names on the map, a few ruins and half-forgotten tales.

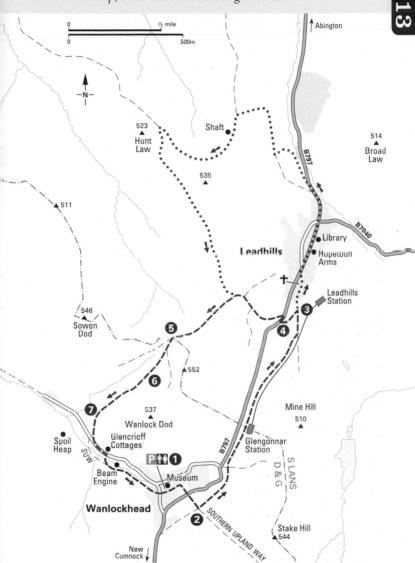

WALK 13 DIRECTIONS

1 With the museum to your back turn left and join the Southern Upland Way. Head uphill on steps then, at the top, cross to

a stone building with a large white door. Turn right on to a rough road, cross the main road and take the public footpath to Enterkine Pass. Follow this to the front of a white house.

WALK 13

❷ Turn left on to the course of an old railway line. Follow this, cross a road then go through a long cutting to reach a fence. Go over a stile to get to Glengonnar Station then follow the narrow path that runs along the left side of the railway tracks from here. Eventually the path runs on to a rough road and in the distance you will see two terraced houses.

❸ At the point where telephone wires intersect the road, turn left at the pole on the left-hand side and follow the line of the fence down to some sheep pens. Turn right at the end of the pens and walk out to the main road.

❹ Turn right then almost immediately left on to a hill road. Walk uphill on this until the road bears sharp right and a dirt track forks off to the left. Turn left on to the track and keep on it until you reach a gate. Cross over, then veer left on to a faint track. Follow the track downhill to the point where it comes close to the corner of a fence on your left.

❺ Cross the fence and go straight ahead on a very faint track picking your way through the heather. Eventually, as the track begins to look more like a path, you will reach a fork. Go to the right here and cross the flank of the hill passing through some disused tips.

❻ The path at this point is little more than a series of sheep tracks and may disappear altogether but

that is not a problem. Ahead of you is a large conical spoil heap and, provided you keep heading towards it, you know you will be going in the right direction.

❼ Towards the end of the hill the track heads left, starts to make its way downhill, then passes behind a row of cottages. Veer right, downhill, after the cottages to join the road. Turn left and continue past Glencrieff cottages, then turn right, leaving the road and heading downhill again. Cross a bridge and climb up on to the Southern Upland Way. Turn left along it and follow this back to the car park.

WHERE TO EAT AND DRINK

The café/tea room attached to the museum is geared towards families and has a splendid menu of light meals, sandwiches, snacks and delicious hot soup. It's a light and airy place conveniently situated where the walk begins and ends. Occasionally in the summer local musicians play traditional music here.

EXTENDING THE WALK

From Point **❸** you can carry on into the mining village of Leadhills, where you will find the first public subscription library in Europe. A pleasant loop can be made by heading across the mining ground on the far side of the village to intersect some hill tracks, which will eventually lead you back into Wanlockhead.

WHILE YOU'RE THERE

A visit to the Museum of Lead Mining will enhance your understanding of the area and your enjoyment of the walk. The entire history of gold and lead mining in this area is covered and the admission fee includes a visit to a former miners' cottage and a trip into one of the mines (wear warm clothing). During the summer there are gold panning demonstrations and courses. The museum is open from April to October, daily.

The Tale of Ardstinchar Castle

The Ayrshire Tragedy, a murder most foul.

DISTANCE 3 miles (4.8km)	**MINIMUM TIME** 2hrs

ASCENT/GRADIENT 295ft (90m) ▲▲▲ **LEVEL OF DIFFICULTY** ✦✦✦

PATHS Country lanes and farm tracks

LANDSCAPE Hillside, pastures and seashore

SUGGESTED MAP OS Explorer 317 Ballantrae, Barr & Barrhill

START/FINISH Grid reference: NX 082824

DOG FRIENDLINESS Mainly farmland, so keep on lead near livestock

PARKING Car park near school on Foreland, Ballantrae

PUBLIC TOILETS Beside car park

If the ruins of Ardstinchar Castle could speak they would tell a tale of a series of events designed to wipe out one branch of Ayrshire's most powerful family, the Kennedys.

Fact or Fiction?

An ancient manuscript lies in a basement in an Edinburgh library. It was written at the time of these events and, although the author remains anonymous, it is believed to be the work of John Mure of Auchindrain House near Ayr. It was the writing of S R Crocket, minister turned novelist, who brought this story to the attention of a wider public when he took it and used it as the basis of his novel *The Grey Man*. This is a work of fiction but woven through the tale is the factual thread of the tragic events which occurred in Ayrshire at the end of the 16th century.

Kennedy Feud

Crocket's novel opens with the fictional burning of Ardstinchar Castle, but he uses this event to outline the origins of the Kennedy feud. This was an attempt by the Earl of Cassillis, the senior Kennedy, to acquire the lands of Crossraguel Abbey. All efforts to persuade Allan Stewart, the Commendator of Crossraguel, having failed, Cassillis seized him, carried him off to his stronghold at Dunure Castle and there in the Black Vault of Dunure 'roasted the hapless Stewart over a slow fire until he signed'. However, Stewart's brother-in-law, Kennedy of Bargany, rescued him and although Cassillis was brought before the High Court and made to compensate Stewart, he was allowed to keep the lands. Cassillis was thereafter intent on destroying the house of Bargany and various plots, intrigues and blood lettings took place culminating in the murder of Bargany by Cassillis near Maybole in 1601.

Bargany was interred in the family vault at Ballantrae and, although Cassillis escaped justice again, Bargany's ally John Mure, the Grey Man of Crocket's tale, took revenge by having an uncle of Cassillis assassinated. Suspicion immediately fell on Mure but he had an alibi. However, there was one witness who could tie Mure to the crime. A young boy had delivered a letter from the intended victim to Mure who read it then told the boy to return it and say he had not found Mure. To protect himself, Mure and his son strangled the hapless boy and threw him into the sea near Girvan. The boy's body washed ashore a few days later, both Mures were arrested, tried and found guilty of murder and also of being involved in the assassination. Sentenced to death for their crimes, they were executed at Edinburgh in 1611, thus ending the feud and leaving Cassillis free of any retribution.

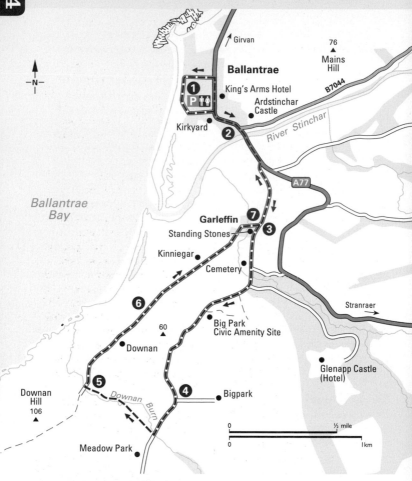

WALK 14 DIRECTIONS

❶ Leave the car park and turn left on to the Foreland. At the T-junction with Main Street cross the road and turn right. Near the outskirts of the village, just before the bridge over the River Stinchar, look up to your left to view the ruins of the former stronghold of the Bargany Kennedy's

Ardstinchar Castle. As the castle walls are considered unstable it is perhaps not advisable to go any closer.

❷ From here cross the Stinchar Bridge and take the first turning on the right, heading uphill on a narrow country lane and past a row of cottages. At a junction in the road keep to the left but

WHERE TO EAT AND DRINK

The Café on the Main Street is a favoured local hang out. It's a cosy wee place, but only open at the weekends. Instead, try the Thistle Tea Room just along the street or the King's Arms Hotel across the road.

look out for one of the Garleffin Standing Stones in the rear garden of the bungalow at the junction.

3 There's another stone in the front garden of this house but you will see that later in the walk. In the meantime continue uphill passing the cemetery, on your right, then Glenapp Castle gates on your left and a little further on the Big Park Civic Amenity Site, on the left.

WHAT TO LOOK OUT FOR

The remaining standing stones of Garleffin formed part of what was a stone circle and it is possible to see the outline by crop marks which are visible from the main Ballantrae to Stranraer road above this hamlet. Local people may tell you that this was once a place of worship for ancient druids but there is no evidence to support that story.

4 The next landmark on the left is the farm road to Bigpark. Continue past this and look out for the next farmhouse on the right. About 300yds (274m) before this house the road dips; there's a stream beside the road here. Turn right on to a farm track that heads downhill between two high hedges.

5 Near the bottom of the hill, just past a large barn on your left, the road splits. Turn right here and continue along this road, through

a farm steading, past Downan farmhouse and uphill. When the road levels out look to the horizon in front of you for the distinctive outline of Knockdolian Hill, often referred to by local mariners as the 'false Craig'.

6 Look over to your left at the same time to see the real Ailsa Craig away to the north-west. Looking along the beach towards Ballantrae is Shellknowe. Continue along this road, past the farm of Kinniegar and through the hamlet of Garleffin. Note that some of the houses have names like Druidslea and Glendruid.

7 In the front garden of Druidslea is another standing stone. Turn left, go downhill on this country lane, turn left on to the main road and return to Ballantrae. Go through a gate on the left-hand side and into the kirkyard. The Kennedy crypt can be found by going up some steps on the right. If the door is locked you can still see inside through a small window on the door. Return to Main Street and turn left, go along the street and take the first turning left past the library. Walk along this street to reach the T-junction and turn left into Foreland and return to the car park where you started.

WHILE YOU'RE THERE

Head along the shore road to Girvan but branch off to the left at Bennane Lea and keep going until you come to a large brick wall built into the rocks to form a cave. This was once home to Snib Scott, a local hermit. His real name was Henry Torbett and he once worked in a bank but for some reason gave it up for a life of solitude. There's a memorial to him, which you will find on the foreshore opposite the cave.

Byne Hill and the Firth of Clyde

Enjoy the views across the sea to Ailsa Craig,
the source of the world's curling stones.

DISTANCE 3.75 miles (6km)	**MINIMUM TIME** 3hrs
ASCENT/GRADIENT 571ft (174m) ▲▲▲	**LEVEL OF DIFFICULTY** ✦✦✦
PATHS Farm roads, dirt tracks and open hillside, 1 stile	
LANDSCAPE Hill, pasture, woodland and seaside	
SUGGESTED MAP OS Explorer 317 Ballantrae, Barr & Barrhill	
START/FINISH Grid reference: NX 187955	
DOG FRIENDLINESS Keep on lead, this is sheep country	
PARKING Ainslie Park car park	
PUBLIC TOILETS At the car park	

The lone sentinel of Ailsa Craig in the Firth of Clyde, which dominates the seaward views on this walk, is the plug of a volcano, extinct since prehistoric times. First mentioned in the charters of the Abbey of Crossraguel in 1404 as the Insula de Ailsay, the island was part of that estate until the Reformation in 1560. Since then it has belonged to the Cassillis family, and has given its name to the senior family member, the Marquis of Ailsa. To generations of immigrant Irish it was known simply as Paddy's Milestone as it is located approximately half-way between Belfast and Glasgow. But Ailsa Craig's main claim to fame is as the source of granite used in the world's supply of curling stones.

The fine micro-granite from Ailsa Craig has been used to make curling stones since the beginning of the 19th century. On the island there are several kinds of granite, Common Ailsa, Blue Hone and Red Hone. All three have been used in curling stone manufacture but the Blue Hone, a finer grained variety, produced the best running surface. Quarrying stopped in 1971 and Welsh granite was substituted. But each stone still had what was known as an Ailsert, a small coaster of Ailsa Craig Blue Hone granite, inserted in the base.

Originally, quarrying on the island was carried out by the Girvan family, who had a lease from the Marquis of Ailsa. They lived in a cottage on the island during the summer months, blasting and extracting the rock for transport back to Girvan harbour and onwards to the curling stone factory in Mauchline. A small railway line was built to carry the rocks to the island pier for loading on to small fishing boats.

During the summer Ailsa Craig was a busy place. As well as the resident lighthouse keepers, the Girvan family and their workforce, there was a constant stream of day-trippers on cruises from Girvan harbour. They could climb to the small ruined castle, take a tour of the lighthouse and wander around the island. Mrs Girvan supplied afternoon teas in a small café. By the 1950s the Girvans had given up quarrying, shut the café and removed their sheep and goats, leaving the rock to the lighthouse keepers and the birds.

BYNE HILL

Kays of Mauchline, the world's only manufacturer of curling stones, started using Welsh Trevor granite to produce their stones with the Ailsert to preserve the smooth running surface. However, in the summer of 2002, Kays removed some 1,500 tons of granite boulders from the old quarries on the island. No blasting or quarrying took place. They simply collected what was already there to avoid disturbing the island's population of seabirds. Now they will be able to make curling stones entirely from Ailsa Craig granite again.

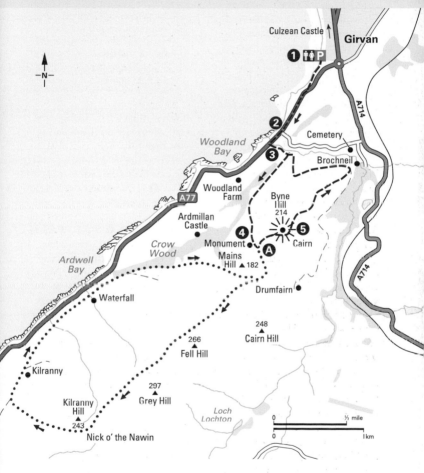

WALK 15 DIRECTIONS

❶ From the car park head south along a pavement alongside the A77. Pass a nursing home on the right, then come to a lane on the left past former Shalloch mill.

❷ The pavement disappears so continue along the verge for

200yds (183m). Just before it reappears cross a bridge, then turn left and cross the road.

❸ Go on to a farm track that runs alongside a burn. Go over a metal gate and turn right. Follow this newly created road which runs behind Woodland Farm and Ardmillan Castle Holiday Park.

15

There are several metal gates to go through on the way. Please ensure that you always close them behind you and leave open any that are not closed.

4 Continue on to the saddle between Mains Hill on your right-hand side and Byne Hill on your left, passing the remains of a monument which was erected to the memory of Archibald C B Craufurd of Ardmillan Estate. As the monument is in poor repair keep a safe distance from it. There used to be a plaque on the front, but some years ago this was removed and dumped in the woods below. Turn left through a gap in the wall and head up the side of Byne Hill to reach a prominent commemorative cairn at the summit. From this vantage point there is one of the finest views of the Firth of Clyde. On a clear day you can see the Antrim coast of Northern Ireland, the island of Arran and the Mull of Kintyre to the north and west, and, about 8 miles (12.9km) out in the sea, the distinctive outline of Ailsa Craig.

5 With the cairn at your back, walk straight ahead. Cross a saddle between the summit and the lower part of the hill, keeping at first to the higher ground then towards the north side of the hill. Descend very carefully and at the

bottom, turn left and follow the wall. Continue until you pass a gate then turn right over a stile and cross the field to then go over the gate on to the farm road at Point **3**. From here retrace your steps to the start.

EXTENDING THE WALK

From Point **A**, an extension loop can be made by following the faint track to a gate, then turning right and heading across rough hill ground to go through the gap known as the Nick o' the Nawin and over rough ground to Kilranny Hill. From here you can pick up the old coach road past the ruins of Kilranny steading, before circling back around the woods to rejoin your original route at Point **A**.

The Gypsy Palace of Kirk Yetholm

This energetic walk takes you over the border to England.

DISTANCE 7 miles (11.2km)	**MINIMUM TIME** 4hrs 30min
ASCENT/GRADIENT 1,600ft (480m) ▲▲▲	**LEVEL OF DIFFICULTY** +++

PATHS Wide tracks and waymarked paths, one short overgrown section, 3 stiles

LANDSCAPE Rolling open hills with panoramic views

SUGGESTED MAP OS Explorer OL16 The Cheviot Hills

START/FINISH Grid reference: NT 839276

DOG FRIENDLINESS Excellent, though keep on lead near sheep

PARKING Car park outside Kirk Yetholm at junction of Pennine Way and St Cuthbert's Way

PUBLIC TOILETS None on route

This is such a lovely walk that you'll want to do it again and again. It's easy to follow, the paths are good and the views have a definite 'wow' factor – so do try to save it for a clear day so that you get the full effect. The walk includes the added thrill of crossing the border from Scotland into England – no, you won't need your passport.

The little village of Kirk Yetholm was noted as a gypsy settlement from at least 1695, although they were probably there before that, as they were in Scotland by the early 16th century. Gypsies were generally regarded with suspicion as they had a reputation for stealing and aggression – it was even said that they kidnapped children and brought them up as their own. However, they were also said to be loyal to those who helped them and never broke their word.

A Royal Family Home

No one is quite sure how the gypsies came to settle in Kirk Yetholm, although many moved to the wild areas of the Borders where they could hide in the hills, after a law was passed in Scotland in 1609 making it legal to kill them. Some say that a young gypsy boy saved the life of a local laird, who showed his thanks by building several homes for gypsies in the village; others, that a gypsy boy helped a local laird to recover a horse that had been stolen and was rewarded with a house in Kirk Yetholm. There were several homes for gypsies in the village, with one cottage being specially built for the royal family – it's called the Gypsy Palace today.

The gypsy royal family had the surname Faa. The first king in Kirk Yetholm was Patrick Faa, who married Jean Gordon. Jean was a powerful character who lived a wild life. Three of her sons were hanged for sheep stealing and she was banned from Kirk Yetholm after attacking another woman. She was said to be the inspiration for Sir Walter Scott's character, Meg Merrilees. She was later immortalised by Keats in his eponymous poem that began: 'Old Meg she was a gypsy; and lived upon the moors: her bed it was the brown heath turf, and her house was out of doors'.

KIRK YETHOLM

The last queen of the gypsies was Esther Faa-Blythe who once said the scattered village was 'sae mingle-mangle that ane micht think it was either built on a dark nicht, or sawn on a windy ane'. Her son, Charles Blythe, was crowned king in 1898 – but the gypsy way of life had gone by then. Today only the Palace remains.

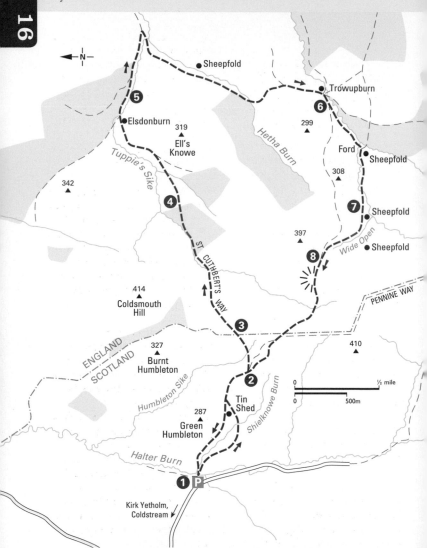

WALK 16 DIRECTIONS

❶ From the car park cross the burn by the footbridge, following the signs to St Cuthbert's Way. Bear right to follow the obvious track uphill, keeping the Shielknowe Burn below on

your left. Eventually the track crosses the burn, then continues uphill, skirting the edge of Green Humbleton hill and eventually reaching a fingerpost.

❷ This is the place where St Cuthbert's Way splits from the

Pennine Way. Take the grassy path on the left to follow St Cuthbert's Way. Continue following this path as it winds uphill, then takes you to a fingerpost by a wall, which marks the border between Scotland and England.

3 Follow the path slantwise over the ridgeline ahead, then straight down into the valley beyond. At the valley floor, cross the right-hand stream to the near corner of a plantation. Cross a stile into the forest, where the path keeps near the foot of the trees, then joins the fence alongside the stream, before slanting slightly right into more open forest of pine. You'll soon walk down an avenue of trees and leave the wood by another stile.

4 Keep ahead across the field. From the gate at its far side a track starts that crosses a small stream, heads briefly uphill, then winds downs to reach Elsdonburn farm. Turn left between the farm buildings and follow the track as it bends round to the right. It becomes a tarred lane, with conifer wood on its left and the burn on its right.

5 Follow this tarred track across a cattle grid to a signpost. Here you leave St Cuthbert's Way to take the tarred track on the right signed 'Trowupburn'. Follow this, passing a sheepfold and then

a conifer plantation. The track eventually winds upwards, skirts a hill, then descends to Trowupburn farmhouse. Continue to walk past the farm buildings then bear right to a fingerpost.

6 Go through the gate here and follow the sign 'Border Ridge 1.5'. Wander along this wide grassy track then cross the ford next to the very large sheepfold. Head upstream with the burn now on your right, then cross the burn again, nip over the stile and join the sheep track that bears left through the bracken.

7 Walk round the hill and, when you are directly above a sheepfold on the left, bear right so that the Wide Open burn is on your left, the sheepfold behind you. Work your way uphill through the bracken to the head of the burn until you reach a fence on the higher ground.

8 Go through the gate at the corner and take the green path ahead across open ground. Walk around the head of a stream valley (the stream drops to the right) to the wall and fence marking the border with Scotland. Cross a stile and bear right to a Pennine Way fingerpost. Here, bear left and follow the green path and waymarkers downhill and past the fingerpost of St Cuthbert's Way (Point **2**). Keep ahead above a tin shed, on a path leading down to the footbridge at the start.

Holy Orders at Jedburgh

Follow waymarked footpaths from this historic town.

WALK 17

DISTANCE 4.5 miles (7.2km)	**MINIMUM TIME** 3hrs
ASCENT/GRADIENT 295ft (90m) ▲▲▲	**LEVEL OF DIFFICULTY** ✛✛✛
PATHS Tracks, meadow paths and some sections of road, 2 stiles	
LANDSCAPE Gentle hills and fine old abbey	
SUGGESTED MAP OS Explorer OL16 The Cheviot Hills	
START/FINISH Grid reference: NT 651204	
DOG FRIENDLINESS Fair, but keep on lead near sheep and on road	
PARKING Main car park by tourist information centre	
PUBLIC TOILETS At car park	

Although it was built back in the 12th century, the beauty and grandeur of Jedburgh Abbey is still clearly evident. It certainly dominates this bustling border town, and sits serene and seemingly untroubled by the hustle and hassle of modern life. It must have seemed still more impressive in medieval times, when the power of the Church was at its height and the population was generally uneducated and superstitious.

The abbey is one of four in the Borders – the others being at Dryburgh, Kelso and Melrose – and all were built after the Norman Conquest. They are stretched across the Borders like a string of ecclesiastical jewels. Jedburgh Abbey is one of the most impressive medieval buildings in Scotland. It was built for French Augustinian canons in 1138 by David I, on the site of an earlier Anglo-Saxon monastery, and was specifically designed to make a visual impact. This was not because the King was exceedingly devout, but was owing to the fact that Jedburgh is very close to the border with England. David needed to make an obvious statement of authority to his powerful Norman neighbours.

Monastic Life

Each of the Border abbeys belonged to a different religious order. The Augustinian canons at Jedburgh were also known as 'Black Canons' owing to the colour of their robes. Unlike monks, canons were all ordained clergymen who were allowed to administer Holy Communion. Dryburgh Abbey was founded by Premonstratensian canons, who wore white robes and lived a more secluded life than the Augustinians. Kelso Abbey, which became one of the largest monasteries in Scotland, belonged to the Benedictine order, while Melrose was founded by Cistercian monks. The Cistercians took their name from the forest of Cîteaux in France, where their first community was established. Often known as 'White Benedictines', Cistercian monks adhered strictly to the Rule of St Benedict. Manual labour in the abbey was carried out by poor, and generally illiterate, lay brothers. These people lived and worshipped separately to the 'choir' monks who devoted their time to reading, writing and private prayer. The Cistercians adhered to a strict regime, designed to purify their lives. They banned the use of practical goods such as bedspreads, combs and even underwear.

Abbeys Under Fire

These medieval abbeys all suffered in the battles that ravaged the Borders for centuries. Jedburgh, for example, was stripped of its roofing lead by Edward I's troops who stayed here during the Wars of Independence. It came under attack many times and was burned by the Earl of Surrey in 1530. After the Reformation, all the abbeys fell into decline and began to decay. Today they remain picturesque reminders of a previous age.

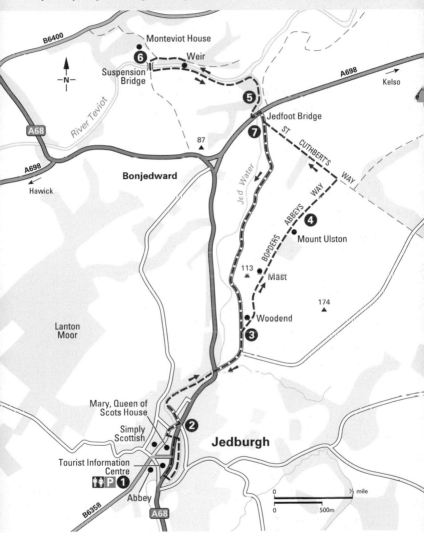

WALK 17 DIRECTIONS

❶ From the car park, walk back to the A68. Cross the road into Duck Row. Take the path on the left to walk beside the river, under an old bridge, then come on to the road. Turn right across the bridge.

Overleaf: Mary, Queen of Scots House in Jedburgh (Walk 17)

WALK 17

2 Turn left, following the sign for Borders Abbeys Way. Where the road divides, turn left and follow the lane beside a builders' yard to join 'Waterside Walk'. When you reach the main road, cross and follow the tarmac lane uphill. Keep straight on, passing a turning on the right, until you reach a fork, just before a farmyard development on the left.

3 Turn right here to walk in front of a small farmhouse called Woodend. Turn left on to a footpath and continue past the front of Mount Ulston house. Your route now runs uphill, taking you past a radio mast. Maintain direction to join the narrow grassy track – this can get very muddy, even in the summer.

4 Continue along this track until you reach the fingerpost at the end, where you turn left to join St Cuthbert's Way. The going becomes much easier now as you are walking along a wide, firm

track. When you reach the tarmac road, turn right and join the main road. Turn left, go over the bridge, then cross the road. Hop over the crash barrier and go down some steps to continue following St Cuthbert's Way.

5 You're now on a narrow, grassy track, which runs beside the river. You then have to nip over a couple of stiles, before walking across a meadow frequently grazed by sheep. Walk past the weir, then go through the gate to cross the suspension bridge – take care as it can get extremely slippery here.

6 You now pass a sign for Monteviot House and walk through the woods to reach a fingerpost, where you can turn right to enjoy views over the river. If you wish to extend your walk, you can continue along St Cuthbert's Way until it joins the road, then retrace your steps. Whatever you choose, you then retrace your steps back over the suspension bridge, along the riverside and back to the main road. Turn left across a bridge, then immediately right down a tarmac lane.

7 Ignoring the track off to the left, follow the road all the way back to Jedburgh. Cross the A68 and return back along 'Waterside Walk' to the car park.

Going the Whole Hogg in Ettrick

An enjoyable tramp in the footsteps of a local poet.

DISTANCE 7 miles (11km)	**MINIMUM TIME** 4hrs
ASCENT/GRADIENT 420ft (1350m) ▲▲▲	**LEVEL OF DIFFICULTY** ✦✦✦
PATHS Hill tracks and grassy paths; pathless grass for Peniestone Knowe loop; 2 stiles	
LANDSCAPE Open rolling hills and loch side	
SUGGESTED MAP OS Explorer 330 Moffat & St Mary's Loch	
START/FINISH Grid reference: NT 2237204	
DOG FRIENDLINESS Keep on lead near sheep	
PARKING On both sides of A708 near Glen Café	
PUBLIC TOILETS At start behind Glen Café	

James Hogg, a shepherd turned writer, was born in this tranquil valley in 1770. He and his beloved dog frequently paced tracks that you follow on this walk, from Ettrick to Tibbie Shiels Inn, to meet Sir Walter Scott.

Hogg is popularly known as the Ettrick Shepherd and a monument to him broods above the start of this walk. However, he would probably prefer to be remembered by his work, as his literary achievements are considerable – particularly for someone who had such humble origins. The son of a poor farmer, he hardly received any formal education – indeed, some reports state that his schooling lasted no more than six months. By the age of seven he had started work as a cowherd on a farm.

But he had ambition and determination, and an artistic streak, perhaps inherited from his grandfather, said to be the last man who could speak to the fairies. By the time Hogg reached his mid-teens he was working as a shepherd and had taught himself to read and write. He began composing poetry while out on the hills, drawing on the tradition of local ballads learned from his mother. He soon came to the attention of Sir Walter Scott, who was travelling the Borders. Scott became Hogg's mentor – although the pronounced differences in their class meant that Scott always regarded him as a bit of a peasant.

Hogg modelled himself on Robert Burns and began to get his poems and songs published. His first collection of ballads, *The Mountain Bard* (1807) was well received, and three years later Hogg moved to Edinburgh to try and make it as a writer. Within a few years he had been recognised as one of the leading poets of the day – the poor country shepherd had become a celebrity.

After a few years Hogg returned to the Borders, where he wrote the work for which he is best remembered – *The Private Memoirs and Confessions of a Justified Sinner* (1824). Contemporary critics felt it was so sophisticated that it could never have been written by such an uneducated man. James Hogg was eventually offered a knighthood, but his wife made him turn it down. He died in 1835 and is buried in Ettrick churchyard.

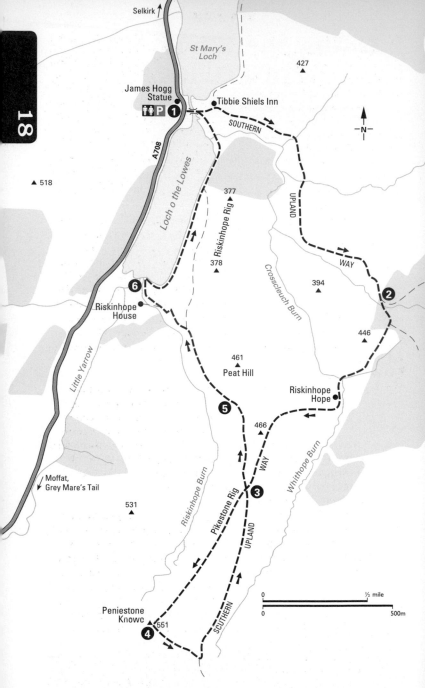

WALK 18 DIRECTIONS

❶ Take the lane across the stone bridge between the two lochs and past Tibbie Shiels Inn, then take the rougher track uphill through

a gate, with the Crosscleuch Burn down on its right. It winds uphill to a gate into plantations.

❷ At once, fork right, at a Southern Upland Way (SUW)

signpost. The path crosses a footbridge, then runs up a tree gap past a signpost, to a stile at the plantation edge. It descends to a footbridge over Whithope Burn, then heads up valley past the ruins of Riskinhope Hope among scattered trees. It then turns uphill, with plenty of waymarkers, to the level ridgeline of Pikestone Rig. Head along the ridge for 550yds (500m) to a small col. Here the SUW bears left, on to the ridge flank; meanwhile another path turns sharp back right out of the col. Later, this will be the descent for Riskinhope.

3 Ignoring both those paths, keep ahead up the grassy ridgeline, on a quad-bike track. Peniestone Knowe's plateau is rough and pathless. The actual summit is marked by a pool, and a slight knoll where three fences and a fallen wall all meet.

4 Don't cross any fence, but follow the fence running downhill to the left. Quad-bike wheelmarks run down fairly steep ground with rushes, to a stile where the SUW crosses the fence. Turn sharp left, away from the stile, and follow the wide, rebuilt path along the flank of Peniestone Knowe to the col on Pikestone Rig (Point **3**). Go slantwise through the col, on

to the path already noted, which slants down the left flank of the ridge. On the left is the notch of Riskinhope Burn and the path runs down along the right wall of this. It is grassy but clear, until it passes below a wide col before Peat Hill. Here it vanishes in a boggy patch, for just a few steps, before reappearing on the bracken slope of Peat Hill.

5 The grassy track slants down the flank of Peat Hill, then zig-zags down through two gates to the valley floor meadow. Before Riskinhope house it reaches a ford of Riskinhope Burn. Follow the burn down to reach the Loch of the Lowes.

6 Turn right along the loch side. Go through a gate above the loch's corner, to a bracken path. This continues alongside the loch to a gate at its northern corner. Bear left to a high footbridge. Cross a field near the river to a gate on to the lane beside the bridge between the lochs and back to your car.

A Beefy Devil of a Walk in Moffat

A hearty walk around the intriguingly named Devil's Beef Tub near the small town of Moffat.

19

DISTANCE 4.5 miles (7.2km)   **MINIMUM TIME** 2hrs

ASCENT/GRADIENT 1,076ft (328m) ▲▲▲   **LEVEL OF DIFFICULTY** +++

PATHS Farm tracks, small paths; narrow path across steep Beef Tub slope

LANDSCAPE Dramatic Beef Tub hollow and views of the Borderlands

SUGGESTED MAP OS Explorer 330 Moffat & St Mary's Loch

START/FINISH Grid reference: NT 057128

DOG FRIENDLINESS Keep on lead when passing sheep and cattle

PARKING Lay-by just south of forest gateway

PUBLIC TOILETS Lay-by just south of forest gateway

WARNING Bull with cows occasionally at Point ❹

Dark, forbidding and dramatic (Sir Walter Scott once described it as a 'black, blackguard-looking abyss of a hole'), the hollow known as the Devil's Beef Tub has a history as turbulent as its name suggests. Over the years this deep, natural bowl has been used as a hiding place by thieves, formed a refuge for the persecuted and witnessed feats of daring – and even murder. Once known as the Corrie of Annan, it gained the name the Devil's Beef Tub in the 16th century when it was frequently used by the Johnstone clan, a local reiving (rustling) family, to hide stolen cattle after a raid. In reference to this it was also sometimes sardonically referred to as the Marquis of Annandale's Beef Stand.

The Covenanting Movement

The Tub was not only useful for sheltering stolen animals, however – it was also used as a hideout by persecuted Covenanters during Charles II's so-called 'Killing Times' (see Walk 5). The origins of the covenanting movement went back to the time when bishops were imposed on the Church of Scotland by James VI. Years later his son, Charles I, who also believed in the divine right of kings, tried to interfere further in Scottish ecclesiastical affairs. This provoked such hostility that there was a riot in Edinburgh, resulting in the signing of the National Covenant in 1638. This document affirmed the authority of the Church of Scotland over the King in all spiritual matters and was circulated throughout Scotland, gaining particular support in the south-west.

Throughout the 17th century, religious fanaticism grew and Covenanters became a powerful force in Scotland. When Charles II, who had Roman Catholic sympathies, was restored to the throne he tried to suppress the movement. There were many battles and prisoners were often brutally treated. Finding themselves outlawed, some ministers of the Church began holding illegal services, known as 'conventicles', in the open air. Persecution only fuelled resistance and during the years 1684 to 1687, the 'Killing Times', hundreds of people were slaughtered by officers of the Crown. The most notorious of these was Graham of Claverhouse, later Viscount Dundee. There's a reminder of these violent times near the car park at the Devil's Beef Tub, where you can see a stone dedicated to John Hunter, a Covenanter who was shot on the hills here in 1685.

A Rebel in the Tub

This violent period in history came to an end when James II's son-in-law, William of Orange, came to the throne in 1689 – but was soon replaced in the following century by the violence of the Jacobite rebellion. In 1746 a prisoner from the Battle of Culloden, which had brought the rebellion to an end the previous year, was being marched to Carlisle for trial.

He escaped his guards by leaping into the Devil's Beef Tub and disappearing in the swirling mist. Once again this great hollow had played its part in Scottish history.

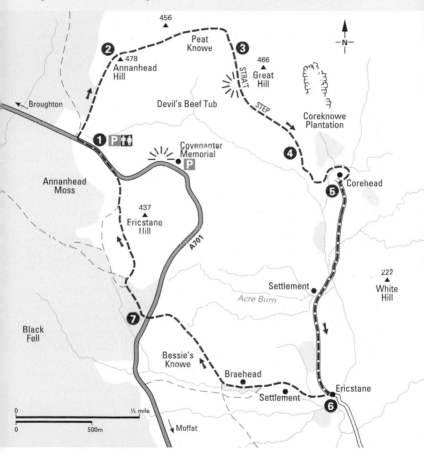

WALK 19 DIRECTIONS

❶ Walk up the A701 to the forest gateway on the right. Don't take the wide gravel track, but a wooden gate on the right-hand side, to a small path to the left of a fence. Climb rails at a fence end, and head up the grassy slope of Annanhead Hill, keeping to the right of the plantation area to the trig point on the summit.

W A L K 19

2 The small path continues around the flank of Peat Knowe, keeping the wall and fence to your left. Follow the path down the grassy slope of Annanhead Hill, keeping to the head of a gully, where your path meets the wall. Walk to the other side of the gully.

WHILE YOU'RE THERE

Moffat has several historical associations. Robert Burns wrote one of his poems at the Black Bull Hotel and Graham of Claverhouse, the scourge of the Covenanters, once stayed here. Of more recent interest is the fact that the town was the birthplace of Air Chief Marshal Lord Dowding, who led Fighter Command in the Battle of Britain.

3 Past the gully head, turn right on a small path that runs just above, and to the left of, the grassy gully. As the slope drops away steeply, the path, called Strait Step, bends left and contours on a level line across the steep slope, below some small craggy outcrops. As the slope eases, the path slants down through bracken, heading towards the Coreknowe plantation at the valley end. Just before the plantation, you'll reach a metal gate leading into a field.

4 A bull occasionally grazes in this field, so if you need to avoid him, pass along above the field and climb an awkward fence into the plantation. Slant down right, under the trees, to a gate into

WHAT TO LOOK OUT FOR

Ericstane Hill, which you pass on the latter part of this walk, was the site of a Roman signal station, used to monitor troop movements along a Roman road that stretched from all the way from Carlisle to the Clyde.

WHERE TO EAT AND DRINK

The Balmoral Hotel and the Ariffe Café on the main square in Moffat are both excellent choices. If you've got a sweet tooth there's always the delights of the Moffat Toffee Shop.

the field with the tiny footbridge mentioned below. Otherwise, go through the grey gate and down beside a grassy bank. Turn left on a rough track to the bottom corner of the plantation. The track reaches a gate above a red-brick house. Through the gate, signed 'Moffat', head out into the field to a tiny footbridge, then bear right to pass to the left of the white buildings of Corehead farm. A fence on the right leads to a gate on to the farm's access track.

5 Follow the farm road along the valley bottom. The small area of undulating land on the right is the remains of an ancient settlement.

6 After a cattle grid, at the start of the buildings, turn up right through a gate signed 'footpath'. A stony track leads past a house and through a gate. Turn right, following the track as it runs above a stone wall. Eventually you'll reach the main A701. Cross over – take care as it's busy – on to a rough track opposite.

7 The route passes over Ericstane Hill. Bear right and follow the track as it runs north round the far side of the hill. On open hill, the track is indistinct, deep ruts half-hidden under rushes. Pass through a slight col to the left of the hill summit, to rejoin the A701. Turn right here to visit the Covenanter memorial, or turn left to return to the start of the walk.

Discover Dunaskin Ironworks

*A hill walk from a 19th-century industrial monument
to a deserted, but not forgotten, village.*

DISTANCE 4 miles (6.4km)	**MINIMUM TIME** 3hrs
ASCENT/GRADIENT 492ft (150m) ▲▲▲	**LEVEL OF DIFFICULTY** +++

PATHS Old rail and tram beds and rough hillside

LANDSCAPE Hill, moorland and industrial buildings

SUGGESTED MAP OS Explorer 327 Cumnock & Dalmellington

START/FINISH Grid reference: NX 440084

DOG FRIENDLINESS Keep on lead near sheep and at lambing time

PARKING Dunaskin Open Air Museum

PUBLIC TOILETS At visitor centre

During the Industrial Revolution, iron was one of the great growth industries. In 1836 Henry Houldsworth, owner of a mill in Glasgow, diversified his business interests and created the Coltness Iron Works. Ten years later he and his son John brought the iron industry to the remote Doon Valley. Henry built his iron foundry on the site of Dunaskin farm and the early Victorian field pattern remains in outline surrounding the works.

New Industry

The area, although rich in iron, coal and water, was almost totally lacking in transport links. Everything for the construction of the foundry had to be brought in by train to Ayr and then by horse to Dunaskin. Twenty-four pairs of horses were needed to haul the great beam for the blast engines alone. Iron was continually produced here from 1848 until 1921, when the buildings became a brickworks and then a processing plant for the coal mines until the late 1970s. One of the most complete Industrial Revolution ironworks in Europe, although restored by a conservation trust and opened as a museum, a lack of funding has resulted in its closure.

At the time the Dunaskin Iron Works were built, the principal industries were agriculture and weaving and the population of the Upper Doon Valley was a mere 250 at Patna and a further 800 in the parish of Dalmellington. Skilled workers were brought in to provide the core of the workforce for the ironworks. They were joined by local men, leaving agricultural work in hope of higher wages, as well as tin miners from Cornwall, itinerant English workers and Highlanders displaced by the Clearances.

New Homes

The company built Waterside village opposite the ironworks to house the large numbers of workers. High above on the Knockkippen plateau, twin villages were built close to the iron ore mines. The twin villages of Lethanhill and Burnfoothill were considered as one, commonly known as the 'Hill, by the close-knit communities. Linked to the outside world by tram and railway lines, this community survived the closure of the mines, the end of smelting at Dunaskin and two world wars. Ironically it was killed off by the post-war drive to improve housing.

Sanitation and overcrowding were a problem on the 'Hill and when the local authority decided to concentrate new building in nearby Patna and Dalmellington, the quality of the new housing and the clean living space it offered was irresistible. No one wanted to leave but gradually the population dwindled until the last man, James Stevenson, departed on 31 August, 1954. All that remains today are the bare outlines of houses among the trees, the war memorial and a simple stone painted white with the poignant inscription 'Long live the Hill 1851–1954'.

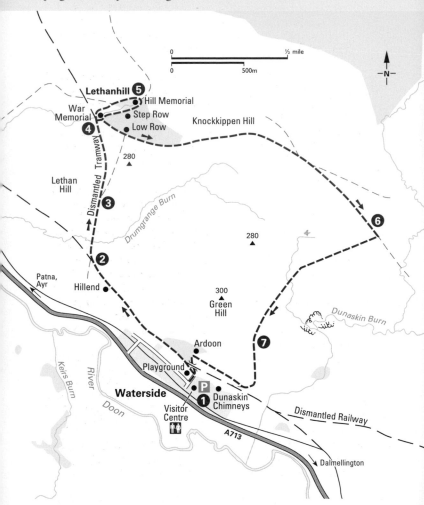

WALK 20 DIRECTIONS

❶ Turn right in front of the visitor centre and follow the road towards the adventure playground. Go uphill on a

track to the right of the playground and through a kissing gate into woodland. Emerge at a T-junction opposite a railway bridge and turn left on to a grassy trail.

2 When you reach a metal gate across the trail, go through a small wooden one at its side. Climb over the next gate, turn right and head uphill following the line of a disused tramway, between the ends of an old bridge. This is the trackbed of the former horse-drawn tramway, which was used in order to bring the iron ore down from the plateau.

WHAT TO LOOK OUT FOR

The foundations of the former church and schoolhouse can be seen on the ground behind the war memorial. The church was sold to a local silver band and was rebuilt in Dalmellington. Look also in the remains of the houses of Low Row for floral tributes hung on the trees by former residents who still walk here on a regular basis.

3 At the top of the hill, when the path divides, keep left and follow the path as it goes through two short sections of wall. The ground to your right in front of the conifer plantation was once the village football field. Where the path is blocked by a fence, turn right and then go left to walk through a gate and right on to a metalled lane.

4 Head along here, past the remains of the miners' houses of Step Row, which are clearly visible amongst the trees. A stone memorial to the 'Hill stands near the site of the former village store. To the right of this, and now within the wood, is the former village square and the remains of more houses.

5 From the stone memorial turn back towards the war memorial, then return to the gate at the corner of the wood and continue along the track beside the wood. In the trees are the remains of Low Row. Go through another gate and continue along the former railway. When it forks, keep right.

6 Continue until the route ahead is blocked by sheets of corrugated iron. Cross the wall and turn right, heading downhill to pick up a faint path. Continue on this to reach a cluster of trees beside a ruined building.

7 Head down from here towards the right of a row of cottages. Go through a gate, turn right then right again at a fork to reach Ardoon. Go past the house, turn left on to a footpath and follow it downhill and under a small, disused railway bridge. Cross the track and carry on, heading back downhill on the footpath which leads back to the visitor centre.

WHERE TO EAT AND DRINK

The Hollybush Inn on the road to Ayr serves reasonably priced bar meals, including bowls of excellent hot soup. Travelling in the other direction you could try one of the hotels in the centre of Dalmellington.

WHILE YOU'RE THERE

Don't miss a visit to one of Scotland's most fascinating railway museums. Just along the road, on the north edge of Dalmellington, is the Scottish Industrial Railway Centre, operated by enthusiasts from the Ayrshire Rail Preservation Group. This is as much part of the local story as the ironworks and every Sunday in July and August they offer trips on a working steam train.

WALK 21

On Old Roads and Rails Around Muirkirk

Walk around a once prosperous moorland town that stood at the crossroads of history.

DISTANCE 3.5 miles (5.7km)	**MINIMUM TIME** 3hrs
ASCENT/GRADIENT 16ft (5m) ▲▲▲	**LEVEL OF DIFFICULTY** +++
PATHS Old railway beds, farm tracks and country lanes, 1 stile	
LANDSCAPE Undulating farmland and dense woodland	
SUGGESTED MAP OS Explorer 328 Sanquhar & New Cumnock	
START/FINISH Grid reference: NX 696265	
DOG FRIENDLINESS Good, locals walk their dogs here	
PARKING Walkers' car park, Furnace Road	
PUBLIC TOILETS None on route	

In the early 17th century Muirkirk was not much more than a crude little settlement called Garan on a dirt track that ran from Ayr to Edinburgh. The building of the Moor Kirk of Kyle led eventually to a name change to Muirkirk. An abundance of natural minerals such as coal, limestone and iron ore in the locality would inevitably make it a centre of industry and bring great prosperity.

'Tar' McAdam

Coal mining was well under way when John Loudon McAdam (1756–1836) came here in 1786 to set up a tar works. Known locally as 'Tar' McAdam, he would later go on to develop his famous method of road construction and this is where he carried out his initial experiments. Furnace Road, leading to the walkers' car park, was used in his first trials and road surfaces are still referred to as 'tarmac' today.

Iron and Coal

Muirkirk became the site of Ayrshire's first ironworks in 1787 when James Ewing & Co opened here. Three years later a canal had been dug to transport ore and coal on a series of barges from the Lightshaw, Auldhouseburn and Crossflat mines east of the works. Tram lines ran to the west and a series of bogie tracks led from the various pits to the canals. The Kames Colliery was opened in 1799 and would become the longest operating coal mine in the area. The canal was eventually replaced by the railway when the Glasgow and South Western Railway Company opened the Auckinleck-to-Muirkirk branch line in 1848. From this main line a maze of spur lines ran to the production areas.

Muirkirk became a prosperous, thriving community. It was the first town in Britain to get gas lighting following the construction of the Muirkirk Coke & Gaslight Co in 1859. At its peak, it had a population in excess of 5,000 with 1,000 employed in the ironworks alone.

But nothing lasts forever. Mines become exhausted, or seams run out and industrial trends change. The ironworks ceased production in 1923, following a strike by the workers. Iron ore mining had stopped some time previously and the ore was shipped in from further afield. During the strike the furnaces cooled with iron still inside them and rather than go to the expense of restoring them the company shut down.

The elaborate façade of the industrial works which locals had dubbed 'The Castle' was demolished in 1968, the same year that the Kames Colliery finally closed. By this time the railway had disappeared under the axe of Dr Beeching in the mid-1960s. With no industry left the population drifted away and Muirkirk gradually declined to the small, close-knit community that remains today.

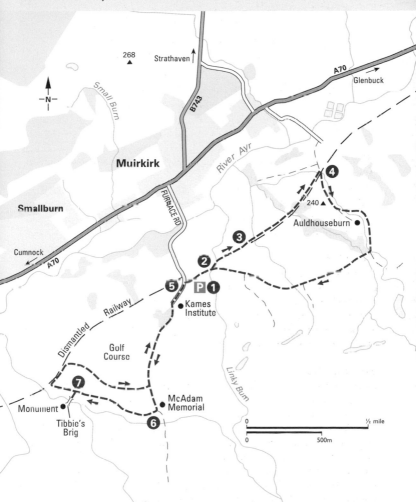

WALK 21 DIRECTIONS

❶ From the car park follow the blue waymarker and exit the car park via a gate on to a rough track with a high wall running along to the right. This continues as a fence and, once past the end of it, look for a waymarker pole on your left.

2 Turn left on to a grass track. Follow this to some steps, go downhill and through a kissing gate. Turn right and walk along what may have been the bank of the 18th-century canal.

3 Go through several kissing gates following the River Ayr Way. This recently constructed path runs between two wire fences, along the trackbed, eventually reaching a kissing gate.

4 Go through the gate and turn right on to the quiet country road. Follow this past the remains of an old railway bridge, past a farm entrance on the right then go through a gate to continue on a farm road. At the next gate turn right, go through four gates and return to the car park.

5 Turn right and exit the car park on to Furnace Road, then turn left. Continue past the clock tower of the derelict Kames Institute and along the edge of a golf course. Go through a gate and continue, passing a cottage on the left, on to the old drove road to Sanquhar. Go through another gate and continue to the McAdam memorial.

6 Just past this head along a green track on the right. Follow this track along the side of a stream until it joins a dirt track just above Tibbie's Brig. Near here, in a small clay dwelling, lived a local poetess, Tibbie Pagan,

who eked out a living by singing, selling her poetry and possibly supplying illicit whisky. She is believed locally to have been the source of the song 'Ca the Yowes tae the Knowes', although Burns himself collected it from a clergyman. In 1803, she published a volume of her collected poems.

7 Go down to the Brig and the monument then return uphill keeping left on the access for the disabled route to McAdam's cairn. Follow this back to the drove road where you turn left to return to the car park.

One of Scotland's Great Scotts at Dryburgh

A gentle walk in the Borders countryside that was much beloved by Sir Walter Scott.

DISTANCE 5 miles (8km)   **MINIMUM TIME** 3hrs

ASCENT/GRADIENT 131ft (40m) ▲▲▲   **LEVEL OF DIFFICULTY** +++

PATHS Firm woodland and riverside tracks, 3 stiles

LANDSCAPE Historic abbey and river banks

SUGGESTED MAP OS Explorer 338 Galashiels, Selkirk & Melrose

START/FINISH Grid reference: NT 592318

DOG FRIENDLINESS Keep on lead on Mertoun Estate and by golf course

PARKING Dryburgh Abbey car park

PUBLIC TOILETS At car park

Walk anywhere in the Scottish Borders and you are probably following in the footsteps of one of Scotland's most celebrated literary figures – Sir Walter Scott. He travelled widely here, writing marvellous books and poetry that would be described as bestsellers if they were published today. Yet, while everyone has certainly heard of Sir Walter Scott, hardly anyone now reads his books.

Wavering over Waverley

The reason for this is almost certainly the somewhat impenetrable nature of the language he uses – impenetrable to non Scots, anyway. Full of enthusiasm, people tend to pick up a copy of *Waverley* (1814), a romantic tale of the Jacobite rebellion, then put it down in defeat after page ten. But those who persist and learn to unravel the old Scots dialect discover tales that were strongly influenced by the ballads, folklore and history of the borderlands – tales that would have died out otherwise.

From Polio to Poetry

Scott was the son of an Edinburgh lawyer but spent a lot of time in the Borders as a child while recuperating from polio. He was fascinated by the stories and ballads he heard and, when he grew older, began to collect material that he later turned into romantic poetry. He was greatly influenced by Robert Burns and became friends with James Hogg, the Ettrick Shepherd (see Walk 18). Scott became a barrister in 1792, but spent his spare time writing poetry. He was appointed Sheriff-Depute of Selkirk in 1799 and in 1811 he moved to Abbotsford, a farmhouse near Melrose, where he lived for the rest of his life. He turned to novel writing, declaring that 'Byron beat me' at poetry.

It was a decision that was to make Scott's fortune – but it was also, ultimately, to cost him his health. After the publication of *Waverley*, he produced several more historical novels, including *Rob Roy* (1817), *The Heart of Midlothian* (1818) and *Ivanhoe* (1819).

DRYBURGH

Scott's novels revived interest in Scottish culture, at a time when it had been in danger of disappearing. In 1818 he discovered the Honours of Scotland, a crown, sword and sceptre, which had been hidden in Edinburgh Castle from the time of Charles II (see Walk 76). And a few years later he was invited to make the arrangements for George IV's visit to Scotland – the King entered wholeheartedly into the spirit of the visit and delighted the crowds by wearing a kilt teamed with some natty pink tights.

Scott should have been able to live in relative wealth and comfort, but in 1825 his publishing house collapsed and he was left with enormous debts. His wife died the same year. Scott worked furiously to pay off his debts, but his health suffered and in 1832 he died at Abbotsford. He is buried in the ruins of Dryburgh Abbey.

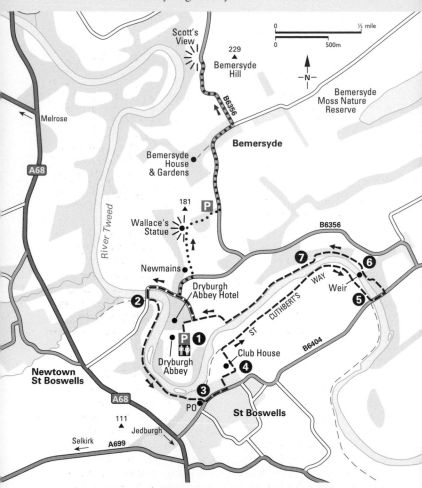

WALK 22 DIRECTIONS

1 From the car park at the abbey walk back to join the road, pass the entrance to the Dryburgh Abbey Hotel and then walk down the dead-end lane in front of you. You'll soon see the river and at the end of the road continue along a footpath and bypass, then cross the bridge over the River Tweed.

2 Turn left immediately and join St Cuthbert's Way. This waymarked trail now leads along the river banks. At some points there are steps, tiny footbridges and patches of boardwalk to assist you. Continue to follow this trail which eventually takes you past two small islands in the river, where it then leads away from the river bank.

3 Follow the trail on to a tarmac track, then left. At the main road in St Boswells go left again and continue to follow the trail signs, passing a post office and later Scott's View chippy on your left. After house No. 101, turn left down Bravheads Road then go to your right along a tarmac track at the end.

WHILE YOU'RE THERE

Abbotsford, west of Melrose, was Sir Walter Scott's home from 1811 until his death. He spent an enormous amount of money turning the original farmhouse into the home you see today. Scott's influence can be felt everywhere, from the library, which contains over 9,000 rare books, to the historic relics, such as Rob Roy's gun. You can visit both the house and grounds and there's a handy tea room too.

4 Follow this, then turn left and walk past the golf club house. Continue walking for a few paces, then turn right and follow St Cuthbert's Way as it hugs the golf course. You now continue by the golf course until your track eventually brings you back down to the river bank. Walk past the weir and up to the bridge.

5 Go up the steps and cross the bridge (take care, there is no footway), then turn sharp left and walk towards the cottages. Before the cottages, go left, over the footbridge, then turn right along the river bank to walk in front of them. At the weir, take the steps that run up to the right, nip over the stile and into a field.

6 Go left now and keep to the track through woodland down to the river bank, following the waymarked trail.

WHERE TO EAT AND DRINK

The Dryburgh Abbey Hotel has a bar and restaurant that is open to non-residents. However if you want more choice, drive into Melrose where there are several pubs and restaurants offering everything from French food to traditional Scottish dishes. Perhaps the best known is Burts Hotel, an 18th-century inn which serves good bar meals and offers a choice of 50 single malts.

7 Follow the river, keeping an eye out for fish leaping up to feed from the water's surface. You'll cross a stile, then pass a greenhouse on your left. Climb another stile here, turn right, walk past the toilets and, at the house ahead, turn left and walk back into the car park.

EXTENDING THE WALK

From the start of this walk, it's less than 2 miles (3.2km) to Scott's View, a vantage point overlooking the Tweed Valley and the Eildon Hills. Walk back along the main road, then take the footpath from Newmains up to the statue of William Wallace. Head for the road from here, and follow it up past Bemersyde House and Gardens to the wide lay-by at the viewpoint. You can return to Dryburgh Abbey by retracing your steps.

22

From Selkirk to the Wilds of Africa

A gentle walk by Ettrick Water, laced with memories of the great explorer Mungo Park.

DISTANCE *4 miles (6.4km)*   **MINIMUM TIME** *1hr 40min*

ASCENT/GRADIENT *131ft (40m)* ▲▲▲   **LEVEL OF DIFFICULTY** ✚✚✚

PATHS *Riverside paths and woodland tracks, town streets, 4 stiles*

LANDSCAPE *Undulating farmland and dense woodland*

SUGGESTED MAP *OS Explorer 338 Galashiels, Selkirk & Montrose*

START/FINISH *Grid reference: NT 469286*

DOG FRIENDLINESS *Good, but don't let them chase ducks*

PARKING *West Port car park in Selkirk*

PUBLIC TOILETS *At car park*

It's hard to imagine that the sleepy town of Selkirk has any connection with the wilds of Africa. But look carefully at the statue in the High Street and you'll see that it commemorates Mungo Park, a local man and noted explorer. Park, who was born in 1771 and educated at Selkirk Grammar, trained as a doctor. Instead of settling down to a comfortable life, he took a post as surgeon's mate on a ship bound for the East Indies. This gave him a taste for travel. He returned from the voyage and promptly set off again, this time heading for Africa to map the Niger.

Wanderlust

His extraordinary journey lasted more than two and a half years. Not only did he become desperately ill from fever and hunger, he was robbed many times, and even captured and held prisoner by a tribal leader. He escaped after four months and continued his travels, following the River Niger to Sillis and only abandoning his journey when he became too ill to carry on. When he returned to Scotland he published a fasinating account of his travels, entitled *Travels in the Interior Districts of Africa* (1799), which quickly became a bestseller. Shortly afterwards he married and took a post as a respectable doctor in Peebles. You'd think he would have had enough excitement to last the rest of his life, but Park longed to return to Africa. As Sir Walter Scott, with whom Park became friends, later wrote: 'He would rather brave Africa and all its horrors, than wear out his life in long and toilsome rides over the hills in Scotland.'

Back to Africa

In 1805, Park set sail again for Africa, this time accompanied by his friend George Scott and brother-in-law Alexander Andersen, both from Selkirk, with the intention of completing the journey along the Niger. When they reached Africa they set off for the Niger, accompanied by soldiers and local bearers. They never came home. Scott, Andersen and many others died from fever. Park refused to give up, writing 'I shall...discover the termination of the Niger or perish in the attempt'.

In his Father's Footsteps

Those words were prophetic. Park continued his journey, together with a few soldiers and native bearers, but disappeared in the jungle. His family searched for him, but it was not until 1810 that they discovered he had died while trying to escape from hostile tribesmen who had attacked his party with poisoned arrows. He had thrown himself into the turbulent waters of the Niger and drowned. He never reached the source of the Niger. About 20 years after his death, his son travelled to Africa. He too disappeared and was never heard of again.

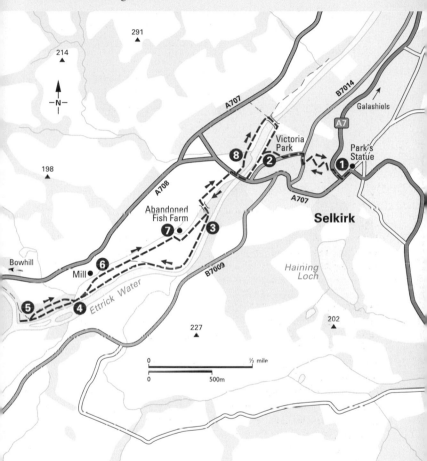

WALK 23 DIRECTIONS

❶ From Park's statue, walk to the Market Place, go right down Ettrick Terrace, left at the church, then immediately sharp right down Forest Road. Follow this downhill, cutting off the corner using the steps after No 109, to Mill Street. Go right, then left on to Buccleuch Road. Turn right following the signs for the riverside walk and continue to walk across Victoria Park to join a tarmac track.

❷ Turn left, walk by the river, then join the road and turn right to cross the bridge. Turn left along Ettrickhaugh Road, passing a row of cottages on your left. Just past them turn left, cross a tiny footbridge, then turn left down some steps and follow the path to the river bank and turn right.

❸ Follow the path along the river margin; it's eroded in places so watch your feet. In spring and summer your way is sprinkled with wild flowers. Eventually you join a wider track and bear left. Follow this until you reach a weir and a salmon ladder. Turn right to cross the tiny bridge.

> **WHILE YOU'RE THERE**
> Bowhill, home of the Duke and Duchess of Buccleuch and Queensberry, is 3 miles (4.8km) west of Selkirk on the A708. This fine Georgian house is stuffed full of art treasures, with paintings by Canaletto, Reynolds, Van Dyck and Gainsborough, as well as elegant furniture, silver and porcelain. It's a good place to bring children as they've also got a restored Victorian kitchen and a country park with an adventure area and nature trails.

❹ Immediately after this go left and continue walking alongside the river until you reach a point at which the Yarrow Water joins the Ettrick Water. Retrace your steps for about 100yds (91m), then turn left at a crossing of tracks.

❺ Your route now takes you through the woods, until you cross over the little bridge by the weir again. Take the footpath to the left and follow the cinder/gravel track round the meadow until you come to the mill buildings.

❻ Bear right (but don't cross the bridge) and continue, walking with the mill lade (small canal) on your left. Where the path splits,

> **WHERE TO EAT AND DRINK**
> There are a few places that you can try in the centre of Selkirk. Among the hotels offering a range of bar meals is the Cross Keys by the Market Place, which serves toasted sandwiches and light snacks. There's also a small tea room. Look out for the famous Selkirk bannock – a type of fruit bread – on sale in the town bakeries.

take the track on the left to follow a straight, concrete path beside the water to reach an abandoned fish farm.

❼ Walk around the buildings, then bear left to continue following the mill lade. Go left over the footbridge, then right, passing the cottages again. At the main road go right to reach the bridge. Don't cross the bridge but join the footpath on the left.

❽ Follow this footpath as it goes past a sports ground, then skirts a housing estate. Continue walking until you reach the pedestrian footbridge on your right-hand side, where you cross over the river, bear right, then retrace your footsteps back over Victoria Park and uphill to the Market Place at the start of the walk.

> **WHAT TO LOOK OUT FOR**
> You've got a great chance of seeing a dipper on this walk, particularly around the river banks at the point where the Ettrick Water and the Yarrow Water meet. Also sometimes known as the water ouzel, it is a pretty little brown bird with a white breast. It feeds on insects, often wading through rushing water and bobbing up and down while searching for them – hence its name.

Remembering the Jacobites at Traquair

You'll find Jacobite connections in an atmospheric old house and a moorland fairy well on this walk.

DISTANCE 7 miles (11.3km)   **MINIMUM TIME** 3hrs 30min

ASCENT/GRADIENT 1,378ft (420m) ▲▲▲   **LEVEL OF DIFFICULTY** +++

PATHS Firm, wide moorland tracks, 1 stile

LANDSCAPE Rolling hills and heather-clad moors – some excellent views

SUGGESTED MAP OS Explorer 337 Peebles & Innerleithen

START/FINISH Grid reference: NT 331345

DOG FRIENDLINESS Can run free for long stretches, but on lead near sheep

PARKING Southern Upland Way car park in Traquair, near village hall

PUBLIC TOILETS None on route; nearest in car park at Peebles

There can be few more romantic places in Britain than Traquair House, just a couple of minutes' drive from the start of this walk. It's the oldest continually inhabited house in Scotland and is still owned by the Maxwell Stuart family, who came here in 1491.

Parts of the house date back to the 12th century, although most of the present building was built in 1680. It's a house full of secret stairways and little windows and even has its own brewery, whose origins stretch back to the 16th century. Traquair House is one of those marvellous places that simply ooze atmosphere largely, I think, because it is still a family home.

All in a Good Cause

The house was always a popular stopping-off point for Scottish monarchs and 27 of them visited over the years, including Mary, Queen of Scots, who stayed here with her husband Darnley in 1566.

The family were traditionally staunch Catholics and when the Protestant William of Orange took the throne in 1689, they joined many others in supporting the Jacobite cause. This demanded that the Stuart King James II (Charles II's brother) be reinstated on the throne and, contrary to popular myth, attracted support among English people as well as Scots. Years of repression and bloodshed followed.

Hiding Out at Traquair

The Jacobite rebellion eventually culminated in the disastrous defeat at Culloden in 1746. You can, of course, visit the site of the battle itself, but it is somehow easier to understand what it must have been like to live during those times when you see the secret priest's room at Traquair. Often called 'priest's holes', these rooms were made in many of the great houses throughout Britain, allowing priests to live in hiding and take Mass for the devout family. The one in Traquair has such a strong atmosphere that it almost feels as if the priest has just stepped out for a moment.

The 4th Earl of Traquair was imprisoned in the Tower of London and sentenced to death for his part in one of the early Jacobite risings. However, he managed to make a story-book escape, when his wife smuggled him out of prison by dressing him as a maid. The cloak he used as his disguise is on display at Traquair. Years later, the 5th Earl was also held prisoner in the Tower for supporting the Jacobites at Culloden.

A Royal Promise

Bonnie Prince Charlie visited Traquair in 1745, passing through the great Bear Gates – so named because of the bear statues that top the gate posts. When the prince left, the 5th Earl wished him a safe journey, closed the gates behind him and promised that they would not be opened again until there was a Stuart monarch on the throne. The gates have remained unopened ever since.

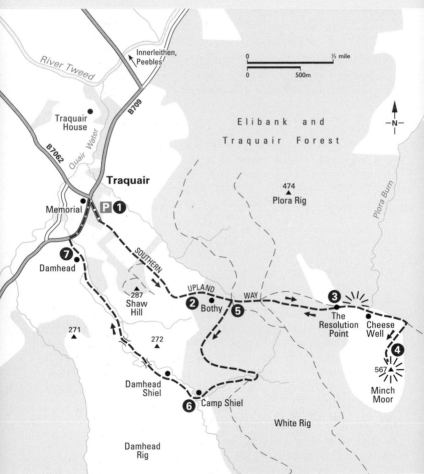

WALK 24 DIRECTIONS

❶ From the Southern Upland Way car park, join the tarmac road and walk left away from Traquair village. Continue ahead and then join the gravel track following signs for the Minch Moor. After you go through a gate the track becomes grassier, then you hop over a stile and enter Forestry Commission land.

2 Continue on the obvious track to pass a bothy on the right. When you come to a crossing of tracks maintain direction, crossing an area of scrub and self-seeded trees. When you reach a forest track, continue ahead, taking a narrow path to the right of a cycleway. The path winds uphill to rejoin the cycle track at 'The Resolution Point'.

WHILE YOU'RE THERE

The mineral waters at St Ronan's Well near Innerleithen have been attracting visitors since the 18th century and inspired the eponymous novel by Sir Walter Scott. The well is covered by a pavilion and you can still sample the waters. Guided walks around the well and garden are available on request.

WHERE TO EAT AND DRINK

In Innerleithen you can get a drink at the Traquair Arms Hotel. They also do cakes and hot drinks, as well as more substantial meals such as filo parcels, pasta bakes and aubergine cannelloni. There's also a restaurant at Traquair House, as well as a Brewery Shop selling Traquair Jacobite Ale to take home with you.

3 Maintain direction, enjoying great views over Walkerburn to the left. It feels wilder and windier up here, with large tracts of heather-covered moorland by your path. When you reach a marker post, turn right and walk up to the cairn on the Minch Moor – the views should be great on a clear day.

4 From the cairn, retrace your steps back to the main track. Then turn left and walk back downhill – stopping to leave some

WHAT TO LOOK OUT FOR

'The Resolution Point' is an artwork created by Charles Poulsen in 2005. From the metal sculptures by the path you will see geometric shapes of grass and heathers etched onto the slopes below. As you move away from the point, you notice that the circles are transformed into ovals as the perspective is distorted.

food when you pass the Cheese Well (see What to Look Out For) on the left – it's by the boggy part of the path. Turn left 20yds (18m) beyond 'The Resolution Point' and return downhill across one forest track to reach a second intersection.

5 Turn left now and walk downhill. The landscape soon opens out on the right-hand side giving you pleasant views of the valley and the river winding away. When you reach the apex of a bend, turn right along a grassy path. Follow this as it bears downhill, go through a gate and walk beside Camp Shiel cottage.

6 Go through another gate, cross the burn, then follow the grassy track and pass Damhead Shiel cottage. Go through another gate and follow the path across a bridge over a burn. You'll pass an expanse of scree on the right-hand side, and an ox-bow lake evolving on the left. Cross another bridge and continue to Damhead farm.

7 Walk past the farm and down to the road, then turn right. You'll now cross the burn again and will walk past some cottages on the right-hand side. When you reach the war memorial on the left, turn right and walk up the track to reach the parking place at the start of the walk on the left.

BROUGHTON

Thirty-Nine Steps in Broughton

A lovely walk through John Buchan country.

DISTANCE 5 miles (8km)	**MINIMUM TIME** 2hrs 30min

ASCENT/GRADIENT 1,575ft (480m) ▲▲▲ **LEVEL OF DIFFICULTY** ✦✦✦

PATHS Hill tracks and grassy paths, 1 stile

LANDSCAPE Rolling hills and exposed ridge

SUGGESTED MAP OS Explorer 336 Biggar & Broughton

START/FINISH Grid reference: NT 119374

DOG FRIENDLINESS Good, but keep on lead because of sheep

PARKING Parking in front of cottage past Broughton Place and art gallery

PUBLIC TOILETS None on route

I had been walking for about half an hour when I spotted a man standing alone on Broughton Heights. I thought nothing of it until he began to wave urgently. Thinking he was in some sort of trouble I climbed the hill. When I reached the top I saw that he was dressed in a tweed jacket and carried a small pack. His piercing blue eyes met mine: 'Hello Hannay,' he said holding out his hand. 'I have a message for you. We need your help.'

John Buchan didn't write those words, but these rugged hills around Broughton were once familiar and often trodden by the author of *The Thirty-Nine Steps* and you can't help but be inspired to flights of fancy by memories of his taut tales of intrigue and derring-do. Although he was born in Perth (in 1875), Buchan has close links with this area as his grandparents lived here and he spent many summer holidays in the village. A keen hillwalker, it is almost certain that he followed the same tracks that you take on this exhilarating circuit.

'Shockers'

Buchan's most famous fictional creation is the upper-class hero Richard Hannay, who featured in the spy thriller *The Thirty-Nine Steps* (1915). But this was not his only novel. He wrote many other adventure stories (or 'shockers' as he liked to call them) – four of them featuring Richard Hannay, as well as a book of poetry and several historical works including biographies of Sir Walter Scott and Oliver Cromwell.

A Career to Envy

He was extraordinarily successful and must have greatly annoyed his contemporaries who could never have hoped to match his achievements. After Oxford University (where he naturally became President of the Union and gained a First), he became a barrister. During the First World War he was appointed Director of Information, and then wrote a 24-volume history of the war. In 1927 he became a Member of Parliament and was made a Companion of Honour in 1932 – publishing more works all the time. As his career flourished he came into contact with many great characters, including Henry James and Lawrence of Arabia.

Buchan must have had immense energy and obviously impressed those around him, for in 1935 he was appointed Governor-General of Canada and was given a peerage — taking the title Baron Tweedsmuir of Elsfield. Tweedsmuir is a hamlet close to the village of Broughton and the area featured in a number of Buchan's works. Broughton was the village of 'Woodilee' in a little-known novel *Witch Wood* (1927), while much of the action in his adventure novels is played out on the moody moors and lonely hills of the Borders. John Buchan died in Canada in 1940. He would probably be surprised to find that his 'shockers' are still being read and enjoyed today.

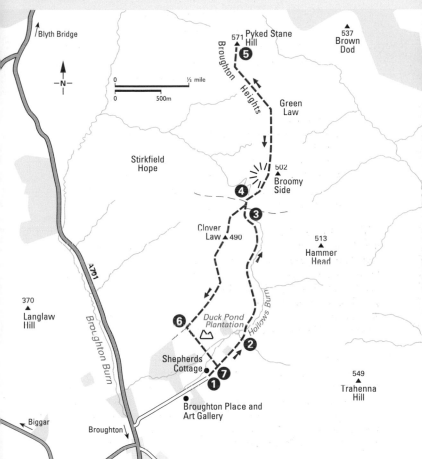

WALK 25 DIRECTIONS

❶ From the parking place, go through the gate and follow the obvious, grassy track that runs in front of the cottage. You'll soon pass a copse on the left-hand side, then pass the attractively named Duck Pond Plantation, also on the left-hand side. The track becomes slightly rougher now, cross a small footbridge over a burn.

2 Your track continues ahead past feathery carpets of heather and bracken — listen for the skylarks in the summer. Continue walking and the path will soon level out and lead you past a gully on the right-hand side. Follow the track until it bends, after which you come to a meeting of tracks.

3 Take the track that bears left and head for the dip that lies between the two hills — Clover Law on the left and Broomy Side in front. You should just be able to spot the fence 100yds (91m) on the skyline. Make for that fence and, as you near it, you'll eventually spot a gate, next to which is a wooden stile.

WHILE YOU'RE THERE

If you're a real John Buchan fan you can make a pilgrimage to the John Buchan Centre, which is at the far end of Broughton village. It's housed in an old church where Buchan and his relatives once attended services. This small museum is full of photographs, books and general memorabilia that illustrate the life and achievements of the author.

4 Cross the stile, then turn right and follow the fence line. You soon get superb views to the left — well, you do on a clear day. Continue following the fence and walk up the track until you reach the trig point on Broughton Heights — the final ascent's a bit of a puff — but it's thankfully not too long.

WHERE TO EAT AND DRINK

The best place for tea is the Laurel Bank tea room, which can be found in the centre of Broughton. It serves home-made soup and light meals such as baked potatoes and toasted sandwiches, substantial meals such as mince and tatties, as well as freshly baked cakes and scones. The atmosphere is friendly and they're used to accomodating walkers.

5 Now retrace your steps to reach the stile again, nip over it, but this time turn right and follow the narrow track that climbs Clover Law. Continue walking in the same direction, following the fence line as it runs along the top of the ridge. When you near the end of the ridge, keep your eyes peeled for a path to the left, down an old earth boundary bank.

6 Follow the track as it runs down roughly in the direction of the cottage — it's quite a steep descent. At the bottom you'll come to an old wall and a burn, which you cross, then continue ahead to cross over another burn and across a field to reach the main track.

7 Turn right here and walk past the little cottage again, through the gate and back to your car. If you want to visit Broughton Place and its art gallery, just continue walking down the track to reach the house on your left.

WHAT TO LOOK OUT FOR

The Broughton Gallery showcases the work of leading British artists and craftspeople. As well as paintings in oil and watercolour, you can find hand-made glass, ceramics, painted silk, carved wood and distinctive jewellery. The goods are for sale so you'd better bring your credit card — you might find a local landscape that you just can't resist.

Darvel's Marvellous Byways

In the footsteps of Sir Alexander Fleming, Darvel's most famous son, and the discovery of penicillin.

DISTANCE 7 miles (11.3km)	**MINIMUM TIME** 3hrs
ASCENT/GRADIENT 459ft (140m) ▲▲▲	**LEVEL OF DIFFICULTY** +++

PATHS Country lanes and pavements

LANDSCAPE Hillside, moorland, pasture and townscape

SUGGESTED MAP OS Explorer 334 East Kilbride, Galston & Darvel

START/FINISH Grid reference: NX 563374

DOG FRIENDLINESS Dogs on lead in lanes

PARKING On-street parking at Hastings Square at start of walk

PUBLIC TOILETS None on route

Lochfield Farm, the birthplace of Alexander Fleming (1881–1955), was the ideal childhood home for a boy with an insatiable curiosity about nature. Together with his brothers, the young Alexander spent much of his time roaming the moors identifying birds, animals and plants and guddling (catching by hand) trout in the nearby burns. He regarded his early education at Loudoun Moor School and later at Darvel as the foundation on which his later career was built.

Medical School

By the age of 13 he had moved to London to live with his brother Tom. Finishing his education at London Polytechnic, Fleming spent four years working as a clerk in a shipping office until the death of an uncle left him a small legacy which enabled him to take a short course of private tuition. He gained first place in the examination which would allow him to enter medical school. Fleming subsequently took first place in every exam he sat. By 1906 he had joined the Inoculation Department at St Mary's Hospital in Paddington and by 1909 was a Fellow of the Royal College of Surgeons. The war interrupted his career at St Mary's but after it he returned there and by 1928 had become Professor of Bacteriology.

A Fortunate Discovery

That year, while clearing up some old virus cultures in his laboratory, Fleming noticed that although all were covered in moulds, one was significantly different. This particular mould was dissolving the virus colonies round about it and was spreading across the dish destroying the rest. The mould was one of a class called penicillium and, as Fleming afterwards stated, 'It was my good fortune that one particular penicillium blew on to a culture plate I was playing with'.

Discovering what we now know as penicillin was just the beginning. Isolating, extracting and finding a means of using it to treat infection would take another ten years and it was the 1940s before this 'magic bullet' was commercially available. Since then it has saved countless thousands of lives and a huge industry has grown round the research and development of other antibiotics. Honours were heaped upon Fleming. In 1944 he was knighted. The following year he was awarded the Nobel Prize for Medicine and on 26 October, 1946, he returned to his native Darvel to receive 'the proudest title I could have... the Freedom of Darvel'. Fleming spent the rest of his life working, lecturing and travelling. His last visit to Darvel was in June 1952 when he presented the Alexander Fleming Dux Medal and addressed the pupils at his old school. On 11 March, 1955, Fleming died from a heart attack; he is buried in St Paul's Cathedral.

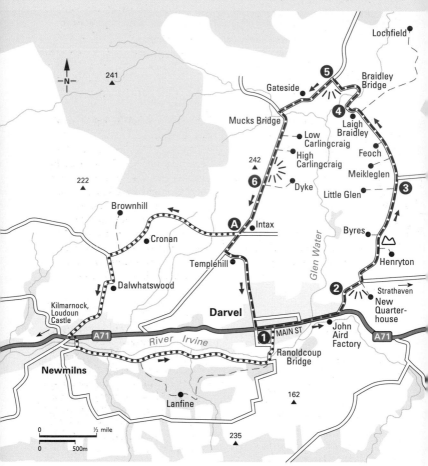

WALK 26 DIRECTIONS

1 From the Alexander Fleming Memorial, cross the square to the pedestrian crossing, cross over the road, turn right and go along Main Street. Near the outskirts of the town go across Darvel Bridge and take the second turning on the left just past the John Aird

factory. Go uphill on this road and pass the cemetery.

2 Keep going uphill to reach a crossroads near New Quarterhouse farm. Follow the waymark arrow pointing left. The road continues uphill, passing Henryton on the right and then Byres on the left. Near Byres there

WHERE TO EAT AND DRINK

Sitting at the foot of Loudoun Hill, with superb views of the surrounding countryside, is the Loudounhill Inn. This family-run establishment is friendly and warm with a good selection of beers and a full restaurant menu. It's just one mile (1.6km) east of Darvel on the A71 and has a real fire in the bar.

is a conveniently situated bench by the roadside if you want some respite on this steep climb.

❸ Little Glen is the next farm on the left-hand side and shortly afterwards the road forks. Take the left turn. The next two farms passed on this road are Mcikleglen and Feoch which come in quick succession. Just before the next farm on the left, Laigh Braidley, a farm road leads off to the right. This is the entrance to Lochfield, Alexander Fleming's birthplace, which is not open to the public. Continue past Laigh Braidley.

❹ After Laigh Braidley the road turns sharply left, then right and goes downhill to cross the Glen Water at Braidley Bridge. As you descend the hill look slightly to the right and uphill and you will see the steading of Lochfield, which is still farmed. Follow the road uphill from the bridge. There's another bench by the roadside at the T-junction near the top of the hill. Enjoy a well-earned rest here and appreciate the splendid view back across the Irvine Valley.

❺ Ignore the waymark and turn left, heading along a lane and past Gateside. When the road forks take the left fork, cross Mucks Bridge and continue uphill. The lane now passes the roads to Low then High Carlingcraig, then levels out. As you continue along the top of this hill look to the left for the distinctive outline of Loudoun Hill.

❻ When you reach Dyke the road heads downhill again. Go over a crossroads at Intax and continue a short distance to some bungalows on the right. Just past here take a left turn. After Hilltop the road turns sharply right and downhill. As you approach the town the lane continues into Burn Street. At the T-junction turn left and follow this back to Hastings Square.

EXTENDING THE WALK

You can extend this walk into the town of Newmilns, once the centre of the Irvine Valley weaving industry. At Intax (Point **Ⓐ**) turn right and follow the lanes down past Cronan and Dalwhatswood into town. You can return to Darvel along a pleasant riverside track before crossing the River Irvine at Ranoldcoup Bridge to get back to Hastings Square.

WHILE YOU'RE THERE

Loudoun Castle, one of the most impressive ruins in Scotland, was built in the early 19th century on the site of a previous keep. Known as the 'Windsor of Scotland' it was destroyed by fire on 1 December, 1941, and lay derelict for years. Now part of a huge theme park, it is an ideal place for families with children.

Lady Flora
of Loudoun

A tragic tale of jealousy, scandal and intrigue.

DISTANCE *7.5 miles (12.1km)* **MINIMUM TIME** *4hrs*

ASCENT/GRADIENT *187ft (57m)* ▲▲▲ **LEVEL OF DIFFICULTY** ✦✦✦

PATHS *Pavements, footpaths and farm roads*

LANDSCAPE *River valley, woodland and town*

SUGGESTED MAP *OS Explorer 334 East Kilbride Galston & Darvel*

START/FINISH *Grid reference: NS 539373*

DOG FRIENDLINESS *Keep on lead at lambing time and near livestock*

PARKING *On-street parking near Lady Flora's Institute*

PUBLIC TOILETS *None on route*

On Wednesday, 10 July, 1839 a strange funeral procession made its way through the streets of London. Strange because it was 4:30am and because this early morning procession had an eerie line of empty carriages following the hearse. The carriages represented the highest families in the land and were preceded by the equally empty state coach of the young Queen Victoria. The hearse was bound for the docks carrying the coffin of Lady Flora Hastings for the sea voyage back to Scotland and burial in the family vault at Loudoun Castle. Despite the hour the streets were lined with people who stoned the state coach as it passed. This was the culmination of a period of deep unpopularity which saw Victoria, Queen for just two years, booed at state events and during theatre visits as a direct result of what the public perceived as her unfair treatment of Lady Flora.

The youngest daughter of the Marquis of Hastings, Flora, had grown up at Loudoun Castle before moving to London to be lady-in-waiting to Victoria's mother, the Duchess of Kent. Following complaints of severe pain and displaying a swollen abdomen she consulted the royal physician, Sir James Clark. He was unable to determine the cause but following his examination a rumour started circulating that Flora was pregnant. Despite an intimate examination by two other doctors the rumours persisted. Lady Flora was ostracised at court and shunned by Victoria. Several newspapers got hold of the story and published a tale of jealousy, scandal and intrigue in court circles, naming the guilty parties.

Flora's brother, Lord Hastings, was incensed and threatened court action and pistols at dawn. Her uncle published a detailed account in another paper and as a result public opinion sided with Lady Flora, who was cheered whenever she appeared. Faced with such hostility Victoria conducted a PR exercise by having Lady Flora attend her in public while continuing to ignore her in private. When Lady Flora died, an independent post mortem revealed that she had suffered from a swollen liver. It may have been Victoria who started the rumour rather than her physician, and Victoria continued to consult him. But in December of 1861 he wrongly diagnosed Prince Albert as suffering from a 'feverish sort of influenza'.

LOUDOUN

By the time William Jenner was called in and discovered Albert in the advance stages of typhoid fever, it was too late to save him and he died on 14 December.

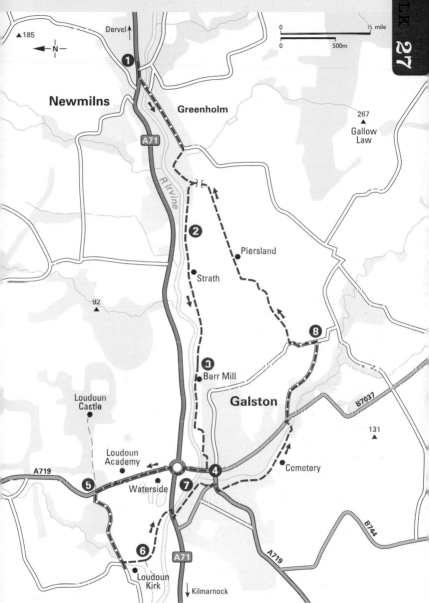

WALK 27 DIRECTIONS

❶ From Lady Flora's Institute, go west along Main Street and turn left into Craigview Road. Cross a bridge, turn right and follow this road to a T-junction. Turn left here, then, where the road forks, keep to the right, go along the side of the factory, turn left into Stonygate Road and follow this to join the Irvine Footpath.

2 Keep on this path, passing Strath and on to the kennels. Turn right at the gate and follow the path round the perimeter. The walkway continues along the river bank on a well-defined, if somewhat muddy, path. Keep on this, going through some woodlands until a white cottage comes into view.

3 Keep right along the riverside path and cross playing fields to go through another gate, then along a street to a T-junction.

4 Turn right, cross the road and continue, heading out of town, crossing the 'Muckle Brig' and the Galston bypass to continue on a pavement heading along the A719 towards Loudoun Academy. Pass the academy on the right, then the entrance gates to Loudoun Castle.

5 Turn left opposite the gates and head along a narrow country lane for 0.5 mile (800m) to Loudoun Kirk Bridge. Turn left and go into Loudoun kirkyard. Return from there, cross a small bridge and turn right on to the signposted footpath to Galston. After 100yds (91m) the path bends right and a narrow grassy footpath forks left. Go left.

6 Keep on this well-trodden path to the T-junction at Galston bypass, then turn right and head

along a pavement, across a bridge, then turn right and head downhill. Turn left at a waymarker and go through the underpass to the other side of the bypass. Turn left and walk along a footpath, which runs beside the river.

7 At the end of the path turn right, head along a narrow lane, then turn left into Titchfield Street. Turn right at the next junction, cross the road and take the next left, passing two school buildings and a cemetery to reach a staggered junction. Cross the B7037 and continue along Clockstone Road.

8 Turn left at the T-junction. Take the next right beside a house and follow this road downhill, then back up to pass Piersland farm. Head downhill from here and cross a gate where the road turns left to go under a railway bridge. Turn right after the bridge and retrace your steps to the start.

A Reference to Peebles

There are reminders of the founders of an encyclopaedia on this lovely walk.

28

DISTANCE 3.5 miles (5.7km)   **MINIMUM TIME** 1hr 20min

ASCENT/GRADIENT 295ft (90m) ▲▲▲   **LEVEL OF DIFFICULTY** ✦✦✦

PATHS Waymarked riverside paths and metalled tracks

LANDSCAPE Rolling borderlands and Tweed Valley

SUGGESTED MAP OS Explorer 337 Peebles & Innerleithen

START/FINISH Grid reference: NT 250402

DOG FRIENDLINESS Great, chance to swim in the river

PARKING Kingsmeadows Road car park, Peebles

PUBLIC TOILETS At car park

Next time you're watching *University Challenge*, listening to *Brain of Britain*, or even taking part in your local pub quiz night, think for a moment about the person who has compiled the questions. They've almost certainly come up with some of them after referring to an encyclopaedia. We tend to take these great tomes for granted, casually assuming that everything they say is correct, giving little thought to the people that produce them. This walk starts and finishes in Peebles – the birthplace of the Chambers brothers, the founding publishers of the famous *Chambers' Encyclopaedia*.

William, the older brother, was born in 1800 and in 1814 was apprenticed to a bookseller in Edinburgh. Robert, born in 1802, later followed him to the city and in 1819 they set up in business as booksellers, then branched out into printing as well. They seemed to have a flair for the trade and, in 1832, William started *Chambers' Edinburgh Journal*, a publication to which Robert contributed many essays. It was a success and later that year the brothers established the publishing house W & R Chambers. Robert, who seemed to be the more literary of the two, continued to write in his spare time and in 1844 anonymously published a book with the less-than-catchy title *Vestiges of the Natural History of Creation*. It was a controversial work, dealing with issues that were then considered blasphemy. Charles Darwin later praised it, saying it had helped to prepare the ground for his book *On the Origin of Species* (1859).

An Encyclopaedia is Born

The first edition of the *Chambers' Encyclopaedia* (1859–68) encompassed ten volumes and was edited by Robert. It was based on a translation of a German work. Robert, who had become friendly with Sir Walter Scott, continued to write, producing books on a wide range of subjects such as history, literature and geology. He also wrote a reference work entitled *A Biographical Dictionary of Eminent Scotsmen* (1832–4).

Although not as prolific as his brother, William too wrote a number of books, including a *History of Peeblesshire*, which came out in 1864. He did not forget his origins in Peebles and in 1859 he founded and endowed a museum, library and art gallery in the town. It's still there today, on the High Street, and is worth visiting, if only for an enormous frieze – a copy of the Elgin marbles that were taken from the Parthenon in Athens. When the brothers died, Robert in 1871 and William in 1883, the company was taken over by Robert's son. The name Chambers is still associated with scholarly reference works today.

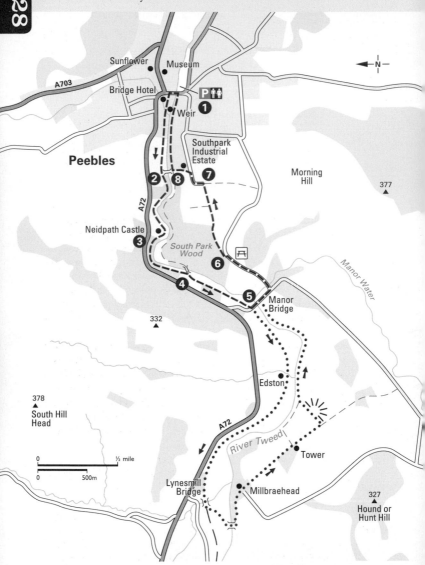

WALK 28 DIRECTIONS

❶ From Kingsmeadows car park, turn right and cross the bridge. Turn left at the Bridge Hotel and walk down the slope, past the swimming pool, to the river. Cross a small footbridge, go up some steps, turn left, descend some steps and follow the riverside track to pass a metal bridge and a children's play area.

② Continue following the obvious path and go over a little bridge over a burn, after which the path becomes a little more rugged. You now enter the woods, going through a gate. Eventually you'll leave the woods and will come to the medieval, romantic-looking Neidpath Castle on the right-hand side.

③ From the castle continue walking by the river to go through another gate. You'll soon come on to higher ground and will get a great view of the old railway bridge spanning the water in front of you. After another kissing gate, maintain your direction to reach the red sandstone bridge.

④ Go up to the right of the bridge, so that you join the old railway line – you now maintain direction and continue following the Tweed Walk. Follow along this disused track until you you find yourself at another attractive bridge – Manor Bridge.

⑤ Turn left here and cross the bridge, then take the turning on the left signed 'Tweed Walk'. You're now on a quiet lane that winds uphill – do stop and look behind you for classic views of the Borders landscape, with lush rolling hills and the wide, busy Tweed. Continue until you reach a track on the left that leads into the woods, opposite a picnic site.

⑥ Follow this path uphill, parallel to the road. Just before the path rejoins the road, continue down a wide, grassy path signposted to Peebles, with woodland to the left. Beyond a gate, the path runs through fields until you join a tarmac road.

⑦ Follow this road and turn left beyond the Southpark Garage into Southpark Industrial Estate, following signs to Riverside Path. Walk between the units, then go down some steps and bear left when you reach the bottom. You'll soon reach a footbridge ahead of you.

⑧ Turn right here and follow the wide track beside the river. This is a popular part of the walk and attracts lots of families on sunny days. Continue walking past the weir, then go up the steps at the bridge and cross over to return to the car park.

EXTENDING THE WALK
A riverside extension adds 3.5 miles (5.7km) to this walk. Instead of crossing Manor Bridge, carry on along the banks of the Tweed to Lynesmill Bridge. You can cross an old railway bridge here then ascend the hillside on the opposite bank for some fine views. Obvious paths will lead you back down to the other side of Manor Bridge where you can resume the main walk back into Peebles from Point **⑤**.

WALK 28

Artful Designs at Manderston

Quiet lanes take you through gentle countryside past ancient monuments to the romantic battlements of Duns Castle.

DISTANCE 4.5 miles (7.2km)	**MINIMUM TIME** 2hrs
ASCENT/GRADIENT 250ft (75m) ▲▲▲	**LEVEL OF DIFFICULTY** +++
PATHS Mostly firm tracks and woodland paths	
LANDSCAPE Parkland, lake and mixed woodland	
SUGGESTED MAP OS Explorer 346 Berwick-upon-Tweed	
START/FINISH Grid reference: NT 787538	
DOG FRIENDLINESS Keep dogs on lead; be considerate of ground-nesting birds	
PARKING Long-stay car park off Market Square, Duns	
PUBLIC TOILETS In South Street, Duns	

Truth, as Oscar Wilde observed, is never pure and rarely simple. The same might be said about some landscapes, as this intriguing walk makes plain. Along the way, you will come across a fascinating record of the past from prehistoric earthworks to a castle that is still a lived-in home. But almost nothing that you see is quite what it appears. Enigmas and legends enshroud the ancient sites; the castle has been altered to enhance its romance, and monuments perpetuate some very doubtful tales. Even the quite natural-looking lake you pass was in fact artfully designed.

Unreliable History

At the start of the walk, a short climb takes you to the hilltop of Duns Law. It's worth it for the views alone, which on a clear day extend down to the Cheviots and Lindsifarne. An Iron Age settlement existed here more than 2,000 years ago, although nothing but faint banks and ditches now remain. A smaller, rectangular enclosure is of much more recent date, forming the stockade in which General Leslie mustered his army of Covenanters in 1639 when Charles I attempted to impose the English Prayer Book on Scotland. You can even see the very stone on which, according to tradition, the Covenanters raised their standard. Two other monuments that you will see along the route are equally the products of tales passed down by word of mouth rather than of documented history. Just off the path back down the hill (a sign points you in the right direction) a cairn claims to mark the spot where the town of Duns originally stood until destroyed by an English raid. But in fact the town has always been exactly where it is today, so perhaps the story may derive from old folk tales about the prehistoric settlement. Then, near the castle gatehouse, another cairn claims to mark the precise birthplace of the medieval philosopher Duns Scotus. In truth, almost nothing of his early life is known.

Landscape Design

Although Duns Castle is not open to the public, its romantic, battlemented towers can be glimpsed from many points along the route. The keep was

DUNS

originally built in 1320, during the reign of Robert Bruce, but much of what you see today was designed by the architect James Gillespie Graham in the 1820s. The park, including the delightful lake that rejoices in the name of Hen Poo, was also laid out in its present form during the early 19th century, although the avenue of limes that you pass on the last stage of the walk was planted in the 1690s. The trees were blown down in a gale in 1880 and even then they were considered of such venerable significance that they were hauled back upright and saved.

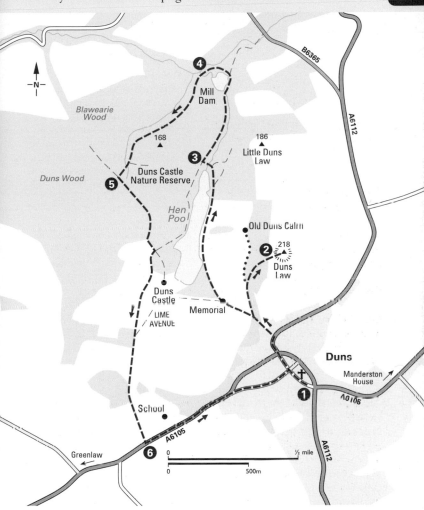

WALK 29 DIRECTIONS

1 From the car park, return to Market Square and continue straight ahead up Castle Street. Cross the main road to follow the continuation of Castle Street, bearing left to enter Duns Castle Estate through an arched gateway. 50yds (46m) along the drive, turn right up a flight of wooden steps and follow the path uphill and through a gate to reach the summit of Duns Law.

WHERE TO EAT AND DRINK

Although Duns is not well-supplied with restaurants, the Pewter Plate in Murray Street offers toasted sandwiches, spaghetti and other light dishes alongside more exotic Thai meals. For a pub lunch, the best bet is the Black Bull, where bar snacks include local smoked salmon.

② From the hilltop, follow your route back down the hill (a sign half-way down points to the alleged site of Old Duns). On reaching the drive, turn right, then fork right at the memorial to Duns Scotus. Follow the drive along the shore of Hen Poo, then fork left through a gate on to a rougher track to the head of the lake, where the path swings left to reach a T-junction.

③ Turn right here to follow the track along a wooded valley and past a pond, Mill Dam, which formerly provided power for the estate sawmill. Shortly beyond the pond, turn left up a woodland path and continue for 100yds (91m) to a footbridge crossing a small stream.

④ Turn left to cross the bridge and climb a flight of rough timber steps. When you reach a wooden bench, bear right to follow the waymarked 'Colonel's Walk'. When you reach an intersection, after approximately 0.5 mile (800m), turn right (signposted to Duns) and continue 100yds (91m) to another intersection.

⑤ Turn left here (again signed to Duns) and follow the driveway until you reach a crossroads. Turn right here, following the waymarked route. After passing Duns Castle and the lime avenue continue down the estate road until you eventually come to the main road.

WHILE YOU'RE THERE

Manderston is an Adam-style Edwardian mansion that was one of the last great country houses to be built in Britain before the First World War. Designed for ostentatious entertainment, it features a silver-plated staircase, lavish décor and a vastly complex 'below-stairs' world that allowed the household to be run with the efficiency of a grand hotel.

⑥ Turn left here and follow the pavement back to Duns. As the main road bears left, continue straight ahead along South Street to reach Market Square, where you turn right to return to the car park at the start of the walk.

WHAT TO LOOK OUT FOR

Duns Castle nature reserve is run by the Scottish Wildlife Trust. The reed-fringed lake provides a perfect habitat for mute swans, mallard and other wildfowl, whilst the woods are home to the green and spotted woodpecker, pied flycatcher, goldcrest and redstart. Roe deer and red squirrels may also be seen and in autumn fungi are plentiful.

A Windy Walk to St Abb's Head

*A refreshing walk along the cliffs
to see some local wildife.*

DISTANCE *4 miles (6.4km)* **MINIMUM TIME** *1hr 30min*

ASCENT/GRADIENT *443ft (135m)* ▲▲▲ **LEVEL OF DIFFICULTY** ✦✦✦

PATHS *Clear footpaths and established tracks*

LANDSCAPE *Dramatic cliff tops and lonely lighthouse*

SUGGESTED MAP *OS Explorer 346 Berwick-upon-Tweed*

START/FINISH *Grid reference: NT 913674*

DOG FRIENDLINESS *They'll love the fresh air, but keep on lead by cliffs*

PARKING *At visitor centre*

PUBLIC TOILETS *At visitor centre*

St Abb's Head is one of those places that people forget to visit. You only ever seem to hear it mentioned on the shipping forecast – and its name is generally followed by a rather chilly outlook – along the lines of 'north-easterly five, continuous light drizzle, poor'. In fact you could be forgiven for wondering if it even exists or is simply a mysterious expanse of sea – like Dogger, Fisher or German Bight.

But St Abb's Head does exist, as you'll find out on this lovely windswept walk which will rumple your hair and leave the salty tang of the sea lingering on your lips. The dramatic cliffs, along which you walk to reach the lonely lighthouse, form an ideal home for thousands of nesting seabirds as they provide superb protection from mammalian predators. Birds you might spot on this walk include guillemots, razorbills, kittiwakes, herring gulls, shags and fulmars – as well as a few puffins. Guillemots and razorbills are difficult to differentiate, as they're both black and white, and have an upright stance – rather like small, perky penguins. However, you should be able to spot the difference if you've got binoculars as razorbills have distinctive blunt beaks. Both birds belong to the auk family, the most famous member of which is probably the great auk, which went the way of the dodo and became extinct in 1844 – a victim of the contemporary passion for egg collecting.

Luckily no egg collector could scale these cliffs, which are precipitous and surrounded by treacherous seas. Do this walk in the nesting season (May to July) and you may well see young birds jumping off the high cliff ledge into the open sea below. Even though they can't yet fly, as their wings are little more than stubs, the baby birds are nevertheless excellent swimmers and have a better chance of survival in the water than in their nests – where they could fall prey to marauding gulls. Neither razorbills nor guillemots are particularly agile in the air, but they swim with the ease of seals, using their wings and feet to propel and steer their sleek little bodies as they fish beneath the waves.

While the steep cliffs are home to most of the seabirds round St Abb's Head, the low, flat rocks below are also used by wildlife, as they are the favoured nesting site of shags. These large black birds are almost indistinguishable from cormorants – except for the distinctive crest on their heads that gives them a quizzical appearance. They tend to fly low over the water, in contrast to the graceful fulmars that frequently soar along the cliff tops as you walk, hitching a ride on convenient currents of air.

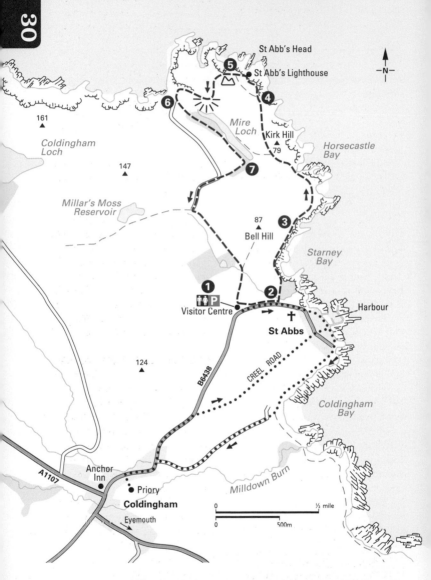

WALK 30 DIRECTIONS

1 From the car park, take the path that runs past the information board and the play area. Walk past the visitor centre, then take the footpath on the left, parallel to the

main road. At the end of the path turn left and go through a gate – you'll immediately get great views of the sea.

2 Follow the track, pass the sign to Starney Bay and continue, passing fields on your left-hand side. Your track now winds around the edge of the bay – to your right is the little harbour at St Abbs. The track then winds around the cliff edge, past dramatic rock formations and eventually to some steps.

3 Walk down the steps, then follow the grassy track as it bears left, with a fence on the left. Go up a slope, through a gate and maintain direction on the obvious grassy track. The path soon veers away from the cliff edge, past high ground on the right, then runs up a short, steep slope to a crossing of tracks, passing a butterfly haven on the right.

4 Maintain direction by keeping to the coastal path which runs up a slope. You'll soon get great views of the St Abb's lighthouse ahead, dramatically situated on the cliff's edge. Continue to the lighthouse and walk in front of the lighthouse buildings and down to join a tarmac road. Take care as this path is steep and eroded.

5 Follow the road down to the bottom of the hill, then 50yds (46m) before a cattle grid, turn left down a narrow path.

6 Continue along the path and over a stile. The path now runs through scrub and woodland

along the edge of a loch. Continue along the path to an intersection with a track.

7 Turn right along the wide track and walk up to the road. Go left now and continue to cross a cattle grid. When you reach a bend in the road, follow the tarmac track as it bears left. You'll soon go through a gate, then pass some cottages before reaching the car park on the left-hand side.

EXTENDING THE WALK

You can add a different dimension to your walk in this area by visiting the priory ruins in Coldingham. From the harbour in St Abbs, head south along the coastal footpath towards Coldingham Bay. A lane will take you up into the village where you can visit the priory. Return to St Abbs by following the main road until you reach the Creel Road path on your right. This will take you down into the back of St Abbs, above the harbour.

Overleaf: Overlooking the sea at the foot of the cliffs of St Abb's Head (Walk 30)

Machrie Moor

*Discover the standing stones of one of Scotland's finest early
settlements on the Isle of Arran.*

31

DISTANCE 5.5 miles (8.8km)   **MINIMUM TIME** 3hrs

ASCENT/GRADIENT 114ft (35m) ▲▲▲   **LEVEL OF DIFFICULTY** ✦✦✦

PATHS Footpaths, rough tracks, road, 3 stiles

LANDSCAPE Forest, seashore, fields and moorland

SUGGESTED MAP OS Explorer 361 Isle of Arran

START/FINISH Grid reference: NS 898314

DOG FRIENDLINESS Keep on lead near livestock and where requested by signs

PARKING King's Cave car park

PUBLIC TOILETS Car park at Blackwaterfoot

Arran is world famous for its archaeological remains dating from the mesolithic period. The island is littered with them, but the greatest concentration can be found on the wild, windswept Machrie Moor. For it was here that humans settled from the earliest of times and have left the remains of their hut circles, chambered cairns and standing stones. The circles of grey granite boulders and tall, weathered red sandstone pillars are an impressive sight against a winter sun on the wide expanse of moor.

Magnificent Monuments

The earliest inhabitants settled here some 8,000 years ago and, across the millennia, later settlements were created and the first simple monuments erected. Within this small area of moor there are over 40 stone circles, standing stones, chambered tombs and hut circles making it the finest neolithic and Bronze Age site in Scotland. Most visitors head straight for the three large red sandstone pillars, the tallest standing slightly over 18ft (5.5m). These stones were once part of a much larger circle, the other stones have fallen or been removed. No one is certain what function these Bronze Age circles performed, but it is likely that they had a religious significance. Many stone circles are precisely aligned to particular celestial events like the rising of the midsummer sun, and they possibly also fulfilled seasonal functions, indicating when to carry out certain rituals or to plant and harvest crops. A survey of the area by archaeologist John Barnatt in 1978 revealed that four of the circles were aligned with a gap in the skyline of Machrie Glen, where the sun rises at midsummer.

Legendary Figures

Other early Arran inhabitants had another explanation for the circles. At a time when people attributed anything they did not understand to legendary figures, the standing stones on Machrie Moor became the province of the giant Fingal, a Scottish form of the Irish warrior Finn MacCumhail and the double circle still has the name of Fingal's Cauldron Seat. According to legend, Fingal put his dog Bran in the outer circle and tied it to a stone

MACHRIE MOOR

with a hole in it to stop it wandering while Fingal had his meal in the inner circle. The dwellers on the moor lived in round huts, the remains of which are still visible. There is no explanation as to why and when they departed, leaving their monuments, but one theory is that climate change forced them to move to a warmer and more sheltered part of the island. In the thousands of years since they left, the area has become covered by a blanket of peat bog. There is undoubtedly more to discover under this protective layer as recent excavations continue to uncover even older structures.

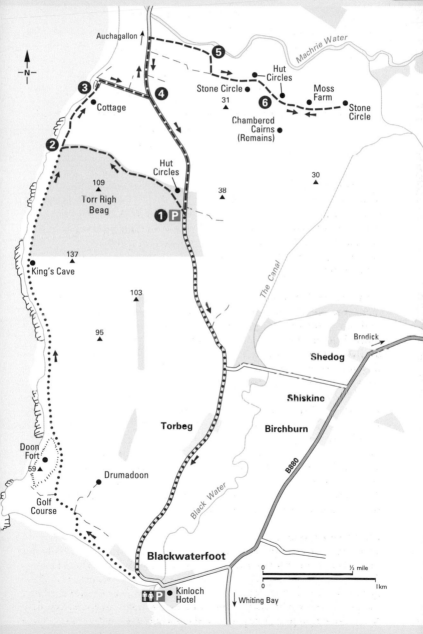

WALK 31 DIRECTIONS

❶ From the car park take the footpath signposted for King's Cave. This goes through an area of woodland, past the site of some hut circles on the right and continues along the edge of the woods until it starts to head downhill towards the sea. Look out for a waymarker on the right pointing back in the direction you have just walked.

❷ Turn right here on to a faint path, which in the summer will be very overgrown with bracken. Plough your way through this and, in a short distance, you will come to a wire fence, which you can easily climb through. Cross this field and go through a gate, then head downhill aiming for the left end of a white cottage overlooking the shore.

❸ As you near the end of the cottage you will see a gate at the corner of the garden wall. Go through the gate and continue along a farm road running between two fences. Keep on this road passing another cottage on the right and then keeping right at the fork.

❹ When the road ends at a T-junction with the A841 turn left. Continue to the signpost for Machrie Moor standing stones. Turn right, go over a stile and follow the access road. This rough track passes through two fields.

❺ In the second field, near the far left-hand corner, is a megalithic site. Nothing is to be seen above ground, the site was only identified when flints were found that were around 7,000 to 9,000 years old. Continue on the road to the Moss Farm road stone circle from around 2000 BC.

❻ From here the track continues, passing the deserted Moss Farm then crossing a stile to the main stone circles of Machrie Moor. When you have finished wandering around them return to the stile and take the Moss Farm road back to the A841. Turn left on to this and walk for approximately 1.5 miles (2km) to return to the car park.

WHILE YOU'RE THERE

A little to the north of Machrie Moor, overlooking Machrie Bay, is Auchagallon Stone Circle. Thought to be a Bronze Age kerbed cairn, it once had a continuous kerb of sandstone blocks around its edge, and is 3,000 to 4,000 years old. Many of the blocks are now missing, but what remains is a stone circle enclosing a burial cairn, the finest burial site on the island.

WHERE TO EAT AND DRINK

Situated at the edge of the car park at Blackwaterfoot and overlooking the beach, the family-friendly Kinloch Hotel is the best pit stop on this walk. The bar and restaurant meals are of a very high quality and served by friendly staff. Seafood isone of their specialities.

EXTENDING THE WALK

Whether King's Cave is actually where Robert Bruce met his fabled spider is not known, but he certainly spent some time hiding there in the Wars of Independence. Visit the cave by walking down the road into Blackwaterfoot then following the coastal path north, behind Doon Fort. Once past the cave, you can either continue on the main walk from Point ❷ or turn right to return to the start.

The Spectacular Falls at Glenashdale

Enjoy this short, scenic woodland walk discovering the Isle of Arran's ancient bedrock.

DISTANCE 2.75 miles (4.4km)   **MINIMUM TIME** 2hrs

ASCENT/GRADIENT 442ft (135m) ▲▲▲   **LEVEL OF DIFFICULTY** +++

PATHS Forest paths and forest roads

LANDSCAPE Woodland, waterfalls, rock

SUGGESTED MAP OS Explorer 361 Isle of Arran

START/FINISH Grid reference: NS 047252

DOG FRIENDLINESS Good, locals walk their dogs here

PARKING Car park opposite youth hostel in Whiting Bay

PUBLIC TOILETS None on route; nearest at Shore Road, Whiting Bay

---

Millions of years ago this area was a hot and barren desert. During what geologists refer to as the Permian period, 270 million years ago, the underlying red sandstone gradually formed from sand dunes. On top of this a sill (layer) of igneous rocks was laid down in the Tertiary period 210 million years later.

The Glenashdale Sill

The Tertiary sill at Glenashdale is about 100ft (30m) thick and composed of several types of igneous rock, the major part being quartz-dolerite. When this is harder than the surrounding rock, it stands proud as the softer rocks are eroded. At Glenashdale continual erosion has created these spectacular waterfalls and, where the stream and the waterfall have cut into the Glenashdale sill, it is easy to examine the now exposed structure of the rocks. Following the stream up from the waterfall the banks and bed of the stream reveal the dark- and medium-grained igneous rocks with a few specks of pyrites – a shiny yellow mineral. South-west of the falls there are veins of a dark basalt. Pack one of those small geological field guides in your backpack, or in a pocket, and use the photographs to help identify the different kinds of rock found on the route.

Native and Exotic Trees

A field guide to trees could also prove useful although several of the trees have been conveniently labelled. There is an abundance of native trees like the alder, hazel, downy birch, oak, ash and rowan. The latter, also called the mountain ash, has bright red berries in the autumn and in Scottish folklore was used for warding off witches.

You'll also find a wide variety of unusual and exotic trees in the glen. The Siberian crab has white flowers and small green berries which may eventually turn into bright red fruits. You'll also come across large specimens of the Douglas fir. This evergreen native of North America is extensively planted in Europe to provide high grade timber but seldom reaches its maximum height of 328ft (100m). Most European specimens tend to be around 180ft (55m). Other North American species include the Great fir and the Sitka spruce. This fast-growing conifer often reaches heights of 197ft (60m) and although it thrives in a range of soils, it is particularly suited to the mild, wet Scottish climate.

Growing on the edge of the path you'll find the heart-shaped leaves of wood sorrel with its long stalked, white, bell-like flowers during April and May. There's a profusion of red campion and the scent of wild honeysuckle and wild garlic mingle with the pine tang of the wood. Look out for the yellow pimpernel, with its star-like flowers, in May and August.

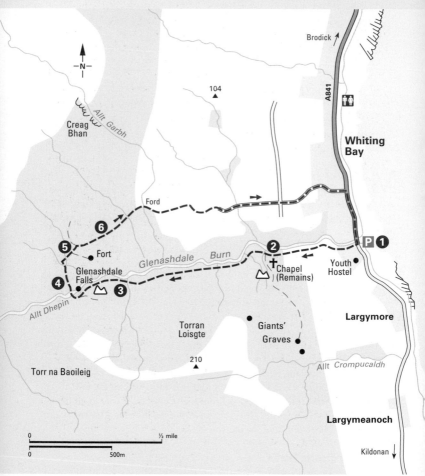

WALK 32 DIRECTIONS

❶ From the car park turn right on to the road, cross it and turn left on to the footpath, signposted 'Giants' Graves and Glenashdale Falls'. Follow this leafy lane until it reaches the rear of a house, then continue on the path along the river bank. Go through a gate, pass a forest walks sign and then continue until you reach a signpost pointing in the direction of the Giants' Graves.

❷ The path forks here. Go right, following the sign to Glenashdale Falls. The path continues, rising gently through a wooded area, where several of the trees are identified by small labels fixed to the trunks. Continue uphill on this path, which is marked by the occasional waymarker, crossing a bridge and fording a shallow section of the burn.

WHERE TO EAT AND DRINK

There are plenty of choices for eating and drinking in Whiting Bay. The Coffee Pot is located at the end of the walk and has hot soup for hungry walkers. The Trafalgar Restaurant, also on Shore Road, serves a variety of main meals and snacks, while the Drift Inn, just off Shore Road by Murchies, does superb bar food.

3 Eventually the path starts to climb steeply uphill and continues to some steps and then forks. Keep right and follow this path to reach the falls. Keep on the path past the falls and continue uphill to cross a bridge. A picnic table situated on the river bank here is a good spot to stop for refreshment.

4 From here follow the path into an area planted with Sitka spruce. Keep to the track marked by the green waymarkers as it heads through this dark part, going through a gap in a wall and eventually arriving at a sign pointing to an Iron Age fort. Turn

WHAT TO LOOK OUT FOR

If you turn left at the sign for the Giants' Graves you can see the remains of Whiting Bay Chapel. In 20yds (18m) on the left look for a raised area covered with vegetation and poke about at the far end. Little remains, but you should be able to find some small gravestones.

off to look at the remains of the ramparts then retrace your steps to the sign and continue your route along the path.

5 Cross over a bridge by another waterfall and then follow more waymarkers to a clearing and a viewpoint. Sit on the bench here and enjoy the panoramic view across the wooded glen. From here you can see the full extent of the impressive Glenashdale Falls as the water cascades over the top. A waymarker points uphill through a densely wooded area before ending at a T-junction with a forest road.

WHILE YOU'RE THERE

Visit the Giants' Graves, an important neolithic site containing several chambered burial cairns of the kind found throughout Arran. Because of their semi-circular forecourts they have been called 'horned gallery graves'. The path to the graves is short but steep, climbing some 173 steps.

6 Turn right on to the forest road and continue, crossing water at a ford and going through three kissing gates until the route continues on a metalled road. Continue along this road, go over a crossroads and wind downhill. Turn right at a T-junction and then walk 200yds (183m) back to the car park at the start.

A Revolutionary Utopia at New Lanark

A rustic walk from a model industrial community.

> **DISTANCE** 6.5 miles (10.4km)   **MINIMUM TIME** 3hrs
>
> **ASCENT/GRADIENT** 476ft (145m) ▲▲▲   **LEVEL OF DIFFICULTY** ✦✦✦
>
> **PATHS** Clear riverside tracks and forest paths, a few steep steps
>
> **LANDSCAPE** Planned industrial town and some stunning waterfalls
>
> **SUGGESTED MAP** OS Explorer 335 Lanark & Tinto Hills
>
> **START/FINISH** Grid reference: NS 883426
>
> **DOG FRIENDLINESS** Mostly off lead
>
> **PARKING** Main car park above New Lanark
>
> **PUBLIC TOILETS** Visitor centre, when open

*... I know that society may be formed so as to exist without
crime, without poverty, with health greatly improved, with little,
if any misery, and with intelligence and happiness increased a
hundredfold...*

          Robert Owen, from a speech made in 1816

If you do this walk you'll get a glimpse of Utopia, for the planned
industrial village of New Lanark was the embodiment of one man's
vision of an ideal world. New Lanark was built as a cotton spinning centre
in 1785 by David Dale and Richard Arkwright, and is so well preserved that
it is now a UNESCO World Heritage Site. It owes its fame to Dale's son-in-
law, Robert Owen, who took over its management in 1798 and made it the
focus of a revolutionary social experiment.

Forward-thinking Pioneer

Owen was a very efficient businessman and ran a strict regime, monitoring
wages, insisting on good timekeeping and dismissing employees for
persistent drunkenness and theft. His methods made New Lanark extremely
profitable. He was also an extremely fair employer and New Lanark was no
'dark satanic mill'.

Owen believed in humane capitalism and felt that businesses were more
successful if the workers were well treated. Unlike most industrialists of his
day, he did not allow children under ten to work in his mills, and established
the world's first nursery school. He also ensured that all children received
a rounded education: by the age of seven they were attending lessons
on everything from history and geography to nature study and dancing.
Education didn't end when children began working in the mills, for all his
employees were encouraged to attend evening classes, lectures and dancing
classes in the wonderfully named Institute for the Formation of Character.
Owen also disapproved of the cruel treatment of his workers and refused to
allow corporal punishment to be used as a form of discipline. His staff were
provided with good housing, free medical care and a co-operative store.

NEW LANARK

Owen tried hard to persuade other industrialists to adopt his caring regime, but failed. Disillusioned, he sold New Lanark in 1825 and travelled to America where he bought a settlement in Indiana, which he named New Harmony. He intended to turn it into a Utopian community, freed from the strictures of 19th-century Britain. The experiment did not work as well as he hoped and he returned to Britain in 1828, where he continued to campaign for workers' welfare, even leading a march protesting against the plight of the Tolpuddle Martyrs, six men who were transported for seven years for forming a trade union. Owen died in 1858. He never managed to create Utopia, but inspired several other model villages such as Saltaire, Port Sunlight and Bournville, and influenced attitudes for years to come.

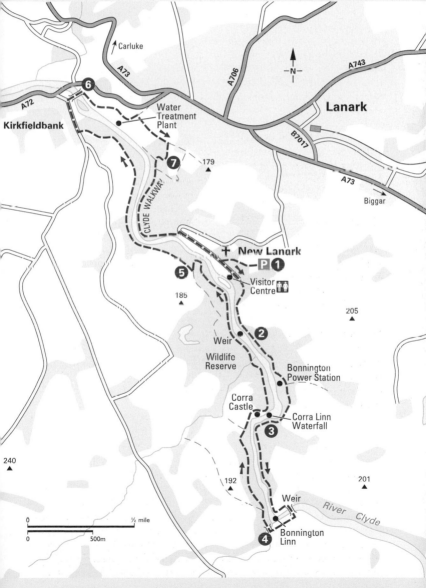

WALK 33 DIRECTIONS

1 From the car park, walk downhill into New Lanark. Bear left and walk to the Scottish Wildlife Trust visitor centre. Turn up the stone steps on the left, following the signs to the Falls of Clyde. The path soon goes down some steps to reach the weir, where there's a lookout point.

2 Continue along the path. You'll pass Bonnington Power Station on your right, where it divides. Take the right-hand path, which takes you into woodland and up some steps. You'll soon come to Corra Linn waterfall, with another lookout point.

WHILE YOU'RE THERE

The ruins of Corra Castle are home to a colony of natterer's bats. These medium-sized bats are found throughout Britain. In winter they tend to hibernate in caves and mines, while during the summer they prefer to roost in old stone buildings and barns. Their limbs have a slight pink tinge, giving rise to their nickname – the 'red-armed bat'.

3 Your path continues to the right, signposted 'Bonnington Linn, 0.75 miles'. Go up some more steps and follow the track to go under a double line of pylons. Follow the path to reach the weir, cross it, then turn right into the Wildlife Reserve.

4 After 100yds (91m), turn right off the track down a narrow path, which crosses a footbridge and then follows the river, rejoining the main path downstream. Bear right here to reach Corra Castle. Continue walking by the river, cross a small footbridge, then follow the wide path through the woods. When you meet another path, turn right.

5 Follow the path to pass houses on your left. At the road turn right, then right again to cross the old bridge, which brings you into a cul de sac. Go through the gate on the right – it looks like someone's drive but is part of the Clyde Walkway.

WHERE TO EAT AND DRINK

There's a self-service café in the village where you can get baked potatoes, sandwiches, cakes and hot drinks. The Mill Hotel also serves bar snacks.

6 Walk past the stables, then turn left through a gate to follow the riverside path. Beyond another gate, continue up some steps beside a water treatment plant and bear right along a tarmac lane. Follow the lane past some houses until you see a sign to Jooker's Johnnie on your left. Just 20yds (18m) further on, turn right down a driveway, then right again at a sign for the Clyde Walkway.

7 Your path zig-zags down to the river. At the water's edge turn left, and follow the forest track back to New Lanark. When the path meets the road turn right, then left at the church for the car park.

WHAT TO LOOK OUT FOR

Peregrines nest near the Corra Linn falls from April to June and high-powered telescopes have been set up to allow you to view their nest without disturbing the birds. They are a protected species, with only around 800 pairs in Scotland, and are sadly threatened by egg collectors, shooting and poisoning.

The Museum of Scottish Country Life

An 18th-century time warp in a late 20th century new town.

DISTANCE 5 miles (8km) **MINIMUM TIME** 3hrs

ASCENT/GRADIENT 262ft (80m) ▲▲▲ **LEVEL OF DIFFICULTY** +++

PATHS *Farm tracks and country roads*

LANDSCAPE *Pastureland, woodland and new town*

SUGGESTED MAP *OS Explorer 342 Glasgow*

START/FINISH *Grid reference: NS 608558*

DOG FRIENDLINESS *Keep on lead near livestock*

PARKING *Car park at Museum of Scottish Country Life*

PUBLIC TOILETS *At museum*

On the outskirts of East Kilbride, Scotland's largest and busiest new town, Wester Kittochside farm sits in a time warp. Preserved as the Museum of Scottish Country Life, it is still a working farm but without any of the high-tech machinery of 21st-century farming – its clock has stopped in the 1950s.

John Reid

In 1567 John Reid, the tenant of Kittochside, bought land from Robert Muir of Caldwell. Muir tried to retake the land by force some 20 years later, attacking the farm 'armed with spears, swords and other fearful wapponis'. Reid was threatened, his possessions seized and his house burned. But the matter was adjudicated by the Privy Council, which found for Reid and ordered Muir to pay compensation.

'Modern' Farming Methods

The agrarian revolution to modernise and industrialise farming was enthusiastically embraced in the 1780s by Reid's descendant, another John. He transformed his arable land and his sheep grazed the moorland. New fields were laid out and enclosed, and drainage was installed to improve the ground. Reid introduced crop rotation, new crops, including turnips and grass for winter feed, and changed the stock emphasis to cattle. By the time he was finished, most of the old buildings on the farm had gone, replaced by the new steading that stands today. The Reid family continued to farm at Wester Kittochside. A dairy and barn were built in the latter half of the 19th century and a threshing mill and horse 'gin' (engine – a large wheel turned by horse power to run machinery) were installed.

Time Stands Still

In 1963 dairy production ceased and the land switched to grazing beef cattle. James Reid, the tenth generation to farm here, never carried out any improvements or modernised his farming in any way and for a period of 50 years Wester Kittochside remained unchanged. Reid continued to farm as his father had and he was taught in the 1950s, so no grain driers, huge silos, slurry tanks or modern cattle units were installed.

A Lasting Legacy

James Reid and his wife had no children and gifted the farm to the National Trust for Scotland. James died in 1982 and Margaret, his wife, carried on until 1992 when she left the house ending nearly four centuries' occupation by a single family. Since the farm opened to the public as a museum, the dairy has been reinstated and the land is farmed as it was in 1950, including the five to six shift crop rotation and grazing supporting milk cattle and working horses. Crops of grass, hay and turnips are still used for winter feed. The techniques and equipment evoke memories of a way of life that has long past, except here at Wester Kittochside farm.

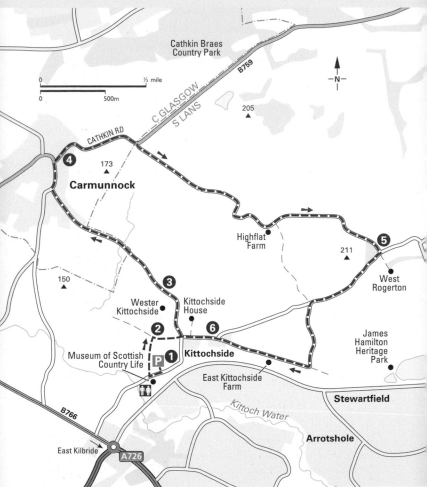

WALK 34 DIRECTIONS

1 Exit the car park and turn right on to the road, heading past the front of the main Exhibition Building then turn right on to a footpath. Continue along this, to reach a T-junction.

② Turn right and follow this to another T-junction with the main road. Turn left and continue along the road, passing the fields and steading of Wester Kittochside.

③ Keep on this quiet road for just over a mile (1.6km), past more of the fields of Wester Kittochside farm, then the fields of more modern farms and finally into the village of Carmunnock. The road ends at a T-junction. Turn right then, a short distance further on, take the next turning on the right into Cathkin Road.

④ Keep on Cathkin Road for about 0.5 mile (800m) then, when it bends sharply to the left, turn right and continue straight ahead on a minor road. Follow this as it twists and turns to reach Highflat Farm after about 0.5 mile (800m) and then continues for another 0.5 mile (800m) to end at a T-junction opposite the road leading to West Rogerton farm.

⑤ Turn right and, in just over 0.5 mile (800m), you will come to a crossroads. On the right is a farm track leading back to Highflat. Turn left here and proceed to the next T-junction. Walk along this country

WHERE TO EAT AND DRINK

The museum Exhibition Building contains an excellent child-friendly café where visitors can enjoy hot soup, sandwiches, snacks and sweet things. Alternatively go into East Kilbride and seek out the heart of the old village and try the bar meals in the 18th-century Montgomery Arms, the oldest pub in the area.

lane passing the farm of East Kittochside on the left.

⑥ Pass a junction on the right, continue through Kittochside, pass the drive to Kittochside House and reach another T-junction. Cross the road and continue along the farm track ahead of you. Take the first turning on the left on to another farm track and, at the end of this, you will then be back in front of the museum Exhibition Building.

WHILE YOU'RE THERE

The Museum of Scottish Country Life is one of the most important and entertaining attractions to have opened in Scotland for decades. The main Exhibition Building has a comprehensive collection covering the entire history of Scottish farming. However, it is the farmstead and the magnificent Georgian farmhouse, unchanged in the last half century and little changed since the 18th century, that turns an interesting visit to a magical experience.

WHAT TO LOOK OUT FOR

The fields at Wester Kittochside remain unaltered since the last century, in marked contrast to those of nearby farms. Compare the hedgerows and fields of Wester Kittochside with Highflat to see the differences in fencing and the abundance and variety of wild flowers growing on each.

Glasgow Harbour's Tall Ship

A pleasant walk by the last of the Clyde-built sailing ships.

DISTANCE 4.75 miles (7.7km) **MINIMUM TIME** 3hrs 30min

ASCENT/GRADIENT 98ft (30m) ▲▲ **LEVEL OF DIFFICULTY** +++

PATHS Pavements and footpaths

LANDSCAPE Riverside, city blocks, park, botanic gardens

SUGGESTED MAP OS Explorer 342 Glasgow; AA Street by Street

START/FINISH Grid reference: NS 569652

DOG FRIENDLINESS Locals walk dogs on part of route, on lead on busy streets

PARKING SECC car park beside Clyde Auditorium (Armadillo)

PUBLIC TOILETS SECC

When she was towed up the Clyde in 1993 the *Glenlee* was a sorry-looking sight. Little more than a derelict hulk, she had been saved from destruction by a group of forward-thinking enthusiasts. Today, restored to her former glory, she is an important part of the regeneration of Glasgow's harbour area.

From Cargo Vessel to Training Ship

Built in 1896 by Anderson Rodger & Co of Port Glasgow, the three-masted steel barque was one of the last sailing vessels launched on the Clyde. She had a long career as a cargo vessel, circumnavigating the globe four times and sailing over a million nautical miles under a British flag. Towards the end of her cargo career, engines were fitted to help keep her on schedule. Three times she ran aground and once almost caught fire, but on each occasion she was rescued. Then in 1921 she became a sail training ship for the Spanish Navy and remained in use until 1981. She sank at Seville, when her sea cocks were stolen to sell as scrap. With her engines drowned and rusted solid it looked like the end.

Lovingly Restored

The Clyde Maritime Trust received a letter from the Spanish Navy giving the ship's details and history and asking if the trust would like to collect the *Glenlee* and save her from being broken up. The trust had very little money but managed to raise enough to purchase, raise her and have her towed back to Scotland. After a short spell in dry dock at Greenock, where an inspection revealed the hull to be sound, she was towed up the Clyde to Yorkhill Quay.

For the next six years volunteers and enthusiasts took on the seemingly impossible task of turning the *Glenlee* back into a sailing ship. The interior cargo holds and accommodation were lovingly re-created. Decking was fitted and Jamie White, a rigging expert from the National Maritime Museum in San Francisco, was called in to restore and reinstall the original rigging. White already looked after the rigging on the *Balclutha*, another Clyde-built sailing ship, so he knew what he was doing. When work was nearly completed in 1999, the *Glenlee* was towed back down the Clyde to Greenock for the final paint job, known as Gunport, when dark patches were painted on the side to look like gun ports. In days gone by this 'deception' was thought to increase the safety of cargo ships. Old photographs of the *Glenlee* show that she was painted in Gunport at one time.

Fully restored, the *Glenlee* went on public display for the first time when the Tall Ships Race came to Greenock in 1999. Then it was a last tow up the Clyde to her permanent moorings at Yorkhill Quay.

WALK 35

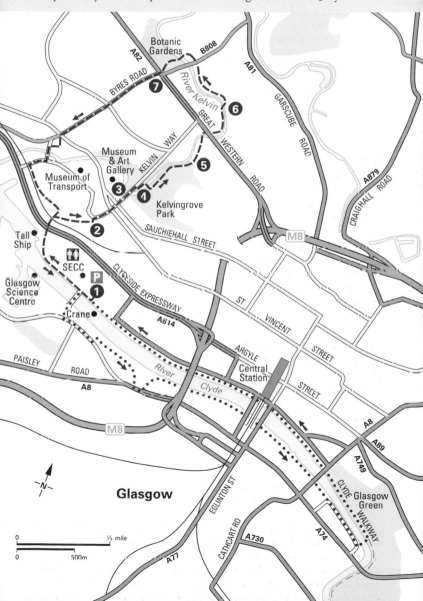

WALK 35 DIRECTIONS

❶ From the Scottish Exhibition and Conference Centre (SECC) car park go on to the Clyde Walkway and turn right, following signs to The Tall Ship' and Museum of Transport (leave the route along here to visit the *Glenlee*). At the roundabout with the Tall Ship on the left, go over a pedestrian bridge to cross the Clydeside Expressway. Go under a bridge into Kelvin Haugh Street.

WHERE TO EAT AND DRINK

Take your pick from the riverside café passed on this walk, coffee bars within the SECC, the restaurant in the Italianate pumping house that forms the visitor centre for the Tall Ship, any one of a number of fine restaurants in Byres Road or the famous art deco University Café on the same street.

❷ Turn west into York Hill Street, then right into Haugh Road and keep ahead, crossing Sauchiehall Street and then along Kelvin Way.

❸ Pass the recently restored Kelvingrove Art Gallery and Museum on your left. This is Scotland's number one top tourist attraction and is free.

❹ Turn right on to the Kelvin Walkway, right again over the second bridge, then turn left at the Memorial to the Highland Light Infantry. Fork left and follow the river bank.

❺ This eventually goes uphill. Just before the top of the hill look for a narrow path on the left. Go left here and under a bridge. Turn left at a cycle path sign to Woodside and Milngavie, go over

a bridge and past a café/bar then continue along the walkway.

❻ Cross another bridge, go left at a junction, still following the river. Go under a bridge and then go left across a humpback bridge leading to the Botanic Gardens. Head up the steps to reach the gardens. Turn right alongside the Kibble Palace, turn left and follow this drive to the gates and then exit the gardens.

❼ Cross Great Western Road at the traffic-lights and walk to the end of Byres Road. Cross Dumbarton Road and turn left into Partickridge Street, right into Dunaskin Street, left at a T-junction then right into Ferry Road. Just before a railway bridge turn left on to a footpath. At its junction with Sandyford Street turn right and continue under the bridge and back to the SECC.

EXTENDING THE WALK

You can do an extra leg from here, along both banks of the River Clyde. From Point ❶ cross the river. Turn left to a riverside pathway, which eventually leads to a suspension bridge near Glasgow Green. Cross back over the river and return to the SECC on the opposite bank, passing the *Waverley* paddle steamer.

WHAT TO LOOK OUT FOR

The massive glass Kibble Palace in the heart of the Botanic Gardens was not always here. Built at Coulport on Loch Long by the engineer John Kibble it was originally part of his own garden. In 1873 he gifted it to the Royal Botanic Institution who had it dismantled, shipped up the Clyde and rebuilt at its present site where it houses plants from the temperate zones.

Right: Kibble Palace at Glasgow's Botanic Gardens (Walk 35)

Alexander 'Greek' Thomson

Discover a Victorian city and the architect who shaped it.

DISTANCE 6.5 miles (10.4km)   **MINIMUM TIME** 3hrs 30min

ASCENT/GRADIENT 98ft (30m) ▲▲▲   **LEVEL OF DIFFICULTY** ✦✦✦

PATHS Pavements

LANDSCAPE City streets

SUGGESTED MAP OS Explorer 342 Glasgow; AA Street by Street

START/FINISH Grid reference: NS 587653

DOG FRIENDLINESS Not great walk for dogs

PARKING Sauchiehall Street multi-storey or on-street parking

PUBLIC TOILETS At Central Station

More than any other architect Alexander Thomson was responsible for the shaping of Glasgow with his innovative use and interpretation of classical Greek designs. Born in 1817, in the Stirlingshire village of Balfron, he moved to Glasgow to live with an older brother. He was apprenticed to an architect and began studying the plans, drawings and engravings of classical architecture. This influence dominated his later style and earned him the nickname 'Greek' Thomson although he never travelled abroad.

Classical Influences

The range of his buildings was extraordinary, from churches to villas, warehouses, tenements and even a set of steps. Much of his work was destroyed by German bombing during the Second World War and even more disappeared in the relentless modernisation of Glasgow during the 1960s and '70s. However, those buildings that have survived provide a fine cross-section of his work. His one remaining church (1857–9) on St Vincent Street is a remarkable building with Grecian columns and an imposing tower, built on the side of Blythswood Hill. Near by, in Union Street, the curiously named Egyptian Halls (1871–3), an enormous stone-fronted building with an interior constructed from cast iron, started life as an early form of shopping centre or bazaar. In the West End, near the Botanic Gardens, Thomson created the Great Western Terrace (1869), the 'grandest terrace in Glasgow' and took the unusual step of placing the tallest buildings in the middle of the row, rather than at the ends, which was more conventional at the time.

Another example of his terraces, Moray Place (1858), is where Thomson took up permanent residence. His home at No 1 is now the contact address for the Alexander Thomson Society and, like most of the houses he designed, is in private ownership. One exception is Holmwood House (1858) in Cathcart, 4.5 miles (7.2km) from the city centre, now owned by the National Trust for Scotland. Built for a wealthy paper manufacturer, it is an asymmetrical villa with a bay window, which looks like a Greek temple attached to the front of the building. It is probably Thomson's finest work.

Left: Kelvingrove Park towards the Glasgow University buildings (Walk 36)

Alexander Thomson Society

Although he gained prominence during his lifetime and had a major influence on later architects such as Charles Rennie Mackintosh and Frank Lloyd Wright, Thomson is little known today. Records of his work are limited to a few drawings held in Glasgow's Mitchell Library. His own office archive has vanished without a trace and were it not for the work of the Alexander Thomson Society, he would have remained in obscurity. However after much campaigning to preserve his remaining 24 buildings within the city and the publication of a book about the man, Thomson is beginning to regain the recognition he deserves.

WALK 36 DIRECTIONS

❶ Exit Central Station and turn right. At the junction with Union Street turn right. The building on the opposite corner is the Ca' d'Oro building, a late 19th-century Italianate warehouse by John Honeyman, based on the Golden House in Venice. The

upper storeys are made of cast iron. A little way down Union Street from here on the same side as the Ca' d'Oro is Thomson's Egyptian Halls, sadly in need of some renovation.

❷ Cross over then head down Union Street turning left into Argyle Street at the next junction.

Cross Argyle Street, then walk along to the junction with Dunlop Street where you will find the Buck's Head building, named after an inn that previously stood on this spot. Cross Argyle Street again, retrace your steps, turning right into Buchanan Street. Turn left into Mitchell Lane, pass the Lighthouse, then turn right.

❸ Walk up Mitchell Street, continue along West Nile Street then turn left into St Vincent Street. Continue on this for just under 0.5 mile (800m), going uphill to the junction with Pitt Street. You are now standing in front of 'Greek' Thomson's St Vincent Street church, one of his greatest achievements. Cross St Vincent Street here then head up Pitt Street to Sauchiehall Street.

❹ On the opposite corner is Thomson's Grecian Chamber (1865) and to the right along Scott Street is Rennie Mackintosh's Glasgow School of Art. From the front of the Grecian Chamber turn left, head down Sauchiehall Street to Charing Cross, then take the pedestrian bridge over the motorway to Woodlands Road. Go along here until it ends at Park Road, turn right, then left again into Great Western Road.

❺ Go right on Belmont Street, left at Doune Gardens, continue

---

WHILE YOU'RE THERE

Thomson designed Holmwood House in Cathcart for James Couper, a paper manufacturer, and everything including the interior design and the furniture came from Thomson's drawing board. Unfortunately the furniture has not survived, but his original paint scheme has been uncovered including a frieze depicting scenes from Homer's *Iliad*. Now in the care of the NTS.

---

along Doune Quadrant, then left again at Queen Margaret Drive. Cross the road and head down past the Botanic Gardens to turn right, back into Great Western Road. Cross the road and continue to Great Western Terrace, another Thomson masterpiece. Retrace your steps back from here to the top of Byres Road and turn right then, near the bottom, turn left into University Avenue.

WHAT TO LOOK OUT FOR

As you exit the station into Gordon Street the first 'Greek' Thomson building is the former warehouse opposite. Look out for the 'Sixty Steps' as you approach Queen Margaret Drive. There are remains of the former Queen Margaret Bridge on the left behind the former BBC buildings. The 'Steps' used to lead from the bridge to Kelvinside Terrace West.

WHERE TO EAT AND DRINK

The Willow Tearoom in Sauchiehall Street was designed by Charles Rennie Mackintosh for Kate Cranston who had a string of tea rooms. Entered through a jeweller's shop, there is always a queue for the 1904, Room de Luxe, where everything is Mackintosh. It's worth the wait and the food is good and reasonably priced.

---

❻ Go left into Oakfield Avenue, pass Eton Terrace on the corner with Great George Street. Turn right into Great George Street, right at Otago Street, left into Gibson Street and keep going when it becomes Eldon Street. Turn right into Woodlands Road and return to Sauchiehall Street. Follow this to the junction with Renfield Street, turn right and head downhill to Central Station.

Soldiers and Saints on the Pentlands

A lovely, bracing walk across the hills and past Edinburgh's reservoirs.

DISTANCE 7 miles (11.3km)   **MINIMUM TIME** 3hrs

ASCENT/GRADIENT 837ft (255m) ▲▲▲   **LEVEL OF DIFFICULTY** ✦✦✦

PATHS Wide firm tracks, short stretches can be muddy, 3 stiles

LANDSCAPE Reservoirs, fields and hills

SUGGESTED MAP OS Explorer 344 Pentland Hills

START/FINISH Grid reference: NT 212679

DOG FRIENDLINESS Good, but beware of ground-nesting birds

PARKING Car park at end of Bonaly Road, beyond Bonaly Tower

PUBLIC TOILETS None on route

Although this walk starts just beyond Edinburgh's busy city bypass, you'll soon think that you're miles from the city. The Pentlands are an uncompromising range of hills, which clasp the city in their craggy, green arms. Their peaks rise 1,500ft (457m) above the sea and offer many great walks where you can easily escape the crowds.

This walk takes you past several reservoirs, which keep Scotland's capital supplied with water. The first you pass is Torduff Reservoir, which was built in 1851 and is 72ft (22m) deep. Later on you come down to Glencorse Reservoir. Beneath its waters are concealed the remains of the Chapel of St Katherine's (or Catherine's) in the Hopes. This dates back to the 13th century and the reign of Robert the Bruce. In the unlikely event that it's been extremely dry and the waters are shallow, you might even see it peering out above the surface.

By coincidence (or perhaps not), in Mortonhall, on the other side of the bypass, is the site of St Catherine's Balm Well, or Oily Well. Tradition has it that St Catherine travelled through here carrying holy oil from Mount Sinai. She dropped a little and the well appeared in answer to her prayers. The oily water was said to heal skin diseases and attracted many pilgrims. The nearby suburb of Liberton is a corruption of 'leper town'. A modern explanation for the oily water was deposits of paraffin shale. James VI visited the spot in 1617 and ordered that the well be protected by a building. This was destroyed by Cromwell's troops when they camped on the surrounding hills in 1650. Cromwell, who had been helped to victory in England by the Scottish Covenanters, had fallen out with them after they decided to recognise Charles II as King.

The Pentlands are full of similar memories. The Camus Stone near Farmilehead commemorates a battle fought against the Danes. And in 1666, General Dalyell of The Binns (an ancestor of MP Tam Dalyell) beat a Covenanting force at Rullion Green on these hills, crushing the so-called Pentland rising. These days you may still see soldiers on the Pentlands, for there are army firing ranges at Castlelaw, while recruits from barracks at Glencorse and Redford are often put through their paces on the hills.

Lord Cockburn's Inspiration

At the start of the walk you'll pass Bonaly Tower, once the home of Lord Cockburn (1779–1854), writer and judge, who was inspired by his glorious surroundings to pen the words: 'Pentlands high hills raise their heather-crowned crest, Peerless Edina expands her white breast, Beauty and grandeur are blent in the scene, Bonnie Bonally lies smiling between.'

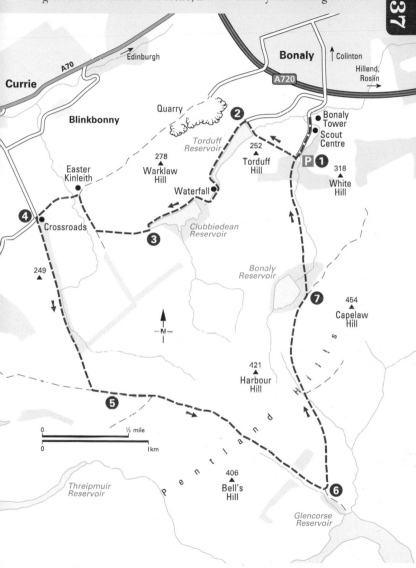

WALK 37 DIRECTIONS

❶ From the car park, go through the gate and take the right-hand path, signposted Torduff Reservoir. Beyond a wooden gate, the path crosses over the reservoir dam to intersect with a tarmac lane.

❷ Turn left along the lane, keeping Torduff Reservoir on your

WHAT TO LOOK OUT FOR

Colinton, close to the start of this walk, has strong associations with Robert Louis Stevenson whose grandfather, Dr Lewis Balfour, was minister at the local church. Stevenson spent many of his holidays here as a child, exploring the hills and nearby Colinton Dell, an extremely picturesque spot.

left-hand side. When you reach the top of the reservoir, walk over the little bridge and follow the metalled track as it bends round to the right beside a waterfall. Walk under a line of electricity pylons, and go over a small bridge, passing a water chute on your left-hand side, and continue past Clubbiedean Reservoir.

3 Your path now bears right, with fields on either side. Pass under another line of pylons and walk to Easter Kinleith farm. Now follow the lane as it bends back to the left, signposted 'Harlaw'. Pass a sign for Poets' Glen and continue ahead, over a bridge and on to a large white house on the left-hand side called Crossroads.

4 Turn left. Follow the track past a conifer plantation on your left-hand side, then go through a small gate. Continue walking ahead until you reach an intersection.

WHERE TO EAT AND DRINK

The Spylaw Tavern in Colinton is worth trying for a light lunch, a cool drink or tea or coffee. They've got a pleasant beer garden where you can sit outside if it's sunny but be warned it can get a bit smelly. Further along the bypass is the Flotterstone Inn, south of Boghall, which serves good pub lunches.

Turn left through a gate, which is signposted to Glencorse.

5 Follow the path across the moor and up into the hills, where you cross a stone stile. Continue in the same direction until you come to a copse of conifers on the right-hand side, with Glencorse Reservoir ahead. Turn left at this point, following the sign to Colinton by Bonaly.

WHILE YOU'RE THERE

If you're feeling fit then make for Hillend Ski Centre on the Pentlands. This is a dry-ski slope, suitable for ski and snowboarding practice. A chairlift takes you to the top if you don't fancy the climb. You're also very close to wonderful Rosslyn Chapel (see Walk 38), which is well worth the visit and just a short drive along the bypass.

6 Walk uphill and maintain direction to go through a metal gate. The track now narrows and takes you through the hills, until it eventually opens out. Continue in the same direction to reach a fence encircling conifers. Keep the fence on your left and walk down to a gate on the left-hand side.

7 Turn left through the gate. Walk past Bonaly Reservoir, then through a kissing gate and walk downhill, getting good views over Edinburgh as you descend. When you reach a wooden gate, go through and continue ahead, walking downhill, with trees on either side. Go through another kissing gate and follow the tarmac path ahead to return to the car park and the start of the walk.

The Romance of Rosslyn Glen

Tree-lined paths take you beside a river to a very special ancient chapel in this glorious glen.

DISTANCE 5 miles (8km)	**MINIMUM TIME** 2hrs 30min

ASCENT/GRADIENT 279ft (85m) ▲▲▲   **LEVEL OF DIFFICULTY** +++

PATHS Generally good, but can be muddy and slippery

LANDSCAPE Woodland and fields, short sections of road

SUGGESTED MAP OS Explorer 344 Pentland Hills

START/FINISH Grid reference: NT 272627

DOG FRIENDLINESS Can mostly run free, steps and climbs might not suit some

PARKING Roslin Glen Country Park car park

PUBLIC TOILETS None on route; nearest at Rosslyn Chapel Visitor Centre

Despite the splendour of its lush woodland, gurgling waters and delicate wild flowers, the most striking feature of romantic Rosslyn Glen is artificial rather than natural. It's Rosslyn Chapel, the exquisite little church that you meet right at the end of this walk. Founded in 1446 by Sir William St Clair, it took 40 years to build and was originally intended to be a much larger structure.

Curious Carvings

The interior of the chapel is full of intricate stone carvings, created by foreign masons commissioned by Sir William, who supervised much of the work himself. The carvings are not just rich in biblical imagery, as you might expect, but also depict masonic and pagan symbols. For instance, there are over one hundred images of the 'green man', the pagan figure that once symbolised great goodness and fertility– as well as great evil. There is also a depiction of a *danse macabre*, an allegorical representation of death's supremacy over mankind.

Crime of Passion

Perhaps the most stunning carving in the chapel is the Apprentice Pillar, an extraordinarily ornate piece of work. It is said that the pillar was carved by a talented apprentice while his master was away. When the master mason returned he was so jealous of the beauty and craftsmanship of the work that he killed the boy in a fit of jealousy.

The Knights Templar

Rosslyn's greatest mysteries come from its associations with the Knights Templar, the medieval order of warrior monks. They were originally formed to protect pilgrims travelling to the Holy Land – and one of their founders was married to a relative of Sir William. The Templars became immensely wealthy and powerful and were eventually persecuted, being accused of immorality and even pagan idolatry. Many fled to Scotland, with help from the freemasons, taking their treasures with them.

ROSLIN

The St Clairs have strong masonic links and Rosslyn Chapel is said to have been built as a memorial to the Templars. Some archaeologists think it hides many of their treasures, such as ancient scrolls from Jerusalem, jewels, perhaps the Holy Grail. Some have even speculated that under the Apprentice Pillar is buried the skull of Christ. This little chapel is certainly full of secrets.

Film buffs will also note that Rosslyn Chapel starred as a crucial location in *The Da Vinci Code*.

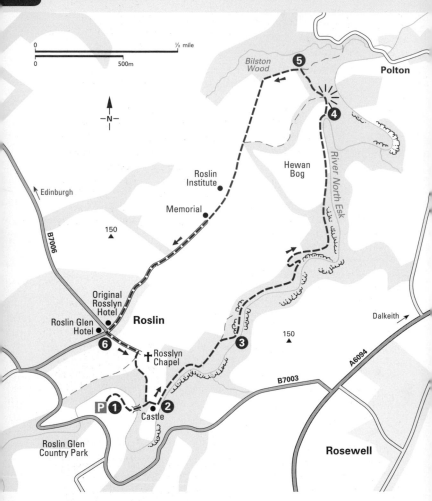

WALK 38 DIRECTIONS

❶ From the country park car park, walk north-east with the sound of the river through the trees to your left. Go up the metal stairs, cross the footbridge, then walk ahead, following the path uphill. In summer, the smell of

wild garlic will soon waft over you. At the bottom of a flight of steps, turn right, walk under the old castle arch, down some stone steps, then turn to your left.

❷ Follow the path through scrub and up some steps into dense woodland. Just by a muddy burn, bear left, keeping to the main path with the gorge to your right. Beyond a line of yew trees growing from an old stone wall, turn right and follow the path that winds steeply downhill until you reach the water's edge.

❸ Walk to your left, then follow the path as it climbs again. At a crossing of paths turn right, following the direction of the river. Your way now takes you high above the river, and you continue ahead to cross a stile. After you cross another stile the view opens out to fields on your left, then takes you closer to the river again, until you reach a kissing gate.

WHAT TO LOOK OUT FOR

The memorial to the Battle of Rosslyn commemorates a battle between Scotland and England. The carnage of the battle gave rise to many local landscape names such as shinbone field, kilburn and stinking rig – a reference presumably to all the dead bodies left in the fields.

❹ Turn left and follow the path up steps with fields to your left. When you reach the top of the ridge there are good views to your right. Continue until you go through a kissing gate

❺ Turn left and follow the wide path. You eventually walk past buildings of the Roslin Institute, where Dolly the sheep was cloned, then pass a memorial to the Battle of Rosslyn on your right-hand side. Keep walking straight ahead, through the outskirts of Roslin and up to the crossroads at the village centre.

❻ Turn left here and walk ahead. After a short distance you see Rosslyn Chapel on the right-hand

WHILE YOU'RE THERE

Butterfly and Insect World is not far from here at Lasswade, near Dalkeith. It's a great place to bring kids as the enclosures contain loads of beautiful and exotic butterflies in a tropical setting. There are also some separate cages in which an interesting variety of creepy-crawlies are kept.

W A L K 38

side. If you don't intend to visit the chapel, take the path that bears downhill to the right, just in front of it. When you reach the cemetery turn left, following the signpost for Polton, and walk between the cemeteries to the metal gate for Rosslyn Castle. Go down the steps on the right-hand side, over the bridge again and return to the car park at the start.

WHERE TO EAT AND DRINK

There's a little café in the visitor centre at Rosslyn Chapel where you can get teas, coffees and cakes. Otherwise there are two reasonable pubs in the centre of the village. The Original Rosslyn Hotel is on your right-hand side as you come into the village and serves bar lunches and high teas. Opposite it, also on the right of your route, is the Roslin Glen Hotel, which also does light bar meals such as baked potatoes.

Poppy Harvest at East Linton

A delightful and varied walk past an old doo'cot and a picturesque mill to fields where poppies grow.

DISTANCE 4.5 miles (7.2km)   **MINIMUM TIME** 2hrs 30min

ASCENT/GRADIENT 295ft (90m) ▲▲▲   **LEVEL OF DIFFICULTY** ✦✦✦

PATHS *Field paths, river margins and woodland tracks. Short section of busy road, 3 stiles*

LANDSCAPE *Cultivated fields, lively river and picturesque village*

SUGGESTED MAP *OS Explorer 351 Dunbar & North Berwick*

START/FINISH *Grid reference: NT 591772*

DOG FRIENDLINESS *Can run free for many sections, watch for sheep though*

PARKING *Main street in East Linton*

PUBLIC TOILETS *Pencraig picnic site*

If you were to design your ideal walk, what would it include? A dash of history; a crumbling castle; perhaps some fields of waving corn and a peaceful river bank? And maybe a pretty village, in which to settle down finally with a cup of tea and a large wedge of home-made cake? Well, this walk's for you then. It takes you on a lovely varied route through the fertile countryside of East Lothian, just a few miles outside Edinburgh. It's the sort of walk that is enjoyable at any time of year – but it is particularly lovely in the summer when you can see all the wild flowers that line your way.

A Phantastic Doo'cot

The first part of the walk takes you past an old doo'cot (dovecote) where pigeons were bred to be used as food. It once belonged to Phantassie house, a local property which was the birthplace of Sir John Rennie in 1761. Rennie was a civil engineer who, after studying at Edinburgh University, moved to London. There he constructed Southwark and Waterloo bridges, as well as designing dockyards, bridges and canals throughout the country. Not far from the doo'cot is the photogenic Preston Mill, owned by the National Trust for Scotland. This is an 18th-century grain mill and was used to process the produce of East Lothian's fertile arable fields. It has a distinctive conical kiln, which was used for drying the grain, and a barn where the grain was ground. The machinery is driven by a waterwheel.

The Symbolism of Poppies

Later on in the walk, as you make your way towards Hailes Castle, you might well see the scarlet heads of poppies waving among the ripening crops. If you see them on a hot day in August, they make a magnificent spectacle.) Sadly, this is a sight you see all too rarely these days, as intensive agriculture has virtually eliminated them from the fields, but it would once have been commonplace. Poppies have been a symbol of blood, harvest and regeneration for thousands of years, as they grow in fields of grain and will rapidly colonise disturbed ground – this was most graphically illustrated in the First World War, and poppies have, of course, also become a symbol of remembrance of lives lost.

Poppies were the sacred plant of the Roman crop goddess Ceres (from whose name we get the word 'cereal'). The Romans used to decorate her statues with garlands of poppies and barley, and poppy seeds were offered up during rituals to ensure a good harvest. Poppy seeds mixed with grains of barley have also been found in Egyptian relics dating from 2500 BC. In Britain it was once believed that picking poppies would provoke a storm and they were nicknamed 'thundercup', 'thunderflower' or 'lightnings'. Whatever you call them, they're a glorious and welcome sight.

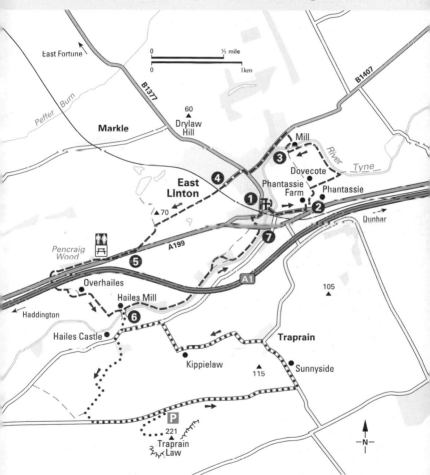

WALK 39 DIRECTIONS

❶ From the Market Cross in the centre of the town, take the lane that runs to the left of the church. When you come to the main street turn left, then walk over the bridge and continue until you reach a garage on the right-hand side. Turn left here into the farm opposite the garage, following the sign for Houston Mill and Mill House.

❷ Follow the path to the right round the farm buildings until you see the old doo'cot (dovecote) ahead of you. Turn right just in front of it and follow the path along the edge of the field. When you reach the footbridge, turn left to continue walking around the edge of the field, with the river on your right-hand side. At the next footbridge, cross over and go through the metal gate.

❸ Take the right-hand path across the field and go through the kissing gate to reach the old mill. Once you've inspected the mill – you can go inside when it's open – continue on to meet the main road, then turn left to walk back into the town. Turn right to walk along the High Street, then cross over the road and turn left to go down Langside.

WHILE YOU'RE THERE

The Museum of Flight at East Fortune, near Haddington, is Scotland's national museum of aviation. You can see wartime memorabilia and lots of old aircraft, including a Tigermoth, all housed in old Second World War hangars. Haddington itself is a prosperous town and was the birthplace of John Knox, one of the founders of the Presbyterian Church.

❹ When you reach the recreation ground, maintain your direction and walk across the grass to reach the railway. Go through the underpass and walk ahead through the fields. Continue in the same direction, crossing over three walls with the help of some steps and two stiles. After you cross the third wall the track starts to become indistinct, but maintain direction until you come to a footpath sign. Bear left here to reach the road.

WHERE TO EAT AND DRINK

Votadini is a coffee shop on the main street in East Linton. There are some comfy seats, and they serve home-made scones and cakes, as well as light meals such as toasted waffles. For a stronger brew than tea try the Crown Hotel, also in the town centre.

❺ Turn right and follow the paved footway through the Pencraig pull-in and on to a signpost to Overhailes. Turn right here and follow it round and under the dual carriageway. From the farm continue down to the end of the lane at Hailes Mill.

❻ Don't cross over the bridge (unless you wish to visit the ruins of Hailes Castle) but instead follow the path that runs to the left of the steps. You're now walking along the river's edge on a narrow path. Follow the path to cross a stile, walk along a field margin and under a new road bridge, then enter some woods. Walk up a flight of stairs, then down some steps, and continue following the path to walk under another road bridge.

❼ The path now runs through a garden and on to the road, where you turn right. Walk under the railway bridge, then turn left and return to the starting point of the walk in the town.

EXTENDING THE WALK

From Point ❻, cross the river to Hailes Castle, then ascend tracks and lanes to Traprain Law. The summit is a fine viewpoint. To return, go down the road into Traprain, then turn left past Kippielaw, which takes you back to Hailes Castle, where you can cross the river and resume the main walk.

Intoxicating Memories in Leith

A gentle linear walk along the Water of Leith to Edinburgh's ancient port, where claret once flowed in freely.

DISTANCE 3.5 miles (5.7km) **MINIMUM TIME** 1hr 30min

ASCENT/GRADIENT Negligible ▲▲▲ **LEVEL OF DIFFICULTY** ✦✦✦

PATHS Wide riverside paths and city streets

LANDSCAPE Edinburgh's hidden waterway and revitalised port

SUGGESTED MAP OS Explorer 350 Edinburgh

START Grid reference: NT 243739 **FINISH** Grid reference: NT 271766

DOG FRIENDLINESS Can run free beside water, keep on lead in Leith

PARKING Scottish National Gallery of Modern Art, Belford Road

PUBLIC TOILETS Near Stockbridge

Visitors always forget to come to Leith, yet Edinburgh's ancient seaport is full of history. Even though the docks have been spruced up and become rather trendy, Leith retains an edgy, maritime atmosphere – like an old sea dog who'll spin you a yarn for a pint.

A Taste for Claret

There has been a port at Leith, where the Water of Leith meets the Forth, from at least the 1st century AD when the Romans stored wine for their legions here. The port grew and by medieval times was facilitating valuable trade with France. Ships would leave loaded with dried local fish and return laden with wines, which were landed by the French monks of St Anthony who were based in Edinburgh. One of the main imports was claret. It rapidly became Scotland's national drink, whereas the most popular drink in England was port. One old verse sums up its popularity, beginning with the words: 'Guid claret best keeps out the cauld an drives awa the winter soon'. When cargoes arrived, some would be sent on a cart through Leith and anyone who fancied a sample simply turned up with a jug, which would be filled for 6d. It didn't seem to matter how large the jug was.

Whisky Makes its Mark

The quality of the claret imported and bottled in Leith was extremely good. One historian said it 'held in its day a cachet comparable to that which one now associates with chateau-bottled wines'. Claret drinking was seen as a symbol of Scotland's national identity and Jacobites drank it as a symbol of independence.

During the 18th century the British government, determined to price the French out of the market, raised taxes on claret. Inevitably traders began to smuggle it into Scotland instead. It was only in the 19th century that claret drinking declined when taxes rose and the Napoleonic Wars made it scarce. While Leith claret was still drunk by the wealthiest people, whisky (a drink from the Highlands) took its place as the people's pick-me-up, going from strength to strength to reach its present state of popularity.

LEITH

The Port of Leith continued to grow in importance and it was from here, in 1698, that the ill-fated Darien expedition set sail, a venture that was eventually to cost Scotland her independence.

The intention was to establish a permanent colony at Darien on the Isthmus of Panama. It cost £400,000 to fund, but it was thought that the venture would give Scotland control of a potentially lucrative trading route. However the terrain was hostile and the colonists rapidly died. The Scottish economy was plunged into crisis and the country was pushed inexorably towards union with England.

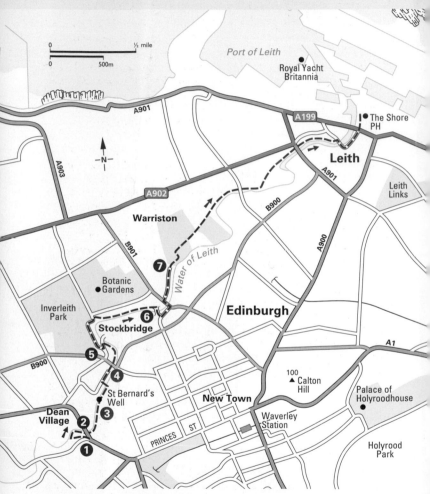

WALK 40 DIRECTIONS

❶ From the junction of the Dean Bridge and Queensferry Street, turn left to walk down Bell's Brae. You are now in the Dean Village, which dates back to 1128. It was once a milling centre and had 11 watermills producing all the meal for Edinburgh. At the bottom, turn right into Miller Row.

❷ Follow this to walk under the impressive arches of the Dean Bridge, which was designed by Thomas Telford and opened in

WHAT TO LOOK OUT FOR

Leith Links is said to be the real home of golf. The rules of the game were established here, only later being formalised at St Andrews. Golf has been played here since the 15th century. In 1641 Charles I was whiling away his time with a round or two when he received the news of the Irish rebellion.

the path beside the river. Where the path ends, climb on to the road, turn left and then right to go down Arboretum Avenue.

5 Walk along this road, then turn right along the path marked Rocheid Path. This runs beside the river and is a popular cycleway and jogging path. Follow this, passing the backs of the Colonies. This low-cost housing was built by the Edinburgh Co-operative for artisans living here in the late 19th century. The idea was to provide houses in a healthy environment away from the dirt of the city. Walk to Tanfield Bridge.

6 Go right, over the bridge, go up the steps, then turn left, walking towards the clock tower. At the end turn left along Warriston Place, cross the road, then turn right down Warriston Crescent. This is lined with town houses. Walk to the end where you'll reach the playing fields.

7 Bear right, around the edge of the park, then follow the path as it bears uphill between trees. Turn left at the top and follow the cycle track marked 'Leith 1.25'. Follow this all the way into Leith, where it brings you out near the old Custom House. Cross the bridge, then turn left to walk along the shore and explore the pubs, before returning to town by bus.

1832. Your path then runs along the bottom of the steeply sided gorge, beside the Water of Leith, and feels extremely rural. You'll pass an old well on your left, followed by the more impressive St Bernard's Well.

WHILE YOU'RE THERE

The former Royal Yacht *Britannia* is moored at Ocean Drive in Leith. It was launched in 1953 and served the Royal Family until 1997, acting as a floating palace and holiday home. Charles and Diana spent part of their honeymoon on the yacht, and the Queen entertained everyone from Bill Clinton to Nelson Mandela. You can go on board the ship and see the accomodation – including the Queen's bedroom, which is surprisingly low key.

3 St Bernard's Well was discovered by some schoolboys in 1760. The mineral water was said to have healing properties and, in 1789, the present Roman Temple was built, with Hygeia – the goddess of health – at the centre. From here continue along the main path, then go up the steps. Turn left, and go right on to Dean Terrace to reach Stockbridge.

4 Cross the road and go down the steps ahead – immediately to the right of the building with the clock tower. Continue to follow

WHERE TO EAT AND DRINK

Newly gentrified Leith is full of bars and restaurants, many of which are along the water's edge. You can get anything from fish to curry. On sunny days you can sit outside and relax. The oldest pub of all is the King's Wark, which is full of atmosphere and serves good food. Also worth trying is The Shore, a lovely old bar with a separate fish restaurant.

Edinburgh's Murky Secrets

A stroll through the atmospheric streets of Edinburgh's Old Town.

DISTANCE 2 miles (3.2km)   **MINIMUM TIME** 1hr

ASCENT/GRADIENT 197ft (60m) ▲▲▲   **LEVEL OF DIFFICULTY** +++

PATHS *City streets, some hill tracks*

LANDSCAPE *Atmospheric ancient city and brooding castle*

SUGGESTED MAP *AA Street by Street Edinburgh*

START/FINISH *Grid reference: NT 256739*

DOG FRIENDLINESS *Keep on lead, watch paws don't get trodden on by crowds*

PARKING *Several NCP car parks in Edinburgh*

PUBLIC TOILETS *At Waverley Station*

Edinburgh is often thought of as an extremely respectable, rather genteel city. But as you'll find out in this walk through the city's ancient heart – the medieval Old Town – it has a darker, more mysterious side to its nature.

The Old Town, the original city, was enclosed by city walls, which protected it from the ravages of conflict – but also stopped it from expanding. This meant that as the population grew, the city became increasingly overcrowded, and was at one time the most densely populated city in Europe. The only solution was to build upwards. People lived in towering tenements known as 'lands', with the wealthy taking the rooms at the bottom, the poorer classes living at the top. Its main street, the Royal Mile, became a complicated maze of narrow 'wynds' or alleyways, which gradually deteriorated into a slum. Cleanliness wasn't a priority and residents habitually threw their rubbish into the street – as well as the contents of their chamber pots. When Dr Johnson stayed in the city with James Boswell, he wrote that they had been 'assailed by the evening effluvia' while walking home from a tavern one night.

However, in the progressive 18th century new public buildings were constructed along the steep slopes of the Royal Mile, using the walls of the old slums as foundations. As the city council chambers were extended over the next century, stories were told of cobbled lanes and long-abandoned rooms that still existed deep below in vaulted basements. It wasn't until late in the 20th century that one of these old lanes was opened to the public. Called Mary King's Close, it is full of atmosphere and, as you might expect, is said to be haunted.

Murder in the Dark

There are more dark secrets in the Grassmarket, where the body-snatchers Burke and Hare used to lure their victims before murdering them. They then sold the bodies to a local surgeon who used them in his research. Then there was Deacon Brodie, the seemingly respectable town councillor who had a secret nocturnal life as a criminal and gambler – and was eventually hanged. He was the inspiration for Robert Louis Stevenson's Dr Jekyll, who turned into Mr Hyde, the vicious werewolf, at night. With such a history, it is hardly surprising that crime writer Ian Rankin sets his Inspector Rebus novels in Edinburgh. He often uses gory historical events in his tales, and has plenty to choose from – even an act of cannibalism (*Set in Darkness*, 2000). As Rankin says of Edinburgh – 'It's a very secretive place.'

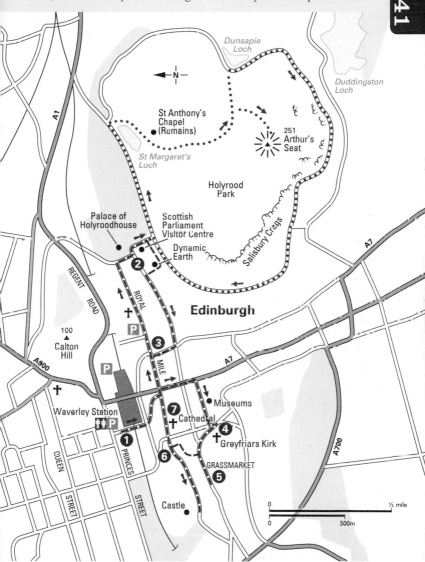

WALK 41 DIRECTIONS

1 From the main entrance to Waverley Station, turn left, go to the end of the street, then cross over and walk up Cockburn Street to the Royal Mile, where you turn left and walk downhill. Continue to the black gates of Holyroodhouse. Turn right and walk to face the new Parliament visitor centre.

WALK 41

❷ Turn left and follow the road to the right, then turn right again past Dynamic Earth (the building looks like a huge white woodlouse) and walk up into Holyrood Road. Turn left, walk past the new buildings of newspaper, *The Scotsman*, and walk up to St Mary's Street, where you turn right and rejoin the Royal Mile. Were you to continue ahead you would join the Cowgate, some parts of which were devastated by fire in December 2002.

❸ Turn left, to the main road, then turn left along South Bridge. At Chambers Street turn right and walk past the museums. At the end of the road, cross and then turn left to see the little statue of Greyfriars Bobby, the dog that refused to leave this spot after his master died.

❹ You can now cross the road and make the short detour into Greyfriars Kirk to see where Greyfriars Bobby is buried close to his master. Or simply turn right and walk down Candlemaker Row. At the bottom, turn left and wander into the atmospheric Grassmarket – once the haunt of Burke and Hare, it's now filled with shops and lively restaurants.

❺ When you've explored the Grassmarket, walk up winding Victoria Street (it says West Bow at the bottom). About two-thirds of the way up look out for a flight of steps hidden away on the left. Climb them and when you emerge at the top, walk ahead at the top to join the Royal Mile again.

❻ Turn left to walk up and visit the castle. Then walk down the Royal Mile again, taking a peek into the dark wynds (alleyways) that lead off it. You eventually pass St Giles' Cathedral on your right, which is well worth a visit.

❼ Next on your left you pass the City Chambers (under which lies mysterious Mary King's Close). Continue until you reach the junction with Cockburn Street. Turn left and walk back down this winding street. At the bottom, cross the road and return to the entrance to Waverley Station.

EXTENDING THE WALK

For the definitive view of the city, leave the main walk at Point ❷, by the Scottish Parliament Visitor Centre and head up the road to St Margaret's Loch. From here a track leads to St Anthony's Chapel and on up to the summit of Arthur's Seat. After admiring the view, drop down to Dunsapie Loch, turn right and follow the road beneath Salisbury Crags back to Point ❷ to resume the main walk.

Right: The sun sets over Edinburgh (Walk 41)

Edinburgh's Elegant New Town

A walk in the footsteps of literary giants.

DISTANCE 3 miles (4.8km)	**MINIMUM TIME** 1hr 30min
ASCENT/GRADIENT 164ft (50m) ▲▲▲	**LEVEL OF DIFFICULTY** ✦✦✦

PATHS Busy city streets

LANDSCAPE Elegant Georgian townscape

SUGGESTED MAP AA Street by Street Edinburgh

START/FINISH Grid reference: NT 257739

DOG FRIENDLINESS Keep on lead, not allowed in Botanic Gardens

PARKING Several large car parks in central Edinburgh

PUBLIC TOILETS At Waverley Station

Don't worry, this is not a walk through some dreary 20th-century housing scheme. Edinburgh's New Town was built in the 18th century and is an elegant development of wide airy streets, punctuated with sweeping crescents and lined with soft grey Georgian buildings. It was a planned development, designed to move the focus of the city away from the filthy, overcrowded streets of the medieval Old Town. It was laid out in the mid 18th century by James Craig, a young architect who won a competition for the design. It is separated from the Old Town by Princes Street, the main thoroughfare and once the smartest shopping street in Scotland. In later years Robert Adam contributed to the development, notably designing Charlotte Square in 1791.

Luring the Literati

Houses in the New Town were soon the most coveted in the city and became the haunt of the Scottish literati. Literary associations abound. Kenneth Grahame, author of *The Wind in the Willows* (1908) was born at 30 Castle Street in 1859; Robert Louis Stevenson grew up at 17 Heriot Row; Percy Bysshe Shelley stayed at 60 George Street with his runaway teenage bride in 1811; and Sir Walter Scott once lived at 39 Castle Street.

The city seems to hold a fascination for writers and many historic meetings have taken place here, including that between Walter Scott and Robert Burns. The war poet Wilfred Owen often came into Edinburgh while he was recuperating from 'shell shock' at nearby Craiglockhart War Hospital. One of his early poems was entitled Six O'clock in Princes Street. It was at Craiglockhart that Owen met Siegfried Sassoon, already an acclaimed poet, who encouraged him in his writing and made amendments to early drafts of some of his greatest works. Owen left Edinburgh in 1917 and returned to the Front, where he died on 4 November, 1918.

Another New Town location, Milne's Bar on Hanover Street, was a favourite haunt of several of Scotland's most influential modern poets. Hugh MacDiarmid (see Walk 2) and his two friends and drinking partners Norman MacCaig and Sorley MacLean are just some of the figures who used to meet here in the last century, and the pub walls are still covered with their memorabilia.

In the latter stages of this walk you will pass a statue of Sherlock Holmes, a tribute to his Edinburgh-born creator Sir Arthur Conan Doyle, who lived near by at 11 Picardy Place (which has now been demolished). Conan Doyle studied medicine at Edinburgh University and modelled his fictional detective Holmes on one of his former lecturers – Dr Joseph Bell. Bell was an extremely observant individual and combined his instincts with science to help the police in solving several murders in the city. Many believe that Conan Doyle assisted Bell with his work in this capacity – acting as Dr Watson to his Holmes.

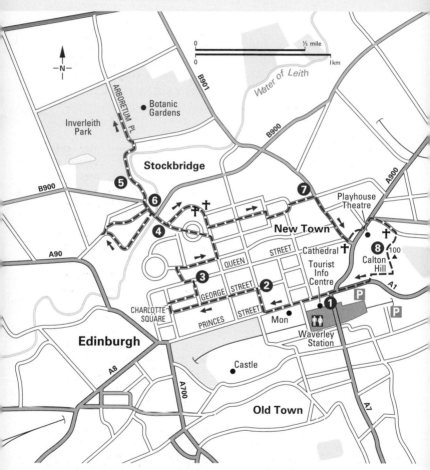

WALK 42 DIRECTIONS

❶ From the tourist information centre, turn left and walk along Princes Street. Just after you pass the Scott Monument on your left, cross the road to reach Jenners department store, Scotland's

answer to Harrods. Continue along Princes Street, then take a right turn up Hanover Street.

❷ Take the second turning on your left and walk along George Street to reach elegant Charlotte Square. Then turn right and right again to go along Young Street. At the end, turn left and walk down North Castle Street to reach Queen Street.

❸ Cross the road, turn left, then right down Wemyss Place and right into Heriot Row. When you reach Howe Street turn left and, before you reach the church in the middle of the street, turn left and walk along South East Circus Place. Walk past the sweep of Royal Circus and then down into Stockbridge.

❹ Cross the bridge, then turn left along Dean Terrace. At the end, turn right into Ann Street. When you reach Dean Park Crescent turn right and follow the road round into Leslie Place and into Stockbridge again. Cross the main road, turn left and then right at the traffic lights down St Bernard's Row. Follow this, then bear left into Arboretum Avenue.

> ### WHILE YOU'RE THERE
> Ann Street in Stockbridge is said to have been the inspiration for J M Barrie's novel *Quality Street* (1901) and was (perhaps still is) one of the most desirable addresses in Scotland. Thomas de Quincey, author of *Confessions of an Opium Eater*, used to visit No. 29, the home of Professor John Wilson, who frequently hosted writers and artists here.

❺ Follow this road past the Water of Leith down to Inverleith Terrace. Cross and walk up Arboretum Place to reach the entrance to the Botanic Gardens on the right. Turn left after exploring the gardens and retrace your steps to Stockbridge again.

❻ Turn left at Hectors bar and walk uphill, then turn left along St Stephen Street. When you

> ### WHERE TO EAT AND DRINK
> Apart from Milne's Bar on Hanover Street, there are plenty more pubs and bars to choose from in the New Town. George Street, which is lined with designer stores, has several bistros and restaurants, while down in Stockbridge you can relax in one of many coffee bars.

reach the church follow the road, cross over Cumberland Street then turn left along Great King Street. At the end, turn right, then immediately left to walk along Drummond Place, past Dublin Street and continue ahead into London Street.

❼ At the roundabout turn right and walk up Broughton Street to reach Picardy Place. Turn left, walk past the statue of Sherlock Holmes, then bear left towards the Playhouse Theatre. Cross over, continue left, then turn right into Leopold Place and right again into Blenheim Place. At the church turn right, walk up the steps and turn left at the meeting of paths.

❽ Go up the steps on the right, walk over Calton Hill, then turn right to pass the canon. Go downhill, take the steps on your left and walk down into Regent Road. Turn right and walk back into Princes Street and the start.

> ### WHAT TO LOOK OUT FOR
> The Royal Botanic Garden covers 72 acres (29ha) and contains many plant species that were discovered by early Scottish botanists. Plants were originally grown here in order to research their medicinal qualities. In spring the grounds are full of rhododendrons in bloom, while the glasshouses contain exotic palms, orchids and cacti.

A Leisurely Circuit of Culross

An easy walk that ends on the cobbled streets of an historic town, where a prosperous trading history is reflected in the buildings.

DISTANCE 3.5 miles (5.7km)   **MINIMUM TIME** 1hr 30min

ASCENT/GRADIENT 180ft (55m) ▲▲▲   **LEVEL OF DIFFICULTY** +++

PATHS Generally firm paths, some muddy woodland tracks

LANDSCAPE Ancient town, fields and woodland

SUGGESTED MAP OS Explorer 367 Dunfermline & Kirkcaldy

START/FINISH Grid reference: NS 983859

DOG FRIENDLINESS Can run free on woodland tracks

PARKING Culross West car park

PUBLIC TOILETS By car park in Culross

Walking through Culross is a bit like stepping on to a film set. With its cobbled streets and immaculately preserved buildings, it gives you the impression that you've stepped back in time. The pretty houses, with their red pantiled roofs and crow-stepped gables, give the place a Flemish look, a typical feature of Scottish architecture of this period. Yet despite its neatly manicured appearance, Culross owes its origins to coal mining.

Monks and Miners

The mining industry was started in the 13th century by the Cistercian monks of Culross Abbey, and a flourishing trade soon developed. Coal production allowed a salt-panning industry to grow up, with fires from inferior quality coal being used to evaporate sea water. By the 16th century Culross was one of the largest ports in Scotland, exporting both coal and salt to the Low Countries and the Baltic. On their return journeys they carried red pantiles as ballast – which were used to give the town's roofs their distinctive appearance. There are reminders of these days throughout the town. The area known as the Sandhaven, for instance, which you pass at the end of this walk, was once the harbour. As you pass it, take a look at the Tron, where officials would weigh export cargoes to assess their tax – you can still see the stone platform that supported the weighing beam.

Culross Palace

Trade brought prosperity to the town, as you can see from the many substantial buildings that dot the streets. Most striking of all is Culross Palace, a beautiful ochre-coloured town house. It was built in 1597 by Sir George Bruce, the local bigwig who owned both the mines and the salt pans – the pine-panelled walls, decorative paintings and period furniture reflect the lifestyle of a rich merchant of the period. If you go on a tour, look out for the Flemish-style paintings on the wooden ceiling in the Painted Chamber.

Eventually the industries in Culross died out and the village went to sleep, its period features preserved like those of an insect trapped in amber.

However, in 1923 the palace was bought by the National Trust for Scotland, which then went on to purchase more properties in the village.

As you near the end of this walk, make time to explore. Walking down the hill you'll pass The House with the Evil Eyes – so named because of the shape of its windows – then the church and the remains of Culross Abbey, before coming into the centre of the village. Look for the street known as The Haggs or Stinking Wynd. If you look carefully you'll see that the centre is higher than the edges. This was 'the crown o' the causie', the place where the local toffs walked. The unfortunate hoi polloi had to walk in the gutters – which would have been swimming with – well, you can imagine.

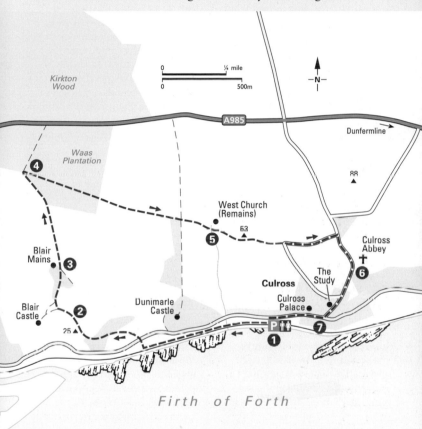

WALK 43 DIRECTIONS

❶ From the car park, take steps up to a tarmac path alongside the railway and turn right. Just beyond a reed bed to the right, turn right down steps and follow the path to the road. Cross over to the entrance to Blair Castle, now a convalescent home for miners.

❷ Walk up the tarmac drive, which is lined with magnificent rhododendron bushes. Walk ahead until you can see Blair Castle on the left. Before you reach it, take the right-hand turning in the trees and follow it as it bears to the right. Continue until you reach Blair Mains farmhouse, which you'll find on the left.

❸ Continue following the track, with fields on either side. Walk ahead until you reach the trees and continue following this track until you reach a metal gate on the left-hand side, just beyond a line of pylons. Look carefully and you should spot a wooden fence post on the right-hand side, with the words 'West Kirk' and 'grave' painted on it in faint white. Take the narrow right-hand path immediately before it, which runs through the trees.

WHILE YOU'RE THERE

Dunfermline Abbey, in nearby Dunfermline, dates back to the 11th century. The only remains of the original church are the foundations as it was ravaged by raiders many times. It is the burial place of six Scottish kings, as well as Robert the Bruce who is buried beneath the pulpit.

❹ Follow this path to go through a kissing gate and continue walking ahead, with trees on your left and fields on your right. Go through another kissing gate, and continue in the same direction. When you reach a crossing of paths, continue ahead along the track and walk under a line of pylons. You will soon pass the remains of a church on the left-hand side.

❺ Continue ahead, past the old cemetery, and walk in the same direction until the track joins a tarmac road. Walk in the same direction until you reach a junction. Turn right here and head downhill – watch out for traffic now as the road can be busy. You will soon reach Culross Abbey on the left-hand side.

❻ It's worth stopping at this point to visit the abbey. You

WHERE TO EAT AND DRINK

There's a café in the Bessie Bar Hall in the palace where you can get home-made cakes and snacks and hot drinks. Still in Culross, the Red Lion Inn serves a selection of salads, ploughman's and other tasty bar meals.

can then continue to walk on downhill, down Tanhouse Brae, and will soon reach the Mercat ('old Market') Cross, with The Study on the right-hand side. Continue walking in the same direction, down Back Causeway, until you reach the main road.

WHAT TO LOOK OUT FOR

The Town House in the Sandhaven was built in 1626 and used to be the seat for local government. The ground floor used to be a prison for debtors, while the attic was used to imprison 'witches'. On one of the houses near by you will find an elegant wall-mounted sundial. Despite the altitude, sundials were highly fashionable in 17th-century Scotland.

❼ Turn right, walk past the tourist information centre, past the Tron (the old burgh weighing machine), then past the large ochre-coloured building on the right, which is Culross Palace. To reach the starting point, continue walking in the same direction – the car park is on the left-hand side, just past the children's play area.

A Fishy Trail in Fife

A linear coastal walk through the villages of Fife's East Neuk.

DISTANCE 4 miles (6.4km)	**MINIMUM TIME** 1hr 30min
ASCENT/GRADIENT 49ft (15m) ▲▲▲	**LEVEL OF DIFFICULTY** +++

PATHS Well-marked coastal path, 3 stiles

LANDSCAPE Picturesque fishing villages and extensive sea views

SUGGESTED MAP OS Explorer 371 St Andrews & East Fife

START Grid reference: NO 613077 **FINISH** Grid reference: NO 569034

DOG FRIENDLINESS Good, but keep on lead near cattle

PARKING On street in Crail

PUBLIC TOILETS Route passes plenty both in Crail and Anstruther

Scotland's James II described the East Neuk (nook) of Fife as 'a fringe of gold on a beggar's mantle'. This corner of the east coast is dotted with picturesque fishing villages, which nestle close together yet retain their own distinctive character.

Crail is perhaps the prettiest village, with a neat little harbour, which attracts many artists and photographers. It was once the largest fishmarket in Europe and, like all the East Neuk villages, used to trade with the Low Countries and Scandinavia; you can see the Dutch influence in the houses with their crow-stepped gables and pantiled roofs.

Further down the coast is Anstruther (known locally as 'Enster'), the largest and busiest of all the villages and home of the local lifeboat. Fishing has always been the focus of life here. The village was the capital of the Scottish herring trade and the harbour was once so busy that you could cross it by stepping over the boats. Look at the houses as you pass and you'll see that many of them have spacious lofts with a pulley outside – designed to store fishing gear and provide an area for mending the nets.

Fishing dominated the lives of people in the past and each of the East Neuk villages was a closely knit community. It was rare for people to marry outside their own village and women were as heavily involved in the work as the men. They prepared the fish, baited the hooks, mended the nets and took the fish to market for sale, carrying enormous baskets of herrings on their backs. They also used to carry their husbands out to sea on their backs so that they could board their boats without getting wet.

Fishing has always had its dangers and many local superstitions are attached to the industry. Women aren't allowed aboard when a boat is working, and it is considered unlucky to utter the word 'minister' on a boat – he had to be referred to as 'the fellow with the white throat' or 'man in the black coat'. Other words to be avoided are 'pig', 'rat' and 'salmon'. These are known as 'curlytail', 'lang-tail' and 'red fish' (or 'silver beastie') respectively. If these words were spoken on a fishing boat the men would cry 'cauld airn' (cold iron) and grab the nearest piece of iron. It's the equivalent of touching wood and is meant to break the bad luck.

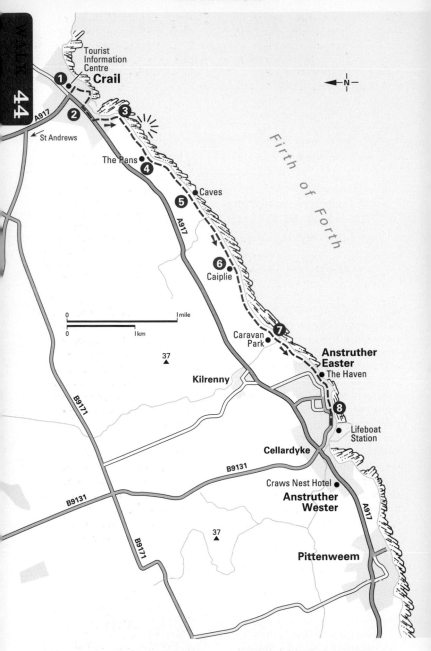

WALK 44 DIRECTIONS

① From the tourist information centre in Crail, walk down Tolbooth Wynd. At the end turn right and, where the road divides, you bear left (a sign says 'no vehicular access to harbour'). You'll now be walking beside the old castle wall to a lookout point, which gives you a grand view of the picturesque harbour. Bear right and then walk on to reach the High Street.

2 Turn left and walk along the road out of the village, passing the two white beacons, which help guide boats into the harbour. Turn left and walk down West Braes, following the signs for the Coastal Path. When you reach Osbourne Terrace turn left down a narrow path, then go down some steps, through a kissing gate and on to a grassy track by the shore.

3 From here you follow the path as it hugs the shoreline. You should soon see cormorants perched on rocks to your left and will also get views of the Isle of May. Go down some steps, over a slightly boggy area, and continue walking until you reach two derelict cottages — an area known as The Pans.

4 Walk past the cottages and continue along the shore, then hop over a stone stile. You'll now pass flat rocks on the left, which are covered with interesting little rock pools. Cross the burn by the footbridge — you'll now be able to see the Bass Rock and Berwick Law on your left and the village of Anstruther ahead, and will soon reach some caves.

5 Pass the caves, then cross a little stone stile on the left-hand side and go over a footbridge. Your track is narrower now and takes you past fields on the right, then some maritime grasses on the left. Stone steps lead to another stile. Climb over it to reach Caiplie.

6 Go through the kissing gate to pass in front of houses, follow the wide grassy track, then go through another kissing gate to walk past a field. The path now runs past a free-range pig farm and up to a caravan park.

WHILE YOU'RE THERE

The Scottish Fisheries Museum opposite the Lifeboat Station is packed full of information on the local fishing industry and tells its story from the earliest times to the present day. There are models of fishing boats and some old vessels in the former boatyard. You can also see a reconstruction of a fisherman's cottage.

7 Continue along the shore, on a tarmac track to reach a play area and war memorial on the right. Maintain direction now as you enter the village of Cellardyke and continue to the harbour. Pass the harbour and The Haven restaurant and continue along John Street, then James Street.

8 At the end of James Street maintain direction, then follow the road as it bends down to the left. You'll walk past a guiding beacon and will come into Anstruther's busy little harbour. You can now either walk back to Crail or take the bus which leaves from the harbour.

WHAT TO LOOK OUT FOR

The Lifeboat Station is often open to visitors. The local lifeboat, manned by RNLI volunteers, is regularly called into service and over 300 lives have been saved since one was first established here.

WHERE TO EAT AND DRINK

There is plenty of choice in Anstruther. Try Anstruther Fish Bar, on Shore Street by the harbour. Brattisanis, also by the harbour, sells great ice creams, while the Ship Inn sells bar meals. In Crail, the Honeypot Tearoom serves tasty snacks.

Academic Traditions at St Andrews

On this easy town trail, discover an ancient university, which observes some very strange traditions.

DISTANCE *4.5 miles (7.2km)* **MINIMUM TIME** *2hrs*

ASCENT/GRADIENT *33ft (10m)* ▲▲▲ **LEVEL OF DIFFICULTY** +++

PATHS *Ancient streets and golden sands*

LANDSCAPE *Historic university town and windy seascapes*

SUGGESTED MAP *OS Explorer 371 St Andrews & East Fife*

START/FINISH *Grid reference: NO 506170*

DOG FRIENDLINESS *Dogs not permitted on beach*

PARKING *Free parking along The Scores, otherwise several car parks*

PUBLIC TOILETS *Several close to beach*

St Andrews is famous for two things – as the home of golf and of an ancient university. A small town on the Fife coast, it has an atmosphere all its own and feels quite unlike any other town in Scotland.

Reasons for Raisins

The university was established in 1410 and is the oldest in Scotland, and third oldest in Britain – after Oxford and Cambridge. The first faculties established here were theology, canon law, civil law, medicine and arts, with theology being of particular importance. In medieval times students could enter the university as young as 13, and a system of seniority soon arose among the student body. New students were known as bejaunus, from the French 'bec-jaune' or fledgling, and were initiated into the fraternity on Raisin Monday, when they were expected to produce a pound of raisins in return for a cheeky receipt. The tradition persists today, with bejants, as they are now known (females are bejantines), being taken under the wings of older students who become their 'academic parents'. On Raisin Sunday, in November, academic 'fathers' take their charges out to get thoroughly drunk. The next day, Raisin Monday, the 'mothers' put them in fancy dress before they and their hangovers congregate in St Salvator's quad for a flour and egg fight.

Elizabeth Garrett, the first woman in Britain to qualify as a doctor, was allowed to matriculate at St Andrews in 1862 but was then rejected after the Senate declared her enrolment illegal. Following this the university made efforts to encourage the education of women, who were finally allowed full membership of the university in 1892. In 1866 Elizabeth Garrett established a dispensary for women in London, which later became the famous Elizabeth Garrett Anderson Hospital.

Treasured Traditions

The university is proud of its traditions and, as you walk around the streets today, you might well spot students wearing their distinctive scarlet gowns. These were introduced after 1640 and some say they were brightly coloured so that students could be spotted when entering the local brothels. They are made of a woolly fabric with a velvet yoke. First-year students wear them over both shoulders, gradually casting them off each year, until in their fourth and final year the gowns hang down, almost dragging behind them.

Other university traditions include a Sunday walk along the pier after church, which continued until the pier was closed for repair, and a mass dawn swim in the sea on May morning (1 May). Given the icy nature of the waters, this is not an activity to be attempted by the faint-hearted.

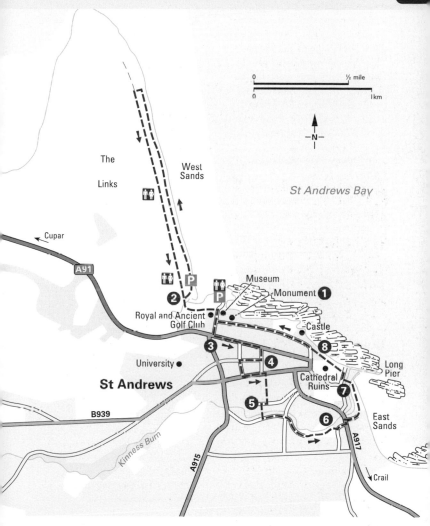

WALK 45 DIRECTIONS

1 With the Martyrs Monument on The Scores in front of you, walk left past the bandstand. At the road turn right, walk to the British Golf Museum, then turn left. Pass the clubhouse of the Royal and Ancient Golf Club on your left, then bear right at the burn to reach the beach.

2 Your route now takes you along the West Sands. Walk as far

WALK 45

as you choose, then either retrace your steps along the beach or take one of the paths through the dunes to join the tarmac road. Walk back to the Golf Museum, then turn right and walk to the main road.

❸ Turn left along the road and walk to St Salvator's College. Take a peek through the archway at the serene quadrangle – and look at the initials PH in the cobbles outside. They commemorate Patrick Hamilton, who was martyred here in 1528 – they say students who tread on the site will fail their exams. Now cross over and walk to the end of College Street.

WHILE YOU'RE THERE

Hill of Tarvit, at nearby Cupar, is an Edwardian mansion house. It has lovely French-style gardens and you can follow a woodland walk through the grounds. The house contains some fine Flemish tapestries, Dutch paintings, porcelain and 2150 elegant items of French and Chippendale furniture.

❹ Turn right and walk along Market Street. At the corner turn left along Bell Street, then left again on South Street. Opposite Holy Trinity Church, turn right down Queens Gardens to reach Queens Terrace.

❺ Turn right then immediately left down steeply sloping Dempster Terrace. At the end cross the burn, turn left and walk

to the main road. Cross over and walk along Glebe Road. At the park, take the path that bears left, walk past the play area and up to Woodburn Terrace.

❻ Turn left to join St Mary Street and cross over the main road to follow Woodburn Place down towards the beach. Just before the slipway, turn left along a tarmac path. Cross over the footbridge and join the road.

❼ Bear right for a few paces, then ascend the steps on the left. These bring you up to the remains of a church and on to the famous ruined cathedral. A gate in the wall on the left gives access to the site.

❽ Your route then follows the beachfront past the ancient castle on the right. A former palace / fortress, it was at the forefront of the Reformation – John Knox preached here. Pass the Castle Visitor Centre, then continue along The Scores to return to the car park at the start.

WHERE TO EAT AND DRINK

There are loads of pubs in St Andrews catering for all those eternally thirsty students, as well as plenty of cafés. Hovies Restaurant in north St Andrews offers a variety of sandwiches and salads. Fisher and Donaldson on Church Street is a bakery famous for its fudge doughnuts (they're very sweet, so hang on to your fillings).

WHAT TO LOOK OUT FOR

The Royal and Ancient Golf Club is the governing body for the rules of golf and overlooks the world-famous Old Course. It's a bastion of conservatism and the clubhouse isn't open to visitors; women guests are permitted to enter on St Andrew's Day. The modern game developed on the east coast of Scotland. It was banned by James II who feared that it distracted men from their archery practice, leaving them unable to defend the country.

Right: The cathedral ruins, St Andrews (Walk 45)

Reinventing the Wheel at Falkirk

*A stroll along Scotland's old canal system to see
a strikingly modern 21st-century wheel.*

DISTANCE	2 miles (3.2km); 4 miles (6.4km) with monument
MINIMUM TIME	1hr
ASCENT/GRADIENT	197ft (60m) ▲▲▲ **LEVEL OF DIFFICULTY** +++
PATHS	Canal tow paths and town streets
LANDSCAPE	Roman wall, 19th-century waterways, 21st-century wheel
SUGGESTED MAP	OS Explorer 349 Falkirk, Cumbernauld & Livingston
START/FINISH	Grid reference: NS 868800
DOG FRIENDLINESS	Good along canals
PARKING	Car park at Lock 16, by Union Inn
PUBLIC TOILETS	At Falkirk Wheel Visitor Centre

The words 'new' and 'unique' are rather overused these days. They seem to be applied to everything from shades of lipstick to formulations of engine oil. But this walk gives you the chance to see something that fully deserves the epithet. The Falkirk Wheel, which opened in the spring of 2002, is the world's first rotating boat lift. It was designed in order to reconnect the Forth and Clyde and Union canals, which stretch across the central belt of Scotland, and so restore a centuries-old link between Glasgow and Edinburgh.

Cruising the Canals

The Forth and Clyde Canal, which ran from Grangemouth to Glasgow, was completed in 1790 and made a great difference to the Scottish economy. It opened up a lucrative trading route to America – raw materials could now easily be transported east, while finished products could be shipped west. It also meant that coal extracted from the mines in Lanarkshire could be sent into the newly industrialised areas of Glasgow. The canal was so successful that merchants in Edinburgh soon felt that they were missing out on trade. A plan was devised for another waterway, running from Edinburgh to Falkirk. Work on the Union Canal began in 1818 and a flight of locks was constructed to link it to the Forth and Clyde Canal.

Rise and Fall

The canals were used to transport not only goods but also people. Many preferred to travel by barge than by stage coach, as they were far less bumpy and decidedly warmer. Night boats even had dining rooms and gaming tables. By 1835 over 127,000 people were travelling on the canal each year. However, shortly afterwards the canal craze began to give way to yet another new innovation – the railways. Train travel, which gained in popularity from the middle of the 19th century, offered cheaper and faster transport, leading to the decline of the canal network. They clung to life until the 1960s, when they were broken up by the expanding network of

WALK 46

roads. However, the canals have now been recognised as an important part of Scotland's industrial heritage and are being restored. The Falkirk Wheel was built to replace the original flight of locks, which had been removed in the 1930s, and it's as much a work of art as a feat of engineering. The Wheel lifts boats from one canal to another and is the only rotating boat lift in the world. Made of sharply glinting steel, it's 115ft (35m) high and looks rather like a set of spanners that have fallen from a giant's tool kit. It can carry eight boats at a time and lift loads of 600 tonnes.

An incongruous sight against the gentle tangle of vegetation beside the canal, the Wheel seems to have re-energised the waterways, drawing people to it like a monumental magnet.

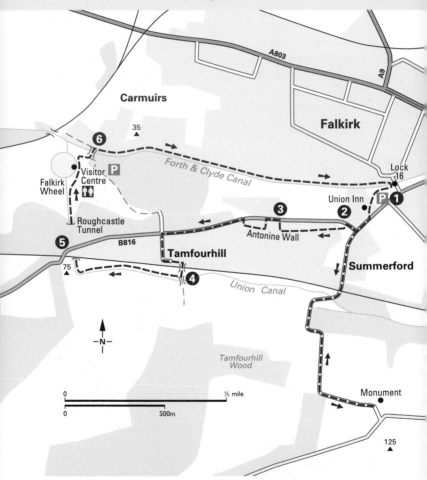

WALK 46 DIRECTIONS

1 Start at the Union Inn by Lock 16. This was once one of the best-known pubs in Scotland and catered for passengers on the canal. Turn right now, away from the canal, then go right along the road. Turn right along Tamfourhill Road and go through the kissing gate on the left-hand side of the road. Alternatively, don't turn up Tamfourhill Road yet, but continue walking uphill to go under the viaduct. Keep walking all the way up until you come to a monument on the left. This commemorates the Battle of Falkirk (1298) in which William Wallace was beaten by Edward I's troops. Retrace your steps, under the viaduct, turn left into Tamfourhill Road, and left through the kissing gate on the left-hand side of the road.

❷ This takes you to a section of the Roman Antonine Wall – there's a deep ditch and a rampart behind it. Walk along here, going parallel with Tamfourhill Road. When you reach the point where you can go no further, climb up the bank on the right-hand side and go down the steps to join the road by a kissing gate.

❸ Go left to continue along the road – you'll soon see another kissing gate on the left leading you

WALK 46

to another, much shorter, section of the wall. Leave the wall, rejoin the road and maintain direction to reach a mini-roundabout. Turn left here, along Maryfield Place. When you reach the end, join the public footpath signed to the canal tow path and woodland walks. Follow this track as it winds up and over the railway bridge, then on to reach the Union Canal.

❹ Don't cross the canal but turn right and walk along the tow path. This is a long straight stretch now, popular with local joggers. Eventually you'll reach Roughcastle tunnel – but remember that it currently closes at 6pm to protect the Wheel from the risk of vandalism.

❺ Walk through the tunnel – it's bright and clean and dry. This will bring you out to the new Falkirk Wheel (and yet another section of the Antonine Wall). You can walk on as far as the Wheel, then walk down to the visitor centre at the bottom. Bear right from here to cross the little bridge over the Forth and Clyde Canal.

❻ Turn right now and walk along the tow path. Lots of dog walkers and cyclists come along here (so take care if you are walking with a dog), while people frequently go canoeing along the canal. Keep walking until you come back to Lock 16, then turn right and cross the canal again to return to the start of the walk at the Union Inn.

Kilsyth and the Forth and Clyde Canal

Travel back in time following along the line of an old Roman wall and an 18th-century canal.

DISTANCE 3.5 miles (5.7km)	**MINIMUM TIME** 3hrs
ASCENT/GRADIENT 344ft (105m) ▲▲▲	**LEVEL OF DIFFICULTY** ✦✦✦

PATHS Tow path, farm road, footpath and road

LANDSCAPE Canal, pastures, hillside and woodland

SUGGESTED MAP OS Explorer 348 Campsie Fells

START/FINISH Grid reference: NS 719770

DOG FRIENDLINESS Take care near livestock

PARKING Car park near old quarry at Kilsyth

PUBLIC TOILETS None on route

Running almost parallel across the central belt of Scotland are two old lines of communication separated in time by some 1,600 years. Despite their antiquity, both have experienced something of a renaissance of interest in recent years.

Water Works

The Forth and Clyde Canal was the first canal built in Scotland and was created for sea-going vessels. Before it was built, ships had nearly 310 miles (498km) to sail, all the way round the coast of Scotland to get from the west to the east coast. When the canal was completed the journey was reduced to 35 miles (56km). Construction began in 1768 with a team of navvies digging at Grangemouth on the Forth, and 22 years later they finally reached Bowling on the Clyde.

To the Heart of Glasgow

This revolutionary engineering achievement linked Scotland's two great waterways – the Clyde and the Forth. It also substantially reduced the cost of, and therefore considerably increased, trade between the country's two most important cities, Glasgow and Edinburgh. Because it was built for shipping it had very large locks, 39 of them in total, each 60ft (18m) long and 20ft (6m) wide. A further 3-mile (4.8km) branch section was constructed from Maryhill to Port Dundas, in order to take trade right into the heart of Glasgow.

New Lease of Life

When it was new the Forth and Clyde Canal boasted the Kelvin Aqueduct, which at 400ft (122m), was the largest structure of its kind then in existence. In 1802 the trials of the *Charlotte Dundas*, the world's first practical steamboat, were conducted along the canal and Scotland's first iron boat, *The Vulcan*, was built for a passenger service on this waterway. It was also the first canal to carry loaded railway wagons and was eventually purchased by the Caledonian Railway in 1868. It continued to operate well into the 20th century and finally closed to navigation on 1 January, 1963. However, a growing interest in the leisure potential of canals has led to a revival of its fortunes and after extensive restoration and the creation of the revolutionary Falkirk Wheel (see While You're There and Walk 46) it is once more open along its entire length.

Roman Barrier

The canal followed the line of the much older Antonine Wall (see While You're There, Walk 46), built in AD 142. Like Hadrian's Wall further south, it was intended as a barrier to keep the warlike Pictish tribes of the north out of Roman-occupied Britain. But what we now call lowland Scotland had not been completely subdued by the imperial occupiers and, on more than one occasion, hostile tribes forced the Romans back behind their more southerly frontier line at Hadrian's Wall. They finally abandoned the land of Scotland in about AD 180. Built from a stone foundation with a turf rampart behind a ditch and with a series of forts and beacon platforms incorporated along its 37-mile (60km) length, the wall lies just north of the Military Way, a Roman road built to allow troop movements between the Clyde and the Forth.

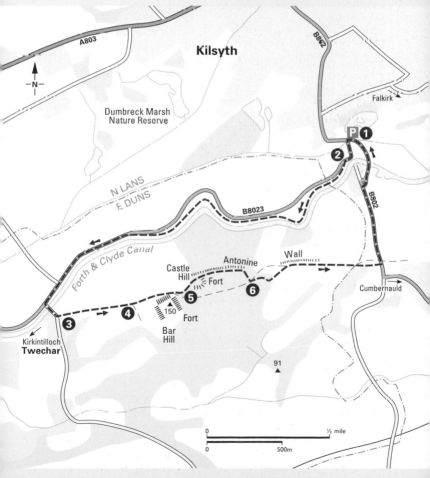

WALK 47 DIRECTIONS

❶ Leave the car park on to the main road and turn right. Cross the road and turn immediately left on to a road signposted for Twechar and Kirkintilloch. Continue along this road for a short while and, when it turns sharply right, veer off the footpath to the left and on to the tow path of the Forth and Clyde Canal.

WHAT TO LOOK OUT FOR

On the summit of Castle Hill are the traces of an Iron Age fort which stood here long before the Romans came to Scotland. All that remain are two low terraces on the north and west slopes. Sometime during the last couple of centuries BC these and other earthen ramparts would have been surrounded by a wooden palisade and a small group would have occupied some wooden huts safe within.

❷ Go round a barrier and keep on along the tow path until it rejoins the pavement beside the main road. Take the next turning on the left, cross the canal via a bridge and enter Twechar. Continue on this road, heading uphill; near the top keep a look out for a sign on the left pointing to the Antonine Wall and Bar Hill.

❸ Take the next turning on the left on to an access road. Continue along here past some houses and continue on a farm track. Go through a gate and uphill. Look back the way you have come for a grand view of the canal as it winds its way towards Glasgow.

❹ When you reach the entrance to the Antonine Wall go left through a kissing gate and along a grassy lane, then go through another kissing gate to access the

WHILE YOU'RE THERE

The Falkirk Wheel is a miracle of modern engineering and the only rotating boat lift in the world. It can carry eight or more boats at a time on a trip taking a mere 15 minutes (see Walk 46). When it opened it reconnected the Forth and Clyde and Union canals making it once more possible to travel from the west to the east coast, overland, by boat.

site. Veer left and uphill to Bar Hill Fort. From the top of the fort you will see some woodland in front of you. Head for an opening in the trees and then on to a well-defined trail.

❺ Follow this trail through the trees, then up on to the summit of Castle Hill. From here head downhill with the remains of the Romans' Antonine Wall on your left-hand side. Turn right when your path is blocked by a dry-stone wall and follow it until you intersect a farm track.

WHERE TO EAT AND DRINK

Buy some sandwiches and a tea or coffee from one of several small baker's shops in Kilsyth town centre and take them with you for a picnic by the canalside.

❻ Turn left and follow this through two kissing gates to reach a T-junction with the main road. Turn left and head down the hill. Keep to the right at the roundabout, still heading downhill to reach another T-junction. From here cross over the road and re-enter the car park.

Exploring The Whangie

Through the hidden opening to the training ground of generations of rock climbers.

DISTANCE 2.5 miles (4km)	**MINIMUM TIME** 3hrs
ASCENT/GRADIENT 515ft (157m) ▲▲▲	**LEVEL OF DIFFICULTY** ✦✦✦

PATHS Hill tracks and well-trodden footpaths, 2 stiles
LANDSCAPE Hill, woodland and lochs
SUGGESTED MAP OS Explorer 347 Loch Lomond South
START/FINISH Grid reference: NS 511808
DOG FRIENDLINESS Suitable for dogs, but keep on lead near livestock
PARKING Queen's View car park
PUBLIC TOILETS None on route

Queen Victoria stood near the start of this walk for her first view of Loch Lomond. She never ventured further up the hill and so missed the opportunity to explore the Whangie, a strange cleft in the rock that has fascinated generations of rock climbers.

A Gash in the Rock

Geologists would have us believe that this gash in the rocks, 50ft (15m) deep and 300ft (91m) long, was caused by a landslide, when the surface layer of black basalt moved slowly over the underlying sandstone. This created stresses within the basalt, which eventually fractured, producing thin slices of slab. However, ask any local about the Whangie and you will be told the truth. It was created by the Devil himself on his way to a witches' coven near Stockie Muir. He got so excited that he gave one flick of his mighty tail and carved a slice out of the hillside creating the Whangie. 'Whang' is a common Lowland Scots dialect word meaning 'a slice'.

Early Pioneers

Whatever its origin, the Whangie is still a valued training ground for Glasgow rock climbers, successors to the mountaineering pioneers of the 1920s and '30s. These working-class men from Glasgow started walking out of the city to explore the surrounding countryside. Clad only in their ordinary clothes and with little in the way of equipment, save perhaps some army surplus kit or an old clothes line, they went looking for adventure.

After a hard week of work they would leave Glasgow late at night, take the last bus to the outskirts and walk into the countryside. They had no tents and found shelter where they could, under a hedge, behind a dry-stone wall or in a cave. Some of the great names in Scottish climbing were among these early pioneers, including W H Murray, the celebrated Himalayan climber and environmentalist, and Tom Weir, who climbed with Murray and went on to make a series of television programmes called *Weir's Way*. Weir continued to write a monthly column of his outdoor adventures in *The Scots Magazine* until his late 80s.

WALK 48

Escaping the Slums

From Glasgow they would head to Milngavie and a campfire near Craigallion Loch. Some, like the legendary Jock Nimlin, were fortunate to have friends who possessed huts at Carbeth (see Walk 49), not far from Craigallion and from there they would walk out, 'up the pipe', to Loch Katrine in the Trossachs. They explored all the glorious countryside they could see from the hills around the Whangie – Ben Lomond, the Kilpatrick Hills and the Arrochar Alps. During prolonged periods of unemployment in the depression years these hardy climbers and others like them took to the hills every week to escape the slums of Glasgow. Some even walked all the way to the Highlands.

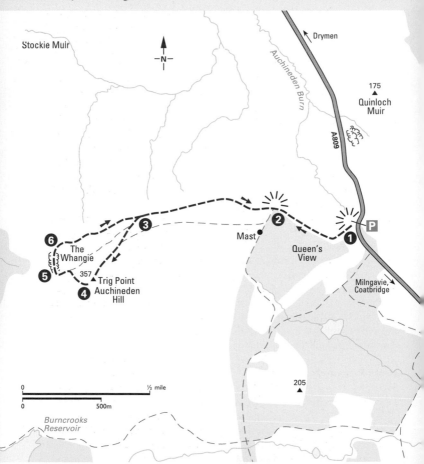

WALK 48 DIRECTIONS

❶ Head toward the left of the car park on to the small hillock where Queen Victoria stood for her first breathtaking view of Loch Lomond. Descend and cross a stile over the wall where a well-

defined path crosses duckboards and meanders uphill. Turn right to follow the edge of a wood. After the duckboards this is a pleasant grassy walk.

❷ As you get to the top, near a fence, stop for a while to admire

THE WHANGIE

the view. Look away to your right for the expanse of Loch Lomond, Ben Lomond towering over it to the right and the Arrochar Hills away to the left. Cross a ladder stile by a tumbledown fence and turn right on to a narrow but well-trodden path. Follow this along the side of the hill.

3 When the path forks go left and head uphill. As you near the top you will see the Ordnance Survey pillar on the summit of Auchineden Hill. Head towards this on a clear path. The ground round here is often boggy and you may have to leave the path to bypass the worst bits. To the south from here are the Kilpatrick Hills and, beyond them, the River Clyde. Look for Burncrooks Reservoir to your right and Kilmannan Reservoir to your left. Beyond that is Cochno Loch, another reservoir and a favourite excursion for the residents of nearby Clydebank.

4 Looking towards Ben Lomond, the area in front of you is the Stockie Muir, where the Devil was

heading for the tryst that created the Whangie. Walk towards the Ben on a path leading away from the Ordnance Survey pillar and go downhill into a dip. Another path runs across this. Turn left on to it and follow it round the side of a small hill. Where the path curves right, look for crags on the right.

5 This is where you'll find the hidden opening to the Whangie. It's easy to miss so look out for a spot on the right where it is simple to climb a few steps up to the crags. It's as if the wall opens up in front of you. Climb into the Whangie and walk to the other end on a path.

6 Exit the Whangie and head to the right on another footpath. Continue on this until it rejoins the path you took on the uphill journey. Go back to the stile then retrace your steps downhill and back to the car park.

The Carbeth Hut Community

*Discover a working-class Utopian dream
near the West Highland Way.*

DISTANCE 3 miles (4.8km)	**MINIMUM TIME** 2hrs 30min
ASCENT/GRADIENT 98ft (30m) ▲▲▲	**LEVEL OF DIFFICULTY** ✦✦✦
PATHS Roads, access tracks and footpaths, 1 stile	
LANDSCAPE Hills, woodland and lochs	
SUGGESTED MAP OS Explorer 348 Campsie Fells	
START/FINISH Grid reference: NX 524791	
DOG FRIENDLINESS Suitable for dogs	
PARKING Carbeth Inn, check beforehand with landlord	
PUBLIC TOILETS None on route	

Situated approximately half-way between Glasgow and Drymen on the A809, an old turnpike road, you'll find an ancient inn. Once called the Halfway House and now the Carbeth Inn, it has served the needs of travellers for over 200 years.

Sir Walter Scott had the character of Baillie Nicol Jarvie in his 1817 novel *Rob Roy* describe the inn as a 'most miserable alehouse'. Things have obviously improved since then and for years it has provided a warm welcome to climbers, bikers, walkers and the nearby community of Carbeth hutters.

Holidays in the Country

The Carbeth hut community started after the First World War, when the owner of the Carbeth Estate let three ex-servicemen found a holiday fellowship camp on his land. At first the visitors lived under canvas but during the depression years unemployed Glaswegians, seeking an escape into the countryside, started to erect more permanent dwellings.

These ingenious and often ramshackle affairs were constructed from any materials that were available free of charge or could be obtained cheaply. Conditions were a bit spartan but met the needs of the people and were probably as good as they had at home. During the summers the area round the Carbeth Inn was alive with activity as whole families decamped to the countryside for their holidays.

Peppercorn Rent

The land was leased from estate owner Barnes-Graham at a peppercorn rent, because of his desire to help people escape from what he saw as a squalid and depressing life in the overcrowded city. They became a tight-knit community with organised games and activities; they even built their own open-air swimming pool, complete with lifebelts and diving boards.

To get to Carbeth the hutters caught the train to Milngavie and then took a path which became known as the Khyber Pass. Coming from the Clydebank area the hutters just hoofed it over the Kilpatrick Hills.

CARBETH

Scottish Social History

Today the swimming pool, simply a dammed stream, is silted up. Fashions and lifestyles have changed but Carbeth still has around 200 huts and an active community. A massive increase in the rents led to a rent strike by many of the hutters and court action was initiated to evict them. Against a background of recriminations and accusations, not to mention unsolved arson attacks on huts, the Carbeth community fought to preserve their foothold in the countryside, campaigning for public support and petitioning the Scottish Parliament to preserve this unique piece of Scottish social history and heritage. At the time of writing, 2007, the situation seems to have stabilised and the community continues to thrive.

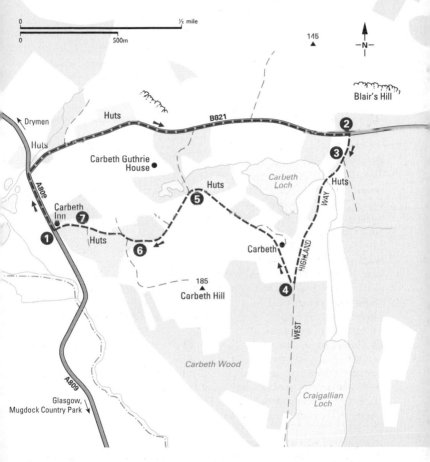

WALK 49 DIRECTIONS

❶ From the car park at the Carbeth Inn turn right on to the A809. After 0.25 mile (400m) take the first turning right on to the B821. Continue on this road for a mile (1.6km), passing a collection of huts on the left and ignoring a public footpath sign to the right.

❷ Turn right at the signpost for the West Highland Way.

There's also a Scottish Rights of Way Society signpost beside this pointing to the Khyber Pass Road to Mugdock Country Park. This was the favoured route of the early walkers heading out of Glasgow to the Campsie Fells and beyond.

3 Go through a gate and continue along a well-surfaced access road. Ignoring the Khyber Pass turn-off, keep right to follow the West Highland Way along the access road to more huts. After passing the first of the huts and reaching a left bend in the path, look out for a partially concealed public path signpost on the right beside a West Highland Way marker post.

4 Turn right here on to a narrow but well-surfaced footpath and continue along it, passing Carbeth Loch on the right-hand side, to reach the junction with the drive leading to Carbeth House. This is a private house and is not open to the public. Turn left, pass a house and some huts on the right then take the next turning on the left.

5 Continue along this lane, then head uphill to reach another grouping of the Carbeth huts. Follow the main route through the huts and when it forks, keep left.

6 Keep on this road as it passes through the main part of the Carbeth huts, an extraordinary assortment of small dwellings, shanties and shacks. Ignore all of the smaller tracks branching off this road. They allow access to individual huts or other parts of the settlement.

7 Eventually reach a T-junction. Turn right and follow the lane as it winds downhill to reach the -junction with the A809 beside the Carbeth Inn. Turn left and return to the car park.

From Puck's Glen to the Benmore Botanic Garden

The story of James Duncan, the man who altered the Cowal landscape.

> **DISTANCE** 4 miles (6.4km)   **MINIMUM TIME** 2hrs 30min
>
> **ASCENT/GRADIENT** 459ft (140m) ▲▲▲   **LEVEL OF DIFFICULTY** ✦✦✦
>
> **PATHS** Mainly forest roads and well-made footpaths, 1 stile
>
> **LANDSCAPE** Woodland
>
> **SUGGESTED MAP** OS Explorer 363 Cowal East
>
> **START/FINISH** Grid reference: NS 142855
>
> **DOG FRIENDLINESS** Keep dogs on lead
>
> **PARKING** Car park at Benmore Botanic Garden
>
> **PUBLIC TOILETS** At Benmore Botanic Garden

Better-known as the Younger Botanic Garden, after Harry George Younger who gifted his estate to the nation in 1925, the Benmore Botanic Garden is 120 acres (48.5ha) of the former estate. Extensive development, since it became part of the Royal Botanic Garden, Edinburgh, has made it world famous for its plant collections. The remainder of the estate, including Puck's Glen, belongs to the Forestry Commission and their afforested hillsides provide a splendid backdrop to the garden's formal collections. Yet none of this would exist without the passionate commitment of a self-made Victorian merchant, James Duncan.

Transforming the Landscape

Duncan, who made his fortune from sugar refining at Greenock, purchased the Benmore Estate in 1870 and laid the foundations of the gardens. When Duncan came to Benmore the landscape was bare and uninteresting. He immediately extended the former Tower House to create the main part of Benmore House. Around the formal gardens he constructed countless ranges of heated glasshouses and, overhanging a ravine in Glen Massan, he established a fernery, the remains of which are still visible today. Acting on the advice of Sir Joseph Hooker, Director of the Royal Botanic Gardens at Kew, Duncan began to plant the collections of shrubs and trees which would provide the basis of the gardens.

Cowal's Golden Gates

Extensive drainage systems were developed throughout the estate and trees were planted on the bare hillsides. Between 1871 and 1883 Duncan planted some 1,600 acres (648ha). The total area stretched from the Strone of Clyde to the head of Loch Eck. When he had done there were a total of 6,480,000 trees, which remain a major feature of the present landscape of this part of the Cowal peninsula. Duncan also commissioned the Golden Gates for the Paris Exhibition of 1865. Made from wrought iron and painted gold with his initials worked into them, they were eventually erected near Glen Massan in 1873. A sociable man, Duncan entertained frequently and welcomed many visitors to Benmore, including Sir Henry Morton Stanley, the explorer, and Charles Haddon Spurgeon, the Billy Graham of his day, who preached to a crowd of 7,000 in the grounds of Benmore in 1877.

Lasting Memorial

Duncan died at Spean Bridge, near Fort William on 12 August, 1905, aged 81. His body was brought back to Cowal and is buried in the historic churchyard at Kilmun. It lies under a pink granite slab on a high part of the steep graveyard with a view looking across the Holy Loch. At the southern limit of his Kilmun estate, on the Strone peninsula at Graham's Point, an obelisk was erected to Duncan's memory and on it can be found the only known likeness of the man, carved in stone. But his real memorial is the garden at Benmore and the surrounding landscape.

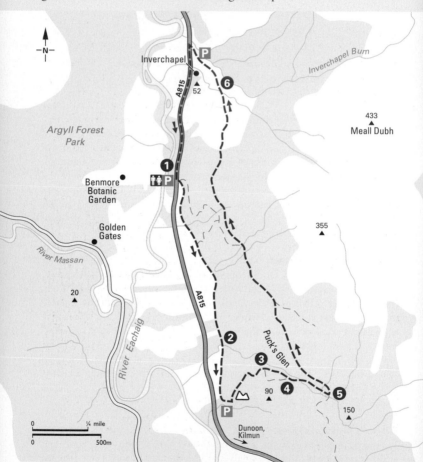

WALK 50 DIRECTIONS

❶ From the car park cross the A815 and follow the footpath past a waymarker for Black Gates. Pass a sign for the Big Tree Walk and

turn right on to a surfaced lane. Continue along this lane for about 1 mile (1.6km) and just after the parapet of a bridge is the first footpath, which leads to Puck's Glen on the left.

BENMORE

WHAT TO LOOK OUT FOR

With care and if you are quiet, you may spot a red squirrel scurrying about in the trees. It's the only species of squirrel native to Britain and is gradually being forced out by the larger American grey squirrel. Red squirrel populations have been in decline since the 1940s owing to competition from the grey for food. Now they are found mainly in Scotland, northern England and parts of Wales.

2 There's a milestone here pointing to 'Dunoon Pier 6 miles'. Ignore this entrance and continue along the lane until you reach the car park. Turn left and along a footpath past the waymarker pole for Puck's Glen. Climb uphill on a steep path.

3 At the top of the hill the path levels out then starts to head back downhill, rather steeply on a series of steps with handrails to the bottom of the gorge. A signpost found at a junction at the bottom of the steps points left for the lower gorge and right for the upper.

4 Turn right, head downhill on another set of steps, then cross a bridge on the left and turn right

WHERE TO EAT AND DRINK

The excellent tea room at the Benmore Botanic Garden can be accessed from the car park without having to pay for admission to the grounds. It's a spacious and delightful area with large glass windows on all sides giving grand views of the fabulous array of trees and shrubs outside and the variety of birds that feed at strategically sited bird tables. The tea room staff are very friendly and the food is of a high quality.

to head along a footpath on the opposite side of the stream. Head uphill, cross another bridge, then go past a series of small waterfalls. Eventually reach yet another bridge to cross before coming to a set of steps that takes you up a steep part of the hillside to another bridge at the top. After crossing it the path levels out a bit and continues through the trees to then reach a T-junction with a forestry road.

5 At the junction is a waymarker post. Turning right will lead you along a forest road to Kilmun Arboretum. However, for this walk you must turn left, following the signs for Black Gates. The Forestry Commission has installed a series of new footpaths and this route can be shortened by taking any of the downhill paths that you'll find to the left.

WHILE YOU'RE THERE

Head out of Dunoon on the Sandbank road for a visit to the Cowal Bird Garden. Not only do they have a large number of exotic birds on display but also some friendly pets to entertain the children. Geese, ducks, parrots and macaws can be seen along with ornamental pheasants and rheas. Goats, pot-bellied pigs, donkeys and a wonderful wee Shetland pony are the animal representatives.

6 Follow the signs to the left and go on to the path for Black Gates car park and, from there, return to the botanic gardens. Otherwise continue on the forest road until you reach a gate located near its end. Continue to reach a T-junction and then turn left on to the A815. Walk along here for 0.5 mile (800m) to return to the start and the car park at Bemore Botanic Garden.

Along the Crinan Canal and Around Mhoine Mhor

A lengthy but easy stroll along a 19th-century canal and around Scotland's last wild peat bog.

DISTANCE 8.25 miles (13.3km)   MINIMUM TIME 5hrs

ASCENT/GRADIENT 176ft (55m) ▲▲▲   LEVEL OF DIFFICULTY ✦✦✦

PATHS Canal tow path, country roads and farm tracks

LANDSCAPE Bog, hillside and pasture

SUGGESTED MAP OS Explorer 358 Lochgilphead & Knapdale North

START/FINISH Grid reference: NR 824908

DOG FRIENDLINESS Keep on lead near livestock

PARKING Dunardry Forest car park

PUBLIC TOILETS None on route

Built just over 200 years ago, the Crinan Canal, just 9 miles (14.5km) in length, with 15 locks, allows easy passage from Loch Fyne to the Sound of Jura, avoiding the lengthy voyage around the Mull of Kintyre. It was designed by John Rennie but later improved by Thomas Telford in 1817. Because it is 69ft (21m) above sea level it needs a constant supply of water to replenish it and its main channels are fed from seven reservoirs in the hills above. But as every single locking operation uses 66,000 gallons (300,000 litres) of water, there have been periods, particularly during long dry summers, when it has run out of water and been forced to close.

The Great Moss

Crinan Canal runs along the southern fringe of Moine Mhor, the Great Moss, one of the last wild, raised bogs in Britain and one of the oldest living sphagnum bogs in Europe. As plants die, their remains become peat. Older than Stonehenge but growing at a rate of only 1mm each year, Moine Mhor is 13ft (4m) in depth and is a protected part of a National Nature Reserve.

Abundant Birdlife

The moss can be visited at any time. A wooden walkway leads from the North Moss car park area and this is the best way to view it. It's a birders' paradise echoing with the distinctive cry of the curlew as it returns to breed each spring. Stonechats, resident year round, are joined by whinchats in summer and you may spot the odd osprey hunting fish in the River Add. Watch too for the hen harrier quartering the moss in search of a quick meal. During the seasons the bog changes colour as heathers and grasses bloom then fade away. Cranberries bear purple flowers in the spring and deep red berries in autumn. Carnivorous plants like the sundew lie in wait to catch unsuspecting insects in their sticky hairs.

Invaders from Ireland

In AD 500 the Scotti tribe from Antrim landed here. To the Scotti, the vast rock of Dunadd in the middle of this great bog would have been the obvious

DUNARDRY FOREST

place on which to build their first fortress and settlement. So the rock became the early capital of Dalriada. Near the summit are rock carvings including the figure of a boar, which may have been the tribe's emblem and some faint lines of ogam (alphabet of straight lines) inscription. A basin and footprint carved from the rock were probably part of early coronation ceremonies. The first recorded coronation here was of Aedann mac Gabhran by St Columba in AD 574. Dunadd, capital of Dalriada until 900, is still regarded as one of the most important historic sites in Scotland.

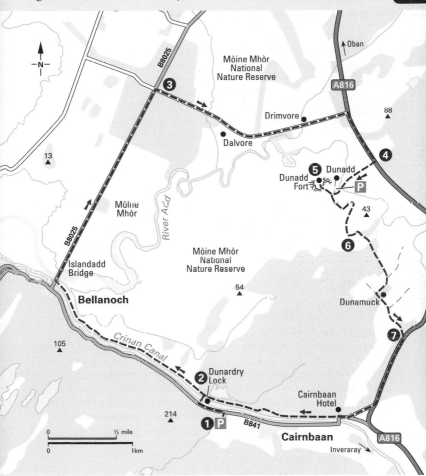

WALK 51 DIRECTIONS

❶ From the car park go down some steps, cross the road and turn left. Keep going until you reach a white cottage on your right. Turn right and on to a dirt track that runs behind the cottage then go through a gap between the fence and a wall. Cross the canal over Dunardry Lock and turn left on to the tow path.

❷ Head along the tow path as far as Bellanoch Bridge and then turn right on to the road, cross over Islandadd Bridge and on to the B8025. This narrow, but not busy, road is long and straight and runs right through the Moine Mhor.

Keep going ahead for nearly 2 miles (3.2km) then turn right on to an unclassified road signposted for Drimvore.

3 Follow this for about 1.75 miles (2.8km) as it runs through the National Nature Reserve and passes the farms of Dalvore and Drimvore. Finally reach a T-junction with the A816 and turn right. After 0.5 mile (800m) an Historic Scotland fingerpost will point you in the direction of Dunadd Fort.

4 Turn right here on to a long straight farm road and keep on it, passing the farm of Dunadd, until your reach the Historic Scotland car park. Make your way towards the hill on a well-trodden path, go past the house on the left and through a kissing gate. Continue on the path, following

the direction arrows, to emerge through a gap in some rocks within the outer ramparts.

5 Continue from here to the summit and after you have admired the views, seen the carvings and tried your own foot in the carved footprint, return by the same route to the car park. Leave it and turn right on to a farm track. Go through a gate then, almost immediately, go left through another gate and follow it as it curves left.

6 Another gate is encountered just before the road turns right and heads uphill. Continue following the road going through another gate until you reach the steading of Dunamuck farm. Turn left through the steading, go through a gate and head downhill on a farm road, continuing along it until you reach a T-junction with the A816.

7 Turn right on to the road and follow it for about 0.5 mile (800m), then turn right on to the road signposted for Cairnbaan and Crinan. After 0.25 mile (400m) turn right towards Crinan. As the road turns left across the swing bridge keep straight ahead and on to the canal tow path. Follow this back to Dunardry Lock and retrace your steps to the car park.

Right: Sailing craft moored at Crinan Canal basin (Walk 51)

The Neolithic Monuments of Kilmartin Glen

A short walk back in time to the stone shrines and monuments in the valley of the ghosts.

DISTANCE 3.5 miles (5.7km)	**MINIMUM TIME** 3hrs
ASCENT/GRADIENT Negligible ▲▲▲	**LEVEL OF DIFFICULTY** ✦✦✦

PATHS Boggy fields, old coach road and country lanes, 3 stiles

LANDSCAPE Pasture, hills, woodland

SUGGESTED MAP OS Explorer 358 Lochgilphead & Knapdale North

START/FINISH Grid reference: NR 835988

DOG FRIENDLINESS Dogs fine on route

PARKING Car park outside Kilmartin church

PUBLIC TOILETS Kilmartin House

Kilmartin Glen with its lush alluvial plains, easy landfalls on the coast near Crinan and an abundant supply of water has attracted human settlers since the earliest times. In around 5000 BC, nomadic hunter gatherers frequented this area but left little evidence of their presence other than piles of bones and shells in caves.

Early Settlers

The arrival of small groups of neolithic people from around 3000 BC provided the first lasting signs of habitation. These early settlers, farmers and skilled weavers and potters, cleared the ground for grazing and erected the first stone shrines and circles. What they were for is not certain, but they were probably an early form of astronomical calendar for determining when to plant and harvest crops or to move cattle. They were probably also part of religious rituals closely related to the seasons and survival. Around Kilmartin Glen 25 different sites of standing stones have been found. Some are simple arrangements, others single stones, while in Temple Wood the monument consists of two stone circles.

Great Monuments

Later, Bronze Age people were responsible for the monuments that can still be seen in the prehistoric linear cemetery, built over the course of 1,000 years, that runs for a mile (1.6km) down the glen. Each of the huge stone-lined burial chambers is slightly different in design and construction.

The Glebe Cairn, which looks like a pile of boulders with a cap stone, is situated near the church and is typical of the burial cairns of the period 1700–1500 BC. At the centre of this cairn were two stone cists for the burials and these contained pottery and a necklace of jet beads. The next tomb south from here, known as the North Tomb, has been rebuilt over a modern shelter that allows access through a hatch and contains a large slab carved with pictures of axe heads and cupmarks. The last cairn in this direction, the South Cairn is the earliest and was originally a chambered tomb dating from 4000 BC.

Left: The Mysterious Standing Stones of Kilmartin Glen (Walk 52)

KILMARTIN GLEN

In the Iron Age, warring tribes ringed the glen with hill-forts and it was on one of these, at Dunadd, that the Scotti tribe from Ireland founded their capital in the 6th century AD (see Walk 51). St Columba came to Kilmartin in the 6th century AD and established the first Christian church here.

Within Kilmartin parish church can be found relics from a later age. The ornately carved Kilmartin Cross depicts one of the most moving images of Christ to have survived from the early Scottish Christian Church and the churchyard has one of the finest collections of ornately carved medieval gravestones in Scotland.

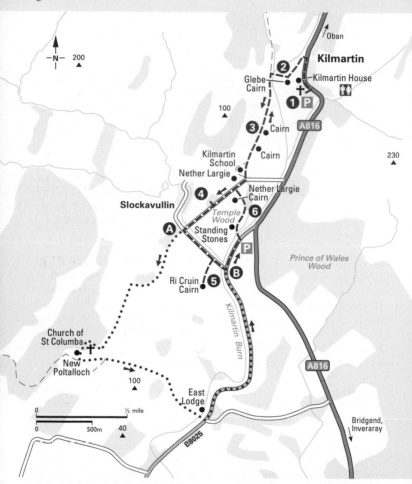

WALK 52 DIRECTIONS

❶ From the car park visit Kilmartin church to marvel at the stones and see the Kilmartin Cross. Leave the church, turn left and walk along the road past Kilmartin House, exit the village and head downhill towards a

garage on the left. Just before the garage turn left, go through a kissing gate and head across the field to the Glebe Cairn.

❷ From the cairn head half right, across the field to cross a stile. In wet weather this can be very boggy so stout footwear is advisable. Cross the stream by a bridge. Go through a gate and turn left on to the old coach road. Follow this to the next cairn. Go left over a stile and follow the path to visit the cairn.

WHILE YOU'RE THERE

Inveraray Jail is one of the most popular attractions in Argyll. Last used in 1930 this ostentatious Georgian courthouse with its prison cells is now an award-winning museum. Within the cells actors recreate the harsh reality of life in the Duke of Argyll's jail. Within the courtroom itself visitors can sit in the public benches and listen to snippets from some of the trials that took place there.

❸ Return to the road and turn left, continuing to the next cairn. After exploring this, follow the coach road to Kilmartin school, where the route becomes a metalled road. Go through a crossroads, past Nether Largie farm and, ignoring the cairn on the left, continue a short distance to Temple Wood ahead on the right.

❹ Go through a gate on the right into Temple Wood, then return by the same route. Turn right on to the road and continue until you reach a T-junction. Turn left and walk along this road until you come to a sign on the right for Ri Cruin Cairn. Cross the wall via a stile and proceed along the well-defined path to see the ancient monument.

❺ Return by the same route and turn right on to the road. Follow it to a T-junction then turn left and keep straight ahead until you reach the car park at Lady Glassary Wood. Opposite this take a path to the left signposted to Temple Wood. Cross a bridge, go

WHERE TO EAT AND DRINK

The Horsehoe Inn at nearby Brigend is a family-friendly establishment serving good food. In Kilmartin itself the café at Kilmartin House is great for soup and sandwiches and the pub just opposite the church offers tasty bar meals.

through a gate and head towards the standing stones.

❻ Turn right and walk across the field away from the stones towards a wood. Go through a gate and follow the fenced path to Nether Largie Cairn. From here continue along the fenced path, go through another gate and turn right on to the road. Continue past Nether Largie farm and Kilmartin school and then retrace your steps back to reach Kilmartin church and the car park.

EXTENDING THE WALK

Extend the walk from Point ❹ by following a dilapidated estate track towards the Church of St Columba and New Poltalloch. The ruins of this enormous neo-Jacobean mansion can be seen to good effect from the estate track on the other side. Continue through to East Lodge, where you should turn left along the road to meet up with the main route again at Point ❸.

WHAT TO LOOK OUT FOR

Look out for the carvings on the tomb stones in Kilmartin church. Intricate Celtic designs indicate an Irish influence on the work of local sculptors or that the sculptors themselves had come from Ireland. Others bear the effigy of armed knights carved in relief. Above the door in the church you'll find what was once the side slab of a tomb chest.

WALK 53

Stirling's Braveheart, William Wallace

Discover the truth about the ultimate Scottish hero on this town trail.

DISTANCE *5 miles (8km)* **MINIMUM TIME** *2hrs 30 min*

ASCENT/GRADIENT *279ft (85m)* ▲▲▲ **LEVEL OF DIFFICULTY** ✦✦✦

PATHS *Ancient city streets and some rough tracks*

LANDSCAPE *Bustling little city topped with magnificent castle*

SUGGESTED MAP *OS Explorer 366 Stirling & Ochil Hills West*

START/FINISH *Grid reference: NS 795933*

DOG FRIENDLINESS *Mostly on lead, not good for those that dislike crowds*

PARKING *On streets near TIC or in multi-storey car parks*

PUBLIC TOILETS *At visitor centre by the castle*

To many Scots he is the ultimate hero, a charismatic patriot who died fighting for his country's freedom. To others he is less exalted – an outlaw and murderer. Discovering the truth about William Wallace is not easy, as few contemporary accounts exist, although we can be reasonably assured that he didn't look like Mel Gibson or paint his face with woad.

Wallace's heroic status is immediately obvious on your arrival in Stirling, which is dominated by the enormous monument erected in his memory. He was born at Ellerslie near Kilmarnock early in the 1270s and little is known of his early life. He might have remained unknown were it not for the fact that in 1286 the Scottish King, Alexander III, was found dead on the sands at Kinghorn, Fife. His only direct heir was Margaret of Norway – and many powerful Scots did not want a woman on the throne. When Margaret died on her way to Scotland, the succession was plunged into further confusion. The only likely contestants were John Balliol and Robert Bruce. Edward I was asked to advise, chose Balliol, and then exerted his authority by demanding revenues from Scotland. Balliol later infuriated Edward by signing a treaty with England's enemy, France, and Edward retaliated by sacking Berwick in 1296, slaughtering thousands. The Scots began to resist, Balliol was deposed as king, and the Wars of Independence began.

Wallace Wages War

Wallace joined the struggle. In 1297 he killed the English Sheriff of Lanark and led a number of attacks on English forces. Later that year he won the battle that was to make his reputation, defeating Edward's army at Stirling Bridge. Wallace's forces killed thousands of English and Welsh troops, driving the wounded into the marshes to drown. Wallace now had considerable power. Faced with the possibility of food shortages in Scotland, he ordered an invasion of northern England to plunder food. Many villagers were murdered, churches were burned and over 700 villages destroyed.

In 1298 Wallace was made Guardian of Scotland, but was defeated by Edward I later that year at the Battle of Falkirk. He resigned the Guardianship and travelled to Rome to enlist support from the Pope for the restoration of Balliol as king. Back in Scotland, he continually refused to accept Edward as King of Scotland and was eventually captured and taken prisoner in 1305 (some say he was betrayed by Scots). He was executed at Smithfield in London (the torture of being hung, drawn and quartered was invented for him) and immediately became a martyr for Scottish independence.

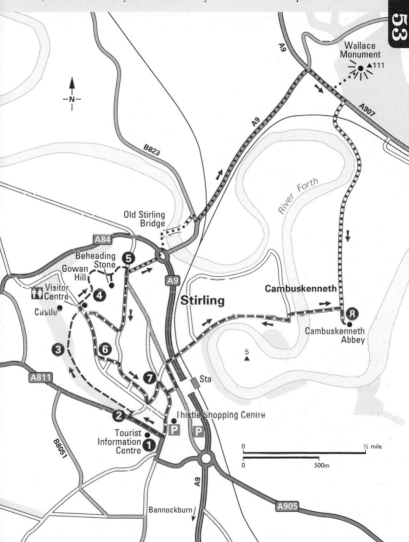

WALK 53 DIRECTIONS

1 From the tourist information centre on Dumbarton Road, cross the road and turn left. Walk past the statue of Robert Burns then, just before the Albert Halls, turn right and walk back on yourself.

Just past the statue of Rob Roy, turn left and take the path along the Back Wall.

2 Almost immediately (20yds/18m) turn right up the flight of steps that takes you on to the Upper Back Wall. It's a steady climb now, up past the Church of the Holy Rude, where James VI was crowned in 1567 and on past Ladies' Rock – where ladies of the castle sat to watch tournaments.

❸ Continue following the path uphill to reach Stirling Castle. Cross the car park to take the path running downhill just to the side of the visitor centre, so that the castle is on your left. At the cemetery, turn right along the footpath signposted to Moto Hill. Continue up steps and across the cemetery to the gap in the wall.

❹ Follow the track downhill on to Gowan Hill. There are several branching tracks but you continue on the main path – heading for the cannons on the hill ahead. At a junction turn right down a track signposted to Lower Bridge Street. Turn on to a grassy slope to the right to see the Beheading Stone. Retrace your steps to the wide track and then follow it to reach the road.

❺ Turn right along Lower Bridge Street, then fork right into Upper Bridge Street. Continue ahead, then 50yds (46m) beyond Settle Inn, turn right up a cobbled lane, it looks a bit like the access to a house. Follow it uphill, then go left at the top. Eventually you'll pass the Castle Esplanade, followed by Argyll's Lodging, and will reach a junction.

❻ Turn left, passing Hermann's Restaurant and the Mercat Cross. Turn right at the bottom down Bow Street, then left along Baker Street. When you reach Friars Street (which is pedestrianised), turn left and walk down to the end.

❼ Turn right now, then first left to reach the station. Turn left, then right over the bridge, then bear

left in front of new development to reach the riverside. Maintain direction and join Abbey Road. Bear left at the end, go right over the footbridge and continue along South Street, turning right at the end to visit the remains of Cambuskenneth Abbey.

❽ Retrace your steps back to the station. Turn right, then left, then right again at the Thistle Shopping Centre. Go along Port Street, then turn right along Dumbarton Road to the start.

EXTENDING THE WALK

You can add a loop to this walk by crossing Old Stirling Bridge and walking up the road to the foot of the Wallace Monument. After you've scaled the heights to the statue, come back to the road and turn left, then right, over the railway to Cambuskenneth Abbey, where you can pick up the main route at Point ❽.

Through the Queen Elizabeth Forest Park

*Walking across the Highland Boundary Fault
and along a 19th-century inclined railway.*

> **DISTANCE** 4 miles (6.4km) **MINIMUM TIME** 3hrs
>
> **ASCENT/GRADIENT** 446ft (136m) ▲▲▲ **LEVEL OF DIFFICULTY** ✦✦✦
>
> **PATHS** Forest roads and footpaths
>
> **LANDSCAPE** Forest and hills
>
> **SUGGESTED MAP** OS Explorer 365 The Trossachs
>
> **START/FINISH** Grid reference: NN 519014
>
> **DOG FRIENDLINESS** Suitable for well-behaved dogs
>
> **PARKING** At visitor centre near Aberfoyle
>
> **PUBLIC TOILETS** At visitor centre

This walk crosses the Highland Boundary Fault, a geological line stretching across the country from Arran to Stonehaven just south of Aberdeen. It is one of Britain's most important geological features and it separates the Highlands from the Lowlands. This weak line in the crust of the earth formed around 390 million years ago when the old rocks of the Highlands were forced up and the Lowland rocks pushed down. North of the fault lie Highland rocks, created over 500 million years ago when land movement on a massive scale squeezed and heated the stone.

Whinstone, which was used extensively as a building stone because it splits easily, formed from pressure on mud and sand. Slate was also formed but was compressed into layers and was valued as a roofing material.

Slate Quarry

Near the walk is the Duke's Pass, one of the largest slate quarries in Scotland. Most of the higher mountains are formed from a rock known as Leny Gritt, which started life as sand and gravel before being moulded into shape by intense heat and pressure. Another group of rocks includes Achray Sandstone, formed when this high mountain area was under the sea. Later earth movement caused the sandstone to tip and stand on its end. Iron minerals present in the formation of the sandstone gave it a reddish brown colour.

Inclined Railway

Given the quality and variety of the rocks found in this part of the forest park it is unsurprising that in the past a great deal of quarrying took place here. Evidence of a once thriving quarry can be found on the steep downhill path (Point ❹ in the Directions), which, at the beginning of the 19th century, was an inclined railway transporting the limestone from Lime Craig Quarry. The limestone was carried on wooden wagons to the lime kilns which used to be at the bottom of the hill.

Heavy wooden sleepers supported the three rails of the wagon way. Full wagons went down using the centre and one outside rail while the empties returned on the centre and other outside rail. The wagons were attached to a wire rope, which was wound round a drum at the top of the hill enabling the weight of the full wagons and gravity to provide the power to return the empty ones to the top. Half-way up the track was a short section of double railing to allow the wagons to pass each other. Brakes at the top of the incline could be used to control the rate of descent. By 1850 the quarry was exhausted and the wagon way no longer needed.

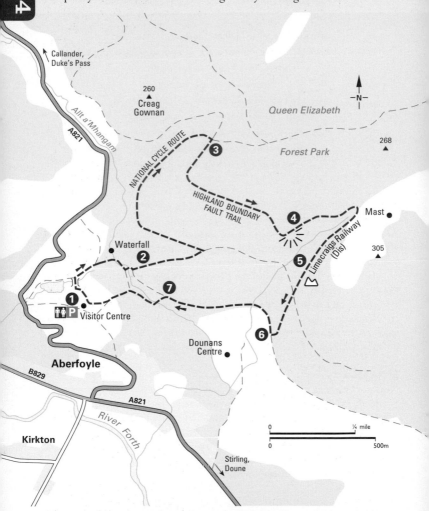

WALK 54 DIRECTIONS

1 From the front of the visitor centre turn left, go down some steps on to a well-surfaced footpath and turn left to follow the blue waymarkers of the Highland Boundary Fault Trail. Continue on this trail to reach the Waterfall

of the Little Fawn with its 55ft (16.7m) drop. Shortly after this turn left to cross a bridge, then turn right following the white arrow left again on to a forest road.

2 This is part of the National Cycle Network (NCN) so look out for cyclists. Head uphill on this waymarked road following the blue Highland Boundary Fault markers and the NCN Route 7 signs. When the road forks at a junction, keep left continuing uphill until you reach a crossroads.

3 Turn right, at the blue waymarker, on to a smaller and rougher road. The Boundary Fault Trail parts company with the NCN Route 7 at this point. The going is easy along this fairly level section. Keep on until you eventually reach a viewpoint on the right with a strategically placed seat.

4 From here the road heads uphill until it reaches a waymarker near a path heading uphill towards a mast. Turn right then go through a barrier and start descending. Although this is a well-made path it is nevertheless a very steep descent through the woods and great care should be taken.

WHILE YOU'RE THERE
Blair Drummond Safari Park, on the road between Doune and Stirling, is a credible day out for the whole family and the only wildlife park in Scotland. Here you'll see animals ranging from lions and elephants, camels and bison roaming free. Other park attractions include a pet farm, pedal boats and a waterfowl cruise.

5 This path follows the line of the Limecraigs Railway, an early 19th-century inclined railway used for transporting limestone. It continues downhill to go through another barrier where the path is intersected by a forest road. Cross this road, go through another barrier and once again continue to head downhill.

WHERE TO EAT AND DRINK
The visitor centre at the Queen Elizabeth Forest Park contains an excellent restaurant where you can enjoy a bowl of hot soup, various hot and cold drinks and a host of other delights ranging from sandwiches to hot meals. As an accompaniment to the food you can enjoy some spectacular views over the forest park.

6 At the bottom of the hill is a set of steps leading to a forest road. Turn right on to the road and follow the blue waymarkers. Stay on this road until you reach a green signpost on the left pointing to the visitor centre. Turn left on to a downhill track and head through the woods.

7 Eventually you'll reach a board announcing the end of the trail. From here the route is signed back to the visitor centre. When the trail forks take the right-hand turning and head uphill beside a handrail and return to the start.

WHAT TO LOOK OUT FOR
The surrounding forest is made up of species such as Sitka spruce, Douglas fir, oak, Scots pine, larch, birch and Norway spruce. In January 1968 a gale destroyed large areas of the woodland and the opportunity was taken to clear and replant. Around these areas are more mature plantings from the 1930s and later ones from the 1980s.

The Great Forest of Loch Ard

One of Scotland's great woodlands, hiding place of the Stone of Destiny and birthplace of the Scottish Parliament.

> **DISTANCE** 3.5 miles (5.7km) **MINIMUM TIME** 2hrs
>
> **ASCENT/GRADIENT** 98ft (30m) ▲▲▲ **LEVEL OF DIFFICULTY** +++
>
> **PATHS** Roads, forest roads and trails
>
> **LANDSCAPE** Fields, hills, forest and loch
>
> **SUGGESTED MAP** OS Explorer 365 The Trossachs
>
> **START/FINISH** Grid reference: NS 521009
>
> **DOG FRIENDLINESS** Keep under control or on lead to avoid disturbing wildlife
>
> **PARKING** Car park at Aberfoyle beside tourist office in centre of town
>
> **PUBLIC TOILETS** Beside tourist office next to car park

Lying between Aberfoyle and the foothills of Ben Lomond this area of woodland is part of the Queen Elizabeth Forest Park. It stretches from just north of Drymen almost to the banks of Loch Katrine. It may look like just another conifer plantation but a walk through any part of it will reveal a surprising variety of landscapes, flora and fauna.

Forestry Management

Most of the forested land was purchased by the Forestry Commission in the early 1930s. It was planted straight away and by the closing years of the century consisted of mature woodland. Ongoing thinning started in the 1950s and areas were felled towards the end of the century. Some 60,000 tons of timber are extracted each year from the park as a whole. With Britain importing about 90 per cent of its timber needs, the increase in harvesting the park's mature trees will help to reduce this figure.

The area south of Lochan Spling was initially planted with Norway spruce, Sitka spruce, larch and Scots pine. Most of the spruce together with some of the larch and pine was felled in the 1980s and replaced with Douglas fir, larch and Sitka spruce. But native broadleaves have been planted too, including 10,000 oak trees to augment the remains of the ancient oak woods that once covered most of the area. Birch and rowan have been regenerating naturally. Part of this area has been left to mature to provide magnificent specimens the equal of anything in European forests. The entire area is enclosed within a deer fence to let the trees establish.

Wilderness Areas

Wildlife is abundant, including red squirrels and capercaillie. Decaying pines, which have been uprooted in gales or just collapsed, support wood-boring insects and provide a ready food supply for a whole host of birds. There are peat bogs and wilderness areas like the one just south of Duchray water in the old wood of Drumore. Here there are no trails, but amidst this jungle-like habitat can be found blueberry, chickweed, wintergreen, cow-wheat and cowberry. You will probably see some evidence of red and roe deer. If you're quiet may see rare birds like blackcock and woodpecker. Changing attitudes to conservation and forestry management have helped to bring about a gradual reshaping of the forest to provide diverse tree species, a wider range of habitats and an environment rich in wildlife.

Stop at the Covenanters' Inn where the Nationalists, led by John McCormick, met in 1949 to launch a petition, which they called the Second Covenant. The signatories called on the government of the day to give Scotland a devolved parliament. Over 2 million people signed the petition but it was not until the closing years of the 20th century, and after much argument, campaigning and voting, that their wishes were granted.

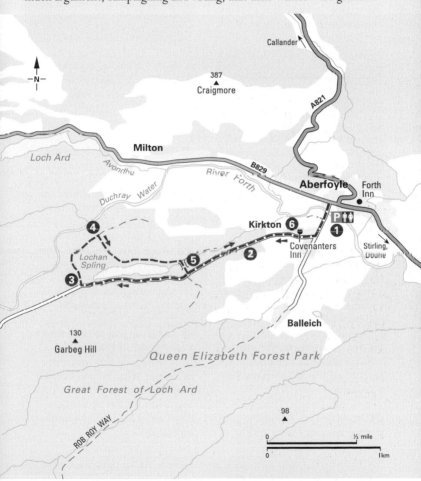

WALK 55 DIRECTIONS

1 Leave from the west end of the car park and turn left into Manse Road. Cross a narrow bridge over the River Forth (the river has its source near here although it is more usually associated with Edinburgh) and continue along the grass beside the road until the first junction on the right. Turn right here and head uphill, passing the Covenanters' Inn. A short distance past here you'll find open countryside and the start of the Great Forest of Loch Ard.

2 Head straight on along the forest road, keeping an ear open for heavy timber lorries. During the week this can get fairly busy, as this is a main forestry extraction route, so keep well into the side. After about 0.5 mile (800m) you will reach a staggered crossroads. Continue straight ahead along the forest road until you come to a turning on the right with a yellow waymarker. Turn right here.

WHAT TO LOOK OUT FOR

The Trossachs is an area rich in wildlife. Roe deer is the animal you have the best chance of seeing on the walk. However with a bit of luck, and by keeping quiet, you could also happen on to some of the rarer beasties which inhabit these woods and hills. This is the southern limit for the elusive pine marten and some have even been spotted round Loch Ard.

WHERE TO EAT AND DRINK

The excellent Forth Inn is reached from the car park. In good weather meals and refreshments are served on picnic tables at the front of the inn or within the spacious restaurant. Delicious home-made soups are served with fresh crusty bread or you can choose from the full menu and specials board. They also have toys and colouring books to keep children amused.

3 Follow this waymarked trail through the forest almost to the banks of Duchray Water. This rises on the north face of Ben Lomond and joins with the Avondhu from Loch Ard to create the River Forth near Aberfoyle. The path now curves right, continues to descend slightly and then reaches a junction.

4 Turn right and follow the path through the trees to the north banks of Lochan Spling. The path then swings left and, at the end of the Lochan, turns right at a waymarker pole, crosses a small stream and heads slightly uphill.

5 When the path reaches the T-junction, turn left and rejoin the main forest access road continuing along it to the Covenanters' Inn. This takes its name not from the activities of the 17th-century Scottish Presbyterians, who were persecuted by the Stuart monarchy for refusing to give up their faith, but from the subsequent activities of 20th-century Scottish Nationalists.

6 Continue past the inn, where a later group of Nationalists temporarily hid Scotland's Stone of Destiny when it was liberated from Westminster Abbey in 1950, and then turn left on to Manse Road at the junction and return back to the start.

WHILE YOU'RE THERE

Visit Doune Castle, 13 miles (20.9km) east of Aberfoyle, built in the 14th century for the Duke of Albany. It was a ruin by the 18th century but has since been restored and now offers a look at what life was like in a medieval royal household. It featured in the film *Monty Python and the Holy Grail* (1974) and more recently the BBC dramatisation of *Ivanhoe*. Although usually associated with Edinburgh, the River Forth actually rises near here where the Duchray Water meets the Avondhu River. It increases in size by the addition of the River Teith near Stirling, then continues its journey to the coast and flows under the Forth Bridges at Queensferry.

The Romance of Rob Roy in Callander

Steep wooded paths lead you through the crags
for superb views of the Trossachs.

DISTANCE 4 miles (6.4km) **MINIMUM TIME** 2hrs 30min

ASCENT/GRADIENT 896ft (273m) ▲▲▲ **LEVEL OF DIFFICULTY** +++

PATHS Forest tracks and some rocky paths

LANDSCAPE Mixed woodlands, great views of hills and lochs

SUGGESTED MAP OS Explorer 365 The Trossachs

START/FINISH Grid reference: NN 625079

DOG FRIENDLINESS Can run free, steep climb and crags might not suit some

PARKING Riverside car park

PUBLIC TOILETS Callander

As you climb through the trees and scramble over the rocks above Callander, it is easy to imagine yourself back in the late 17th century, when Rob Roy (see Walk 62) and his clansmen lived as outlaws in the heart of The Trossachs. His name has for centuries been tied up with myth and legend, and has inspired authors and film makers – including Sir Walter Scott, who wrote a romantic account of his life in his eponymous novel of 1818. For some, Rob Roy is a Highland hero, for others a notorious cattle thief – whatever the truth behind the myth, he is certainly one of the most colourful characters in Scottish history.

The Wicked Clan Gregor

Rob Roy (the Gaelic for Red Robert) was more properly known as Robert MacGregor. Born in 1671, he was the son of Donald MacGregor of Glengyle. This clan – the 'wicked Clan Gregor' – had been outlawed in 1603, and was known as 'the nameless clan' as they were even forbidden to use their name. The MacGregors had a violent reputation, as they defended their lands and cattle vigorously against assaults from neighbouring clans, which included the rival Campbells, who acted as government agents. Rob Roy, living as a cattle herder in Balquhidder, kept an armed band of men to protect him and his cattle – and extended their services to neighbours who paid him protection money. He began to extend his influence and eventually made a claim to be the chief of the clan.

In 1712 he borrowed money from the Duke of Montrose for a speculative cattle deal, and suffered heavy losses, which caused a terrible rift between them. His lands were seized, his properties plundered and his wife and children were turned out of their home despite it being the middle of winter.

These were already troubled times, for the Jacobite rebellion had begun in 1689 and there were frequent battles between government forces and the supporters of James. Rob Roy, who had fought on the Jacobite side at Sheriffmuir, now gathered his clansmen and took revenge on the Duke of Montrose, supporter of the government.

Loved by the Good

As a result, Rob Roy was outlawed and stories began to appear about his dramatic escapes from his pursuers. He even began to be seen as a sort of Robin Hood figure, generously helping the poor by stealing from the rich. Local people would help him and warn him if troops were in the area.

However, Rob Roy's luck didn't last – he was captured in 1727 and was sentenced to transportation. He was later pardoned and went back to Balquhidder, where he seems to have settled down and lived quietly for the rest of his life. He died in 1734 and is buried in Balquhidder churchyard.

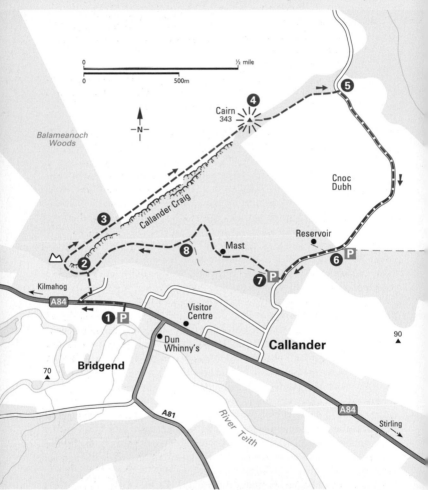

WALK 56 DIRECTIONS

1 From the Riverside car park, walk back to the main road, then turn left. Follow this, then turn right along Tulipan Crescent. Just in front of some modern flats, turn left and follow the wide

track. Where the track splits, take the path on the left that is signposted 'The Crags'.

2 Your path now winds steeply uphill through the trees and can get slippery if there's been a lot of rain. Keep following the path and cross a footbridge. Climb to reach a wall on the left-hand side, after which your path narrows. Follow it to pass a large boulder.

3 Continue following the path, which eventually bears left, up some steps to a fence. Cross another footbridge, scramble over some rocks and go through a metal kissing gate. You eventually come to a memorial cairn, created in 1897 for Queen Victoria's Diamond Jubilee. On a clear day there are stunning, panoramic views of the surrounding countryside from here.

4 Leaving the cairn, your path now begins to wind downhill. It's rocky in places and you'll need to take some care as you descend. Follow the path down to the road.

5 Turn right along the road – you'll see the Wallace Monument near Stirling in the far distance. You'll soon pass a sign on the right-hand side for the Red Well, where the water runs a distinctly reddish colour owing to the presence of iron traces in the local rock. Continue until you reach a car park on your left. You can make a detour here to see the Bracklyn Falls.

6 After the car park, stay on the road for about 0.25 mile (400m) passing a track up to a reservoir

on your right, then turn right into the Forestry Commission car park (signposted 'The Crags').

7 Continue to walk through a car park on to a broad Forestry Commission track. Continue walking past telecommunications next to the end of the track. At the end of the track, turn left and then walk downhill until you reach a wooden seat and a footbridge.

8 Take the path that runs to the right of the seat (don't cross the footbridge). Follow the path as it runs downhill and takes you back to the place at which you entered the woods. Turn right, then go left along the main road and walk back into Callander to the car park at the start of the walk.

Climbing to the Castle of Cups

*Dun na Cuaiche offers a fine view of Inveraray,
Campbell capital of Argyll.*

DISTANCE *4 miles (6.4km)* MINIMUM TIME *2hrs 15min*

ASCENT/GRADIENT *900ft (274m)* ▲▲▲ LEVEL OF DIFFICULTY +++

PATHS *Clear, mostly waymarked paths, no stiles*

LANDSCAPE *Steep, wooded hill, some rocky outcrops*

SUGGESTED MAP *OS Explorer 363 Cowal East*

START/FINISH *Grid reference: NN 096085*

DOG FRIENDLINESS *Must be under control, not necessarily on lead*

PARKING *Pay-and-display, Inveraray Pier*

PUBLIC TOILETS *Inveraray Pier and Castle*

Inveraray is the seat of the Duke of Argyll, chieftain of Clan Campbell. Thus it became, in the eyes of Campbells anyway, the capital of the southern Highlands.

The Campbells Have Come

Until about 1600, the main power in the Highlands was MacDonald, Lord of the Isles. The Duke of Argyll aimed to take his place – by the normal methods of intrigue and armed attack on neighbouring clans, but also by collaboration with the legal government in Edinburgh and the King in London. Clan Campbell would hit you with fire and the sword, but also with a writ from the Privy Council. As a result they became the most powerful and the most universally disliked of all the clans.

In 1691, King William demanded an oath of loyalty from the rebellious Highland chieftains. MacIan of the Glen Coe MacDonalds was required to sign his oath in Inveraray. He hesitated over this visit to the capital of his hated rivals, and eventually arrived two days after the deadline. His delay was made the pretext for the Campbell-led Massacre of Glen Coe (see Walk 70). When a Campbell was murdered in Appin 60 years later, the suspect, James Stewart of the Glens, was tried at Inveraray before a jury of Campbells, with Argyll himself as judge. The hanging of Stewart, who was almost certainly innocent, is still resented in the MacDonald country.

Argyll Rebuilds

With the breaking of the clan system in 1745, Argyll felt confident enough to pull down his fortified castle and rebuild in a grand residential style that suited a wealthy landowner who no longer needed to resort to violence to keep control over his lands.

The present building, greatly admired by Sir Walter Scott, is described as a country house in the style of a castle. Its grey stone, quarried from just above the town, is sombre, but tones well with the muted green and blue of the Campbell tartan. To go with his new castle, Argyll decided he needed a new town. Some say that old Inveraray was simply too close to the castle.

INVERARAY

But in its present position, curved around its bay, it's a magnificent and early example of a modern, planned town. It is dominated by the Court House where James of the Glens stood his trial, and by the white arches of the Argyll Hotel. One of these arches is a passageway for the A819.

The Duke of Argyll completed his ambitious rebuilding scheme with avenues and bridges; one of the bridges forms an elegant entry to the town on the A83. This walk crosses the Garden Bridge, designed by John Adam (1721–92) of the Scottish family of architects. The whole layout of castle and town is seen from the summit of Dun na Cuaiche (Castle of Cups).

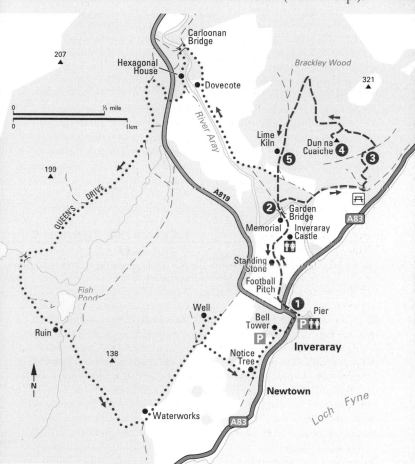

WALK 57 DIRECTIONS

① Follow the seafront past the Argyll Hotel and bear left towards Inveraray Castle. At the first junction, turn right past a football pitch with a standing stone. After the coach park on the left and the end wall of the castle on the right, the estate road on the left is signed 'Dun na Cuaiche Woodland Walks'. It passes a memorial to clansmen who were killed for religious reasons in 1685. Cross the stone-arched Garden Bridge to a junction.

② Half-right now is the uphill path with coloured waymarkers that will be the return leg of the walk. During the coming summers this may be affected by timber lorries, in which case there will be a notice closing this path. If you should see such a notice, it is fine to continue with the route described below up to Dun na Cuaiche, Point ❹, before returning by the way you came up, via Point ❸. Turn right on a riverside track and follow it to a picnic table with a view back to the castle. A rough track runs up left, but turn off instead on to a small path just to right of this, beside a stone gatepost. It climbs quite steeply through an area where attempts have failed to eradicate rhododendron.

❸ At a green track above, turn right, slightly uphill, for 100yds (91m) to a turning circle. Turn left up a muddy path under trees. This improves, bending left and slanting uphill across a stream. The path continues directly uphill under birch trees, with a stream nearby on its left through woods. As the slope eases, the path crosses a grassy clearing to meet a wider one. Turn left, in zig-zags, to reach the summit of Dun na Cuaiche. The tower offers outstanding views.

❹ Return down the path to the clearing, but this time keep ahead. The path, rather muddy, bends left then enters the plantation and becomes a clear track. It passes between two dry-stone pillars

where a wall crosses, turns back sharp left, and passes between two more pillars lower down the same wall. Continue down the track, ignoring side-tracks on the left, to a lime kiln on the right.

❺ Past the lime kiln, a gate leads into a field. Fork right off the track, re-crossing it below to a gate beyond. This leads into a wood. The path runs down to the track junction before the Garden Bridge (Point ❷). Return along the castle driveway to Inveraray.

EXTENDING THE WALK
From Point ❺, you could take the track on the right, to head upstream to the right of River Aray, past a white dovecote and through Carloonan farm. Cross Carloonan Bridge and head back downstream on a track that bends right to the A819. Turn right on an old road opposite to a path on the left. At a T-junction, turn left over a stream. With the track about to rejoin A819, turn right and keep right at the next fork to follow Queen's Drive through Coille-bhraghad Wood. It passes to the right of a large fishpond. In 440yds (402m) keep ahead on a smaller track, down a pretty wooded glen to a waterworks. Turn left along the wooded footpath. With a metal turnpike gate on the right, fork up left to visit the ornamental well. Return to the turnpike gate, which leads out towards Newtown. At the notice tree turn left to Inveraray.

The Shores of Loch Katrine

Glasgow's water supply in the heart of The Trossachs.

> **DISTANCE** 6.75 miles (10.9km)   **MINIMUM TIME** 4hrs 30min
>
> **ASCENT/GRADIENT** 420ft (128m) ▲▲▲   **LEVEL OF DIFFICULTY** ✦✦✦
>
> **PATHS** Water board roads, hill tracks
>
> **LANDSCAPE** Hills, woodland, lochs and heather
>
> **SUGGESTED MAP** OS Explorers 364 Loch Lomond North; 365 The Trossachs
>
> **START/FINISH** Grid reference: NN 404102 (on Explorer 364)
>
> **DOG FRIENDLINESS** Keep on lead near loch and livestock
>
> **PARKING** Car park at Stronachlachar Pier
>
> **PUBLIC TOILETS** At car park

Loch Katrine takes its name from the Gaelic 'cateran', a Highland robber – a fitting place then for the birthplace of Rob Roy MacGregor, the bandit, who was born at Glengyle at the western end of the loch. This is the heart of MacGregor country and a clan graveyard lies near the head of the loch. Rob Roy's lasting fame is due to a novel written by Sir Walter Scott and the loch, too, owed its early popularity to one of Scott's poems, *The Lady of the Lake*. First published in 1810, Scott's description of the scenery encouraged tourists to visit the Trossachs. Coleridge and Wordsworth were inspired by its beauty and Queen Victoria enjoyed a sail upon the loch in 1869. But the pure water of the loch was destined to be a crucial element in the growth of Glasgow as well as a rural escape for its citizens.

By the start of the 19th century Glasgow's population of over 80,000 depended for their drinking water on a few public wells. Later, private companies supplied water from large barrels. But the poor quality of the water, combined with dreadful overcrowding and poor sanitation, led to thousands of deaths from cholera in the 1830s and '40s.

By the mid-19th century Glasgow resolved to provide a municipal waterworks and commissioned John Frederick Bateman, an English engineer. Bateman identified Loch Katrine as the best source of water for Glasgow because of the quality of the water, the large catchment area and its remote, rural, location, but it required a massive feat of engineering. Bateman first built a large dam to raise the level of the loch. Then he constructed an aqueduct 26 miles (41.8km) long to transport the water to a huge reservoir at Mugdock, on the outskirts of the city. A further 26 miles (41.8km) of main piping and 46 miles (74km) of distribution pipes were installed to take the water to all quarters of Glasgow.

After three and a half years, it was officially opened by Queen Victoria in 1859. Bateman was mightily impressed by his scheme and told the city fathers that he had left them 'a work which I believe will, with very slight attention, remain perfect for ages, which for the greater part of it, is indestructible as the hills through which it has been carried'.

LOCH KATRINE

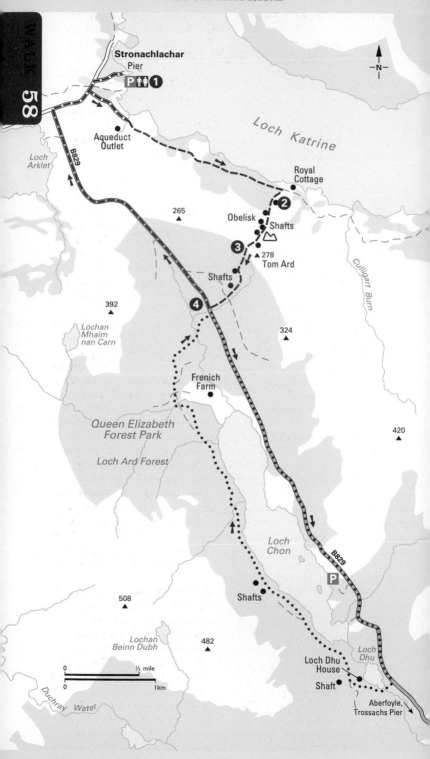

WALK 58 DIRECTIONS

❶ From the car park follow the road back towards the B829 and take the second turning on the left. This is an access road for Scottish Water vehicles only. Continue along the access road until you come to a cattle grid with green gate posts at the building known as Royal Cottage. Turn right just before this on to a rough gravel track that heads through some dense bracken.

WHILE YOU'RE THERE

Head round to The Trossachs Pier and take a trip on the SS *Sir Walter Scott*, the last of the screw-driven steamships in service on Scotland's inland waters. The trip sails via Stronachlachar and passes Royal Cottage, Ellen's Isle, the Factor's Island and Rob Roy's birthplace at Glengyle House.

❷ As the path emerges on to open hillside you will see the first of several ventilation shafts and beyond it, on the hill, a strange obelisk. Follow the path along this line. When you reach the obelisk be sure to look back for a magnificent view over Loch Katrine below and across to the hills with their narrow passes. This is where Rob Roy and his

WHERE TO EAT AND DRINK

This is one of those occasions where a picnic appears to be the only practical option. There are lots of excellent spots on the route to sit down, pour a cup of hot soup from your flask and enjoy your sandwiches while you gaze in awe at the scenery. Alternatively head back into Aberfoyle to the Forth Inn next to the car park there.

men moved from Loch Katrine to Balquhidder and beyond, moving cattle or escaping from the forces of law and order. Continue following the line of the ventilation shafts towards a chimney-like structure on top of a hill. Skirt this hill to the right and then continue around its left-hand side, following an obvious forestry track.

❸ Follow this well-defined track past another ventilation shaft. Keep left at the shaft. It can be very muddy on this short stretch. Continue on the path until it intersects a forest road by a stream. Cross the road and look for a faint track continuing downhill in the same direction. In summer this path may be difficult to find because it's hidden by bracken. In this case follow the line of the telephone poles. Eventually after working downhill through more woodland the track emerges on to the B829.

❹ Turn right here and follow the road. It will eventually emerge from Loch Ard Forest into open countryside. Loch Arklet can be seen on the left; it is now connected to Loch Katrine by an underground pipeline. When the road reaches a T-junction with the Inversnaid road, turn right. When this road forks, turn right again and return to Stronachlachar Pier.

EXTENDING THE WALK

From Point ❹ you can make a pleasant circular extension by turning left, along the road towards Aberfoyle. Turn back when you pass Loch Dhu, cross over a bridge and join a woodland track, which will take you along the opposite bank of Loch Chon back to Point ❹, where you can resume your walk to Stronachlachar.

A Trail Through the Sallochy Woods

*A gentle stroll by the bonnie
banks of Loch Lomond.*

DISTANCE *2 miles (3.2km)* MINIMUM TIME *1hr 30min*

ASCENT/GRADIENT *131ft (40m)* ▲▲▲ LEVEL OF DIFFICULTY +++

PATHS *West Highland Way, forest trail and forest road*

LANDSCAPE *Loch, hills and woodland*

SUGGESTED MAP *OS Explorer 364 Loch Lomond North*

START/FINISH *Grid reference: NS 380957*

DOG FRIENDLINESS *Suitable for dogs*

PARKING *Sallochy Woods car park*

PUBLIC TOILETS *None on route*

One of Scotland's best-known songs, 'The Bonnie Banks of Loch Lomond', was reputedly written by a soldier of Prince Charles Edward Stuart's army during the Jacobite rising of 1745. During the long, slow retreat from Derby the soldier was captured and taken to Carlisle Castle and it was here that he wrote the song for his love, while languishing in prison awaiting execution. It tells of their joy in each other's company on the banks of Loch Lomond and how she would make the lonely journey home to Scotland by the 'high road'. Meanwhile his soul would be instantly transported at the moment of death back to his beloved loch along the 'low road' of the underworld and reach there before her. It's a poignant song of love and parting and a nostalgic remembrance of a landscape that the soldier will never see again in life.

Loch Lomond

Loch Lomond is the largest freshwater lake in Britain. It is 24 miles (38.6km) long, 5 miles (8km) wide and, at its deepest point is 623ft (190m) deep. Within its banks are approximately 38 islands, some of which are inhabited while others form sanctuaries for birds and wildlife. Most of them are in private ownership and not open to visitors. Inchcailloch is part of the National Nature Reserve and Bucinch and Ceardach are National Trust for Scotland properties. They can be visited and in summer a ferry and mail boat operate a regular passenger service from the boatyard at Balmaha, allowing island exploration and the opportunity to lunch at the Inchmurrin Hotel on Inchmurrin.

Geological Fault

The loch straddles the Highland Boundary Fault, a fracture caused by movement of the earth's crust millions of years ago, and the geological differences between Highland and Lowland Scotland formed at this time are clearly visible from its banks. Here the fault runs from Conic Hill on the south east shore through the islands of Inchcailloch, Torrinch, Creinch and Inchmurrin.

LOCH LOMOND

Forest Park

Most visitors rush up the busy A82 along the west side of Loch Lomond, but on the more secluded eastern shore there is a largely unspoilt area of tranquillity and beauty, even in the height of summer. The diverse woods here are part of the Queen Elizabeth Forest Park and contain walking and nature trails and isolated picnic spots. The variety of animals and plants which can be found is staggering. Over a quarter of the plants that flourish in Britain can be found around the loch. You may well spot the rare capercaillie (it's the size of a turkey), ptarmigan or even a golden eagle. On Inchcailloch white fallow deer have been spotted in the past. While on Inchconnacan you might encounter a wallaby. They were transported here from the Australian outback some years ago, by Lady Arran.

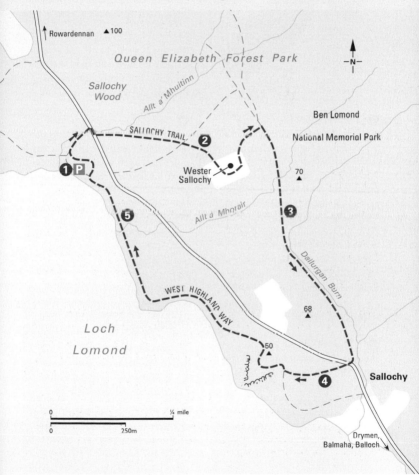

WALK 59 DIRECTIONS

❶ From the car park head towards the entrance on to the main road. Go right on to a track beside the starting post to the Sallochy Trail. Cross the road with care and continue along the trail on the other side. Follow red, green and blue waymarkers. At the second junction turn right and follow the green waymarkers.

WHILE YOU'RE THERE

Head for Loch Lomond Shores, a new gateway visitor attraction situated at Balloch. Within Drumkinnon Tower are viewing galleries and shops as well as two informative shows and a street theatre troupe. Here you can journey with a young otter through some of the myths and legends of the loch, or watch and listen as the scenery becomes the backdrop to the story behind the well-known song.

tthe main road. Cross the gate, then cross the main road. Look carefully for a faint path running through the woods to your left.

2 The trail goes through the wood and passes into the ruined 19th-century farm steading of Wester Sallochy which the Forestry Commission has now cleared of trees. Several buildings can be seen and its worth spending some time investigating these old ruins and trying to imagine life in those times. When you have finished, circle the buildings to the left and follow the well-worn trail until it ends at a T-junction beside a waymarker post. Turn right on to the forest road here.

3 Follow the forest road for about 0.5 mile (800m) to reach a gate just before the junction with

4 Follow the faint path back towards the loch (if you miss the track then enter the wood at any point and head west towards the loch). When the track intersects with a well-surfaced footpath, turn right. You are now on the West Highland Way. Follow the waymarkers, keeping on the main path and ignoring any subsidiary tracks branching off it.

WHAT TO LOOK OUT FOR

Large oak trees remain from when these woods were used to provide a constant supply of timber. They were under a coppice system of management throughout the 18th and 19th centuries which divided the area into a series of sections or 'hags'. Each hag was felled every 24 years but the best 400 trees would be left another 24 years and eight of these were spared to go on growing.

WHERE TO EAT AND DRINK

Try the tea room of the garden centre on the shores of the loch at Balmaha. Here you'll find friendly service, food that is hot, tasty and nourishing and some dreadfully fattening cakes. Alternatively eat in one of several cafés and restaurants at Loch Lomond Shores where, as well as superb views, you'll find everything to tempt you from snacks to seafood.

5 Follow the path uphill through a rocky section and then, as it levels off, through a wood. Eventually the trail passes through the Sallochy Woods car park returning you to the start.

The Holy Island of St Columba

A circuit of Iona to the marble quarry and the saint's landing place in Coracle Bay.

DISTANCE 5.25 miles (8.4km)	**MINIMUM TIME** 3hrs 30min
ASCENT/GRADIENT 650ft (198m) ▲▲▲	**LEVEL OF DIFFICULTY** +++
PATHS Tracks, sandy paths, some rugged rock and heather	
LANDSCAPE Bare gneiss rock and Atlantic Ocean	
SUGGESTED MAP OS Explorer 373 Iona, Staffa & Ross of Mull	
START/FINISH Grid reference: NM 286240	
DOG FRIENDLINESS Keep on lead near sheep	
PARKING Ferry terminal at Fionnphort on Mull	
PUBLIC TOILETS Beside Martyr's Bay Bar	

In the early summer of AD 563, a middle-aged cleric crossed over from Ireland with 12 companions and the intention of setting up a monastic community on the remote and windswept island of Iona.

Flight of the Dove

Columba (in Gaelic, Colum Cille, 'the Dove of the Church') did not intend to bring Christianity to a new country, indeed he had left his native Ireland under a cloud. It had started with a dispute over copyright. Columba had secretly copied a psalter owned by St Finnian of Clonard, and Finnian had claimed ownership of the copy. The dispute became more complicated when a young prince accidentally killed an opponent during a game of Irish hockey and claimed sanctuary with Columba. A battle followed, for which Columba felt responsible. In penance for these events he accepted 'white martyrdom', perpetual exile.

Irish Poetry

At the centre of Columba's settlement on Iona was a church of oak logs and thatch and, around it, huts for the individual monks. Columba himself slept on the bedrock with a stone for a pillow. Larger huts of wattle were used as the dining hall, guest house, library and writing room. The monks' lives consisted of prayer, simple farming and study, and here Columba composed poetry in Latin and Irish.

Celtic Calendar Calculations

Columba's Celtic Christianity spread from Iona across Scotland, and led to the Northumbrian foundation of Lindisfarne, with its rich tradition of illustrated documents such as the *Lindisfarne Gospel*. Here it came into contact with the Roman-style Christianity of continental Europe, brought to England by Augustine in AD 597. While the outward dispute was on the correct hairstyle for monks and the way to calculate the date of Easter, it seems that the Celtic Christianity was more personal and mystical, the Roman more authoritarian. The Roman version eventually dominated, but the Celtic was never suppressed. Columba, never officially canonised as a saint, is venerated in Scotland and Ireland to this day.

Iona Today

Columba's church vanished beneath a later Benedictine abbey, itself heavily restored in the 19th century. But the spirit of Columba still dominates the island. From the low hill called Dun I, on the day of his death, he blessed the island and community. The monks grew kale and oats at the machars (coastal lowlands) of Bay at the Back of the Ocean (Camus Cuil an t-Saimh), over what is today the golf course. At the southern tip of the island is Coracle Bay, traditionally named as the saint's landing place.

'That man is little to be envied, whose patriotism would not gain force upon the plain of Marathon, or whose piety would not grow warmer among the ruins of Iona,' said the renowned English writer and critic Samuel Johnson, who visited the island in 1773. Today's Iona Foundation is ecumenical – tied to no single denomination of Christianity – and has restored the buildings within a tradition of simple craftsmanship and prayer. The grave of John Smith, Labour leader in the 1990s, lies in the north-east extension of the burial ground.

WALK 60 DIRECTIONS

1 Ferries cross to Iona about every hour. Once on the island, take the tarred road on the left, passing Martyr's Bay. After a second larger bay, rejoin the road as it bends right. Follow the road across the island to a gate on to the Iona golf course (dogs on leads).

2 Take the sandy track ahead, then bear left past a small cairn to the shore. Turn left along the shore to a large beach. At its end, bear left up a narrow valley. After 100yds (91m) you pass a small concrete hut to join a stony track. It passes a fenced reservoir and drops to the corner of Loch Staoineig. Walk along to the left of the lochan on a path, improved in places, that runs gently down to Coracle Bay. You cross to the left of an area that shows the furrows of lazybed cultivation – fields drained to improve crop yields – and reach the shore just to the left of a rocky knoll.

3 Take the route ahead following an indistinct path. If your ferry to the mainland leaves in 2 hours time or earlier, return by the outward route and leave exploring the marble quarries for another visit. Otherwise, return inland for 200yds (183m) and bear right into a little grassy valley. After 100yds (91m), go through a broken wall and then bear slightly left, past another inlet on the right. Cross heather to the eastern shoreline

of the island. Bear left, above the small sea cliff, for 0.25 mile (400m). Turn sharp right into a little valley descending into the remnants of the marble quarry.

4 Turn inland, back up the valley to its head. Pass the low walls of two ruined cottages and continue in the same direction for about 200yds (183m) to a fence corner. Keep the fence on your left, picking a way through heather Dun I with its cairn appears ahead – aim directly for it to reach the edge of fields, where a fence runs across ahead. Turn right along it to a small iron gate.

5 This leads to a track that passes Ruanaich farm to the tarred road of the outward walk. Cross on to a farm track, which bends to the right at Maol. It reaches Baile Mor (Iona village) at the ruined nunnery. Just ahead is the abbey with its squat square tower, or turn right directly to return to the ferry pier.

Overleaf: Harbour front at Baile Mor on Iona (Walk 60).

The Hill with the Hole

*Looking along Loch Awe from Cruachan Reservoir,
Britain's biggest energy storage system.*

DISTANCE 2 miles (3.2km)   **MINIMUM TIME** 1hr 45min

ASCENT/GRADIENT 1,200ft (365m) ▲▲▲   **LEVEL OF DIFFICULTY** +++

PATHS Steep rugged paths, 2 ladder stiles

LANDSCAPE Wooded slopes and high corrie

SUGGESTED MAP OS Explorer 377 Loch Etive & Glen Orchy

START/FINISH Grid reference: NN 078268

DOG FRIENDLINESS Good, but high and steep ladder stiles to negotiate

PARKING Two pull-ins on north side of A85, below railway station.
Also lay-by 0.5 mile (800m) west. Not visitor centre car park

PUBLIC TOILETS Cruachan Visitor Centre

The Cruachan Reservoir collects rainfall from a fairly small catchment, 9 square miles (23sq km) bounded by the rocky ridge of Ben Cruachan. Even with Cruachan's 116in (2,945mm) of rain a year only 4 megawatts of power are generated, not enough to supply Oban, to the west.

The Big Battery

But Cruachan is more than just a rather small power station. It's a rechargeable storage system for electrical energy, a very big electric battery. The demand for electric power varies from day to day, and even from minute to minute. There's the surge at the advertising break during your favourite soap, as a million kettles get switched on at once. Coal and oil power stations can be stoked up or cooled off, but only quite gradually. Nuclear stations run at the same rate day and night. And the greenest energy sources, wind and wave generators, give power according to the weather. So there has to be a way of taking electricity out of the National Grid when there's too much, and putting it back when it's most needed.

Cruachan Power

Fortunately, an electric generator running backwards becomes a motor, and a turbine turns into a pump. At 'white-meter' (off-peak) times of day, water is pumped from Loch Awe up to Cruachan Reservoir, 1,000ft (305m) above. And at 7:15 on a weekday evening, it flows back down again.

The stored energy in the battery of your car is sufficient to keep it running for about half a minute, but that's enough to start it in the morning and run the CD deck when the engine's off. Full to the brim, Cruachan Reservoir, with the capacity of about half a billion car batteries, in theory holds enough potential energy to supply the UK's peak demand for 10 minutes. In fact the water can't be drawn down that fast, but at full flow Cruachan can supply 400 megawatts, enough for most of Glasgow. Time your arrival for 7:15pm, and you could see the reservoir sinking at an inch (2.5cm) per minute. The same amount of water will be flowing out into

CRUACHAN

Loch Awe, just beside the visitor centre. The whole process – pumping up and then retrieving the potential energy – is not much more than 50 per cent efficient. The waste heat ends up in Loch Awe, where it benefits the fish farm opposite the visitor centre.

The Secret Source
The Cruachan powerhouse makes a fairly small impact on the outer world. Around 12 miles (19km) of pipes bring water into the reservoir, and the outgoing or incoming electricity loops across the hill on high pylons. The 1,030ft (315m) dam is only visible once you reach the corrie; the power station itself is actually buried deep in the heart of the mountain.

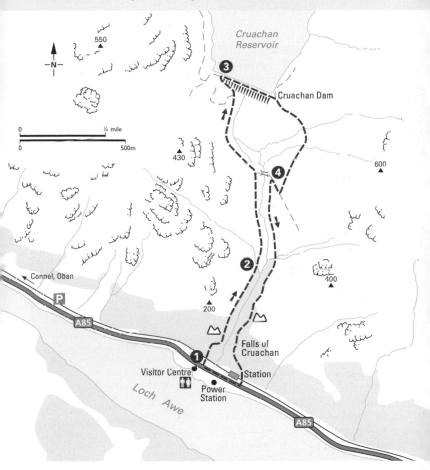

WALK 61 DIRECTIONS

❶ Two paths run up on either side of the Falls of Cruachan. Both are initially rough and steep through woodland. The western one starts at a tarred lane opposite the entrance to the power station proper (not the visitor centre, slightly further to the west). This diminishes to a track, which becomes rough and crosses the railway as a level crossing. A path continues uphill in steep zig-zags through birch, rowan and oak. There are various points to stop and admire Loch Awe, which disappears glittering in the distance. White speckled stones in the path are Cruachan granite. The path continues on steeply to the top of the wood.

❷ Here a high ladder stile crosses a deer fence. With the stream on your right, continue uphill on the small path to a track below the Cruachan dam. Turn left, up to the base of the dam, which measures 1,030ft (315m) wide and 150ft (46m) high. Because it's tucked back into the corrie, it can't be seen from below, but it is clearly visible from the top of Dun na Cuaiche (see Walk 57), 12 miles (19.3km) away. The hollows between the 13 huge buttresses send back a fine echo. Steps on the left lead up below the base of the dam, then iron steps take you on to the dam's top.

❸ From here you can look across the reservoir and up to a skyline that's slightly jagged at the back left corner, where Ben Cruachan's ridge sharpens to a rocky edge. In the other direction, your tough ascent is rewarded by a long view across Lorn. Turn right to the dam end, where a track leads down right to a junction, then right for 50yds (46m).

❹ At this point you could stay on the track to cross the concrete bridge just ahead, leading to the top of the path used for coming up. Otherwise there is a clear path as you go down to the left of the stream, to reach a high, steep ladder stile. (There's a useful dog flap in the deer fence alongside.) Below this there is a clear path that descends grassy slopes and gives a good view of some of the Falls of Cruachan. Inside the wood, the path becomes steep and rough for the rest of the way down. Just above the railway, it turns left, then passes under the line by a low tunnel beside Falls of Cruachan Station, to the A85.

From Balquhidder to Creag an Tuirc

On the trail of the Highland outlaw, Rob Roy, a 'MacGregor despite them', and on to his final resting place.

DISTANCE 2.5 miles (4km)	**MINIMUM TIME** 2hrs
ASCENT/GRADIENT 328ft (100m) ▲▲▲	**LEVEL OF DIFFICULTY** ✦✦✦
PATHS Forest roads and hillside, 2 stiles	
LANDSCAPE Hills, loch and woodlands	
SUGGESTED MAP OS Explorer 365 The Trossachs	
START/FINISH Grid reference: NN 536209	
DOG FRIENDLINESS Dogs ok on this route	
PARKING At Balquhidder church	
PUBLIC TOILETS None on route	

The romantic myth of the life of Rob Roy MacGregor (see Walk 56) was immortalised by Sir Walter Scott in his novel *Rob Roy* (1817).

Prosperous Cattle Dealer

Born in 1671, the third son of Lieutenant Colonel Donald MacGregor of Glengyle, Rob Roy was exceedingly strong, with long arms. Roy, from the Gaelic 'rhuadh', meaning 'red', denoted the colour of his hair. After his marriage to Mary Campbell he acquired land on the east shore of Loch Lomond and rented grazing at Balquhidder. Soon he was a prosperous cattle dealer but an arrangement with the Marquis of Montrose led to his downfall. In 1711 the Marquis gave Rob Roy £1,000 to buy cattle, one of his men absconded with the money and Rob Roy was charged with embezzlement. Failure to answer the court summons led to him being outlawed and a warrant issued for his arrest. Meanwhile Montrose's factor (his agent handling his business affairs), Graham of Killearn, evicted Rob Roy's wife and family from their home at Craigroyston.

To Outlaw

The Earl of Breadalbane gave Rob Roy some land in Glen Dochart, but as an outlaw he was unable to trade as a cattle dealer. Undeterred he turned to sheep and cattle rustling and offering protection. He harried far and wide, lifting cattle and demanding blackmail. His most vicious attacks were always reserved for the Marquis of Montrose, stealing his cattle and lifting his rents. He was even known to give money to a tenant facing eviction and then ambush the factor to steal it back. Twice Rob Roy was captured but both times he managed to escape. Once in a daring escapade, while fording the River Forth and tied to a horse behind his captors, he severed his bonds and plunged into the fast flowing river. His captors were powerless as the current swept him down river.

In 1715 he raised Clan Gregor for the Jacobite rising of the Old Pretender. When it failed, Rob Roy was charged with high treason but again he managed to give his pursuers the slip and retain his freedom.

BALQUHIDDER

Government forces burnt his house in Glen Dochart, but in 1716 the Duke of Argyll let him build another in Glen Shira.

Pardoned

After years of being a wanted man he finally turned himself in to General Wade in 1725 and was pardoned by the King. His remaining years were spent in his house at Inverlochlarig at the head of Balquhidder Glen. He died there, peacefully, on the 28 December, 1734. His funeral procession came down the 15-mile (24km) glen on New Year's Day 1735, led by the MacGregor piper. His grave is beside the ruined church in front of the present Balquhidder parish church.

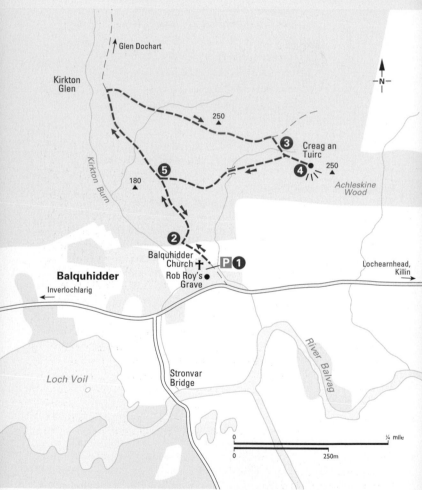

WALK 62 DIRECTIONS

❶ The walk starts at the car park at Balquhidder church. From here, walk along a dirt track, go past a shed and turn on to a path on

the right-hand side which gives access into the forest. Follow the direction arrows on the green signposts pointing to Creag an Tuirc, along a forest track and heading up the hill.

BALQUHIDDER

2 Continue on this obvious trail for about 0.5 mile (800m) and then turn right, alongside a green building, again following the clearly signposted and waymarked route along a forest road. After another 0.5 mile (800m) go through a gate on the right-hand side, go slightly downhill on some stone steps and across a small stream.

WHILE YOU'RE THERE
Take a trip to nearby Kirkton and visit the Breadalbane Folklore Centre. Here in a restored watermill overlooking the Falls of Dochart you can trace the stories of the Scottish clans.

3 The path now heads uphill on some stone steps, through old pine trees and on towards the summit of a knoll. Here is a cairn erected by the Clan Maclaren Society in 1987 to commemorate their 25th anniversary. The plaque proclaims that this place is the ancient rallying point of their clan.

4 A seat below the cairn is a grand place to rest after the climb up here. Sit for a while and enjoy the magnificent views over the meandering line of the River Balvag and the length of Loch Voil with the Braes of Balquhidder rising steeply above it. You can see

WHERE TO EAT AND DRINK
If you're in need of some refreshment after your walk, visit the Kings House Hotel on the entrance road to Balquhiddher. Set against the superb Highland scenery, the inn dates back to 1571 and was once the hunting lodge of King James VI. Today, the Kings House offer open fires, a traditional ambience, daily specials and tasty bar food.

the route that Rob Roy's funeral procession would have taken from Inverlochlarig down to the village itself, and the churchyard where his body lies. From here, retrace your steps back down the hill but before reaching the top of the stone steps on which you came up, take the path to the left signposted 'Forest Walk'. This continues downhill following waymarked poles, down some steps and across a small bridge. The path goes through some bracken, over a small stream and then across a stile. Eventually it will pass through a small wood of young native trees before emerging on to the forest road.

WHAT TO LOOK OUT FOR
The forest road continues past the junction where you turn off at the green building. Following this will take you on a longer walk up through the Kirkton Glen and into the hills on an ancient route to Glen Dochart where Rob Roy also had a house. Once up in these hills and amongst the heather it would have been impossible for soldiers to catch him.

5 Turn left here and retrace your steps back downhill over the stile and then turn left to return to reach the car park. From here enter the churchyard and turn left. Rob Roy's grave is on the left in front of the ruins of a pre-Reformation church.

Along the
Tay to Scone

*A town trail of Perth with views
over Scotland's ancient capital.*

DISTANCE 4 miles (6.4km)	**MINIMUM TIME** 2hrs

ASCENT/GRADIENT Negligible ▲▲▲   **LEVEL OF DIFFICULTY** +++

PATHS City streets and wide firm tracks

LANDSCAPE Historic city and wide, lazy river

SUGGESTED MAP OS Explorer 369 Perth & Kinross

START/FINISH Grid reference: NO 114237

DOG FRIENDLINESS They'll enjoy the river but might not like busy streets

PARKING On street in Perth

PUBLIC TOILETS Off Kinnoull Street in Perth

An ancient description of one of Scotland's most potent symbols – the Stone of Scone, also known as the Stone of Destiny – reads: 'No king was ever wont to reign in Scotland unless he had first sat upon this Stone at Scone.' Scone Palace, of which you get excellent views on this walk, was the crowning place of Scottish kings, including Macbeth and Robert the Bruce. The Stone, which was placed on Moot Hill, by the palace, served as their throne – until it was stolen. The last monarch to be crowned on the Moot Hill was Charles II in 1651 – he was recognised as King in Scotland before he was restored to the throne in England a few years later, in 1660.

Origins of the Stone

Scone was the capital of the Pictish kingdom and was the seat of Kenneth MacAlpin, who united Scotland, from AD 843. The Stone, a piece of red sandstone over 400 million years old, was possibly already in place and could have formed an important part of a pagan ceremony. Geological studies have shown it to be virtually identical to other rocks in the Scone area. The Stone was seen as a symbol of Scotland's nationhood and its significance was to increase after it was stolen by Edward I in 1296. Edward had taken the Stone as a war trophy, determined to exert his authority and crush the independence of the Scots. He had it removed and taken to Westminster Abbey, where in 1297 it was installed beneath the Coronation Chair. Some have claimed that Edward was palmed off with a fake – perhaps even a drainage cover. However this is unlikely, as his officials had already seen the Stone, which has a smooth surface and some distinctive markings.

Return of the Stone

The Scots appealed to the Pope to help them get the Stone returned and, because it apparently had no intrinsic value or aesthetic appeal, the lawyer arguing their case embellished his story of how important it was by claiming that the Stone had been brought to Scotland from Egypt by a pharaoh's daughter. Further myths began to spring up and some even claimed that the Stone was Jacob's pillow.

PERTH

The Stone continued to play its role in history, as all English monarchs from 1297 were crowned upon it. It also continued to be seen as a symbol of Scottish independence and many resented its presence in London. In 1950 some Scottish students managed to steal it from Westminster Abbey, but it was retrieved and replaced. However, in 1996 the Stone was returned to the Scots. It was escorted with due ceremony and put on display in Edinburgh Castle. Many hope that one day it will return to Scone.

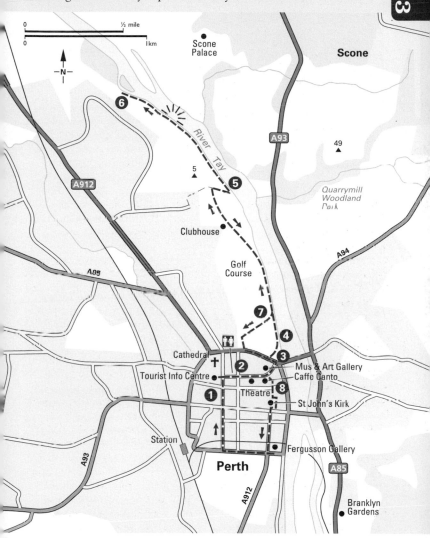

WALK 63 DIRECTIONS

1 From the tourist information centre turn right, then take the first right so you walk round the building. Turn right again and walk down to the road. Cross into Murray Street, passing the bus stops and continue across Kinnoul Street into Mill Street.

2 Continue down Mill Street, passing Perth Theatre on the right-hand side. Keep walking ahead, pass Caffe Canto (see Where to Eat and Drink) on the right-hand side, and join Bridge Lane. You'll pass the museum and art gallery on the left-hand side and will come on to Charlotte Street. Turn left here.

WHAT TO LOOK OUT FOR

St John's Kirk was founded in 1126 – though most of the present building dates from the 15th century. It gave the town its original name 'St John's town' – now the name of the local football team, St Johnstone. John Knox gave a sermon here that inspired local people to sack the nearby monasteries.

3 At the corner you can turn left if you wish to visit the Fair Maid's House. Otherwise, cross over the road and turn right through the park. Walk past a statue of Prince Albert then bear left to join the riverside path. This will give you good views of the smart houses along the opposite bank.

4 Continue ahead on the path, passing the golf course. When you reach the sign for the 14th tee, turn right and follow the track, with a wall to your left when you reach the water's edge. You can either follow the cycle track to the left of the wall, or walk along the river bank.

5 Follow your chosen track until the two tracks meet, just past an electricity substation. Walk by the

WHERE TO EAT AND DRINK

Caffe Canto on George Street is a chic café and a good spot to enjoy a cappuccino and a cake or a panini. Pubs worth trying include the Auld Hoose, Mucky Mulligan's or the Cherrybank. All serve bar meals.

riverside now to enjoy great views of Scone Palace on the opposite bank – there's a seat so you can sneak a rest. This is a lovely spot on a warm, summer's day.

6 Retrace your steps now, walking back beside the river or along the cycle track and back to the golf course. Turn left and walk back towards Perth until you reach the cricket and football pitches on the right-hand side.

7 Turn right and walk between the pitches to join Rose Terrace – John Ruskin once lived here. Turn left, then bear left at the end into Charlotte Street and right into George Street, then right again into Bridge Lane. Turn left along Skinner Gate, the site of the oldest pub in Perth, and walk along to the end.

WHILE YOU'RE THERE

If you like gardens, make for Branklyn Gardens on Dundee Road. This 2-acre (0.8ha) private garden contains lots of unusual and rare plants, including gorgeous Himalayan poppies – they're the bright blue ones. There are more plants at Bell's Cherrybank Centre, the home of Bell's Scotch Whisky and the National Heather Collection. There are over 900 varieties of heather on display.

8 Cross over to pass around St John Kirk, through an archway into South Street and across Princes Street. (see What to Look Out For). At Marshall Place turn left and walk to the Fergusson Gallery on the left-hand side. Then turn back along Marshall Place, walk up to King Street and then turn right. Maintain direction now, then turn left into West Mill Street and return to the start.

The Mysterious Stones of Aberlemno

This linear walk takes you through agricultural land once inhabited by the Picts, a fascinating ancient British tribe.

DISTANCE 5 miles (8km) **MINIMUM TIME** 1hr 45min

ASCENT/GRADIENT 394ft (120m) ▲▲▲ **LEVEL OF DIFFICULTY** ✦✦✦

PATHS Mainly quiet roads but one extremely overgrown area

LANDSCAPE Quiet agricultural land and ancient carved stones

SUGGESTED MAP OS Explorer 389 Forfar, Brechin & Edzell

START/FINISH Grid reference: TQ 522558

DOG FRIENDLINESS Overgrown area makes this unsuitable for dogs

PARKING Car park by school in Aberlemno

PUBLIC TOILETS None on route; nearest in Forfar

Had history turned out differently, you would have been doing this walk in Pictland, not Scotland. The Picts inhabited this northern part of Britain for thousands of years, yet today we know little about them. Neither their language nor manuscripts have survived and their culture remains a mystery. The best reminders we have of them are the intriguing carved stones that dot the landscape of eastern Scotland – the greatest concentration being in Angus and around the Moray Firth. You can see several of these beautiful pieces of ancient art on this walk, which takes you through the heart of the land of the Picts.

The Painted Ones

Mystery surrounds the origins of the Picts. The only thing that seems to be certain is that they occupied what we now call Scotland when the Romans arrived and they may have been here for over 1,000 years before that. The Roman Empire soon stretched from southern England to the central belt of Scotland, and the culture and language of the tribes living under the occupation gradually began to alter under their influence. However, the Romans never spread north of the Forth–Clyde line, and so the tribes there kept their distinct language and customs. The Romans called them the Picti, Latin for 'painted ones' – a reference to their warriors' continued habit of daubing themselves in woad.

After the fall of the Roman Empire, new tribes began to invade Britain, with the Angles and Saxons gradually conquering the south, and Gaelic speakers from Ireland, who called themselves Scotti – or Scots – moving into the far north-west.

The Picts were pagans, but they had been exposed to Christian ideas from AD 400 onwards, brought into the country by the great Celtic missionaries Ninian, and later Columba. In AD 565 Columba travelled to Inverness to meet a powerful Pictish king, Bridei. The two men had a competition to see whether Columba's Christian miracles could beat the wiles of Pictish magic. It isn't clear who won, but gradually the Picts converted to Christianity.

ABERLEMNO

Of course there were wars between the various tribes, the Picts fighting the Gaels and Angles, as well as battling among themselves. The carved stone that you pass in Aberlemno churchyard is thought to commemorate one of Bridei's major victories. Stone carving became more and more important in their culture, with increasingly intricate patterns being created, often combined with a Christian cross. However, in AD 794 the Vikings began to raid northern and western Scotland, weakening the Pictish kingdom. The Gaelic-speaking Scots saw their opportunity – in AD 843 a Scot called Kenneth MacAlpin seized their throne, and the Pictish nation died.

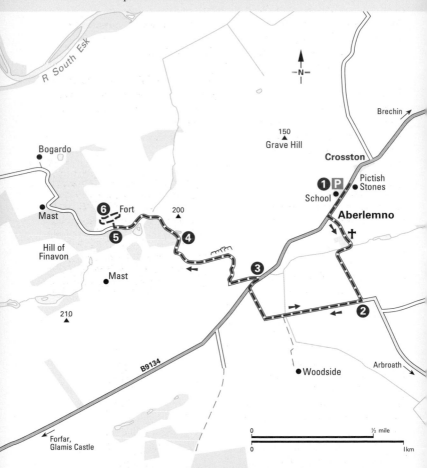

WALK 64 DIRECTIONS

❶ From the car park, opposite the Pictish stones, turn right and walk along the road, then go first left, signed 'Aberlemno church and stone'. Walk past the church – another Pictish stone is found

in the churchyard – and follow the road as it bends round to the right. Follow the road until you reach a T-junction.

❷ Turn right and follow this road, passing the entrance to Woodside on the left. At the corner, follow the road as it bends right. Walk down to join the B9134, turn right and follow this a short distance until you reach a turning on the left.

❸ Turn left along this road, signed 'Finavon Hill'. The road winds uphill, past several outcrops, then under a line of pylons. Continue on this road as it skirts a hill.

❹ Continue following the road uphill, passing a small loch half-hidden in woodland to the left. Shortly after this, you reach an old stone wall on your right. Just beyond a rusty gate in the corner of a field, you will see a section of the wall has collapsed. Hop over here, taking care to avoid the strand of wire.

❺ Head uphill now to explore the turf-covered ramparts of Finavon vitrified fort. Dating from the Iron Age (1000 BC), the hilltop stronghold had walls built of stones that were fused together

by tremendous heat. As you walk around the summit, keep a sharp eye out for vitrified material found in the bank.

❻ From the hilltop, return to the road and turn left to retrace your steps back to the start of the walk in Aberlemno.

WHERE TO EAT AND DRINK

There are several places to choose from in nearby Forfar. The Royal Hotel serves lunches such as sandwiches, filled baguettes and baked potatoes, as well as dishes like lasagne and vegetable curry. It also offers substantial evening meals such as steak-and-Guinness pie and traditional haggis.

WHILE YOU'RE THERE

Glamis Castle is just a few miles away and well worth a visit. The seat of the Earls of Strathmore and childhood home of the late Queen Elizabeth, the Queen Mother, it is a wonderfully atmospheric castle, with towers, turrets and tiny windows. It is also said to be haunted by a 'grey lady' who appears in the chapel. You can take a tour of the castle, the grounds and stop at the café.

The Sweet Fruits of Alyth

This varied walk takes you through the fertile heart of Scotland.

DISTANCE *5 miles (8km)*   **MINIMUM TIME** *3hrs*

ASCENT/GRADIENT *787ft (240m)* ▲▲▲   **LEVEL OF DIFFICULTY** ✦✦✦

PATHS *Wide grassy tracks, some rougher paths on hill*

LANDSCAPE *Mixed woodland, overgrown pasture and gentle hills*

SUGGESTED MAP *OS Explorer 381 Blairgowrie, Kirriemuir & Glamis*

START/FINISH *Grid reference: NO 236486*

DOG FRIENDLINESS *Can run free in many places – keep on lead near shee*

PARKING *Car park in Alyth Market Square*

PUBLIC TOILETS *Alyth Market Square*

If you do this walk in the summer or early autumn, put some plastic bowls in the car before you go. That's because Alyth is close to Blairgowrie, and is surrounded by the soft fruit fields of Strathmore. Although you don't pass any strawberry fields on the walk, there are many just a short drive away and you'll see 'Pick your own' signs everywhere.

Fabulous Fruits

This part of Scotland has long been famed for the quality of its soft fruit, particularly its strawberries and raspberries. The land is fertile and the climate mild – perfect for raising sweet, juicy berries. You will see many fields covered in a layer of fine fleece, placed there to protect the strawberry plants, particularly from birds. Fruits from the fields used to be picked to serve the jam-making industry of nearby Dundee. The area's importance for fruit growing is reflected in the names of many varieties of berry. There's the Tayberry (a cross between a blackberry and a raspberry), which refers to the nearby Tay, as well as varieties of raspberry such as Glen Clova and Glen Prosen (both glens being just a short distance from Alyth).

These soft fruits have played an important part in the British diet for a long time, providing valuable vitamin C. Wild strawberries and raspberries are both native to Britain. Strawberries were cultivated in Elizabethan times, although the cultivated ones you buy today are more likely to come from non-native stock: a Chilean species, for example, was introduced in the 1800s and produced larger, more brightly coloured fruits.

Today we tend to use soft fruits for jam or simply eat them fresh or with cream as a treat. However, they were once used in much more complicated recipes. An Elizabethan book, first printed in 1596 and entitled *The Good Huswifes Jewell*, describes a recipe for Tarte of Strawberries that begins: 'Take strawberries and washe them in claret wine, thicke and temper them with rose-water, and season them with cinamon, sugar, and ginger...'

Not only were soft fruits eaten, they were once used to make medicines. Culpeper, the famous 17th-century physician and herbalist, described the versatile healing properties of strawberries in some detail, declaring that the plants were ruled by the planet Venus and that the berries were 'excellent good to cool the liver, the blood, and the spleen, or an hot choleric stomach'. He declared that lotions made from the leaves and roots of strawberries could help ulcers in the 'privy parts' and were also good 'to fasten loose teeth, and to heal spungy foul gums'. Even today, raspberry leaf tea is drunk by women to help them in the final stages of pregnancy and during labour, while raspberry vinegar makes an excellent gargle for soothing sore throats.

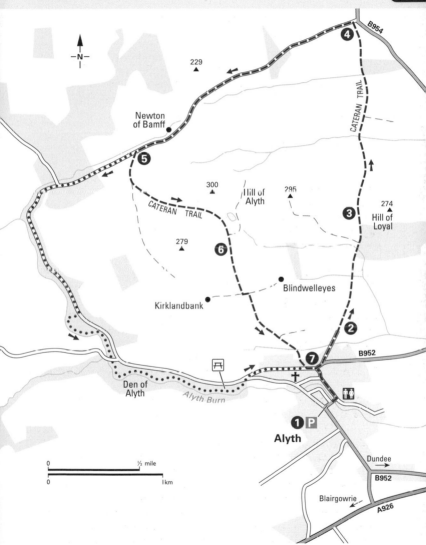

WALK 65 DIRECTIONS

❶ From the Market Square, cross the burn, then turn left along Commercial Street, so that the river is on your left. Turn right up Toutie Street, right again up Hill Street, then left on Loyal Road. Continue walking uphill to reach a sign for the Cateran Trail.

2 Walk uphill now, go through a gate and continue in the same direction, walking past a wood on the right-hand side. You'll go through a kissing gate, passing an area that in summer is a mass of purple foxgloves. Eventually your path levels out and then starts to bear downhill. Maintain your direction to go through a kissing gate and over a burn.

WHERE TO EAT AND DRINK

The Bridges Coffee Shop in Alyth serves a range of snacks, such as baked potatoes and salads, whilst the Alyth Hotel, also in the Market Square can provide more substantial fare.

3 From this point the path becomes narrower and bears uphill again, becoming muddier and more overgrown. You'll walk under trees now, through a gate, and will then leave the birch and oak woodland. Keep an eye out for deer here, as you might spot one bounding into the trees, just a few feet away from. Maintain your direction through the grass, then go through a kissing gate to reach the road.

4 Turn left and walk along the road, following the signs to the Hill of Alyth Walk. It's pretty quiet along here, so you should meet few cars. The road takes you past a conifer plantation, past a house on the right-hand side and over a cattle grid. Soon after this, you turn left and follow the signs for the Cateran Trail.

5 Walk uphill and, at a crossing of tracks, turn to the right. Then, within 50yds (46m), turn left uphill. When you reach another crossing of paths, turn right. There are lots of paths traversing the hill, so you can choose your own

WHILE YOU'RE THERE

Explore Alyth, which was once the home of James Sandy. Never heard of him? Well, not only was he the inventor of the invisible hinge (an item we never give a thought to today, probably because it's invisible), but he was also something of a mechanical genius, copying all sorts of items with great success. For some reason he also took to incubating and hatching birds' eggs using the warmth of his body – the young fledglings would then sit on his head and sing.

route at this point, but essentially you must keep the ponds on your left and don't walk as far as the beacon. At the pond, bear right at a waymark sign, aiming for a small copse until you go through a gate.

6 Walk downhill along the enclosed track – you'll see the spire of the church below you. When you reach another track turn left and then right to continue walking downhill on a metalled track. Walk under a line of pylons and past a farm to eventually reach the village.

7 Your path now bears left along a residential road and takes you downhill. Turn right and retrace your steps along the side of the burn to the start of the walk in the Market Square.

EXTENDING THE WALK
Instead of traversing the Hill of Alyth, carry straight on at Point **5**, following the road into the Den of Alyth. A footpath on the right takes you down into this ancient woodland, from where you can follow the burn to a pleasant picnic area before rejoining the lane into town.

An Ancient Yew in Fortingall

*Discover the history of an extraordinary tree on
this easy walk amidst stunning mountain scenery.*

DISTANCE 3.5 miles (5.6km)	**MINIMUM TIME** 2hrs
ASCENT/GRADIENT 33ft (10m) ▲▲▲	**LEVEL OF DIFFICULTY** ✦✦✦
PATHS Quiet roads and firm farm tracks, 1 stile	
LANDSCAPE Picture postcard Scottish scenery, ancient tree	
SUGGESTED MAP OS Explorer 378 Ben Lawers & Glen Lyon	
START/FINISH Grid reference: NN 741470	
DOG FRIENDLINESS Best to keep them on lead in case of cars	
PARKING Fortingall village	
PUBLIC TOILETS None on route; nearest in Aberfeldy	

Take a good look at the yew tree in the churchyard at the start of this walk. It is the oldest living thing in Europe – possibly even the world. No one knows exactly how old it is, as yews are notoriously difficult to date (their heartwood dies and they become hollow after around 500 years). However, it is generally reckoned to be around 5,000 years old. Some people think it could even be older – up to 9,000 years. In 1769 the tree's girth was measured and found to be 56ft (17m).

A Special Tree

Long before Christianity, yew trees were held sacred by the Druids and the Celts. This must surely be because of the tree's extraordinary powers of regeneration; they can enter long periods of 'hibernation' when they hardly grow at all – and then suddenly sprout new leaves. Some think yews were planted over graves to protect and purify the dead – others think that sacred sites and burial grounds grew up beside existing yew trees. What is certain is that they have a special place in our culture. Like many pagan symbols, the significance of yew trees was retained and sanctified by the early Christian Church and you will often see yew trees in churchyards today. There are at least 500 churchyards in England and Wales that have yews as old as the church itself, and many of the trees are much undoubtedly older than the building.

Rock a Bye Baby

During medieval times, yews were often placed in churchyards alongside the route that coffins would take. Some think trees were also planted here to provide wood for longbows, while keeping their poisonous branches out of the reach of cattle. The branches of yew trees were also used as church decoration. One famous yew tree in Derbyshire is said to have provided the inspiration for the nursery rhyme 'Rock a Bye Baby'. It's known as the Betty Kenny tree and was once the home of a local family. A child's cradle was created in one of the boughs. Yew trees were also sometimes planted beside inns as a sign to travellers. Two yews were said to indicate that accommodation was available. Three yews meant that the inn was able to make provision for the travellers' animals as well.

Pilate Was Here?

Fortingall is also said to have been the birthplace of Pontius Pilate, who is reputed to have played under the branches of the tree. Apparently Pilate's father was an officer in the Roman army and was stationed here with his wife during the Roman occupation. The family supposedly left Scotland when Pilate was young. However, some claim that Pilate eventually returned to Fortingall and is buried in the churchyard.

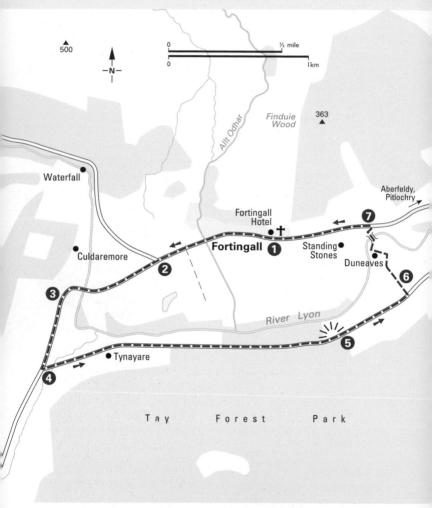

WALK 66 DIRECTIONS

❶ With your back to the Fortingall Hotel, turn right to walk along the road, passing several pretty thatched cottages

(an unusual sight in Scotland) on the right-hand side. Follow the road over a burn and then walk past the entrance to Glen Lyon farm. Eventually you'll reach a fork in the road.

FORTINGALL

2 Ignore the right-hand fork and maintain direction. The road will soon take you over a bridge that crosses the River Lyon.

3 Cross over the bridge and continue along the road (it's tarmacked but very quiet), and walk past some little cottages on the right-hand side. Continue until you reach the sign for Duneaves.

4 Turn left and follow the road – the river is on your left-hand side. You feel as if you're in a secret valley as you walk along here, and in late summer you can stop to pick the wild raspberries that grow by the roadside. Continue past an area of woodland, after which you get views across the valley to Fortingall.

5 Continue to follow the road until you see a white house on the right-hand side. Leave the metalled track and turn left 50yds (46m) before the house, down a track signposted to Duneaves Farmhouse – the views of the surrounding hills are great.

6 Follow the wide, stony track as it leads down to Duneaves. Just before you reach the farmhouse go through the gate in the wall on the right-hand side. Then turn left, following the path around the fields and along the river bank to a rather bouncy footbridge. Bear right after crossing the bridge, then continue through the gate and join the road.

7 Turn left and walk back along the road. You'll soon pass two sets of standing stones in the field on the left – six stones in a ring near the road, and three further away. Walk back into Fortingall to reach your starting place.

The Braes o' Killiecrankie

A deeply wooded riverside leads from the famous battlefield to Loch Faskally.

DISTANCE 8.75 miles (14.1km)	**MINIMUM TIME** 4hrs
ASCENT/GRADIENT 492ft (150m) ▲▲▲	**LEVEL OF DIFFICULTY** +++

PATHS Wide riverside paths, minor road, no stiles

LANDSCAPE Oakwoods on banks of two rivers

SUGGESTED MAP OS Explorer 386 Pitlochry & Loch Tummel

START/FINISH Grid reference: NN 917626

DOG FRIENDLINESS Off lead on riverside paths

PARKING Killiecrankie visitor centre

PUBLIC TOILETS At start

Ye wouldna been sae swanky o
If ye'd hae seen where I hae seen
On the braes o Killiecrankie o'

The song commemorating the victory of the Battle of Killiecrankie in July 1689 is still sung wherever anyone with an accordion sits down in a pub full of patriotic tourists. In fact, both sides in the battle were Scots. When James II was ousted from England in a bloodless coup in 1688, the Scots Parliament (the Estates) voted to replace him with William of Orange. The Stuarts had neglected and mismanaged Scotland, and had mounted a bloody persecution of the fundamentalist Protestants (Covenanters) of the Southern Uplands.

'Bluidy Clavers'

John Claverhouse, 'Bonnie Dundee', had earned the rather different nickname 'Bluidy Clavers' in those persecutions. He now raised a small army of Highlanders in support of King James. The Estates sent a larger army north under another Highlander, General Hugh Mackay, to sort things out. Dundee, outnumbered two to one, was urged to ambush Mackay in the Pass of Killiecrankie. He refused, on the grounds of chivalry. The path above the river was steep, muddy and wide enough for only two soldiers; a surprise attack on such difficult ground would give his broadsword-wielding Highlanders too great an advantage against Mackay's inexperienced troops. Just one of the Lowlanders was picked off by an Atholl sharpshooter at the Trouper's Den (below today's visitor centre), and the battle actually took place on open ground, to the north of the pass.

Claymore Victorious

Killiecrankie was the last time the claymore conquered the musket in open battle, due to a deficiency in the musket. Some 900 of the 2,500 Highlanders were shot down as they charged, but then the troopers had to stop to fix their bayonets, which plugged into the muzzle of the musket.

LOCH FASKALLY

By this time the Highlanders were upon them, and they broke and fled. The battle had lasted just three minutes. Half of Mackay's army was killed, wounded, captured or drowned in the Garry. One escaped by leaping 18ft (5.5m) across the river: the 'Soldier's Leap'. Dundee died in battle. A month later his army was defeated at Dunkeld, and 25 years later, when the Highlanders next brought their claymores south for the Stuarts, the troupers had learnt to fix a bayonet to the side of a musket where it didn't block the barrel.

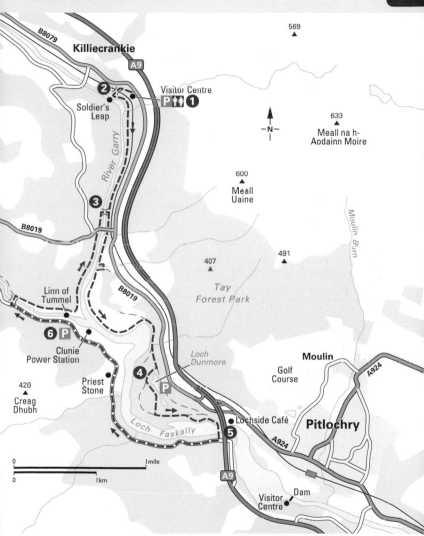

WALK 67 DIRECTIONS

❶ From the back corner of the visitor centre steps, signed 'Soldier's Leap', lead down into the wooded gorge. A footbridge crosses the waterfall of Trouper's Den. At the next junction, turn left ('Soldier's Leap'). Ten steps down, a spur path on the right leads to the viewpoint above the Soldier's Leap.

239

2 Return to the main path, signed 'Linn of Tummel', which runs down to the River Garry below the railway viaduct. After 1 mile (1.6km) the path reaches a footbridge.

3 Don't cross this footbridge, but continue ahead, signed 'Pitlochry', along the riverside under the tall South Garry road bridge. The path bears left to a footbridge. Cross and turn right, signed 'Pitlochry', back to the main river. The path runs around a huge river pool to a tarred lane; turn right here. The lane leaves the lochside, then passes a track on the right, blocked by a vehicle barrier. Ignore this track; shortly afterwards turn right at a signpost, 'Pitlochry'.

> ### WHILE YOU'RE THERE
> At the Pitlochry dam that forms Loch Faskally, Scottish and Southern Energy has a small visitor centre celebrating its hydro-electric schemes. It also has a window into the salmon ladder beside the dam. From March to October you can watch the fish battle their way up towards Killiecrankie.

4 Immediately bear left to pass along the right-hand side of Loch Dunmore, following red-top posts. A footbridge crosses the loch, but turn away from it, half

> ### WHAT TO LOOK OUT FOR
> Loch Faskally is artificial, and you'll pass the Clunie power station on the walk. Its stone arch commemorates the five people who tragically died during the construction of the Clunie Tunnel, which brings water from Loch Tummel down to Killiecrankie.

> ### WHERE TO EAT AND DRINK
> There are cafés at the start and at Lochside, Pitlochry. Pitlochry itself is the town of the tea room. One of them is Macdonald's, on the main street, which serves traditional Scottish high teas to the very hungry.

right, on to a small path that becomes a dirt track. After 270yds (250m) it reaches a wider track. Turn left, with a white/yellow waymarker. After 220yds (201m) the track starts to climb; here the white/yellow markers indicate a smaller path on the right, which follows the lochside to a point below the A9 road bridge.

5 Cross Loch Faskally on the Clunie footbridge below the road's bridge and turn right, on a quiet road around the loch. In 1 mile (1.6km), at the top of the grass bank on the left, is the Priest Stone. After you pass the Clunie power station, you reach a car park on the left. Here a sign indicates a steep little path down to the Linn of Tummel.

6 Return to the road above for 0.5 mile (800m), to cross a grey suspension bridge on the right. Turn right, downstream, to pass above the Linn. A spur path back right returns to the falls at a lower level, but the main path continues along the riverside (signed 'Killiecrankie'). It bends left and goes down wooden steps to the Garry, then continues upstream and under the high road bridge. Take the side-path up on to the bridge for the view of the river, then return to follow the descending path signed 'Pitlochry via Faskally'. This runs down to the bridge, Point **3**. Return upstream to the start.

Right: View across Loch Faskally (Walk 67)

The Black Wood of Rannoch

*Looking between the branches of the ancient
Caledonian forest to Loch Rannoch and Ben Alder.*

DISTANCE 3.75 miles (6km)   **MINIMUM TIME** 2hrs 30min

ASCENT/GRADIENT 1,150ft (350m) ▲▲▲   **LEVEL OF DIFFICULTY** ✦✦✦

PATHS Forest roads, rough woodland paths, no stiles

LANDSCAPE Birch wood, plantations, ancient pine forest

SUGGESTED MAP OS Explorer 385 Rannoch Moor & Ben Alder

START/FINISH Grid reference: NN 590567

DOG FRIENDLINESS Off lead in woodland, but at heel in Black Wood

PARKING Small pull-in just west of Rannoch School

PUBLIC TOILETS Carie (forest car park), 2 miles (3.2km) east

The Black Wood of Rannoch gets its sombre name simply because it consists of pines, rather than more colourful birch or oak. None of its trees has been planted by human hand; surrounded by spruce plantations, and damaged by grazing deer, it still represents an existing remnant of the ancient Caledonian forest.

The Great Wood of Caledon

As the ice retreated during the last Ice Age, the trees moved in. Once the climate had stabilised, Scotland was one forest almost to the mountain tops. In the warmer west, the tree-cover consisted of oak (see Walk 71); in the north-eastern valleys it was the birch. But the slopes of the Grampians were clothed in magnificent Scots pine.

A warm wet spell after the Ice Age, with the build-up of soggy inhospitable peat, contributed to the decline of the pine. But their main enemy has been humans. Forest that once stretched from Rannoch to Inverness was destroyed piece by piece for various reasons. In the 14th century, the Wolf of Badenoch (the brother of King Robert the Bruce) roamed and plundered this country, burning large areas of forest because they made it easier for his enemies to escape. In the 1500s, Queen Elizabeth of England prohibited iron smelting in parts of her kingdom, which drove the fuel-hungry smelters north into the Highlands. A hundred years later, forests were being destroyed around Rannoch to prevent their giving shelter to MacGregors, wolves and other undesirables.

Nibbled to Death

After the Jacobite rebellions, English timber companies moved in, and as clan chieftains became absentee landlords, they needed timber cash to support their lavish new lifestyles. The felling of ancient pines continued through the two world wars. The coming of sheep meant that where ancient forest still stood, any seedlings would be nibbled to death. However, two centuries of non-regeneration aren't enough to extinguish a pine wood. Today such remnants are being fenced and protected, and are coming alive again with new growth.

243

Left: The Black Wood of Rannoch (Walk 68)

Proper Forest and Granny Pines

As you reach Point ❹ of this walk, your spirits should suddenly rise. You have passed from what the Forestry Commission calls a forest, where trees destined to become pulp for paper stand trunk to trunk in grey gloom, to emerge under a more open canopy, where views are wide and where sunlight reaches the pine-needle floor and brightens the undercover of bilberry and heather. The cheerful reddish bark complements the dark green of the foliage above.

Here and there you'll come across an old pine that's too twisted to be of any use in shipbuilding, which has been spared – a so-called granny pine. The lifespan of a pine is 300 years or more, so these trees will have seen the last of the wolves pass by, and sheltered broken men after Bonnie Prince Charlie's failed rebellion in 1746.

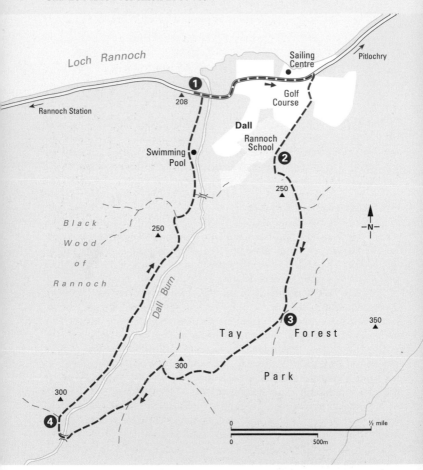

WALK 68 DIRECTIONS

❶ From the pull-in, walk back along the road with Loch Rannoch on your left and Rannoch School on the right. You pass its commando climbing tower on the right, its sailing centre on the left and its golf course. At the former school's goods entrance, a Scottish Rights of Way Society (SRWS) signpost points up to the right –

LOCH RANNOCH

this is an old and unused through route to Glen Lyon. Follow the tarred driveway past tennis courts to the first buildings and turn left at another SRWS signpost.

❷ A sketchy path runs up under some fine birch trees. At an empty gateway in a decomposing fence it enters spruce trees and becomes a narrow track that's a little damp in places. Avoid a lesser path turning off to the left; the main one becomes a pleasant green path contouring across the slope with glimpses of Loch Rannoch on the right. The path runs up to a wide forest road.

❸ Ignore the path continuing opposite and turn right, contouring around the hill. Clear-felling has opened up views to

WHAT TO LOOK OUT FOR

A low, star-like flower below the birches at the walk's start could be mistaken for the common wood anemone, but is actually chickweed wintergreen. It can be identified by the rosette of leaves half-way up the flower stem. Most flowering plants die back in autumn to allow them to escape the frosts and winds, but on the sheltered forest floor, evolution has programmed this plant to keep its leaves through the winter – hence the name.

Loch Rannoch and the remote hills beyond. The highest of these, with a steep right edge, is Ben Alder, the centre of the southern Highlands. This hill is glimpsed from many places, notably the A9 at Dalwhinnie, but isn't easily reached from anywhere. After 0.5 mile (800m), keep ahead where another track joins from the left. The joined tracks descend to a triangle junction. Turn left, gently uphill and, after 120yds (110m), bear right on to a little-used old track. This descends to a bridge over the Dall Burn.

WHERE TO EAT AND DRINK

From the head of Loch Rannoch, the former 'Road to the Isles' runs on for 5 miles (8km) to Rannoch Station. The great moor featured briefly in the film *Trainspotting* (1996), perhaps to show that the countryside can be as bleak as any run-down corner of Edinburgh. The austere impression is rather spoilt by the warm and friendly little café in the listed Swiss chalet-style station building. It's open from March to October.

❹ Some 120yds (110m) after the bridge, the track bends left; here a path descends on the right. This is the Black Wood of Rannoch, now a forest reserve. The path runs under beautiful pines and birches. On the right, the Dall Burn is sometimes in sight and can always be heard. The path is quite rough, but unmistakable as it cuts through deep bilberry and heather. After a mile (1.6km), the path bends left to a track. Turn right to leave the Caledonian Reserve at a notice board. At a T-junction, turn left, away from the bridge leading into the former school. The track improves as it runs past the school's indoor swimming pool and back to the lochside road.

Around the Small Shepherd

*Two valley passes through the high mountains
at the head of Glen Coe.*

DISTANCE *8 miles (12.9km)*   **MINIMUM TIME** *4hrs 30min*

ASCENT/GRADIENT *1,300ft (396m)* ▲▲▲   **LEVEL OF DIFFICULTY** +++

PATHS *Rough, unmade paths, some boggy bits, no stiles*

LANDSCAPE *Remote high valleys into heart of hills*

SUGGESTED MAP *OS Explorer 384 Glen Coe & Glen Etive*

START/FINISH *Grid reference: NN 213559*

DOG FRIENDLINESS *Good, some streams to cross*

PARKING *Large parking area on south side of A82, marked by yellow
AA phone post*

PUBLIC TOILETS *Glencoe village*

WARNING *Fords in Lairig Eilde can be impassable or dangerous after heavy rain*

This walk uses two through routes on either side of Buachaille Etive Beag, the 'Small Herdsman of Etive'. The Gaelic word 'Lairig' means a valley pass through the mountains. We follow Lairig Gartain for the outward part of the journey, and Lairig Eilde for the return, with a final link along the old Glen Coe road.

Passing Deer

This land is owned by the National Trust for Scotland, and there hasn't been any deer stalking for 65 years. If you are really lucky, you might hear the mountain walls echoing with the roaring of the stags as you walk through Lairig Eilde ('Pass of the Deer'). It's an unforgettable sound – rather like a lion, but a little like a cow too.

For most of the year the hinds gather in small family groups with their calves of the last two years, while the stags go around in loose gangs. Deer dislike midges, so in summer they'll be on the high tops, though they may come down at night or in bad weather. In winter they'll be in the valley bottom or even at the roadside. The calves are born in early June; they are dappled to camouflage them on the forest floor, which is their natural home. Within a few days they're running with the herd. The grace and speed of a week-old deer calf across a peat bog is the envy of any hillwalker.

The hinds have no antlers. The stags lose theirs in early summer and grow new ones ready for the rut: the September mating season. Large, many-branched antlers do not make a stag a better fighter, and are a serious drain on his system. They have probably evolved as display items, for intimidating other males and attracting females. A mighty roar may gain the stag the harem of a dozen hinds that he's after. If not, a quick clash of antlers will usually settle the matter. These displays are a way of determining which stag would have won without putting either to the risk of injury. However, the stag is sometimes prepared to fight for his wives and such fights can end in the death of one or even both males.

GLEN COE

Red deer owe their widespread survival in Scotland to the men who preserved and nurtured them in order to hunt them every autumn. For ancient aristocrats and newly rich Victorian manufacturers, the sport of sneaking up on a stag with a rifle was exciting, virile and also impressively expensive. With no predators, deer must still be culled by shooting, even on NTS land where no sport stalking takes place. Such culling will be done at dawn, before walkers start disturbing the hill.

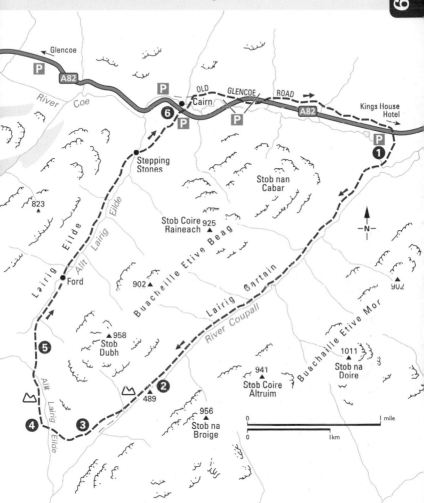

WALK 69 DIRECTIONS

❶ A signpost to Glen Etive, at the edge of the car park, marks the start of the path into Lairig Gartain. The path is clear, but very boggy in places. It heads up-valley with the River Coupall down on the left. Gradually it draws closer to the river, but does not cross it. A large cairn marks the top of the path, which is slightly to the right of the lowest point of the pass.

❷ The descending path is steeper, first down boggy grass, then stony and eroded to the right of the stream. After 0.5 mile (800m) the main path bears off right, and slants down the right-hand wall of the valley. Eventually it emerges on to the steep south ridge of Stob Dubh.

❸ Here a path runs down to a gate in a deer fence just below, but there's no need to go any further downhill. Follow a path above the deer fence, descending to cross the Allt Lairig Eilde. If the stream is too full to cross, you can return and go down through the deer fence to a wider but shallower crossing, 200yds (183m) downstream. Alternatively, you can head up on a small path to the right of the stream, hoping to find a safer crossing higher up. Having crossed the stream, follow the fence up to pass its corner. Turn right up a wide path that rises out of Glen Etive.

WHAT TO LOOK OUT FOR

The lousewort is a low plant with purple flowers, which slightly resembles heather but flowers earlier, in June and July. Its less common white variety outnumbers the pink on the way up Lairig Gartain. On the Etive side of the pass, only the pink form is seen. Once past the top of Lairig Eilde, almost all the plants are white. This would indicate that the very tops of the two passes are barriers to this plant, allowing separate valley types to develop.

WHILE YOU'RE THERE

The Glencoe Folk Museum occupies a heather-thatched house in the centre of the village. It has items of interest rather than value, such as china, toys and medical utensils from the Victorian age, and weapons that were hidden away after the Battle of Culloden.

❹ The path ascends to the left of the stream, passing several waterfalls. Eventually it crosses the stream, now very much smaller, then continues straight ahead, crossing the col well to the right of its lowest point. A large cairn marks the top of the path.

❺ The new, descending stream is also, confusingly, the Allt Lairig Eilde. The path crosses it by a wide, shallow ford and goes down its left bank. A mile (1.6km) further on, the path recrosses, using large boulders as stepping stones. It runs down to join the A82 near the cairn that marks the entry into Glen Coe.

❻ Cross the road, and the river beyond, to join the old Glencoe road at an arched culvert. Turn right along the firm track, which soon rejoins the new road, then cross diagonally, on to a damp path. This runs to the right of the new road, then recrosses. It soon rejoins the A82 opposite the beginning of the walk.

WHERE TO EAT AND DRINK

The Kings House Hotel was built in 1590 as a hunting lodge for James VI (later James I of England). But its status as a 'king's house' dates from 1799, when a squad of redcoats was stationed there to protect travellers. Kingshouse was an overnight stop for the drovers bringing cattle south to market every autumn. The green flats, popular today as an informal camp ground, were overnight grazing. Today it's a much-appreciated stop-off for people on the West Highland Way, and for hillwalkers, climbers and skiers.

Into the Lost Valley

A rugged waterfall walk into the hidden hollow where the MacDonalds hid their stolen cows.

DISTANCE 2.75 miles (4.4km) **MINIMUM TIME** 2hrs 15min

ASCENT/GRADIENT 1,050ft (320m) ▲▲▲ **LEVEL OF DIFFICULTY** +++

PATHS Rugged and stony, stream to wade through

LANDSCAPE Crags and mountains

SUGGESTED MAP OS Explorer 384 Glen Coe & Glen Etive

START/FINISH Grid reference: NN 168569

DOG FRIENDLINESS Dogs must be reasonably fit and agile

PARKING Lower of two roadside parking places opposite Gearr Aonach (middle one of Three Sisters)

PUBLIC TOILETS Glencoe village

The romantically named Lost Valley is 'Coire Gabhail' in Gaelic, the 'Corrie of Booty'. Here, during the centuries leading up to the famous massacre of 1692, the MacDonalds hid their stolen cattle when the owners came storming in over the Moor of Rannoch with torch and claymore. It seems incredible that even the sure-footed black cattle of the clans could have been persuaded up the slope to Coire Gabhail. The corrie entrance is blocked by two old landslides from the face of Gearr Aonach, the middle hill of Glen Coe's Three Sisters.

Noble Profession of Cattle Thief

The economic system of Highland Scotland, until 1745, was based on the keeping and the stealing of cattle. It was an unsettled and dangerous lifestyle, and its artform was the verse of the bard who celebrated the most ingenious or violent acts of thievery and kept track of blood feuds.

The clan, gathered under its chieftain, was an organisation for protecting its own glen and for stealing from its neighbours. The MacDonalds of Glen Coe were particularly good at it. They raided right across the country, passing the fringes of the Cairngorms to steal from Aberdeenshire and Moray. In 1689, when Campbell of Glen Lyon was a guest in the house of MacIan, chief of Glen Coe, his cold blue eyes may have dwelt on a particular cooking pot. Twice in the previous ten years, MacIan had come raiding into Glen Lyon, dishonoured the women by cutting off their hair and, on the second occasion, stolen that pot from Campbell's own mother.

The Massacre

By the late 1600s, the clan and the claymore were being replaced by a legal system backed by the central government and its army. But because they were so good at cattle thieving, the MacDonalds of Glen Coe continued the practice long after everyone else had, reluctantly, started to move into the modern world of cash. As a result, the government decided to make an example of them.

GLEN COE

On a cold February day, a squad of soldiers arrived in the valley. Traditional hospitality meant that even its leader from Glen Lyon, a Campbell and an enemy, was welcomed into the house of MacDonald. Five nights later, at a given signal, the soldiers rose and murdered their hosts. The Glen Coe Massacre was either incompetent or mercifully half-hearted. Of the valley's population of 300, just 40 were killed, with the remainder escaping through the snow to the Lost Valley and other high corries.

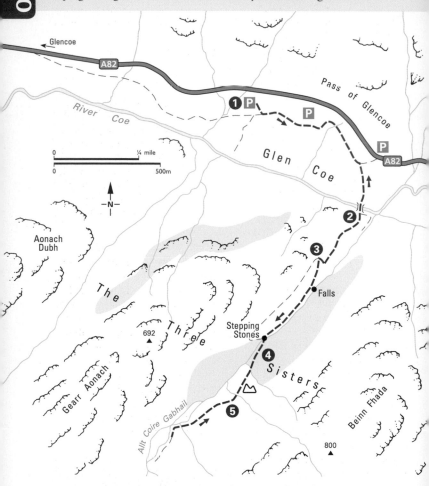

WALK 70 DIRECTIONS

❶ From the uphill corner of the car park, a faint path slants down to the old road, which is now a well-used wide path. Head up the valley for about 650yds (594m). With the old road continuing as a green track ahead, your path now bends down to the right. It has been rebuilt, with the bog

problem solved by scraping down to the bedrock. The path reaches the gorge where the River Coe runs in a geological dyke of softer rock. Descend here on a steep wooden step ladder, to cross a spectacular footbridge.

❷ The ascent out of the gorge is on a bare rock staircase. Above, the path runs through regenerating birch wood, which can be very wet on the legs; sheep and deer have been excluded from the wood with a temporary fence. Emerge from this through a high gate. The path, rebuilt in places, runs uphill for 60yds (55m). Here it bends left; an inconspicuous alternative path continues uphill, which can be used to bypass the narrow path of the main route.

3 The main route contours into the gorge of the Allt Coire Gabhail. It is narrow with steep drops below. Where there is an alternative of rock slabs and a narrow path just below, the slabs are more secure. You will hear waterfalls, then two fine ones come into view ahead. After passing these, continue between boulders to where the main path bends left to cross the stream below a boulder the size of a small house. (A small path runs on up to right of the stream, but leads nowhere useful.) The river here is wide and fairly shallow. Five or six stepping stones usually allow dry crossing. If the water is above the stones, then it's safer to wade alongside them; if the water is more than knee-deep the crossing should not be attempted.

4 A well-built path continues uphill, now with the stream on its right. After 100yds (91m) a lump of rock blocks the way. The path follows a slanting ramp up its right-hand side. It continues uphill, still rebuilt in places, passing above the boulder pile that blocks the valley, the result of two large rockfalls from under Gearr Aonach opposite. At the top of the rockpile the path levels, giving a good view into the Lost Valley.

5 Drop gently to the valley's gravel floor. The stream vanishes into the gravel, to reappear below the boulder pile on the other side. Note where the path arrives at the gravel, as it becomes invisible at that point. Wander up the valley to where the stream vanishes, 0.25 mile (400m) ahead. Anywhere beyond this point is more serious hillwalking than you have done up to now on this walk. Return to the path and follow it back to the start of the walk.

Ariundle Oakwoods and the Elements of Chemistry

Through the shades of green Sunart to the hillside site of an old lead mine.

DISTANCE 7 miles (11.3km)	**MINIMUM TIME** 3hrs 45min
ASCENT/GRADIENT 950ft (290m) ▲▲▲	**LEVEL OF DIFFICULTY** +++

PATHS Good through woodland, sketchy on open hill, no stiles

LANDSCAPE Ancient oakwood, open and remote hill ground

SUGGESTED MAP OS Explorer 391 Ardgour & Strontian

START/FINISH Grid reference: NM 826633

DOG FRIENDLINESS Keep on lead in reserve

PARKING Nature Reserve car park at Ariundle

PUBLIC TOILETS Tourist Information Centre, Strontian

What does Strontian have in common with the hamlet of Ytterby in Sweden, with Paris (Lutetia) and Copenhagen (Hafnia), with the planet Uranus and the Sun (Helios)? Chemical elements – the fundamental materials of nature. Seventeen of them are named after places, including ytterbium, lutetium, hafnium, uranium, helium – and strontium.

Davy the Namer

A new mineral was discovered in the lead ores of Strontian in 1793, and named strontites. Sir Humphrey Davy visited the mines in 1808 and isolated the new element strontium. Davy is remembered as the inventor of the safety lamp for miners, but he also identified and named the elements calcium, magnesium and chlorine. Strontium (Sr) comes in at number 38 in the list of chemical elements. When heated its salts burn with a crimson flame, and it is used in making fireworks. The radioactive form strontium 90 does not occur in nature at Strontian or anywhere else, but is produced in nuclear explosions, including the Chernobyl reactor disaster. Because of its chemical similarity to calcium, strontium 90 is absorbed into the bones, where its radioactive breakdown damages the bone marrow.

The Older New York

The lead mines around Strontian, including the Bellsgrove mine reached on this walk, opened in the early 18th century. The villages around them came to be known as New York, after the York Building Company that built them. Some 60 tons of Strontian lead – one tenth of the year's output – went in 1753 to roof the new castle at Inveraray (see Walk 57). As the more accessible veins were worked out, these remote mines became uneconomic and eventually closed in 1871. They have been reopened in a small way for the extraction of the mineral barytes. The element barium, a chemical relative of calcium and strontium, is used in drilling muds for the oil industry.

On its way to the lead mine and the waterfalls of Strontian Glen, the walk passes through the Ariundle National Nature Reserve. In the mountains, the native wild wood of Scotland was the Scots pine (see Walk 68). Here on the warm, damp sea coast, the wild wood is of oak. The Ariundle oakwood owes its survival to human interference. The livestock and deer that destroyed Scotland's forest were kept out so that the oaks could be coppiced – harvested on a seven-year cycle. The timber went to the iron smelters of Bonawe on Loch Etive and the bark to the tanners.

The wild oakwood is being repaired, with the felling out of commercial spruce. Beneath the dense canopy of leaves, it is carpeted in soft, glossy moss that even climbs the trees, and rich in ferns and primitive plants called liverworts. While we expect the natural world to be green, it's not often quite so green as Ariundle.

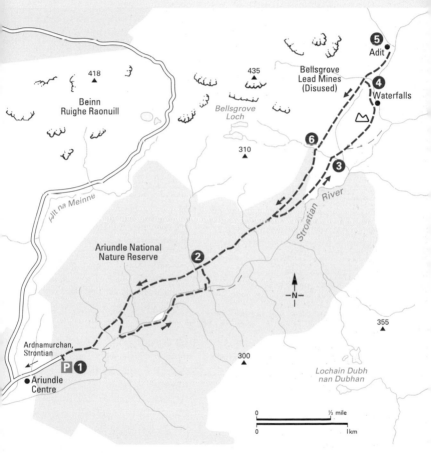

WALK 71 DIRECTIONS

1 From the car park, continue along the track into oakwoods. After 0.25 mile (400m), ignore a pony path on the right. In another 0.25 mile (400m) a footpath turns off right. It crosses the Strontian River and heads upstream along

it. After a pleasant 0.75 mile (1.2km) it recrosses the river, following a duckboard section to rejoin the oakwood track.

2 Turn right, away from the car park, to reach a high gate in a deer fence. The track immediately forks. Take the downward branch

WALK 71

WHERE TO EAT AND DRINK

The Ariundle Centre, 0.5 mile (800m) from the start of the walk, has craft displays and a café with excellent home-made cakes. Dogs are welcome in the covered outdoor eating area.

on the right to emerge into open grazings at river level. The track passes through a high gate and ends at a gateway and stream.

❸ Ford the stream on to a rough path. This crosses two more small streams, then forks (small cairn). The lower, right-hand branch continues alongside the Strontian River, but take the left-hand one, which is quite faint. It slants up to the left to a solitary holly tree. Here it turns straight uphill for 50yds (46m), then bends right to slant up as before, passing 200yds (183m) below a bare rock knoll. The remains of wooden steps are in the path and a few cairns stand beside it. It steepens slightly to pass below a small crag with three different trees growing out of it – rowan, hazel and oak. With a large stream and waterfalls ahead, the path turns uphill to the brink of the small gorge. Above the waterfalls, the slope eases. Just above, the path reaches the broken dam wall of a former reservoir.

❹ A green path runs across the slope just above. You can turn right on this, heading up beside

the stream for about 0.25 mile (400m). Here you will find a spoil heap; a heather bank marks the entrance to an adit – a mine tunnel running into the hill.

❺ Return along the green path past Point ❹, with the remains of the Bellsgrove Lead Mines above and below. The path improves into a track, following a stream down a small and slantwise side valley. As this stream turns down to the left, the track contours forward, to cross a wooded stream valley by a high footbridge above a waterfall.

WHILE YOU'RE THERE

Ardnamurchan is one of the most green and beautiful corners of the Highlands, with empty beaches and wildlife cruises, either escorted or in hire boats. The remote Ardnamurchan Lighthouse, built in the 1840s, was designed by Alan Stevenson, the uncle of Robert Louis Stevenson. It is the westernmost point on the Scottish mainland and houses the Kingdom of Light visitor centre (April–October). You can see its 0.5 megawatt lens, as well as spot whales and dolphins if you're lucky.

❻ A wide, smooth track continues ahead through a gate. After 0.5 mile (800m) it rejoins the outward route at the edge of the nature reserve. Follow the track back to eventually reach the car park at Ariundle.

WHAT TO LOOK OUT FOR

You're unlikely to spot the shy pine marten, though there's a stuffed one behind the bar at the Nether Lochaber Hotel, on the mainland side of the Corran Ferry. The animal is like a large furry ferret and lives in the trees, eating baby squirrels. (Given the chance, pine martens actually prefer chocolate and jam.) A notice board on the nature trail points out, after you've passed it, that the duckboard section of the path is a place where they sometimes leave droppings – imagine a very small dog that's been on a diet of black treacle and you get the idea.

Grey Mare's Tail and Mamore Lodge

A waterfall, a shooting lodge and a ramble down the West Highland Way.

DISTANCE 3.5 miles (5.7km)   **MINIMUM TIME** 2hrs 15min

ASCENT/GRADIENT 984ft (300m) ▲▲▲   **LEVEL OF DIFFICULTY** +++

PATHS Well-made paths, one steep, rough ascent, no stiles

LANDSCAPE Birchwoods leading to long views along Loch Leven

SUGGESTED MAP OS Explorer 384 Glen Coe & Glen Etive or 392 Ben Nevis & Fort William

START/FINISH Grid reference: NN 187622 on OS Explorer 384

DOG FRIENDLINESS Off lead unless sheep near by

PARKING Grey Mare's Tail car park, Kinlochleven

PUBLIC TOILETS Kinlochleven, at bridge over River Leven

Aluminium is a very common metal: around eight per cent of the earth's crust is made up of it. But, it's very reactive, which means that it's extremely difficult to extract the aluminium atoms out of the ore called bauxite. There is no chemical method for this process. Instead, it's done by dissolving the ore in molten cryolite (a fluoride mineral) and applying vast quantities of electricity. As a result, aluminium processing doesn't take place where you find the bauxite, but where you find the electricity, with lots of water coming down steep hillsides, and a deep-water harbour at the bottom, such as Kinlochleven.

The village of Kinlochleven was built around the smelter. Two lochs above have been dammed for hydro-electricity, and six huge pipes bring the water down from a control station above the Devil's Staircase footpath.

Pipeline or Path

A pipeline on the OS Landranger map is a dotted line, rather like a path. And it may be that the path of this walk happened by mistake, as walkers mistook the pipeline for a path, walked along it and so created the path that they thought was there in the first place.

The pipeline path leads from the outflow of Loch Eilde Mor, around the head of Loch Leven along the 1,100ft (335m) contour, giving superb views towards the Pap of Glencoe and the loch's foot. Eventually, it carries Loch Eilde's water to the Blackwater Reservoir.

Why has the water from Loch Eilde been taken all the way round this hillside to the Blackwater Reservoir, instead of straight down to the turbines where it's actually needed? You need to glance across the valley at the six descending pipes for the answer. At the foot of those huge reinforced pipes the water is under 30 tons per square foot (300 tonnes/sq m) of pressure. A second such set from Loch Eilde would cost far more than the much longer, unpressurised pipe to the other reservoir.

The Kinlochmore smelter started as one of the largest in the world, but by the end of the 1900s it was the world's smallest. It closed in 2000, although its turbines continue to generate electricity, which is now diverted to the smelter at Fort William or into the National Grid. The smelter had been the reason for Kinlochleven, and its main employer. Projects to keep Kinlochleven alive include the fine, newly constructed path system, the visitor centre and the Atlas Brewery on the site where carbon electrical connectors were once made.

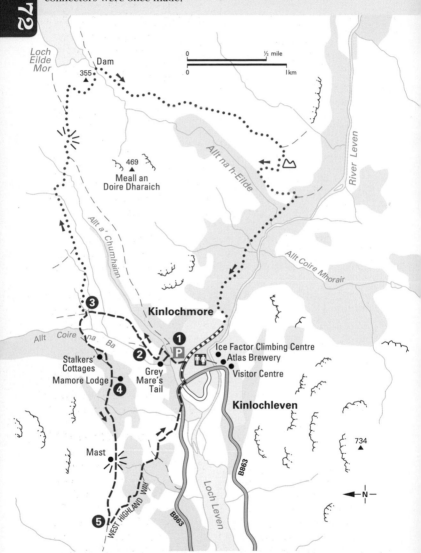

WALK 72 DIRECTIONS

❶ A smooth gravel path leads up out of the car park to multicoloured waymarkers pointing left. The path rises to a view through trees of the

Grey Mare's Tail waterfall, then descends to a footbridge. Here turn left (blue waymarker) to visit the foot of the spectacular waterfall, then return to take the path on the right (white, yellow and green waymarker). Follow the stream up for 100yds (91m), then turn left at a waymarker. The path, quite steep and loose, zig-zags up through birches to reach more open ground.

2 Here the path forks. Take the right-hand branch, with a yellow and green waymarker, to pass under power lines. The path runs through scattered birch to a gate in a deer fence, then bends left to cross over two streams. Immediately after the second stream is another junction.

3 The confusing waymarker here has eight arrows in four colours. Turn left, following a white arrow slightly downhill, to cross a footbridge above a waterfall and red granite rocks. The path leads up under birches. Here the ground cover includes the aromatic bog myrtle, which can be used to discourage midges. When the path reaches a track, turn left. Below the track is a tin deer used by stalkers for target practice: it's more convenient than the real thing as it doesn't wander off just when you're creeping up on it. A signed footpath bypasses the Stalkers' Cottages on the left, then rejoins the track beyond, to a junction above Mamore Lodge.

4 Keep ahead, above the lodge, climbing gently past two tin huts, self-catering accommodation labelled 'stable' and 'bothy'. At the high point of the track there is a TV mast on the right, a bench

on the left and a view along Loch Leven ahead. The track descends gently, with slabs of whitish quartzite above. The wide path of the West Highland Way (WHW) can be seen below and gradually rises to join the track, with a large waymarker planted in a cairn.

5 Turn left down the West Highland Way path, which drops into the woods below. Watch out for a junction where the main path seems to double back to the right; take the smaller path, continuing ahead with a WHW waymarker. After crossing the tarred access track of Mamore Lodge, the path fords a small stream to reach the village. Turn left along the pavement and fork left into Wades Road to regain the car park.

EXTENDING THE WALK

For a longer walk, turn right instead of left at Point **3** on a path rising to a high track. Turn right on this and follow until it crosses a wide pass. After 0.25 mile (400m) downhill, with Loch Eilde Mor in sight ahead, turn right on a cairned path to the dam at the loch's outflow. Turn right on a wet track following a concrete pipeline. After 1 mile (1.6km), with the track running below the pipeline, turn down right on a steep path to join a path in woods above River Leven. Follow it to the right, into Kinlochmore.

Blair Castle and Glen Tilt

*Following Queen Victoria into the great
through route of the Grampians.*

DISTANCE 6.5 miles (10.4km)   **MINIMUM TIME** 3hrs 15min

ASCENT/GRADIENT 852ft (250m) ▲▲▲   **LEVEL OF DIFFICULTY** ✚✚✚

PATHS Estate tracks and smooth paths, 1 stile

LANDSCAPE Castle grounds, woodland, wild river valley and mountains

SUGGESTED MAP OS Explorers 386 Pitlochry & Loch Tummel;
394 Atholl

START/FINISH Grid reference: NN 866662 (on Explorer 386)

DOG FRIENDLINESS Keep lead on open grazing land

PARKING Blair Castle main car park

PUBLIC TOILETS Blair Atholl Centre; Blair Castle

WARNING Track goes through firing range and is closed on a few days each
year. Consult Atholl Estate Ranger service

Since humans first arrived, Tilt has been a natural highway. Robert the Bruce marched down Glen Tilt in 1306 on his way to a minor defeat near Tyndrum. Some 200 years later James V and Mary, Queen of Scots attended a deer drive in 1529, but the next monarch to complete the whole route was Queen Victoria. She came this way with Prince Albert on the third of their 'great expeditions' from Balmoral. Along with the Christmas tree and the 'Scottish Baronial' style of architecture, multi-day hill walks were ideas introduced by the Prince Consort. Today we'd call it backpacking, except that then the packs were carried by ponies and so were the people for much of the way. Even so, 69 miles (111km) from Dalwhinnie to Balmoral in a day was a considerable trek. Two bagpipers forded the Tarff side-stream waist deep, playing all the time, while the Queen came behind on her pony, led by John Brown.

An Angry Duke

Kings and cattle thieves, soldiers and shepherds have used Glen Tilt for thousands of years, and its right-of-way status is self-evident. But in 1840, the then Duke of Atholl, whose castle lay at its foot, felt he could make his own law. He did, after all, boast Britain's only private army. He tried to turn back a botanical expedition lead by Professor Balfour. The professor won the right to walk here, and his victory is commemorated in a ballad:

> *There's ne'er a kilted chiel*
> *Shall drive us back this day, man.*
> *It's justice and it's public richt*
> *We'll pass Glen Tilt afore the nicht,*
> *For Dukes shall we care ae bawbee?*
> *The road's as free to you and me*
> *As to his Grace himself, man.*

GLEN TILT

Responsible Access

Today a general right of responsible access to all hill ground has been made law by the Scottish Parliament. An 'Access Code' defines responsible access. During the deer-stalking season, from mid-August to October, polite and reasonable requests from the estate will be respected by hill walkers. Such a request is made at Gilbert's Bridge (Point ❹).

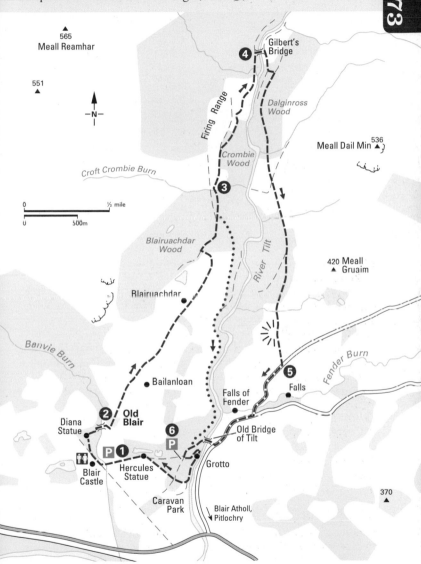

WALK 73 DIRECTIONS

❶ Turn right in front of the castle to a six-way signpost, and bear right for a gate into Diana's Grove. Bear left on a wide path to Diana herself. Turn right on a path that leads to a giant redwood tree and then bear left, to cross Banvie Burn on a footbridge alongside a road bridge. Soon a gate leads you to the road.

2 You are now at Old Blair. Follow Minigaig Street ahead uphill. It eventually becomes a track and enters forest. Ignore a track on the left and, in another 0.25 mile (400m), fork right. In 60yds (55m) you pass a path down to the right with a green waymarker. This is the return route if the firing range ahead is closed. Otherwise keep ahead to emerge from the trees at the firing range gate.

3 A red flag flies here if the range is in use, but read the notice carefully as on most firing days the track route through the range may be used. Follow the main track gently downhill, well below the firing range targets, until you get to the riverside, then fork right to reach Gilbert's Bridge.

4 Cross and turn right over a cattle grid. Follow the track for 220yds (201m), then turn left up

a steep little path under trees to a stile. A green track now runs down-valley with fine views. It passes along the top of a larch wood. Once through a gate into the birchwood, keep on the main track, gently uphill. After the gateway out of the wood, there's a view across Blair Castle to Schiehallion. Another gate leads to a gravel track, then a tarred road.

5 Turn right, down a long hill, crossing some waterfalls on the way down. At the foot of the hill turn right, signed 'Old Blair', to cross the Old Bridge of Tilt, then turn left into a car park.

6 Just to the right of a signboard, yellow waymarkers indicate a path that passes under trees to the River Tilt. Turn right through an exotic grotto until wooden steps on the right lead up to the corner of a caravan park. Head directly away from the river under pines. Ignore a track on the right and, at the corner of the caravan park, keep ahead under larch trees following a faint path. Cross a track to take the big beech avenue towards Blair Castle. Bear left when you reach a statue of Hercules, passing the Hercules Garden to the front of the castle.

The Black Gold of the North Sea

A walk around the old fishing port to discover the tragedy and prosperity that oil has brought to Aberdeen.

DISTANCE 3.75 miles (6km)	**MINIMUM TIME** 2hrs

ASCENT/GRADIENT Negligible ▲▲▲   **LEVEL OF DIFFICULTY** ✦✦✦

PATHS Mainly pavements; along beach (underwater at high tide)

LANDSCAPE Old fishing port

SUGGESTED MAP OS Explorer 406 Aberdeen & Banchory

START/FINISH Grid reference: NJ 954067

DOG FRIENDLINESS Keep on lead

PARKING Esplanade at Fun Beach or Linx Ice Arena

PUBLIC TOILETS Upperkirkgate, opposite Marischal College

Aberdeen was a major maritime centre throughout the 19th century, starting when a group of local entrepreneurs purchased an ageing paddle tug and launched it as the first steam-powered trawler.

From small beginnings the steam trawling industry expanded and by 1933 Aberdeen was Scotland's top fishing port, employing nearly 3,000 men with 300 vessels sailing from its harbour. By the time oil was coming on stream, much of the massive trawling fleet had relocated to Peterhead. An early morning visit to the fish market will verify that Aberdeen still brings in substantial catches, but the tugs, safety vessels and supply ships for the offshore rigs packed into the harbour far outnumber the trawlers.

Black Gold

Geologists had speculated about the existence of oil and gas in the North Sea since the middle of the 20th century, but tapping its deep and inhospitable waters was another story. However, with the Middle Eastern oil sheiks becoming more aware of the political and economic power of their oil reserves and government threats of rationing, the industry began to consider the North Sea as a viable source of oil. Exploration commenced in the 1960s and the first major find in the British sector was in November 1970 in the Forties field, 110 miles (177km) east of Aberdeen.

By late 1975, after years of intense construction, the hundreds of miles of pipes, massive oilshore rigs, supply ships, helicopters and an army of oil workers were finally in place. In Aberdeen, at BP's (British Petroleum) headquarters, the Queen pressed the button that would set the whole thing moving. Oil flowed from the rig directly to the refinery at far-away Grangemouth. While many ports have suffered decline, Aberdeen remains busy due to oil trade, as the influx of people connected with the industry and a subsequent rise in property prices have brought prosperity.

The Human Cost

The human cost of oil prosperity was brutally brought home on the night of 6 July, 1988. A huge fire lit the sky as the Piper Alpha oil platform,

120 miles (193km) offshore, exploded. Helicopters flew all night bringing the dead and injured to Aberdeen. In all 167 died; many of the survivors live with the scars of that night and the horrific memories of escaping the burning rig. A memorial to the dead stands in Hazlehead Park. The subsequent inquiry revealed that safety regulations had been ignored. The industry learned a bitter lesson, and the rigs are now safer places to work.

The industry still supports about 47,000 jobs locally and known reserves are such that oil will continue to flow well into the 21st century.

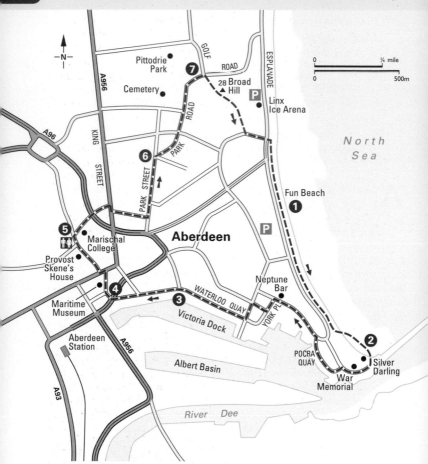

WALK 74 DIRECTIONS

❶ From your parking place, head southwards on the promenade, walking beside the shore with the sea on your left. Go down the slipway on to the beach for a short distance to wooden steps on the right and leave the beach to enter a children's play area. (But if the tide is high at the slipway:

clamber over the sea wall on your right, and pass along a row of fishermen's cottages.)

❷ Walk past the Silver Darling restaurant and into the harbour area. Continue past the war memorial, keeping the blue storage tanks to your left, and along Pocra Quay as it bends right. Turn left into York Street and then at the Neptune bar, turn left into York Place. Take the first right, the first left and second right to emerge on Waterloo Quay.

❸ Where Waterloo Quay becomes Commerce Street, turn left into Regent Quay and then at the T-junction cross the dual carriageway at pedestrian lights. Turn left and then first right to reach Aberdeen Maritime Museum and John Ross's House, Provost of Aberdeen between 1710 and 1711). If you have time visit the Maritime Museum.

❹ From here head along Exchequer Row, to turn left into Union Street. At once turn right into Broad Street, where you will find Provost Skene's House on the left, reached by passing underneath an office block.

❺ Continue ahead past Marischal College (which houses the Marischal Museum), turn right into Littlejohn Street, and then cross North Street. At the end of Meal Market Street turn right into King Street and then left into Frederick Street. At the junction with Park Street turn left and keep walking ahead until the road crosses a railway.

❻ Shortly after the crossing is a roundabout. Head slightly right along Park Road. Follow the road through the Trinity Cemetery and towards Pittodrie Park, which is the home of Aberdeen Football Club, to the junction with Golf Road.

❼ At the junction with Golf Road, turn up right, on the well-made path over Broad Hill. There are wide views of the sea and Aberdeen. At the path end, turn left to a roundabout with subtropical plants on the Esplanade. The shoreline promenade leads back to your car.

The Inspirational Landscape of Auchenblae

Walk through the fields and woods of the Howe of Mearns, which inspired a Scottish writer.

DISTANCE *6.75 miles (11km)*   **MINIMUM TIME** *3hrs 30min*

ASCENT/GRADIENT *459ft (140m)* ▲▲▲   **LEVEL OF DIFFICULTY** ✦✦✦

PATHS *Established footpaths, overgrown woodland tracks*

LANDSCAPE *Acres of arable fields and cool forests*

SUGGESTED MAP *OS Explorer 396 Stonehaven, Inverbervie & Lawrencekirk*

START/FINISH *Grid reference: NO 727787*

DOG FRIENDLINESS *Fallen trees make it unsuitable except for fit dogs*

PARKING *On street in Auchenblae*

PUBLIC TOILETS *Off main street in Auchenblae and at Drumtochty Castle car park*

…you'd waken with the peewits crying across the hills, deep and deep, crying in the heart of you … almost you'd cry for that, the beauty of it and the sweetness of the Scottish land and skies'
'Sunset Song', 1932

Those words were written by James Leslie Mitchell and sums up the immense love and affection he had for his native Howe of the Mearns in north-east Scotland. It is fertile land, south of Aberdeen. This walk introduces you to this little-walked part of the country, an area that will forever be associated with the author. Mitchell is better known by his pen name of Lewis Grassic Gibbon. He was born in 1901 into a crofting family and had no illusions about the toughness of life on the land. He once wrote: 'My mother used to hap me in a plaid in harvest time and leave me in the lea of a stook while she harvested.' In his books he portrayed the breakdown of crofting life, but did not gloss over its hardships.

Crofter to Author

Gibbon became a journalist at the age of 16 and joined the *Aberdeen Journal*, and later the *Scottish Farmer* in Glasgow. He became ill and moved back home to work in the fields before joining the army as a clerk, later moving into the RAF. He travelled to Central America to see the remains of the Maya civilisation, and later claimed that his digestion was forever affected by the enforced local diet of maize.

Gibbon left the forces in 1929 and returned to Britain, living in the south of England and trying to make his name as a writer. His first book was *Sunset Song*, set in the Howe of the Mearns and telling the tale of Chris Guthrie, who was torn between her desire to escape her small community and her love for the land. He wrote it in six weeks. It was the first of a trilogy, known as *A Scots Quair* (or 'quire' – a volume) and was rapidly followed by the other books *Cloud Howe* (1933) and *Grey Granite* (1934).

AUCHENBLAE

A Short but Prolific Life

Gibbon was extremely disciplined and driven – it was as if he knew he did not have much time to make his name. He divided each day into three and aimed to write 1,500 words in each session. He made some mistakes at first and tried to sell some of his short stories to the wrong type of magazines. However, H G Wells took an interest in his work and suggested different publications for him to try. Lewis Grassic Gibbon eventually died in 1935 of a duodenal ulcer. He was just 34 and had written 16 books.

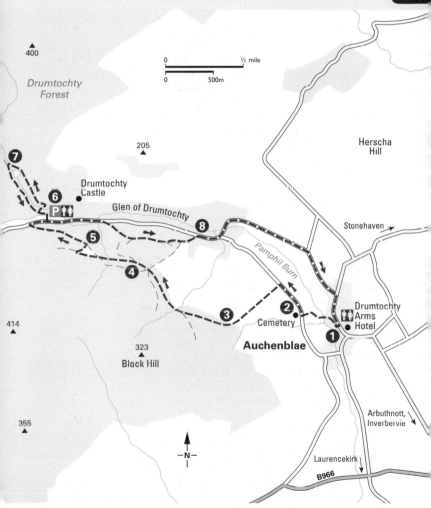

WALK 75 DIRECTIONS

1 Half-way up the steep High Street, turn left, signed 'Woodland Walks'. The lane runs steeply downhill and crosses Pamphil Burn beside a play area; then runs uphill to a T-junction.

2 Turn right to walk past a cemetery and then take a grassy track on the left. The track runs up between arable fields to reach the plantation above. Scramble over or past a rusty gate (take care here) and then walk through long grass to reach a track.

❸ Turn right and follow the thickly vegetated track along the bottom edge of the forest. There are a couple of fallen trees to clamber over or walk around. At a wider gravel track, turn right and then continue with fields still visible through the trees below. Above where these fields end, ignore a side-track up left. In another 220yds (200m), fork left on a fainter track.

❹ The track runs level then gently uphill. Where a pylon rises on the right-hand side of the track, strike downhill through the cleared ground under the electric wires – this is awkward going, with brushwood underfoot.

❺ At the bottom left corner of the cleared ground, a small path strikes left taking you into the forest. The path becomes clearer as it slants gradually down to join the valley road below. Turn sharp right along the road, passing a huge Sitka spruce tree, to Drumtochty car park on the left.

❻ Take the track through the car park, bending up left past toilets. After a stiff climb on tarmac, turn right (red waymarker) down a zig-zag path to a mill lade. Turn left along this, to a footbridge above a weir. A little way upstream, the path climbs out of the steep valley, and contours upstream to pass above a small reservoir.

❼ At the track beyond, turn left and return to Drumtochty car park. Turn left along the road until a path forks up right past a vehicle barrier. This leads to a forest track, which joins a larger one. Keep ahead, now level, until the track descends left to rejoin the road below.

❽ Turn right and walk along the road, to a junction where you turn left, signed 'Auchenblae', and cross Pamphil Burn. At the following junction bear right, to reach the top end of Auchenblae's High Street.

The Hidden Treasure of Stonehaven

A lovely walk along the cliffs to Dunnottar Castle, which once housed Scotland's crown jewels.

DISTANCE 3.5 miles (5.7km)	**MINIMUM TIME** 1hr 30min
ASCENT/GRADIENT 377ft (115m) ▲▲▲	**LEVEL OF DIFFICULTY** +++
PATHS Cliff edges, metalled tracks, forest paths	
LANDSCAPE Striking seascapes, ancient castle	
SUGGESTED MAP OS Explorer 396 Stonehaven & Inverbervie	
START/FINISH Grid reference: NO 874858	
DOG FRIENDLINESS Keep on lead along cliffs	
PARKING Market Square, Stonehaven	
PUBLIC TOILETS Market Square and harbour, Stonehaven	

There's more than a dash of romance on this windswept walk to Dunnottar Castle. One of Scotland's lesser known castles, it is deliciously picturesque, a glowering ruin perched on cliff edge and sprayed by the chilly northern seas. It was the setting for one of the most fascinating and little known episodes in Scotland's history, for Dunnottar Castle was the hiding place of the country's greatest treasures – the crown jewels.

Symbols of Independence

Scotland's crown jewels are among the oldest in Europe. Also known as the Honours of Scotland, they comprise a crown, a sword of state and a silver sceptre. The crown was created in 1532 for James V. It is made of gold encrusted with precious stones and pearls, and rimmed with ermine. The sword was fashioned in 1507 for James IV and has a silver encrusted scabbard lined with red velvet, while the sceptre, which was made in 1494 and lengthened in 1536, has a pearl-topped globe of rock crystal which some say has magical properties. Together they are powerful symbols of Scotland's independence, and today the Honours are on display at Edinburgh Castle, but you can only see them thanks to the bravery of some patriotic Scots.

Lost and Found

The Scottish regalia were taken to George Ogilvie at Dunnottar Castle when Cromwell invaded Scotland. Cromwell intended to destroy them, as he had done with the English crown jewels, but they were spirited away from Edinburgh for safe keeping. Cromwell came to Dunnottar and besieged the castle for nearly a year, but when it finally fell the jewels had gone. They had been smuggled out by the wife of the Revd James Granger, the minister of nearby Kineff, and her maid. They'd visited a friend in the castle and managed to leave with the jewels hidden in their clothes. They took the Honours to Kineff, further down the coast, where they hid them, sometimes stashing them under the church floor, sometimes pushing them under their bed. The jewels remained there for eight years, and though

STONEHAVEN

Cromwell's men tried everything they could to find them, imprisoning the Grangers, and even tortured Ogilvie's wife, no one gave the secret away. Go to Kinneff Old Church and you'll see a memorial to the Grangers.

The crown jewels were returned to Edinburgh after the Restoration in 1660. Following the Act of Union with England in 1707, they were walled up in a sealed room in a tower in Edinburgh Castle. People eventually forgot where they were and many believed they had been stolen by the English. It was Sir Walter Scott who rediscovered them, locked inside a chest covered with dust.

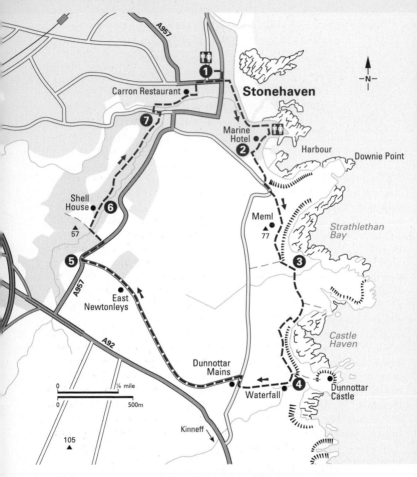

WALK 76 DIRECTIONS

❶ From the Market Square in Stonehaven, walk back on to Allardyce Street, turn right and cross over the road. Turn left up Market Lane and, when you come to the beach, turn right to cross over the footbridge. Turn right at a sign to Dunnottar Castle to

reach the harbour. Cross here to continue down Shorehead, on the east side of the harbour. Pass the Marine Hotel, then turn right into Wallis Wynd.

❷ Turn left into Castle Street. It becomes a steep path, to emerge at the main road, then maintain your direction walking along the road until it bends. Continue ahead, following the enclosed tarmac path, between arable fields and past a war memorial on the right-hand side. Cross the middle of the field, then above Strathlethan Bay.

3 The path turns right across the middle of a field and then over a footbridge. You now pass a path going down to Castle Haven and continue following the main path around the cliff edge. Cross another footbridge and bear uphill. You'll soon reach some steps on your left that run down to Dunnottar Castle.

4 Your walk bears right here inland, past a waterfall, through a kissing gate and then up to a house. Pass the house to the road into Stonehaven by the Dunnottar Mains, turn right, then take the first turning left, to walk alongside the farm. Follow this wide, metalled track past East Newtonleys on the left-hand side, to the main A957.

5 Turn right and walk downhill, then take the first road on the leftt signed 'Dunnottar Church'. Follow this over the Burn of Glaslow to a path on the right signed 'Carron Gate'. Take this path into the woods but at once fork right, following the lower path that runs by the burn. Continue until you reach the Shell House on the left.

6 Just past the Shell House, continue along the lower path, which turns uphill to join a higher path. Bear right here, to reach the end of the woods at Carron Gate. Walk through a housing estate to join Low Wood Road and the River Carron.

7 Turn left, then right to cross the footbridge with the green railings. Turn right and walk by the water. You'll soon pass the striking art deco Carron Restaurant on the left-hand side, and then come to a cream-coloured iron bridge. Bear left here, then turn first right to return to the Market Square.

Overleaf: Stonehaven harbour in the Old Town (Walk 76)

Banks of the Caledonian Canal

A walk alongside — and underneath — Thomas Telford's masterpiece of civil engineering.

DISTANCE 4.5 miles (7.2km)	**MINIMUM TIME** 1hr 45min

ASCENT/GRADIENT 100ft (30m) ▲▲▲ **LEVEL OF DIFFICULTY** ✦✦✦

PATHS Wide tow paths, no stiles

LANDSCAPE Banks of wide canal, shore of tidal loch

SUGGESTED MAP OS Explorer 392 Ben Nevis & Fort William

START/FINISH Grid reference: NN 097768

DOG FRIENDLINESS Sensible dogs off lead on tow path

PARKING Kilmallie Hall, Corpach

PUBLIC TOILETS None on route

The first survey for a coast-to-coast canal was made in 1767 by James Watt, the steam engine inventor, in the aftermath of Culloden. The Commissioners of Forfeited Estates had land aplenty, and a canal fitted with their plans of bringing the Highlands into the industrialised world.

War Footing

But it was the Napoleonic War that finally sent the men with the wheelbarrows up to Fort William in 1803. Despite the fact that nature had already provided 38 miles (61km) of the route, the canal was still a tremendous feat of civil engineering. Roughly 200 million wheelbarrow loads of earth were shifted over the next 19 years. Each of its 29 locks was designed to accommodate the width and length of a 40-gun frigate of Nelson's navy, four aqueducts let streams and rivers pass below the waterway, and there was a dam on Loch Lochy and diversion of the rivers Oich and Lochy. Loch Oich needed to be deepened, and for this task a steam dredger had to be not just built, but invented and designed. And before a single turf was shifted, the first essential, a brewery was required to supply the thousands of thirsty navvies.

Thomas Telford

For this great enterprise, only one name was seriously considered: Thomas Telford. Scotland has a tradition of self-made men, but even here Telford's beginnings were unusually unhopeful. His destitute mother raised her boy supported by neighbours and by casual work as a milkmaid. Apprenticed to a stonemason, Telford worked on a new bridge for his home town of Langholm, while educating himself in Burns, Milton and chemistry from books lent by the local gentry. The poet laureate Robert Southey referred to him as 'Pontifex Maximus', the Biggest Bridge-builder.

As well as the old-style stone, Telford became a master of two entirely new techniques — the cast-iron arch and the first suspension bridges. While working on the Caledonian Canal, he was also building 600 miles (nearly 1,000km) of new roads and enlarging most of Scotland's harbours.

CORPACH

Waterways for the Future

Even Telford's masonry crumbles eventually, and after a century of neglect, the canal at the end of the 1900s was on the verge of closure. In 1996 the government promised £20 million for a complete refurbishment: 'Canals have a great future'. And for those without boats, the tow path has been resurfaced as a cycleway from coast to coast, with a new National Trail, the Great Glen Way, running in parallel.

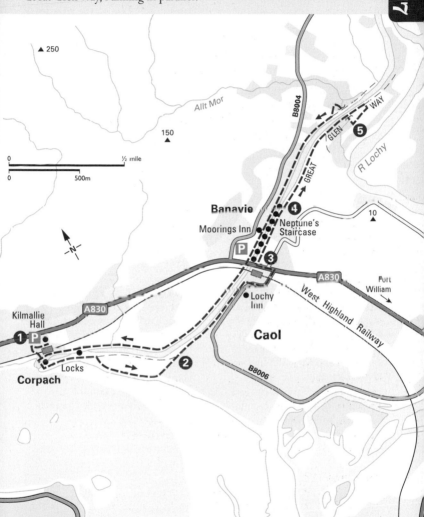

WALK 77 DIRECTIONS

1 Go down past Corpach Station to the canal and cross the sea lock that separates salt water from fresh water. Follow the canal (on your left) up past another lock, where a path on the right

has a blue cycle path sign and a Great Glen Way marker. It passes under tall sycamores to the shore. Follow the shoreline path past a football pitch and then turn left, across damp grass to the end of a back street. A path ahead leads up a wooded bank to the tow path.

❷ Turn right along the tow path, for 0.5 mile (800m). Just before the Banavie swing bridge, a path down to the right has a Great Glen Way marker. Follow waymarkers on street signs to a level crossing, then turn left towards the other swing bridge, the one with the road on it.

WHILE YOU'RE THERE

Much to Telford's distress, the canal was a loss-making enterprise from the day it opened. One reason was the coming of the railways. At Banavie, the West Highland Railway is Britain's most beautiful. During the summer, the steam-powered Jacobite Steam Train runs daily to Mallaig and back.

❸ Just before the bridge, turn right at signs for the Great Glen Way and the Great Glen Cycle Route and continue along the tow path to Neptune's Staircase. The fanciful name was given to the locks by Telford himself. The 60ft (18m) of ascent alongside the eight locks is the serious uphill part of this walk, but more serious for boats of course. It takes about 90 minutes to work through the system. As each lock fills, slow roiling currents come up from underneath, like bath water emptying but in reverse,

WHERE TO EAT AND DRINK

The Moorings Inn at Banavie offers restaurant and bar meals to canal users and visitors. On the other side of both the A830 and canal, the unassuming Lochy family pub has picnic tables and promises 'massive portions'. At the walk start, a Keystore shop on the main road sells hot pies and the Kilmallie Hall has a community garden with picnic tables to eat them at.

and as each empties, water forced under pressure into the banks emerges from the masonry in little fountains.

❹ A gate ends the basin above the locks. About 200yds (183m) later, a grey gate on the right leads to a dump for dead cars; ignore this one. Just 220yds (200m) later the canal crosses a little wooded valley, with a black fence on the right. Now comes a second grey gate. Go through, to a track turning back sharp right and descending to ford a small stream.

❺ On the right, the stream passes right under the canal in an arched tunnel, and alongside is a second tunnel which provides a walkers' way to the other side. Water from the canal drips into the tunnel, which has a fairly spooky atmosphere – try not to think of the large boats sailing directly over your head! At the tunnel's end, a track runs up to join the canal's northern tow path. Turn right, back down the tow path. After passing Neptune's Staircase, cross the A830 to a level crossing without warning lights. Continue along the right-hand tow path. After a mile (1.6km) the tow path track leads back to the Corpach double lock.

WHAT TO LOOK OUT FOR

From Fort William, Britain's biggest hill appears as a mere hump. The canalside, however, gives the best view into the great Northern Corrie of Ben Nevis. On its right-hand side, ranged one behind the other, rise the buttresses of the country's largest crag. Across the back runs a narrow edge of granite, linking it to the neighbouring Carn Mor Dearg. This arête is the mountaineers' preferred route to the big Ben.

The Nevis Gorge and its Waterfalls

*A walk beside Scotland's Himalayan lookalike
leading to an enormous waterfall.*

> **DISTANCE** 2.5 miles (4km) **MINIMUM TIME** 1hr 30min
>
> **ASCENT/GRADIENT** 270ft (82m) ▲▲▲ **LEVEL OF DIFFICULTY** ✦✦✦
>
> **PATHS** Well-built path with drops alongside, no stiles
>
> **LANDSCAPE** Deep wooded gorge, wet meadow above
>
> **SUGGESTED MAP** OS Explorer 392 Ben Nevis & Fort William
>
> **START/FINISH** Grid reference: NN 168691
>
> **DOG FRIENDLINESS** Off lead, beware of steep slopes alongside path
>
> **PARKING** Walkers' car park at end of Glen Nevis road
>
> **PUBLIC TOILETS** Glen Nevis Visitor Centre

The Nevis Gorge, it's been said, is where Scotland pays its little tribute to the Himalayas. High walls of crag and boulder rise on either side. The path runs through a narrow gap where forest clings to the steep hillside and the river crashes below among its boulders.

Rocks and Falls Galore

Four different types of rock make up this scenery, and three of them are obvious from the walk. The crushed and ancient rocks of the Central Highlands (the Dalradian series) are mostly grey schist, but here there is also the pale-grey quartzite of Sgurr a'Mhaim, above the bend of the glen. The grinding of the continents at the time the Caledonian mountains were formed caused great bubbles of melted rock within the schist. These now appear at the surface as the granite on the lower slopes of Ben Nevis. It's grey on the outside, but pink when freshly broken or washed by streams. The granite was formed deep underground, but above it volcanoes were pouring out the black lava that now forms the summit of Ben Nevis and its formidable northern crags.

As the glen bends east towards the gorge, stop at the Polldubh car park (grid ref NN 145683). The first waterfall is hidden underneath the road bridge. The riverbed is the pinkish Nevis granite, cut by two dykes – vertical intrusions of volcanic rock – which the river has eroded into twin channels. Continue up the road to its end at the second car park, where the walk starts. Glen Nevis has the rounded outline of a glacial valley.

Glacier-smoothed rock below the car park has become an informal 'symbolic cemetery', commemorating those killed by the mountains they loved. Once above the gorge, the depth of the former glacier is shown by the rocks of Meall Cumhann, on the Ben Nevis (north) side. These are obviously smoothed by the ice that has passed right over the top of them.

Steall Fall

Steall Fall is about 300ft (91m) high. In a good winter it freezes completely and climbers ascend it in spiked crampons with an ice axe in each hand.

NEVIS GORGE

The valley above the fall, the Allt Coire a'Mhail, once flowed gently out into a higher version of Glen Nevis. From above, it still appears to unwary walkers to do so. Ice deepened Glen Nevis by 750ft (228m). In the following 10,000 years, the side-stream has barely started its task of eroding the hanging valley down to the level of its new endpoint.

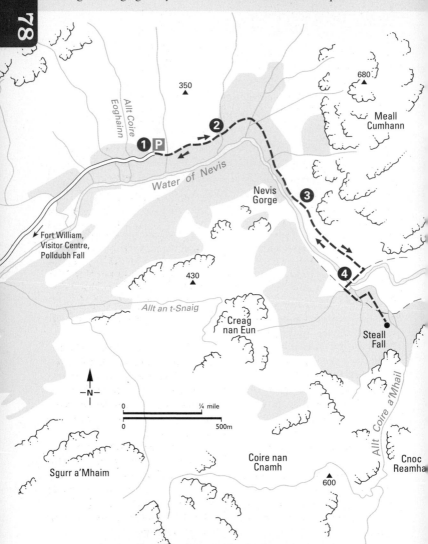

WALK 78 DIRECTIONS

❶ It should be noted that the waterslide above the car park is the Allt Coire Eoghainn – if you mistake it for the Steall Fall and set off towards it you are on a difficult and potentially dangerous path. The path you will take on this walk is much easier, but even here there have been casualties, mostly caused by people wearing unsuitable shoes. At the top end of the car park you will see a signpost that shows no destination closer than the 13 miles (21km)

to Kinlochleven – accordingly, this walk will be a short out-and-back. The well-made path runs gently uphill under woods of birch and hazel, across what turns into a very steep slope. For a few steps it becomes a rock-cut ledge, with a step across a waterfall side-stream. The path at this point is on clean pink granite, but you will see a boulder of grey schist beside the path just afterwards. Ahead, the top of the Steall Fall can now be just glimpsed through the notch of the valley.

2 The path continues downhill to cross a stream with big rock blocks; the rock now is schist, with fine zig-zag stripes of grey and white. A short rock staircase leads to a wooden balcony section. From here the path is just above the bed of the Nevis Gorge. Here the river runs through some huge boulders, some of which bridge it completely.

3 Quite suddenly, the path emerges on to a level meadow above the gorge. Ahead, the Steall Fall fills the view. The well-built path runs along the left-hand edge of the meadow to a point opposite the waterfall.

4 The walk ends here, beside a footbridge which consists simply of three steel cables over a very deep pool. Those who wish to attempt the crossing should note that it gets wobblier in the middle; it's hard to turn round, but the return journey is rather easier. From the wire bridge, the driest path runs alongside the main river round one bend before heading up to the foot of the waterfall. The view from directly beneath is even more spectacular.

Half Ben Nevis

*The half-way lochan and the great
north corrie of Nevis.*

DISTANCE *10 miles (16.1km)*   MINIMUM TIME *6hrs 15min*

ASCENT/GRADIENT *2,000ft (610m)* ▲▲▲   LEVEL OF DIFFICULTY +++

PATHS *Hill paths, well-built, then very rough, 4 stiles*

LANDSCAPE *Slopes of Britain's biggest hill*

SUGGESTED MAP *OS Explorer 392 Ben Nevis & Fort William*

START/FINISH *Grid reference: NN 123731*

DOG FRIENDLINESS *Keep on lead through Achintee grazings, by River Nevis*

PARKING *Large car park at Glen Nevis Visitor Centre*

PUBLIC TOILETS *At start*

For 21 years in the 19th century, an observatory was sited on the summit of Ben Nevis. It recorded, to the surprise of few, that this is one of the wettest spots in Britain. Averaged over the year, the summit is sunny for about two hours per day.

This walk of half the hill shows you the mountain's great northern crags and the rocky hollow of Coire Leis. The further edge of the corrie is the jagged line of Tower Ridge, Britain's longest rock climb. In early spring the damp Atlantic winds coat the crags in thick hoar-frost, over which climbers with crampons and ice axes have created hundreds of routes.

Charles Wilson, a grammar school teacher turned Cambridge professor, came to Ben Nevis on holiday in 1894. The Scottish-born professor was so struck by the effects of sunlight on the clouds above Coire Leis that he attempted to reproduce them in the Cavendish Laboratory. In so doing he invented the Wilson cloud chamber, for which he was awarded the Nobel Prize for Physics in 1927.

In summer, the moist Atlantic air that sweeps into Coire Leis condenses into cloud, and then rain. Each droplet forms around a 'nucleation centre' such as a speck of dust. Perfectly clean air can become supersaturated: it has more than enough moisture to form clouds, but can't. When moist air rises up Ben Nevis it expands due to the drop in pressure. As it expands it cools, allowing the water droplets to appear. In Wilson's cloud chamber, the pressure drop was achieved with a bicycle pump working backwards. One pull of the pump handle, and any passing particle became suddenly visible as a pencil-line of white cloud. The step-up in size is astonishing: it's as if a model aeroplane left a vapour trail as wide as the solar system, visible to an observer on another star! High energy particles can be seen zipping through the cloud chamber. Thus the positron (the positive electron) was discovered in 1932 and the muon (an exotic heavy electron) in 1937. It is actually possible to make your own Wilson cloud chamber – simply cool air with dry ice and shine a torch in. The successor to the cloud chamber was devised while gazing into a glass of beer. Donald Glaser earned the Nobel Prize for his bubble chamber in 1960.

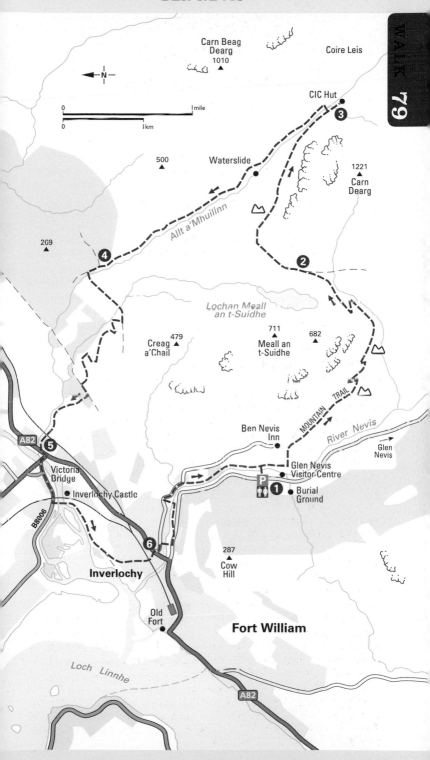

Carn Beag Dearg
1010 ▲

Coire Leis

—N—

0 ━━━━━━━━━━━ 1 mile
0 ━━━━━━━━━━━ 1 km

CIC Hut
3

500 ▲

Waterslide

1221 ▲
Carn Dearg

Allt a'Mhuilinn

269 ▲

4

2

Lochan Meall an t-Suidhe

711 ▲
Meall an t-Suidhe

682 ▲

479 ▲
Creag a'Chail

MOUNTAIN TRAIL

River Nevis

Glen Nevis

A82

5

Victoria Bridge

● Inverlochy Castle

Ben Nevis Inn ●

Glen Nevis Visitor Centre

B8806

P
1 ● Burial Ground

6

Inverlochy

287 ▲
Cow Hill

Old Fort

Fort William

Loch Linnhe

A82

WALK 79 DIRECTIONS

1 At the downstream corner of the car park, a bridge crosses the River Nevis. The path turns upstream, then crosses fields to a track. Cross on to the signed 'Ben Path' to Ben Nevis. After a long climb, a notice points you to a zig-zag up left on to the half-way plateau. The path passes above Lochan Meall ant-Suidhe, the Halfway Lochan, down on the left.

2 The main path takes a sharp turn back to the right, heading for the summit. Your path descends ahead, behind a wall-like cairn. After 0.25 mile (400m), bear right on a very rough path that climbs gently over peat bog to a cairn on the skyline. Here it becomes rough and rocky as it slants down across the steep slide slope of the valley of Allt a'Mhuilinn. Eventually it joins the stream and runs up beside it to the Charles Inglis Clark (CIC) Hut.

3 Return for 100yds (91m) and cross the stream on the right to join a clear path which leads downhill. This descends a rocky step with a waterslide and reaches a ladder stile into plantations.

4 Go down a forest road, which bends left across a bridge, then contours across open hill. After 0.5 mile (800m) the main track turns downhill in zig-zags. At the slope foot, it passes under power lines. In another 220yds (200m), take a smaller track on the right, signed 'Distillery', soon to rejoin the Allt a'Mhuilinn. Pass out between distillery buildings to reach the A82.

5 Cross the River Lochy on Victoria Bridge opposite and turn left into a fenced-off side road and left again along a street. It rises to a railway bridge. Turn left here on the long Soldiers Bridge back across the Lochy. At its end, turn right over a stile for a riverside path. This soon joins the hard surfaced Great Glen Way path. This becomes a built path into woodland. After two footbridges, bear left on a smaller path to the edge of Inverlochy. Turn right, then left into a street with copper beeches. This leads through Montrose Square to the A82.

WHERE TO EAT AND DRINK

The Ben Nevis Inn, at the bottom of the Mountain Trail, offers food and music to returning walkers. It's the local of the Lochaber mountain rescue team, and featured in the BBC programme *Rockface*. Children are welcome, and dogs in the beer garden. The walk also passes Nevisport (at the north end of Fort William, with a bar and self-service restaurant) and the Ben Nevis Takeaway, Inverlochy.

WHILE YOU'RE THERE

From Fort William's Town Pier, a passenger ferry across Loch Linnhe lets you explore the woods of Camusnagaul. Longer cruises visit the fish farms and seal island, while the evening cruise along Loch Eil gives, if it's clear, the best views of Ben Nevis' great northern corrie.

6 The street opposite is signed 'Ben Nevis Footpath'. Shortly, take a stone bridge to the Glen Nevis road. Turn left for 0.25 mile (400m) to a track on the left. Recross the Nevis on a green footbridge and turn right to a small riverside footpath. This rejoins the road briefly, then leads up-river to the footbridge at Glen Nevis Visitor Centre.

A Happy Birch-day in Coire Ardair

Regenerating woodlands lead to a high pass where Bonnie Prince Charlie escaped through the window.

DISTANCE 8 miles (12.9km)   **MINIMUM TIME** 4hrs 15min

ASCENT/GRADIENT 1,400ft (427m) ▲▲▲   **LEVEL OF DIFFICULTY** +++

PATHS Very good, rough around the loch, no stiles

LANDSCAPE One-ended valley leading to lochan under crags

SUGGESTED MAP OS Explorer 401 Loch Laggan & Creag Meagaidh

START/FINISH Grid reference: NN 483872

DOG FRIENDLINESS No dogs allowed as they disturb wildlife

PARKING Nature reserve car park at Aberarder track end beside Loch Laggan

PUBLIC TOILETS None on route or near by

As the path curves westward after Point ②, you'll see the crags of Creag Meagaidh ahead of you. When well iced up, these create many famous winter climbs. On the right, they're bounded by a narrow pass high on the skyline.

Bonnie Prince Charlie

After the defeat of the Jacobite cause at Culloden Moor on 16 April, 1746, Prince Charles Edward Stuart went on the run in the Scottish Highlands. From then until 18 September he sheltered in caves and bothies (shepherds' huts) and in the open heather. He was often hungry, usually wet, hunted by redcoat soldiers and plagued by midges. His flight took him across the country to Mallaig, for an 80-mile (129km) journey by open boat in a storm to the Outer Hebrides. He came back to Skye disguised as the maidservant of Miss Flora MacDonald. The prince adapted well to the life of a long-distance backpacker, living for weeks in the same dirty shirt and greasy black kilt, growing a long red beard and learning to enjoy the oat bread and whisky of the country. In a bothy on South Uist, he out-drank all of his companions and then proceeded to intone a penitential psalm over their unconscious bodies.

In the face of the weather and a barbarous and implacable enemy, he showed not just strength and courage, but good humour as well. He made jokes with Flora MacDonald – 'they'll never guess what I've got hidden up my skirts' (it was a pistol).

The prince came to know Scotland like no monarch before or since, and at the same time, Scotland's people – from clan chieftains to crofters and fishermen, and even outlaws like the Seven Men of Glenmoriston. Despite a price on his head of £30,000, equivalent to more than a lottery jackpot of today, not one of them betrayed him.

Back on the mainland, in July he was encircled by Hanoverian soldiers, but slipped between two sentries in the dark. By mid-August the manhunt had been abandoned. Soon afterwards he heard of a French boat waiting near Mallaig. Travelling away from the main roads, on 18 September he passed along the route of the walk, up to Coire Ardair and then through the high pass alongside Creag Meagaidh into the empty country around Glen Roy. That pass is called Uinneag Coire Ardair. Translating it into English we can say that Prince Charlie left Scotland through the Window.

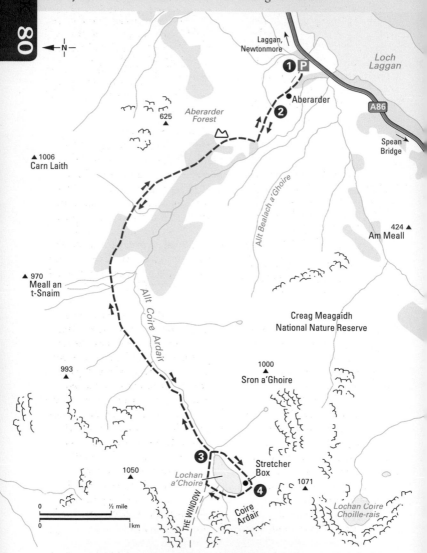

WALK 80 DIRECTIONS

❶ A new path runs alongside the grey gravel track, leading to Aberarder farm. Here there's an information area and a bench under a roof. Pass to the right of the buildings following a footprint waymarker on to a rebuilt path.

❷ The well-built path rises through bracken, then crosses a boggy area. It heads up the valley of Allt Coire Ardair, keeping a little way up the right-hand side, becoming steeper as it ascends through an area of regenerating birch trees. Now the crags of Coire Ardair come into sight

COIRE ARDAIR

ahead. The path crosses many small streams – here it is still being reconstructed. It bends left, slightly downhill, to join the main river. Tiny rowan trees can be seen attempting to regenerate among the heather. Wild flowers in the boggy ground include the pink or white pyramids of the heath spotted orchid (the leaves have the spots). The path winds gently near the stream, then suddenly to the outflow of Lochan a' Choire.

3 The outflow is a fine viewpoint for the crag walls of Coire Ardair. These walls are too loose and overgrown for rock climbing, but when covered in snow and hoarfrost give excellent sport for winter mountaineers. The circuit of the lochan is considerably more rugged than the path up the glen, and could be omitted if the outflow stream is too full, or if a picnic is preferred. Cross the outflow stream near where it emerges from the lochan and follow a trace of path round the

shore to the notable clump of boulders marked by a stretcher box. (The stretcher is used for removing mountain casualties from the foot of the crags.) One of the boulders forms a small cave, with a spring running through it. A vigorous rowan tree, seeded where deer can't get at it, shows that without grazing pressure this glen would be wooded even at this altitude of 2,000ft (610m).

4 After the boulder cave you must cross rocks and scree. This short section is awkward. Once past the head of the lochan, slant up away from the shore. A path descends from high on the left, coming out of the notch called the Window. Join this and turn down to the loch's outflow (Point **3** again). Quite clearly there's no way out of this dead-end valley that doesn't involve serious mountain walking – or one of those winter climbs up the icy gullies. Return down the valley by the outward path.

Up and Down the Corrieyairack

Above the Great Glen on the road the English built and Bonnie Prince Charlie marched over.

DISTANCE 7.25 miles (11.7km) **MINIMUM TIME** 4hrs

ASCENT/GRADIENT 1,300ft (395m) ▲▲▲ **LEVEL OF DIFFICULTY** +++

PATHS Tracks, one vanished pathless section, 2 stiles

LANDSCAPE Foothills of Monadhliath, birchwood hollows

SUGGESTED MAP OS Explorer 400 Loch Lochy & Glen Roy

START/FINISH Grid reference: NH 378080

DOG FRIENDLINESS Off lead, unless passing sheep

PARKING Southern edge of Fort Augustus, signed lane leads off A82 to burial ground

PUBLIC TOILETS Fort Augustus

The most striking feature of Scotland's geography is the 2,000ft (610m) deep Great Glen. It runs perfectly straight from Fort William to Inverness as if a giant ploughshare had been dragged across the country.

Scotland's San Andreas

Around 400 million years ago, the northern part of Scotland slipped 65 miles (105km) to the left. Looking across from Corrieyairack you'd have seen ground that's now the Island of Mull. The Great Glen represents a tear-fault, similar to the San Andreas Fault in California, but no longer active, so that there isn't going to be any Fort Augustus Earthquake. Where two ground masses slide past each other, the rock where they touch is shattered. Rivers and glaciers have worn away this broken rock to make the striking valley.

Wade's Ways

After the uprising of 1715, General Wade became the military commander of Scotland. He constructed and repaired forts along the Great Glen at Fort William, Fort Augustus and Inverness, as well as at Ruthven on the present A9 and Glenelg (see Walk 86). To link them, he built 260 miles (around 418km) of roads across the Highlands. The most spectacular of these was the one through the Corrieyairack Pass, rising to 2,500ft (762m) to link the Great Glen with the Spey. The construction was little changed since Roman times. Large rocks were jammed together into a firm bed, up to 15ft (4.5m) wide, and then surfaced with smaller stones and gravel packed down. Modern path-builders know that however well you build it, if it's got water running down it turns into a stream. Wade paid particular attention to drainage. The 500 soldiers working through the summer of 1731 got a bonus of 6d a day – about £5 in today's money – and celebrated its completion with a barbecue of six oxen.

The chieftains worried that the roads would soften their people, making them unfit for raids across rough country. But they soon came to appreciate the convenience. 'If you'd seen these roads before they were made, You'd lift up your hands and bless General Wade.'

And when Prince Charles Stuart landed 14 years later, it was the Jacobite army that marched triumphantly across the Corrieyairack. At the Speyside end of the pass, a small and ill-prepared force under General John Cope fled before him into England. And a new Wade rhyme was inserted, temporarily, into the National Anthem itself: 'God grant that Marshal Wade, May by Thy mighty aid, Victory bring, May he sedition hush, and like a torrent rush, Rebellious Scots to crush, God save the King.'

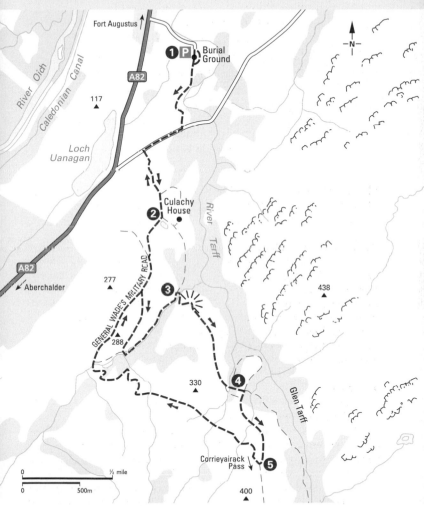

WALK 81 DIRECTIONS

❶ A track leads round to the left of the burial ground to meet a minor road. Turn right for about 0.25 mile (400m) to the foot of a rather rubbly track signposted for

the Corrieyairack Pass. After some 50yds (46m) the track passes through a gate, getting much easier, and, soon, the right of way joins a smoother track coming up from Culachy House.

2 After another 0.25 mile (400m), a gate leads out on to the open hill. About 350yds (320m) further on, the track passes under high-tension wires. At once bear left across a grassy meadow. As this drops towards a stream, you will see a green track slanting down to the right. Bear left off the track to pass the corner of a deer fence, where a small path continues down to the stream. Cross and turn downstream on an old grassy track. It recrosses the stream and passes under the high power line to a bend with a sudden view across deep and wooded Glen Tarff.

WHILE YOU'RE THERE

You will find a rather specialised take on the life of the Highlanders at the Clansman Centre in Fort Augustus, which focuses on their techniques of doing away with one another. In a simulated turf house, staff will teach the 'art of killing or maiming using ancient weapons', and will even make the weapons.

3 Turn right across a high stone bridge. A disused track climbs through birch woods then, as a terraced shelf, across the high side of Glen Tarff. A side stream forms a wooded re-entrant ahead. The old track contours in to this and crosses below a narrow waterfall – the former bridge has now disappeared.

4 Contour out across the steep slope to pick up the old track as it restarts. It runs gently uphill to a gateless gateway in a fence. Turn up the fence to another gateway, 150yds (137m) above. Here turn left for 20yds (18m) to the brink of another stream hollow. (Its delightful Gaelic name – Sidhean Ceum na Goibhre – means 'Fairy Goat-step'.) Don't go into this,

WHERE TO EAT AND DRINK

The Lock Inn at Fort Augustus is not misspelled: its upstairs restaurant (April–October) overlooks the locks of the Caledonian Canal. Bar meals are served downstairs, year round. Children welcome, but not dogs.

but turn uphill alongside it, through pathless bracken, to its top. A deer fence is just above; turn left alongside it to go through a nearby gate, then left beside the fence. When it turns downhill, a green path continues ahead, gently uphill through heather. Far ahead and above, pylons crossing the skyline mark the Corrieyairack Pass. The path bends right to join the Corrieyairack track just above.

5 Turn right. The track passes a knoll on the right and this heathery rise marks the highest point of this walk. It then descends in sweeping curves for 1.25 miles (2km). The pass is still technically a road, and it is now a scheduled ancient monument and protected by law. Any person found damaging it will be prosecuted. From here the track climbs gently to rejoin the upward route. At the final bend, a stile offers a short cut through (rather than round) the ancient burial ground.

WHAT TO LOOK OUT FOR

Despite the road's preservation, you will see little of General Wade's work, apart from its ambitious uphill line preserved by the modern track on top. You may be more interested in the burial ground at the start of the walk. Here is buried 'John Anderson, my Jo', subject of a poem by Robert Burns; and Gilleasbuig MacDonald, bard of North Uist, who died on his way to his publisher in Inverness.

Moorland on Morrone

*The hill at the back of Braemar gives
a taste of the Cairngorms.*

DISTANCE 6.75 miles (10.9km) MINIMUM TIME 4hrs 15min

ASCENT/GRADIENT 2,000ft ▲▲▲ LEVEL OF DIFFICULTY +++

PATHS *Well-made but fairly steep path, track, 1 stile*

LANDSCAPE *Rolling heather hills*

SUGGESTED MAP *OS Explorer 387 Glen Shee & Braemar*

START/FINISH *Grid reference: NO 143911*

DOG FRIENDLINESS *Keep on lead in reserve, also on hill during grouse
nesting May/June*

PARKING *Duck pond, at top of Chapel Brae, Braemar*

PUBLIC TOILETS *Braemar centre (opposite Fife Arms)*

Coming down the back of Morrone Hill, you descend through several plant zones, and the home of two distinctive Grampian birds.

Ptarmigan Pterritory

On the windswept, often snow-covered summit plateau, gravel alternates with shrubby plants that grow barely ankle-high. These are food for the ptarmigan, a member of the grouse family that's rather like a small hen. Uniquely among British birds it turns white in the winter, and in spring and early summer it will still be white in patches. Its late summer plumage is paler than the grouse, and more speckled. But the easy way to recognise it is by where it lives – a grouse above the heather line is a ptarmigan – and by its behaviour. It relies on camouflage, and when you notice it, will probably be standing on the gravel only a few yards away. Even then, it doesn't fly away, but will probably wander off round the back of a boulder. In springtime, the male bird's soaring display flight is accompanied by a soundtrack of belches and cackles. The 'P' at the beginning of its name is purely ornamental – in Gaelic it's 'tarmachan'.

Heather and Grouse

At the 2,000ft (610m) mark, bilberry and some grass grow, along with dwarf heather. Once you reach slightly more sheltered ground, the heather springs up twice as high. At around 1,500ft (457m), it is deep enough to hinder off-path walking. Wild flowers like yellow tormentil and white woodruff grow, and you may see meadow pipits and mountain hare.

A small brown bird – or more likely three or four – leaps up out of the heather with a squawking cry that seems to say 'go back, go back!' Grouse go with heather, like pandas go with bamboo and koalas with gum trees. Red grouse are found only in the British Isles, and unfortunately their heather country, however familiar and tiresome to Scottish walkers, is rare and vanishing in a world context. The grouse need old leggy heather to nest in, but shorter, younger plants to eat. As a result, grouse moors are burnt in a ten-year cycle to provide tall heather with short heather. The piebald effect of 'muirburn', as it's called, gives these hills an attractive texture.

Eighty per cent of the grouse's diet is heather, the rest being the insects that live in it. As birds lack teeth they require small stones in their gizzards to help grind their food up and aid digestion. For grouse, sharp quartz grit is ideal, and you may spot small piles of this beside the track.

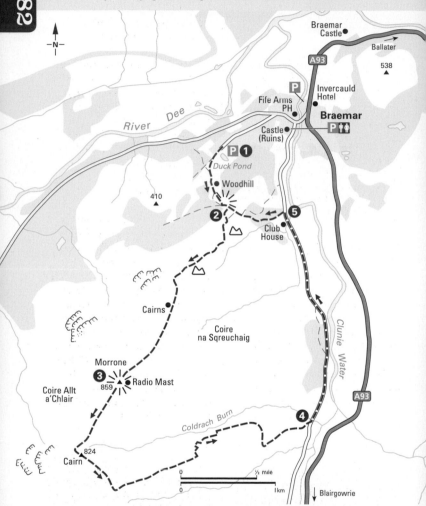

WALK 82 DIRECTIONS

❶ Take the wide track uphill, to the right of the duck pond at the top of Chapel Brae, bearing left twice following blue waymarkers to Woodhill house. The house can be bypassed by taking a small footpath on the right which rejoins the track just above. When

the track forks again, bear left to a viewpoint indicator.

❷ Cross a track diagonally to a hill path marked 'Morrone'. The path has been rebuilt with rough stone steps. Higher up, it slants to the right along a line of rocky outcrops, a geological dyke of harder rock. At the top of this it turns directly uphill, passing five sprawling cairns. These are the turning point in the Morrone Hill Race that is part of the Braemar Games. The wide, stony path runs up to the radio mast and other ugly constructions on top of the summit.

3 The summit, if you turn your back on the buildings, has fine views across Deeside to the high Cairngorms. On the main tops, Ben Macdui and Beinn a'Bhuird, snow may show right through the summer. To the east you will see Loch Callater and the White Mounth plateau. A notable hump is Cac Carn Beag, one of the summits of Lochnagar. Morrone's summit area is bare stones, but if you go past the buildings you'll

find the start of a wide track. It runs down to a shallow col and climbs to the cairn on the low summit beyond. Here it bends left towards a lower col, but before reaching it, turns left again down the side of the hill. A gentle zig-zagging descent leads to the road by the Clunie Water.

4 Turn left, alongside the river, for 1.5 miles (2.4km). Ben Avon with its row of summit tors fills the skyline ahead. After a snow gate and golf clubhouse comes a road sign warning of a cattle grid (the grid itself is round the next bend). Here a track, back up to the left, has a blue-topped waymarker pole.

5 Go up between caravans to a ladder stile with a dog flap. A faint path leads up under birches, bearing right and becoming clearer. After a gate in a fence the path becomes quite clear, leading to a Scottish Natural Heritage signboard and blue waymarker at the top of the birchwood. The path becomes a track with a fence on its right and, in 220yds (201m), reaches the viewpoint indicator, Point **2**. From here you can return to the duck pond and the start of the walk.

Crombie Water and the Whisky Hills

A walk through a green valley and bare heather moor in the smugglers' country of Glenlivet.

DISTANCE 6.25 miles (10.1km)   **MINIMUM TIME** 3hrs 15min

ASCENT/GRADIENT 1,000ft (305m) ▲▲▲   **LEVEL OF DIFFICULTY** +++

PATHS Waymarked, muddy and indistinct in places, 11 stiles

LANDSCAPE Birchwoods, heather, rolling hills

SUGGESTED MAP OS Explorer 420 Correen Hills & Glenlivet

START/FINISH Grid reference: NJ 218257

DOG FRIENDLINESS Keep on lead except in plantation

PARKING Track opposite church at Tombae runs up to quarry car park

PUBLIC TOILETS NOTE None on route or near by

WARNING Grouse shooting in August/September – consult Glenlivet Ranger Service at Tomintoul

Long before the coming of licensed distilleries, whisky was part of the economy of the Highlands. After the hard work of the barley harvest came the quieter occupation of mashing and distilling. The draff (dregs) from the mash-barrel went to feed the cows, while the spirit itself warmed the crofter through the snows of winter.

As rents came to be paid in money rather than in kind, whisky was an easily transported product for cash. It was also convenient to tax, but this simply meant that the Highlanders moved their operation into the hills. The barley fields of Strathspey, the clear mountain water of the Cairngorms and the convenient smuggling routes to Aberdeen and Inverness made Glenlivet a famous whisky country. Even as his redcoats were hunting the smugglers through the Ladder Hills, King George IV was demanding the illicit Glenlivet by name.

Water, Malt – and Mystery

The old word 'Scotch' is only applied to whisky – the people are 'Scottish' and the language is 'Scots'. And whiskey with an 'e' comes from Ireland or the United States. Barley is the start-point. The grain is allowed to germinate in the warm, damp environment of the malting floor, which converts some of its starch to sugar. The malt is heated, under the pagoda-like copper roof of the malting kiln, then boiled and fermented into the 'mash', a kind of sweet insipid beer. The mash is passed three times through the onion-shaped copper stills and stored in barrels for at least eight years. That's the technical process; the added mystery happens almost by accident. The killing of the malt, traditionally done over a peat fire, adds a smoky aroma, but it's the second-hand sherry barrels used for storage that add the golden colour, much of the flavour and the bite of the oakwood.

Blended whiskies, such as Bells, Teachers and Famous Grouse, are made of cheaper corn spirit with malt whisky mixed in. More serious are the 'single malts', each a product of a named distillery. From Glenlivet comes the Glenlivet itself, and also Tomnavoulin, Tomintoul, Cragganmore and Glenfarclas. These are Speyside malts – smooth and subtle. From the islands of the west come wilder whiskies like Lagavoulin and Talisker, with overtones of peat, seaweed and even old fish crates. An educational tasting session could start in the hotels and whisky shops of Tomintoul.

WALK 83

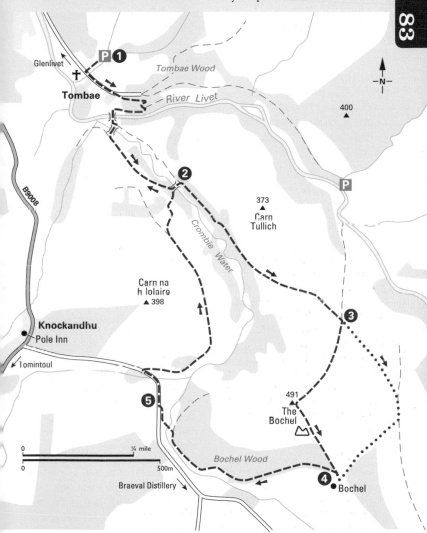

WALK 83 DIRECTIONS

❶ At Tombae church, turn left to walk for 330yds (300m) to a stile on the right – signposted as Walk 10. A track leads down into birchwoods. Bear right at a waymarker and follow the main track to reach a bridge

and cross over the River Livet. After 60yds (55m), turn right to another bridge, this time over the Crombie Water. Turn half left, up to a stile beside a field gate. The walk now follows the top of the low wooded bank above the Crombie Water to reach a footbridge (grid ref 226245).

WALK 83

2 Across the footbridge, a small path runs across a meadow into a wood, slanting up to the right to a green track. Turn right and follow this gently up through the wood, then bend left on to heather moorland. Below the abrupt hill of The Bochel the track forks. Keep ahead, with a waymarker. The way becomes a peaty path. At the top of the first rise is a stile with a gate alongside. The path, with a waymarker, leads to a gateway in another fence. Don't go through, but turn right, with the fence on your left, to a stile with a signpost.

3 For an easier alternative, follow the sign for Walk 10, ahead. Just before a house, turn right at another signpost and follow a track towards Bochel farm. But the main route goes over The

Bochel itself. Across the stile, turn uphill on small sheep paths to the summit cairn. Turn left, to descend towards the white Braeval distillery below the Ladder Hills. As the slope steepens, you'll see Bochel farm below. Head down the left-hand edge of the nearer pine wood to join the rough track leading into the farm.

4 At once a gate on the right leads to a faint path into the plantation. This soon becomes a green track running just above the bottom edge of the wood. It becomes more well-used and then runs out to a road.

5 Turn right, over a bridge to a waymarked gate on the right. A track rises to open fields above the river. At its highest point, a waymarker points down to the right. Go down to a fence, with a waymarked stile on the left, then through heather with a fence on your left. Turn downhill to a stile at the bottom. Cross this and turn left, ignoring another stile on the left, to reach the footbridge, Point **2**. Retrace the first part of the walk back to Tombae.

Right: Ducks on a lake behind the Glenlivet distillery (Walk 83)

Loch an Eilein's Castle and Ord Ban

The castle on the island in the loch is the heart of Rothiemurchus Forest.

DISTANCE 4.25 miles (6.8km)   **MINIMUM TIME** 1hr 45min

ASCENT/GRADIENT 100ft (30m) ▲▲▲   **LEVEL OF DIFFICULTY** ✚✚✚

PATHS Wide smooth paths, optional steep hill with high ladder stile

LANDSCAPE Ancient pine forest around loch

SUGGESTED MAP OS Explorer 403 Cairn Gorm & Aviemore

START/FINISH Grid reference: NH 897084

DOG FRIENDLINESS Keep on lead on Rothiemurchus Estate

PARKING Estate car park near Loch an Eilein, charges apply

PUBLIC TOILETS Visitor centre

An island castle, surrounded by ancient pines, and the mountains rising behind – you hardly have to bother with the rest of Scotland, Loch an Eilein has it all.

Castle for Cattle Thieves

Loch an Eilein Castle was built by John Comyn II, known as the Red Comyn, in the 13th century. It guards the strategic cattle-stealing route which runs along the shore of the loch. Locals used to keep a cow tied to a tree in hope that the raiders would take that and leave the rest alone. The three murderers of a Macintosh chieftain were imprisoned in chains here for seven years, before being executed in 1531. The castle was most recently fought over in 1690, when Grizzel Mhor (Big Grizelda), the chieftain's wife, held it for Clan Grant against the king. There is said to be an underwater zig-zag causeway leading out to the island.

Life in the Pines

Walk quietly with binoculars and you may see some of the unique birdlife of the forest. The crested tit resembles the more familiar coal tit, with brown body and striped head, but with the Mohican hair-style effect of its crest. It nests in holes in old, rotten trees, so will only be found in wild forest. The Scottish crossbill, found only in Scotland, has a parrot-like beak, adapted for cracking open pine cones. The capercaillie is the large grouse of the forest and its name means 'horse of the woods'. The male challenges and intimidates other males with a noise like the clip-clop of hooves, or like a wine-bottle being opened. Your only real chance of seeing it in the wild is at dawn, in spring, at the RSPB reserve at Loch Garten (better known for its ospreys).

Osprey Island

Ospreys used to nest in the castle ruins. An egg collector once swam across wearing nothing but his cap, which he used to bring back his plunder. Ospreys are back in the Cairngorms, and though they won't return to

Left: Loch an Eilein, Cairngorms National Park (Walk 84)

this over-public island, you might see them elsewhere plunging feet-first as they strike for a trout. Try the trout farm at Inverdruie, on the edge of Aviemore. Sadly, the egg-collectors are back as well. In 2000, a man in Leicester was caught with three stolen osprey eggs.

Romantic Setting

In the romantic novel *The Key above the Door* by Maurice Walsh (1926), the hero and heroine spend half the book gazing at each other from cottages on opposite sides of Loch an Eilein before accidentally getting shipwrecked on the island. More recently, Archie and Katrina, from the popular TV series *Monarch of the Glen*, enjoyed their own romantic encounter on the island.

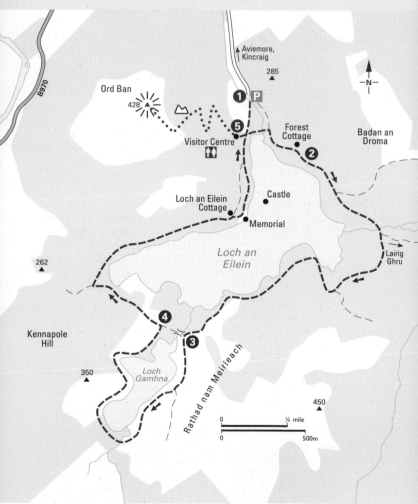

WALK 84 DIRECTIONS

1 From the end of the car park at the beginning of the walk, a made-up path leads to the visitor centre. Turn left to cross the end of Loch an Eilein, then turn right on a smooth sandy track. The loch shore is near by on the right. There are small paths leading down to it if you wish to visit. Just past a red-roofed house, a deer fence runs across, with a gate.

2 The track now becomes a wide, smooth path, which runs close to the loch side. After a bridge, the main track forks right to pass a bench backed by a flat boulder. The smaller path on the left leads high into the hills and through the famous pass of the Lairig Ghru, eventually to Braemar. After crossing a stream at a low concrete footbridge, the path bends right for 120yds (110m) to a junction. Just beyond you'll find a footbridge with wooden handrails.

WHAT TO LOOK OUT FOR

At the foot of the loch, you walk across a low loggers' dam. Timber men used to release the water to carry the tree trunks down to the Spey. We usually think of the log-rafts of the great Canadian rivers, but the skill was carried there by Highlanders from Rothiemurchus.

3 To shorten the walk, cross this footbridge and continue along the main track, passing Point **4** in another 170yds (155m). For a longer walk, turn left before the footbridge on to a narrower path that will pass around Loch Gamhna. This second loch soon

appears on your right-hand side. Where the path forks, keep right to pass along the loch side, across its head (rather boggy) and back along its further side, to rejoin the wider path around Loch an Eilein. Turn left here.

4 Continue around Loch an Eilein, with the water on your right, to a reedy corner of the loch and a bench. About 55yds (51m) further, the path turns sharply right, signposted 'footpath'. After a gate, turn right to the loch side and a memorial to Major General Brook Rice who drowned here while skating. Follow the shore to the point opposite the castle, then back up to the wide track above. A deer fence on the left leads back to the visitor centre.

5 From here, a stiff climb (500ft/152m) can be made on to the rocky little hill of Ord Ban, a superb viewpoint. Cross a ladder stile immediately to the right of the toilet block and follow the deer fence to the right for 150yds (137m), to a point behind the car park. Just behind one of the lowest birches on the slope, a small indistinct path zig-zags up the steep slope. It slants to the left to avoid crags, then crosses a small rock slab (take care if wet) and continues on to the summit. Descend by the same path.

WHERE TO EAT AND DRINK

Smiffy's Fish & Chips at Aviemore is celebrated across Scotland by hillwalkers and climbers. For even hungrier ones, La Taverna offers a pizza and salad 'eat as much as you can' buffet, as well as more formal Italian restaurant fare. You can find it at the south end of Aviemore, opposite the turn-off to Glenmore.

WHILE YOU'RE THERE

Careful observers might see the wildcat, pine marten and capercaillie, but it's several centuries too late to spot the extinct wolf, bison and lynx. However, all these can be seen at the Highland Wildlife Park at Kincraig. It's an outpost of Edinburgh Zoo, where all the Cairngorms' wildlife past and present is kept under fairly natural conditions.

WALK 85

The Pass of Ryvoan and the Thieves' Road

*Following cattle thieves and drovers to the lochan
used by the fairies for their laundry.*

DISTANCE 5 miles (8km) **MINIMUM TIME** 2hrs 15min

ASCENT/GRADIENT 400ft (122m) ▲▲▲ **LEVEL OF DIFFICULTY** ✦✦✦

PATHS Smooth tracks, one steep ascent, no stile

LANDSCAPE Views over Rothiemurchus Forest to Cairngorm

SUGGESTED MAP OS Explorer 403 Cairn Gorm & Aviemore

START/FINISH Grid reference: NH 980095

DOG FRIENDLINESS Off lead but under close control

PARKING Bridge just south of Glenmore village

PUBLIC TOILETS Glenmore village

The Pass of Ryvoan has all the atmosphere of a classic Cairngorm through-route. It's a scaled down version of the famous and fearsome Lairig Ghru that cuts through the Cairngorm range southwards from Aviemore. You pass from the shelter of the forest to a green lochan, trapped between two high and stony mountainsides. Once through the narrow gap, you'll find wide moors and a ring of peaks around the horizon.

Thieving Ways

Ryvoan marked the exit of the Thieves' Road that ran out of Rannoch and Lochaber by secret ways through the Rothiemurchus Forest. The MacDonalds of Glen Coe used to come raiding here in the 17th century, as did Clan Cameron from Loch Eil near Fort William. Once through the pass, they could take their pick from the rich lands of Moray and Aberdeenshire. In more settled times, the raiding chieftains became landlords, and their rents were paid in the small black cattle of the glens. Every autumn, the drove herds assembled for their long walk to the markets of Falkirk, Perth and northern England.

The Old Drove Road

The drovers used the same road as their thieving grandfathers, but once through the pass they turned sharp right across the flank of the mountain. The Lairig an Lui, the Pass of the Calves, crosses the dangerous ford of the Avon and runs down Glen Derry to Braemar. It's 30 miles (48km) to the next grazing and shelter – two full days for the drove. Overnight the cattle would snatch some grazing from the rough grasses, while the drovers cooked their oatmeal and potatoes, before rolling themselves in their woollen plaids on a bed of heather. As late as 1859, Queen Victoria found the Lairig path torn up by hooves and scented with fresh cow pats.

The Sith and Others

Lochan Uaine means 'Green Loch'. Some say the green colour is caused by flecks of mica. Others claim that it's where the fairies wash their green garments. The Highland fairies, the Sithe (pronounced 'Shee'), don't dance around with wands and grant you wishes. They are touchy and vengeful, and if you meet one it is best to address him politely in good Gaelic. Precautions you can take are to avoid wearing green, which is known to annoy them, and never to address your friends by name while under the trees.

The Bodach Lamh-dearg is a spectre who appears wrapped in a grey plaid with one bloodstained hand, challenging passers-by to a fight and leaving their bodies for the foxes. Big Donald, the King of the Fairies, lived beside Loch Morlich. While wolves and bears may one day return to the forest, we should be more alarmed about the return of the Sithe.

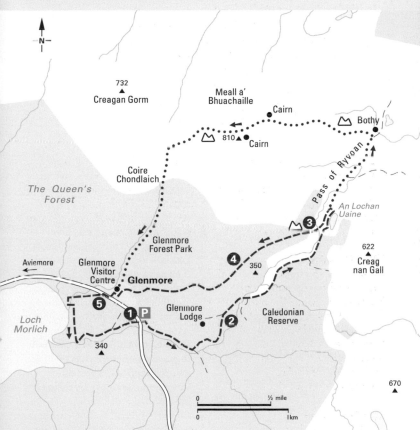

WALK 85 DIRECTIONS

1 Head upstream on a sandy track to the left of the river. Interpretation signs explain the flowers of the forest you may come across, many of which are ferns and mosses. After 550yds (503m), turn left on a wide smooth path with blue/yellow waymarkers. Ahead is a gate into Glenmore Lodge rifle range; here the path bends right, to a wide gravel track.

2 Turn right, away from Glenmore Lodge, to cross a concrete bridge into the Caledonian Reserve. Immediately keep ahead on a smaller track (marked by a blue waymarker) as the main one bends right. The track narrows as it heads into the Pass of Ryvoan between steep wooded slopes of pine, birch and scree. At this, the most scenic part of the route, a path turns left, with a blue waymarker, which you take in a moment. Just beyond this, steps on the right lead down to Lochan Uaine. Walk round to the left of the water on the beach. At the head of the loch a small path leads back up to the track. Turn sharp left, back to the junction already visited; now turn off to the right on to the narrower path with the blue waymarker.

❸ This small path crosses some duckboard and heads back down the valley. Very soon it starts to climb steeply to the right, up rough stone steps. When it levels off the going is easier, although it's still narrow with tree roots. The path reaches a forest road at a bench and a waymarker.

❹ Continue to the left along the track. After a clear-felled area with views, the track re-enters trees and slopes downhill into

WHERE TO EAT AND DRINK

The Forestry Commission's visitor centre has a café serving baked potatoes and snacks. Across the road, the Glenmore Café offers chips, toasties and red squirrels – the squirrels are outside, using a feeder placed directly opposite the windows.

Glenmore village. Just above the main road turn right, through a green barrier, to reach Glenmore Visitor Centre. Pass through its car park to the main road.

WHILE YOU'RE THERE

Reintroduced to the Cairngorms after an absence of around 1,000 years, the Glenmore reindeer herd is based at Glenmore village. From the Reindeer Centre you'll be taken up the hill to visit the herd. Some of the reindeer pull sleighs in Christmas parades.

❺ Cross to Glenmore shop. Behind a post-box, steps lead down to the campsite. Pass along its right-hand edge to a path into woods. Head left across a footbridge to the shore of Loch Morlich and follow the beaches until another river blocks the way. Turn left along the river bank. Ignore a footbridge, but continue on the wide path with the river on your right. Where the path divides, the smaller branch continues beside the river through bushes to the car park.

EXTENDING THE WALK

In good weather you can continue through the Pass of Ryvoan. Return to Glenmore by taking a hill path from the bothy, over the summit of Meall a' Bhuachaille and then down through the Coire Chondlaich.

WHAT TO LOOK OUT FOR

Elsewhere in Britain, red squirrels are being supplanted by their big grey cousins which were introduced from America. However, the red squirrel's smaller teeth are better adapted to life among the pines, and it is widespread in the Rothiemurchus Forest. Typically they'll run up the side of a tree trunk facing away from you, but then you'll see them escaping through the branches overhead. Close up – as at the Glenmore Café – you may notice their vicious little claws and teeth and realise they're nothing more than fluffy orange rats.

Looking Over the Sea to Skye

*A coast walk along Loch Alsh with views of Skye,
the sea and a fish farm.*

> **DISTANCE** 8.5 miles (13.7km)   **MINIMUM TIME** 4hrs
>
> **ASCENT/GRADIENT** 1,000ft (300m) ▲▲▲   **LEVEL OF DIFFICULTY** +++
>
> **PATHS** Tracks, grassy shoreline, minor road, 4 stiles
>
> **LANDSCAPE** Wooded coast, moorland pass, stony paths
>
> **SUGGESTED MAP** OS Explorer 413 Knoydart, Loch Hourn & Loch Duich
>
> **START/FINISH** Grid reference: NG 795213
>
> **DOG FRIENDLINESS** Off lead most of walk
>
> **PARKING** Above pier of Glenelg ferry
>
> **PUBLIC TOILETS** None on route or near by

Two hundred years ago, Scotland's rivers were full of salmon, and smoked salmon was the crofter's winter food store. When wild salmon became scarce it was considered a luxury food, and today, if you buy salmon, it's almost certainly from a fish farm.

Fish Farming

A fish farm should be sheltered from storm waves, but in water at least 30ft (9m) deep so that fish droppings don't poison the fish. There should be a vigorous tidal flow to carry oxygen-rich water into the pens, no pollution and the water should be cool, but should not freeze. In other words, it should be in a Scottish sea loch. Scotland's farms now produce salmon with a fish-counter value of one billion pounds each year, they employ 8,500 people and produce 160,000 tonnes of fish a year, enough to give every Briton a 4oz (100g) steak every week.

Fish farming is a tough life. Mending a net that's 3ft (90cm) underwater is not comfortable when the water is still, but it invariably isn't, because the day when it's blowing half a gale is the very day the nets break. Hauling the cages out of the water for cleaning is the toughest job of all – seaweed grows on fish farms just as it does on the shoreline, and after two years it starts to hinder the flow of water. And a single storm, or even a passing whale, can tear the nets and lose the work of two years.

Mass Catering

During its first 40 years, fish farming tried to produce as much as possible, as cheaply as possible. Salmon were stocked like battery hens and fed a high-fat diet. Antibiotics keep them alive if not altogether healthy, and dyes give their flesh the pink colour. One result has been pollution from their droppings poisoning nearby shellfish beds. Fish farms act as reservoirs of disease, in particular of the parasitic sea-lice. There are many reasons for the decline of the wild salmon and infection from fish farms is one of them.

Scottish fish farming has now reached the point where it has to clean up its act. A recent development is the organic fish farm, where the fish are stocked less densely and are fed a more natural diet. Fish pens are circular because the salmon prefer to swim round and round. If they were put in a square enclosure, the corners would be wasted. More importantly, the fish would hit the sides, and this would damage their scales.

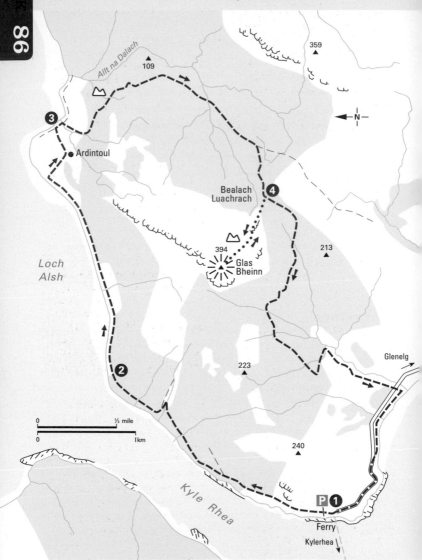

WALK 86 DIRECTIONS

1 A track runs out of the car park, signed for Ardintoul and Totaig. It descends gently through two gates, then goes up through a third into a plantation. With high power lines just above, the track

forks. Take the left-hand one, downhill, passing an arrow made of stones. The track runs between the feet of a tall pylon and then climbs again to contour through a birch wood. It runs in and out of a tiny stream gorge, then gently descends towards the shore.

On the other side of Loch Alsh, the white houses of Balmacara are directly ahead.

② At the shoreline, the track disappears into an open field strip. Follow the short grass next to the shingle beach, passing a salmon farm just offshore. When the trees once more run down to the sea, a green track runs next to the shore to reach an open field below a small crag with birches. Keep along the shore, outside field walls, and sometimes taking to the stripy schist shingle, towards a square brick building on the point ahead. As you pass the end of the birch crag, you come to a wall gap. Here a track that's simply a pair of green ruts runs directly

inland through a grey gate to meet a gravel track. Turn left, away from the abandoned Ardintoul farm to pass sheds and a house to regain the shoreline at Ardintoul.

❸ The track runs along the shoreline, then turns inland to climb the hill behind. The steeper uphill sections are tarred. Below on the left, the Allt na Dalach runs into Loch Alsh, with, at low tide, a clear example of a gravel spit where river debris runs into tidal water. The track enters plantations, crosses a stream and bends right to complete its climb to the Bealach Luachrach. Here you may see fresh peat workings on the left.

❹ The energetic can make a diversion on to Glas Bheinn – a tough little hill, but a fine viewpoint. The grading and timing given for this walk don't take account of this side-trip. From the road's high point, turn right up a wet tree gap to reach open hillside. Follow the remains of an old fence up the first rise. Where it bends right, continue straight uphill to the summit, returning by the same route. The old fence makes a useful guide back into the tree gap. Continue downhill from Point **❹** on the unsurfaced road, which reaches the tarred public road a mile (1.6km) north of Glenelg village. Grassy shoreline, then the road, leads back to the ferry pier.

Heart of the Cuillins

*Classic rock-climbing country below the
Cioch and the Inaccessible Pinnacle.*

DISTANCE 5.75 miles (9.2km)   **MINIMUM TIME** 4hrs

ASCENT/GRADIENT 1,900ft (580m) ▲▲▲   **LEVEL OF DIFFICULTY** +++

PATHS Mountain paths, one boggy and tough, 2 stiles

LANDSCAPE Peaty slopes into spectacular crag hollow

SUGGESTED MAP OS Explorer 411 Skye – Cuillin Hills

START/FINISH Grid reference: NG 409206

DOG FRIENDLINESS Signs indicate on lead in sheep country below corrie

PARKING Walkers' pull-off before gate into Glenbrittle campsite

PUBLIC TOILETS At campsite

The Black Cuillin Hills, seen through Skye's moist Atlantic air, appear blue and under romantic sunset light almost purple. This land is like nowhere else, even in Scotland, for crag, boulder and jagged horizon.

The Glory of Gabbro

The special quality of Skye is obvious to the eye, but even more so to the foot. The black rock grips the foot like velcro. This is gabbro, formed in the magma chamber of a volcano about the height of Mount Fuji that stood here 50 million years ago. Skye's screes are the steepest, its crags the craggiest, and its ridges look out across the Hebrides and the Atlantic.

As you approach Point ❹ on the upward journey, you are looking towards the buttress of Sron na Ciche. High on the face is a smooth, diamond-shaped slab and, at its right-hand corner, a famous rock-projection. It long went unnoticed, until a famous climber, Professor Norman Collie, spotted the shadow it casts across the slab in the afternoon. This is A'Chioch, 'the Breast'. Its flat top was the scene of a sword-fight in the film *Highlander*. The top is reached by a spectacular, but fairly straightforward climb.

Behind Lagan

In the upper corrie, more famous bits of rock come into view. At the back right corner is the long scree called the Great Stone Shoot. It is strenuous and frustrating but not technically difficult, and it brings climbers up to the ridge just to the right of Skye's highest peak, Sgurr Alasdair. The skyline to the left of the Stone Shoot is dominated by Sgurr Mhic Choinnich, with its near-vertical right profile. This step, 200ft (61m) high, can be avoided by a remarkable ledge that crosses below the summit, to emerge on the mountain's gentler left-hand ridge.

To the left again, you can just see the rock-prow of the so-called Inaccessible Pinnacle. This forms the summit of Skye's second highest peak, Sgurr Dearg. Its easiest route is very scary, but only moderately difficult and not particularly inaccessible. It must be climbed by anyone wishing to complete the Munro summits, Scottish peaks over 3,000ft (914m).

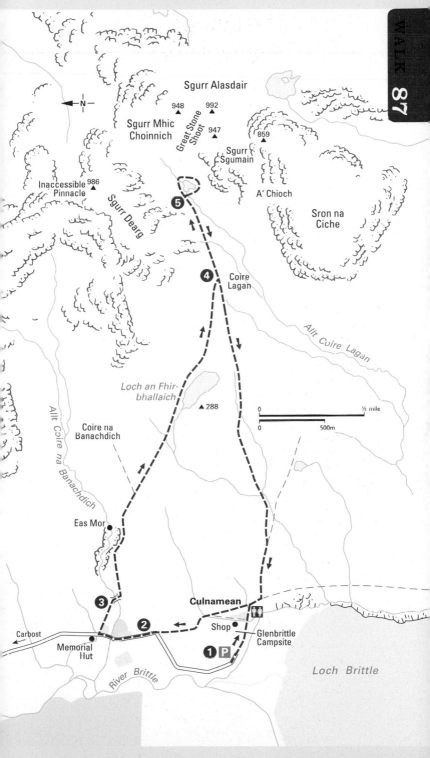

WALK 87

Sgurr Alasdair

948
992
Sgurr Mhic
Choinnich
947

Great Stone Shoot

859

Sgurr
Sgumain

A' Chioch

Inaccessible 986
Pinnacle

Sron na
Ciche

Sgurr Dearg

5

4 Coire
Lagan

Allt Coire Lagan

Loch an Fhir-
bhallaich

▲ 288

0   ½ mile
0   500m

Coire na
Banachdich

Allt Coire na Banachdich

Eas Mor

Culnamean

3

2

Shop

Glenbrittle
Campsite

Carbost

Memorial
Hut

1 P

Loch Brittle

River Brittle

WALK 87 DIRECTIONS

❶ From the parking area, the track leads on through Glenbrittle campsite to a gate with a kissing gate. Pass left of the toilet block to cross a stile. Turn left along a stony track just above, which runs gently downhill above the campsite, to rejoin the Glenbrittle road.

WHAT TO LOOK OUT FOR

After the gabbro formed, molten basalt was forced sideways into any cracks. The picnic rocks at the outflow of Loch Coire Lagan are crossed by basalt dykes, about 1ft (30cm) wide. The basalt is the same black colour as the gabbro around it, but smooth and blocky in texture. Basalt dykes form the cracks and narrow gullies that run up and down the rock faces.

❷ Keep ahead to cross a bridge with the white Memorial Hut just ahead. On the right are some stone buchts (sheep-handling enclosures) and here a waymarked path heads uphill to reach a footbridge which crosses the Allt Coire na Banachdich.

❸ Cross the footbridge and head up to the right of the stream's deep ravine, with a great view of the waterfall at its head. Its Gaelic name, Eas Mor, means simply 'Big Waterfall'. Above, the path bears right, to slant up the hillside. Below the spur of Sgurr Dearg the path forks. Here keep right, aiming for the right-hand of the two corries above, which is Coire Lagan. The path passes above Loch an Fhir-bhallaich. After a short steepening, the rebuilding works currently end and the path becomes rough. It rounds a shoulder into the lower part of Coire Lagan and meets a much larger path at a big cairn.

❹ Turn uphill on this path, until a belt of bare rock blocks the way into the upper corrie. This rock has been smoothed by a glacier into gently-rounded swells, known as 'boiler-plates'. A scree field runs up into the boiler-plate rocks. The best way keeps up the left edge, below a slab wall with a small waterslide, to the highest point of the scree. Head up left for 50ft (15m) on bare rock, then back right on ledges to an eroded scree above the boiler-plate obstruction. Look back down your upward route to note it for your return. The trodden way slants up to the right. With the main stream near by on the right, it goes up to the rim of the upper corrie.

WHERE TO EAT AND DRINK

The Sligachan Hotel serves the Skye-brewed Black Cuillin beer along with walker-size meals in its barn-like bar. No dogs, but children are welcome.

❺ The boiler-plate slabs at the lochan's outflow are excellent for picnics. Walking mainly on bare rock, it's easy to make a circuit of the lochan. For the return journey, retrace your steps to Point ❹. Ignoring the right fork of the route you came up by, keep straight downhill on the main path. It runs straight down to the toilets at Glenbrittle campsite. Turn left over a rustic footbridge to finish along the beach.

WHILE YOU'RE THERE

There's an easier way into the Cuillins. Loch Coruisk is shut in by the horseshoe-shaped mountains. However, it can be reached by boat from Elgol *Bella Jane* or *Misty Isle* gives you 1hr 30min or 4hrs 30min ashore, returning past Scavaig seal colony.

Seeing Sea Eagles at Portree Bay

A coastal walk to a raised beach called the Bile,
then returning by way of Ben Chracaig

DISTANCE 3.5 miles (5.5km)   **MINIMUM TIME** 1hr 15min

ASCENT/GRADIENT 459ft (140m) ▲▲▲   **LEVEL OF DIFFICULTY** ✦✦✦

PATHS Smooth, well-made paths, farm track, 3 stiles

LANDSCAPE Views across Minch from wooded coast and hill above

SUGGESTED MAP OS Explorer 409 Raasay, Rona & Scalpay or
410 Skye – Portree & Bracadale

START Dogs on lead through farmland, scoop poop on shore path

PARKING On A855 (Staffin Road) above Portree Bay. Another small parking
area near slipway

PUBLIC TOILETS Town centre, just off village square

While walking beside Portree Bay, keep at least one eye looking out to sea. You may spot what has been described as Britain's greatest conservation story – ever.

Sea Eagle Story

The last sea eagle in Scotland died on Skye in the early 1900s. Like all large raptors, it was shot at by shepherds and gamekeepers. An attempt to reintroduce them in 1959 failed. In 1975, a secret RAF mission flew four young birds from Norway to the island of Rum. Over the next ten years, they were joined by 80 more. Today, about a dozen pairs are nesting here, with a total population of around 100 spread up along the western coast and the Hebrides.

In Gaelic it is called 'iolaire suil na greine' – the eagle with the sunlit eye – as its eye is a golden colour. In English it's also called the white-tailed eagle, the white-tailed fish eagle and the European sea eagle; it hasn't been back here long enough to finalise its name. Its nickname is the 'flying barn door' because it's so big, but it's not a heavy bird. Even with its 8ft (2.4m) wingspan, it weighs in at just 7lb (3kg). The sea eagle nests in cliffs. One nest, with an RSPB hide, is at Loch Frisa on Mull, another here at Portree. The Aros visitor centre has a closed-circuit TV camera trained on the nest, and the Portree fishermen have taken to throwing seafood to the birds outside the bay. The eagle feeds by snatching fish out of the sea – but even more spectacular is its mating display, when the two birds soar and cartwheel high above the water.

Was that an Eagle?

The first few eagles you think you see are almost certainly buzzards. When you see a real eagle, and even though you can't tell how far away it is, you'll know it for what it is. It's four times the size of a buzzard and its wingbeats are so slow and powerful. That's when it isn't gliding from one horizon to the other apparently without moving a feather. The sea eagle is even bigger than the golden one, and has a white tail – but so does a young golden

309

eagle. But if the eagle is flying over the sea, and specially if it's over the sea at Portree, then it's a sea eagle.

Naturalists believed that the bird's main problem would be the golden eagle, which during the years of extinction has taken over the nest sites. But sadly, the real enemy is still humans. In 2000, and despite a 24-hour guard, thieves took the two eggs from the Mull pair.

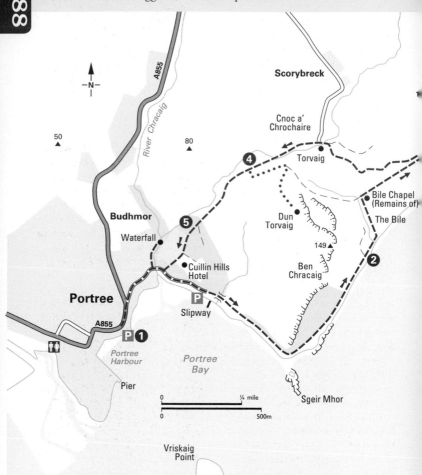

WALK 88 DIRECTIONS

❶ Turn off the main A855 on to a lane signed 'Budh Mor', to walk down to the shoreline and then continue to a small parking area. A tarred path continues along the shore past a slipway. After a footbridge, it passes under hazels which show the typical ground-branching habit of bushes formerly coppiced,

cut back every seven years for firewood. The path passes below a viewpoint with flagpoles and then rounds the headland to reach the edge of a level green field called The Bile.

❷ A wall runs up the edge of The Bile. A sign points up left for Scorybreck but ignore it and go through a small gate ahead. A rough path leads into the corner

of The Bile field. Go up its left edge and turn across its top, to a stile just above a field gate. Cross the top of the next field on an old green path, to a stile at its corner. You will see a track just beyond.

3 Turn sharp left, up the track. At the top it passes through two gates to reach a stony road just to right of Torvaig. Turn left past the house and cross the foot of a tarred road into a gently descending track. It runs down between two large corrugated sheds and then through to a gate with a stile.

4 The grassy path ahead leads down into Portree, but you can take a short, rather rough, diversion to Dun Torvaig (an ancient fortified hilltop) above. For the dun, turn left along the fence, and left again on a well-made path above. It leads to a kissing gate above the two sheds. Turn sharp right along the fence for a few steps, then bear left

around the base of a small outcrop and head straight up on a tiny path to the dun. Remnants of dry-stone walling can be seen around the summit. Return to the well-made path, passing above Point **4** to join the wall on the right. The path leads down under goat willows into a wood where it splits; stay close to the wall.

5 At the first houses (The Parks Bungalow 5), keep downhill on a tarred street. On the left is the entrance to the Cuillin Hills Hotel. A few steps later, fork right on to a stony path. At the shore road, turn right across a stream and at once right again on a path that runs up for 60yds (55m) to a craggy little waterfall. Return to the shore road and turn right to the walk start.

A Raasay Roundabout

*Seaside and woodland lead to Raasay's
old iron-mining railway.*

DISTANCE 7.75 miles (12.5km) **MINIMUM TIME** 3hrs 45min	
ASCENT/GRADIENT 820ft (250m) ▲▲▲ **LEVEL OF DIFFICULTY** ✦✦✧	
PATHS Small but clear paths, some tracks, 1 stile	
LANDSCAPE Shingle beaches, woodland and moorland	
SUGGESTED MAP OS Explorer 409 Raasay, Rona & Scalpay or 410 Skye – Portree & Bracadale	
START/FINISH Grid reference: NG 555342	
DOG FRIENDLINESS Close control in woodland and moor, keep on lead near livestock	
PARKING Ferry terminal at Sconser, Skye (or lay-by to east)	
PUBLIC TOILETS Sconser ferry terminal and start of walk	

In his *Journal of a Tour to the Hebrides with Dr Johnson* (1773), Scottish biographer James Boswell described the island of Raasay. 'It was a most pleasing approach to Raasay. We saw before us a beautiful bay, well defended with a rocky coast; a good gentleman's house, a fine verdure about it, a considerable number of trees, and beyond it hills and mountains in gradation of wildness. Our boatmen sung with great spirit.'

Boswell and Macleod

Boswell found Raasay a delight. He enjoyed the company of Macleod the laird and his ten beautiful daughters, he was impressed by the fine food and the two pet parrots, he enjoyed the landscape and he very much enjoyed his walk. He rose before six and, after a light breakfast of dry bread and whisky, set off with the laird. The aim was the island's highest point, Dun Caan. Once there, they lunched on cold mutton and brandy, and danced a Highland reel on its flat summit. They returned by way of Beinn a' Chapuill, and in the afternoon 'there came a heavy rain, by which we were a great deal wet'. Their walk totalled 24 miles altogether (nearly 40km). By way of a warm-down, Boswell 'exerted himself extraordinarily in dancing, drinking porter heavily'.

'If I had my wife and little daughters with me, I would stay long enough,' said Boswell. And today Raasay, with its well-laid paths (22 of them, all together), its woodlands and moors and small beaches, offers walking for everyone, with none of the mainland's turgid bog and skin-shredding gabbro.

Boswell and his companion Dr Johnson felt highly honoured by the boatman who ferried them to Raasay, for just 27 years before, the sailor had carried the Bonnie Prince in the opposite direction. Prince Charles Stuart had sheltered on Raasay for as long as was safe, then crossed to the mainland and walked across the moors to Strath. The boatman told Boswell that the prince had been a stronger walker than himself, but that he'd had to

RAASAY

dissuade him from littering the countryside with his empty brandy bottle. Even today, some walkers need similar education.

As punishment for sheltering the prince, the island was stripped of its cattle and every house burnt. The restoration of Raasay House was almost complete when Boswell visited. He had just one complaint. While the ruins of the former castle boasted an ancient garderobe, the new house had no such 'convenience', and Johnson reproached the laird accordingly. 'You take very good care of one end of a man, but not of the other!'

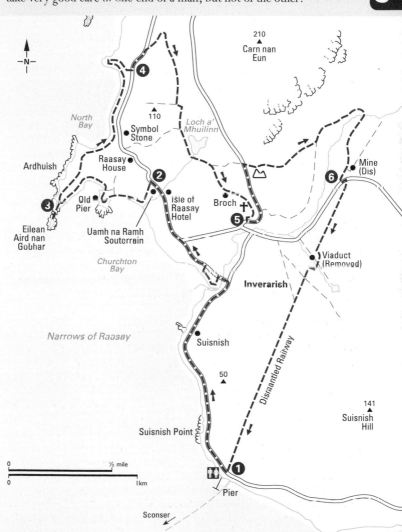

WALK 89 DIRECTIONS

1 CalMac ferries run roughly hourly during the day to the island of Raasay. Turn left on the island's small road. At Inverarish, turn left over a bridge and divert left past cottages and along the shore. After a playing field you then rejoin the road, which leads past the Isle of Raasay Hotel to another road junction.

2 Uamh na Ramh souterrain is over a stile on the left. Continue ahead past the superb but neglected stable block (ahead now is Raasay House, an outdoor centre). At the corner of the stable, turn left, signed 'Clachan'. A track continues below the ramparts of an old gun battery decorated with two stone mermaids. From the pier, follow a path around the bay, until a gate leads to a pleasant shoreline path to Eilean Aird nan Gobhar. Check the tides before crossing the rocks to this tidal island.

3 Head inland over a rock knoll, then pass along the left-hand edge of a plantation on a muddy path overhung by rhododendron. Continue along the shore of North Bay, with a pine plantation on your right, round to a headland. Go up briefly through the low basalt cliff and return along its top. Head along the left edge of the plantation, to emerge through a decorative iron gate on to a road.

4 Turn left for 180yds (165m) to a grey gate on the right. A green track leads up and to the right into a craggy valley. At a walled paddock it turns left and right to join a tarred track. Follow this down past a lily lochan (Loch a' Mhuilinn) and turn left across its dam. Join a wide path running up under larch and rhododendron

WHILE YOU'RE THERE

'A little off the shore is a kind of subterranean house. There has been a natural fissure or separation of the rock, running towards the sea, roofed over with long stones, and above them turf... in that place the inhabitants used to keep their oars.' Forgotten since Boswell's time, this souterrain has been rediscovered at Point **2**.

WHAT TO LOOK OUT FOR

Seals and otters play in North Bay. A seal will usually show only its dark brown head, often lifting it far out of the water. An otter sighting is less common, although shoreline otters are less timid than river ones.

but, in 100yds (91m), bear right, waymarked 'Temptation Hill Trail'. Look out for a side path on the right which leads up to Dun Bhorogh Dail, the remains of an Iron Age broch (tower). The main path leads down to pass an austere white church, then bends to the right and drops to a tarred road.

5 Turn sharp left up the road for 0.25 mile (400m), then right at a signpost for Burma Road. The track shrinks to a path as it bends left and climbs quite steeply. It becomes a forest track, passing white waymarkers, finally reaching the abandoned buildings of an old iron mine.

WHERE TO EAT AND DRINK

Raasay House is now an outdoor centre and at its Dolphin Café you can enjoy fresh coffee where James Boswell and Dr Samuel Johnson dined on chops and claret, and danced with the ten beautiful Macleod daughters.

6 When you get to the tarred road beyond, turn up left to a signpost for the Miners' Trail. Here turn right on the green track of a former railway. Where a viaduct has been removed, a new-built path descends steeply and then climbs again to regain the railbed. The blue-waymarked Miners' Trail turns off, but your route follows the railway onwards, across a stretch of moor and down to the ferry terminal.

Waterstein Head

*Through crofting country and peat moors
to a 1,000ft (300m) sea cliff.*

DISTANCE 5.75 miles (9.2km)   MINIMUM TIME 3hrs 30min

ASCENT/GRADIENT 1,500ft (457m) ▲▲▲   LEVEL OF DIFFICULTY +++

PATHS Grassy clifftops and moorland, 2 fences and 1 gate

LANDSCAPE Cliff tops high above Atlantic Ocean

SUGGESTED MAP OS Explorer 407 Skye – Dunvegan

START/FINISH Grid reference: NG 163443

DOG FRIENDLINESS On short lead – risk of scaring sheep over cliff edges

PARKING Ramasaig road end or pull-ins at pass 0.75 mile (1.2km) north

PUBLIC TOILETS Glendale village hall

After the defeat of Bonnie Prince Charlie's uprising in 1746, the clan system was swept away. But the clansmen were still there, transformed into crofters. Elsewhere, such subsistence smallholders go by the honourable name of 'peasant farmers', with 25 acres (10ha), a kailyard, a cow and some sheep on the hill.

Rents rose, partly to support the landlords' new London lifestyles. Crofting lands were cleared to make way for sheep, and the crofters were forced to relocate, first to the shore and later right out of the country to Canada and Australia. By the late 1800s, they were starting to fight back. In 1882, crofters at the Braes, south of Portree, resisted an eviction. Fifty Glasgow policemen were sent to restore order, and in the 'Battle of the Braes' the crofters retaliated with sticks and stones.

In Glendale, land-starved crofters deliberately let their cattle stray on to neighbouring farms. Government forces and the gunboat *Jackal* were defied by 600 crofters. There were four arrests, including John Macpherson, the 'Glendale Martyr', and a minister, the Reverend D MacCallum. The 'martyrs' received two-month prison sentences. The public outcry that followed saw a newly formed 'Crofters' Party' – distant forerunner of today's New Labour – send four MPs to Westminster. The first of the Crofting Acts, passed by Gladstone's government, led to less unfair rents and security of tenure.

Today, thanks to those battles of long ago, Glendale and the Braes are inhabited lands where so much of Scotland is bleak and empty. Crofters now have the right to buy and enjoy subsidies and grants from the government. Few crofts provide enough to live on, without a part-time job on the side. As a result there's a series of small-scale, off-beat and interesting tourist enterprises along the Glendale Visitor Route.

Peat became the crofters' fuel supply and in a few places it is still being worked today. Above Loch Eishort on this walk you'll see the little triangular stacks, each made from four peats, drying in the wind (and of course getting wet again in the rain). And when it burns, it brings the smell of the wild bog-moss right into the house.

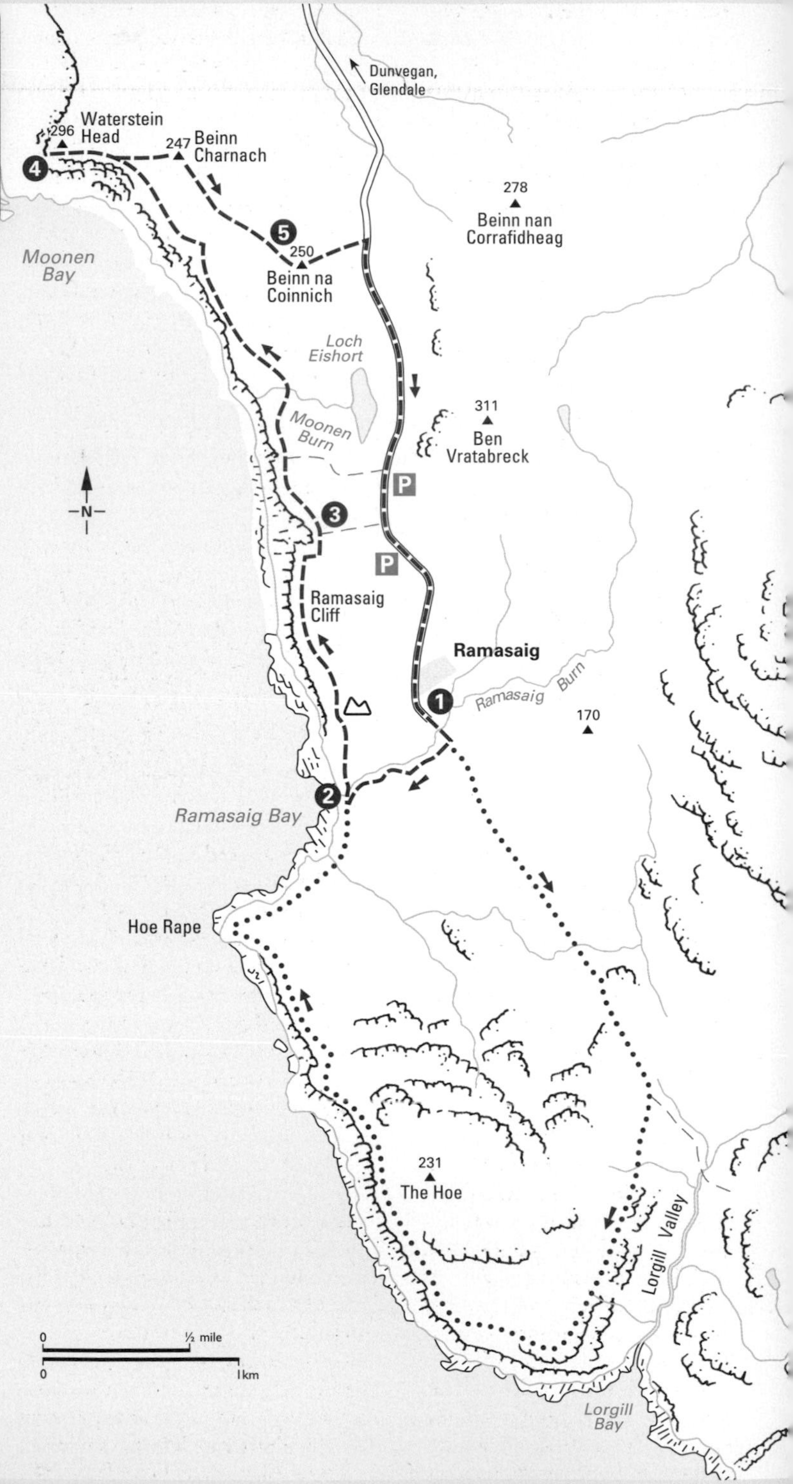

296
Waterstein
Head
247 Beinn
Charnach
④
5
250
Beinn na
Coinnich

Moonen
Bay

Dunvegan,
Glendale

278
Beinn nan
Corrafidheag

Loch
Eishort

Moonen
Burn

311
Ben
Vratabreck

−N−

P

③

P

Ramasaig
Cliff

Ramasaig

① Ramasaig Burn

170

②

Ramasaig Bay

Hoe Rape

231
The Hoe

Lorgill Valley

Lorgill
Bay

0   ½ mile

0   1km

WALK 90 DIRECTIONS

① From the end of the tarmac, the road continues as a track past farm buildings, with a bridge over the Ramasaig Burn. After a gate it reaches a shed with a tin roof. Bear right and follow the left bank of Ramasaig Burn to the shore.

WHILE YOU'RE THERE

Dunvegan Castle is one of Scotland's most visited attractions. For those who prefer the quirky and out-of-the-way, the Glendale Visitor Route includes the small Colbost Folk Museum and the centre devoted to the famous MacCrimmons of Borreraig, hereditary clan of pipers. The Giant MacAskill Museum, Dunvegan, in a re antiquated black house, is a small museum to a man, whose height of 7ft 9in (239cm) got him into the Guinness Book of Records.

② Cross the burn at a ford and head up a very steep meadow beside the fence that protects the cliff edge. There's an awkward fence to cross half-way up. At the top, above Ramasaig Cliff, keep following the fence on the left. It cuts across to the right to protect a notch in the cliff edge. From here, you could cut down to the parking areas at the nearby road pass.

③ Keep downhill along the cliffside fence. At the bottom, a turf wall off to the right provides another short-cut back to the road. The clifftop walk now bears slightly right around the V-notch of the Moonen Burn. A small path crosses the stream and slants up left to rejoin the clifftop fence, which soon turns slightly inland around another cliff notch. The cliff-edge fence leads up and to the left, to reach Waterstein Head.

Here there is a trig point, 971ft (296m) above the sea – the second highest cliff on Skye. Below, you will see Neist Point lighthouse.

④ Return for 0.25 mile (400m) down to where the fence bends to the right, then continue through a shallow grassy col for the slight rise to Beinn Charnach. Here bear right to follow a gently rounded grass ridge-line parallel with cliffs. The highest line along the ridge is the driest. A fence runs across, with a grey gate at its highest point where it passes through a col. Climb over the gate and on up to a cairn on Beinn na Coinnich.

WHERE TO EAT AND DRINK

An Strupag Gallery and café at Glendale sells home-made cakes. Dunvegan's hotels all serve food. The Misty Isle Hotel is inexpensive and Dunvegan Hotel's restaurant has a sea view and seafood shellfish dishes on the menu'.

⑤ Continue along the slightly rocky plateau for 300yds (274m) to the south-east top. Now the Ramasaig road is visible 0.25 mile (400m) away on the left. Go down to join a quad-bike track heading towards the road. Just before reaching the road, the bike track crosses a swampy col. This shows old and recent peat workings. Turn right, along the road, passing above Loch Eishort to the start.

EXTENDING THE WALK

For more big cliff scenery, you can extend this walk from the start by heading out on the track towards Lorgill. At a gate overlooking Lorgill Valley, turn off right and contour along the valley rim to a clifftop corner overlooking Lorgill Bay. Follow the cliff tops to Hoe Rape and Ramasaig Bay, Point **②**.

Prison and Pinnacle

*Exploring the weird lava landscape
of Skye's northern peninsula.*

DISTANCE 5.25 miles (8.4km)   **MINIMUM TIME** 3hrs

ASCENT/GRADIENT 1,200ft (365m) ▲▲▲   **LEVEL OF DIFFICULTY** ✦✦✦

PATHS Well-used path, 2 stiles

LANDSCAPE Rock towers and pinnacles

SUGGESTED MAP OS Explorer 408 Skye – Trotternish & the Storr

START/FINISH Grid reference: NG 440679

DOG FRIENDLINESS Keep on lead passing sheep, take care on cliff top

PARKING Pull-in, top of pass on Staffin–Uig road. Overflow parking at cemetery 0.25 mile (400m) on Staffin side (not available during funerals)

PUBLIC TOILETS Brogaig

The rocks of Scotland vary from ancient – about 400 million years – to a great deal older than that, but along the western edge is something quite different. The great eye of the Atlantic Ocean opened at a time that, geologically speaking, is this morning just before breakfast. A mere 60 million years ago, the mid-Atlantic ridge lay just off the Scottish coast. And all along that ridge, new seabed emerged in exotic and interesting volcanic rocks that now form the Arran granite, the basalt of Mull and Skye, and the Skye gabbro.

Lava Landscape

Stir together butter and sugar in a saucepan, take the mixture off the heat and it crystallises into fudge. But take the same ingredients and cool them quickly, by tipping them into cold water, for example, and you get the glassy solid we call toffee. Now take a basic silicaceous magma, let it cool over thousands of years deep inside a volcano, and you'll get the rough crystalline gabbro that featured on Walk 87. But let it erupt suddenly at the surface, and it congeals into basalt, which is black, shiny and slippery. It forms a completely different sort of scenery – that of northern Skye.

Basalt lava is a slippery liquid, like milk rather than treacle. This makes it quite different from the lumpy rhyolite lava that formed Glen Coe and the craggy side of Ben Nevis. Basalt lava spreads in wide, shallow layers across the country. After erosion, you get a flat-topped landscape, with long low cliffs at the edges and wide grassy plateaux. Macleod's Tables and Dun Caan on Raasay (see Walk 89) are lava-layer hills.

North of Portree, the lava flowed out over older, softer rocks of Jurassic (dinosaur) age. All along the Trotternish peninsula, the sea has been steadily removing those softer rocks, and the basalt above has been breaking off in hill-sized chunks and slipping downhill and eastwards. The chunks lean over, split apart and erode: the result is some extraordinary scenery, of which the queerest is the Quiraing. Some of its rock forms, with intriguing names such as The Prison, The Needle and the Fingalian Slab, have been a tourist must-see since Victorian times. As a result, a wide, well-made path leads below these pinnacles, then back along the top. Here you will find a gently undulating lawn, which would be quite suitable for a spot of croquet, that's called the Table. Spread your picnic cloth on The Table, and then peep out between the rock architecture to the Sound of Raasay and the distant hills of Torridon.

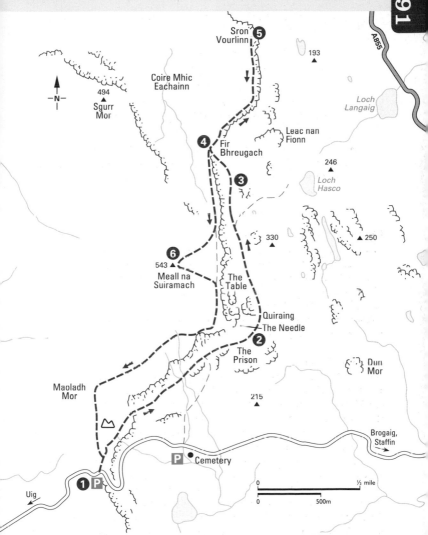

WALK 91 DIRECTIONS

1 A well-built path starts at a small green signpost opposite the lay-by, where you can park. The jagged tower of grass and rock on the skyline is the Prison. The path crosses over the steep landslip slope towards it, with an awkward crossing of a small stream gully on bare rock and then passes a small waterfall high above and heads to the right, rather than up into a rocky gap. It turns uphill into the wide col to the left of The Prison.

WHAT TO LOOK OUT FOR

Basalt rock is alkaline and relatively rich in lime and minerals, so its soils support meadow flowers such as would more usually be seen in the English countryside. Yellow rattle, a flower of ancient pastureland, has been spotted here. Sron Vourlinn grows daisies like any suburban lawn. Global warming has encouraged the marbled white butterfly, blotchy brown and white, to move north from England as well.

2 The main path does not drop, but goes forward, slightly uphill, crossing a new fence at a stile and then dodging below a crag foot. It crosses the foot of steep ground, then passes above a small peat pool. Ignore a path forking down right; the main path slants up to the left into a col where an old wall runs across.

3 The path descends into a landslip valley that runs across rather than down the hillside, then slants up left to a col with a stile.

4 Cross and turn right for the excursion to Sron Vourlinn. Follow the crest over a slightly rocky section with a short descent beyond, then join the main path along a grassy meadow with a very sudden edge on the right. After

WHILE YOU'RE THERE

Kilt Rock is seen from a clifftop viewpoint at Staffin. The warning (in Gaelic and five other languages) not to climb over the fence seems scarcely necessary as immediately beyond is a 500ft (152m) drop to the sea. Lean over to see the startling waterfall and columnar basalt cliff. Some of the six-sided blocks have fallen off and lie in the sea directly below the platform.

the highest point, continue slightly downhill to the north top. Here you can see that the land is still slipping, with a crevasse beside the cliff edge where another narrow section is shortly to peel away. The shelter of the rock crevice grows luxuriant rock rose, rowan and valerian.

WHERE TO EAT AND DRINK

The Pieces of Ate café at Brogaig, at the foot of the hill road, serves home-made snacks and soup from a small shack (closed on Sundays, as is most of the island). Magnificently sited below the Quiraing crags, the Flodigarry Hotel offers evening meals and Sunday lunch at its restaurant, bistro and terrace, specialising in local lobster and other seafood.

5 Return to the col with the stile (Point **4**) and continue uphill. The drops are now on your left, as you look down towards the pinnacles surrounding The Table. After passing broken ground on the right, you come to a fallen wall, part of which appears from below as a cairn. The path continues next to the cliff edge on the left; you can fork off right, directly uphill, to the summit trig point on Meall na Suiramach.

6 Follow a broad faint path slightly downhill to a cairn at the cliff edge. You now look straight down on to The Table, 100ft (30m) below. Turn right on the wide path alongside the crag drop. After 0.25 mile (400m) as the path steepens, you'll see a fence on your right with a kissing gate. Once through this, the path becomes much clearer, contouring across the steep slope of Maoladh Mor. Above the car park, it turns straight downhill for a final ascent.

Sir James Grant's Town

Ancient pine wood, the banks of the Spey and an 18th-century planned town.

DISTANCE *7 miles (11.3km)* **MINIMUM TIME** *3hrs*

ASCENT/GRADIENT *200ft (60m)* ▲▲▲ **LEVEL OF DIFFICULTY** ✦✦✦

PATHS *Tracks and smooth paths, 1 stile*

LANDSCAPE *Open pine forest, wide river*

SUGGESTED MAP *OS Explorer 419 Grantown-on-Spey*

START/FINISH *Grid reference: NJ 035280*

DOG FRIENDLINESS *Close control in Anagach woods, on lead on golf course*

PARKING *Grantown-on-Spey Museum*

PUBLIC TOILETS *At start*

Sir Ludovic Grant and Mr Grant of Grant propose a TOWN should be erected, and will give Feus or long Leases, and all proper Encouragement to Manufacturers, Tradesmen or others...

In about 1750, young Mr James Grant returned from his Grand Tour of Europe. He'd seen Edinburgh New Town, just then being built, and thought Speyside could do with something of the sort. Somehow he persuaded his father, Sir Ludovic. The new town was set out, above the new military bridge over the Spey. Merchants, tradesmen and artisans were invited in. They were to build their own houses, to a set pattern, roofed with slate and walled with pale speckled granite from the surrounding fields. The town was to be supported by a linen factory.

In 1766 the market cross was ceremonially moved in procession from old town to new. To persuade the townsfolk away from whisky, a brewery was set up. The Grants put up a handsome orphanage, and established a daringly modern school where the young people were chastised with birch and the leather tawse only now and then. What James Grant was playing was the modern computer game of 'Sim City', but with real people and real money. And he lost the game. First he was obliged to subsidise the building of most of the houses, then he had to pay for the linen factory. Grantown was not handy for transport, and the Industrial Revolution in England was just starting to churn out cheap cloth. 'A Highlander never sits at ease at a loom, 'tis like putting a deer in the plough', and in 1774 the linen factory failed. By 1804 the town was threatened with economic collapse, and Sir James had to sell his London house to buy meal.

But Grantown continued as a market town for the barley lands of the Spey. And in September 1860, Queen Victoria stopped off at the Grant Arms. Her ghillies got rather drunk, her secretary General Grey went shopping and bought himself a watch, and the Queen enjoyed some excellent porridge.

With the arrival of the railway, middle-class Victorians came in the steps of their Queen. The inhabitants of Grantown moved into cottages in their own gardens, while the middle-class families of doctors and lawyers moved in for the summer, with 'Pater' becoming a weekly commuter back to Aberdeen or Edinburgh. 'I know of no more attractive mountain resting place,' said Prime Minister Ramsay Macdonald. And Sir James Grant's handsome granite town has been attracting tourists ever since.

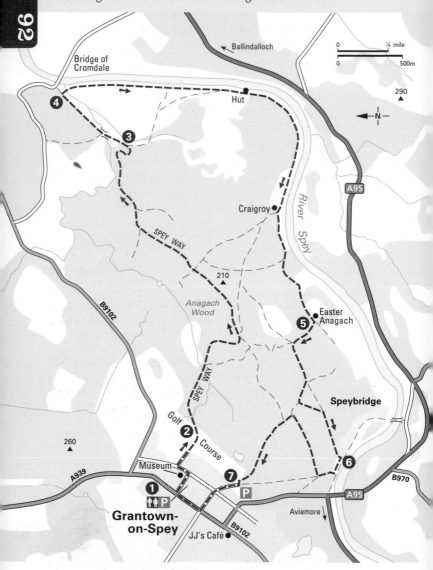

WALK 92 DIRECTIONS

1 Go down past the museum. Turn left into South Street, then right into Golf Course Road. A tarred path crosses the golf course to a small gate into Anagach Wood.

2 The wide path ahead has a blue/red waymarker. At a junction, the blue trail departs to the right; turn left, following a Spey Way marker and red-top poles. Keep following the red markers, turning left at the first junction and bearing left at the next. When the track joins a new fence and a bend in a stream is on the left, keep ahead, following a Spey Way marker.

③ The track emerges into open fields. After crossing a small bridge, turn to the right through a new hunting gate. A path with pines on its left leads to a track near the River Spey. (Bridge of Cromdale is just ahead here.)

④ Turn sharp right on this track, alongside the river. At a fishers' hut it re-enters forest. About 0.75 mile (1.2km) later it diminishes to a green path and slants up past the cottage of Craigroy to join its entrance track.

⑤ At Easter Anagach, a grass track on the right has red waymarkers and runs into a birchwood. With a barrier ahead, follow marker poles to the left, on to a broad path beside a falling fence. At the next junction, turn right, following the red poles, over a slight rise. Descending, turn left just before a blue-top post, on to a smaller path with blue and red posts. This runs along the top of a ridge, to reach a bench above a lane. To the left down the lane is the handsome stone bridge built by Major Caulfield as part of the military road system.

⑥ The path bends right, alongside the road, to meet a wide track which is the former military road. Turn right, to a path on the right with green-top posts. At a small pool, the main path bends left for 150yds (137m), with blue and green posts; take the path ahead, with green posts. A very old tree in the middle of the path was once used for public hangings. Once at a five-way junction bear left to find the next green post. At the edge of the golf course turn left to a small car park and information board.

⑦ Follow the tarred street uphill, past the end of the golf course, to Grantown's High Street. Turn right to The Square. Just past the Grant Arms Hotel, a sign points right, to the museum.

Farigaig Forest and Loch Ness

*Overlooking Loch Ness and past the home of
a different monster, the Beast of Boleskine.*

WALK

93

DISTANCE 4.25 miles (6.8km)	**MINIMUM TIME** 2hrs 15min
ASCENT/GRADIENT 700ft (213m) ▲▲▲	**LEVEL OF DIFFICULTY** ✦✦✧

PATHS Waymarked paths and tracks, no stiles

LANDSCAPE Hillside of mixed woodland

SUGGESTED MAP OS Explorer 416 Inverness, Loch Ness & Culloden

START/FINISH Grid reference: NH 522237

DOG FRIENDLINESS Keep on lead for short stretch past Easter Boleskine

PARKING Forest Enterprise car park

PUBLIC TOILETS At start

With so many fine sights in Scotland, it's a shame that such large numbers of people take the trouble to see one that doesn't exist. The first encounter with the Loch Ness monster was back to the 6th century AD, when St Columba was crossing the River Ness. One of his companions was attacked by a water beast. When the saint ordered it to go away, it did. The onlookers, pagan barbarians whose friend had already been eaten, promptly converted to Christianity. The account was set down 100 years later by Adomnan, an abbot of Iona. It sounds suspiciously like an earlier incident from the life of a different holy man, St Martin of Tours, and also like a story about how Christianity took over a site where human sacrifice had been offered to a river god.

Later confirmation came during the Lisbon earthquake of 1755. A shock wave, freakishly magnified along Loch Ness, sent breakers crashing against the shore at Fort Augustus – clearly Columba's monster was still down there disturbing the water.

The Beast of Boleskine

Authentic sightings of a rather different monster did, however, take place in the early 1900s. Finding it fashionable to be Scottish, Alexander Crowley changed his name to Aleister and bought the nearby hall to become the Laird of Boleskine. In his time, he was known as 'The Beast of Boleskine', the 'wickedest man alive'. He identified himself with the Great Beast described in the final book of the Bible, the seven-headed monster that was to battle with the angels at the end of time.

In pursuit of his precept 'do what thou wilt shall be the whole of the law', he debauched minor film stars, when given the opportunity, betrayed his friends and became an alcoholic and heroin addict. At Boleskine, as he studied his magical books, the sky darkened at midday so candles had to be lit, and the lodge keeper went mad.

We might take the darkening of the sky as a normal Scottish summer raincloud, but we can still see the rowan trees his neighbours planted to protect themselves from his dangerous magical influence.

LOCH NESS

Apart from seducing his neighbours and brightening the Inverness-shire scene with various exotic mistresses, Crowley contributed to local life by prankishly reporting to the Society for the Suppression of Vice the prevalence of prostitution in Foyers (where there wasn't any). He also made an impassioned plea against the plan to enclose the Falls of Foyers in hydroelectric water pipes.

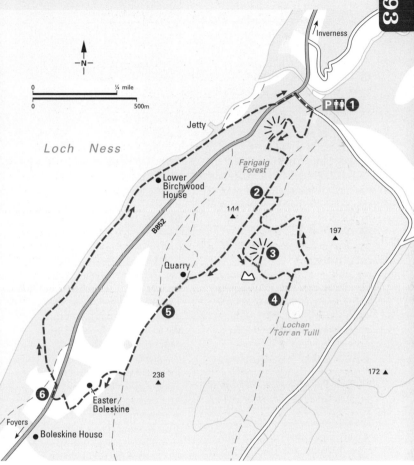

WALK 93 DIRECTIONS

❶ From the car park follow yellow waymarkers uphill near a stream. After 100yds (91m), a path on the right has a yellow-top waymarker. After a bench, the path contours briefly then turns up left, to a higher viewpoint. It then turns back sharply right and descends on earth steps through a little crag to a forest road. Turn right for 200yds (183m).

❷ Turn up left on a footpath with more yellow waymarkers. The path has a low, heavily mossed wall alongside as it bends up to a higher forest road. Turn right and walk for about 150yds (137m) until you reach a sharp left-hand bend. Turn off right here, on a small footpath walking through an area of small self-seeded trees, then go steeply up to the left underneath mature trees. At the top, bear left along a little ridge,

WALK 93

dropping gently downhill to a fine viewpoint.

❸ Return for 100yds (91m) and bear left down the other side of the ridge. The path now descends steeply until it reaches a forest road. A sign indicates Lochan Torr an Tuill, near by on the left, with a picnic table.

❹ Return along the forest road, past where you joined it. It climbs gently and then descends to the sharp right bend where you turned off earlier – the waymarker says 'to Carpark' on the side now facing you. After 150yds (137m), at another 'to Car Park' waymarker, turn left down the path with the low mossed wall to the forest road below (Point ❷). Turn left, past a red/green waymarker. The track kinks left past a quarry.

❺ Where the main track bends right, downhill, keep ahead on a green track with a red/green waymarker. It emerges from

the trees at a signpost. Follow this down to the right towards Easter Boleskine house. Green waymarkers indicate a diversion to the left of the house, to join its driveway track below. Follow this down to the B852.

❻ Turn right for 50yds (46m). Below the left edge of the road is a tarred track. Turn down a faint path between the trees to cross this track, with a blue waymarker leading into a clearer path beyond. This passes down to the right of electricity transformers. At the foot of the slope, the main path bears right with a blue waymarker. It runs above the loch shore and joins a gravel track just below Lower Birchwood House. At a tarmac turning circle, an overgrown jetty on the left is great for monster-watchers. The tarred lane ahead leads up to the B852, with the car park just above on the right.

WHERE TO EAT AND DRINK

Craigdarroch House Hotel at Lower Foyers is an upmarket country house, but it offers very good bar meals at normal bar prices. Its restaurant is a conservatory with views of Loch Ness. The Red Squirrel Bistro is in Upper Foyers, at the top of the path to the waterfall.

WHILE YOU'RE THERE

The Falls of Foyers are reached by a short but quite exciting walk from Upper Foyers. In September 1803, the poet Samuel Taylor Coleridge wrote about them – 'The plumage of the fall, the puffs of smoke in every direction from the bed of plumy foam at the bottom, the restless network of waves on its pool.' Although the stream above has now been dammed for the Foyers Power Station, a reasonable spell of wet weather leaves plenty of water for the fall. Otherwise you can see it in an old print in the bar of the Craigdarroch House Hotel.

The Shores of Loch Shieldaig

A walk around the many inlets of the Shieldaig peninsula.

DISTANCE 3.25 miles (5.3km) **MINIMUM TIME** 1hr 45min

ASCENT/GRADIENT 500ft (152m) ▲▲▲ **LEVEL OF DIFFICULTY** ✦✦✦

PATHS Well-made old paths, 1 rough section

LANDSCAPE Saltwater views up Loch Torridon and down Loch Shieldaig

SUGGESTED MAP OS Explorer 428 Kyle of Lochalsh

START/FINISH Grid reference: NG 814538

DOG FRIENDLINESS Keep on lead in village and when passing livestock

PARKING South end of Shieldaig village, opposite shop and hotel

PUBLIC TOILETS North end of village (another car park)

The Shieldaig peninsula separates inner and outer Loch Torridon, and at every turn there's a new view – up the loch to Liathach and the less-known hills to the south, out across the sea to Skye and Raasay, or into a sheltered bay with a cluster of eider or the sleek head of a seal. But on a warm, grey summer's day you may wish to complete the walk quickly and not linger too long.

Scotland's Scourge

The reason? In Gaelic she's 'meanbh-chuileag', the tiny fly, but she's better known as the mighty midge, Scotland's scourge. I say 'she' as the male is an altogether weaker creature, content with a suck of bog myrtle, a brief dance in the summer haze and death among the heather stalks. It's the female that needs a blood meal in order to lay her eggs. The blood host could be a deer, a sheep, a grouse, or, of course, you. The larvae hatch in wet peat moss, which is all too common in western Scotland. They have the evil ability to absorb oxygen even from such waterlogged surroundings.

Midgie Prince

Bonnie Prince Charlie, wandering Scotland in the damp summer of 1746, was mildly inconvenienced by the pursuing redcoats. But his real enemy was the midge. On Benbecula, crouching under a rock in the rain, on a muggy June day, he lost his customary poise and gave way to 'hideous cries and complaints'. His remedy was brandy when brandy was to be had, and otherwise whisky. During his flight through the heather he got through as much as a bottle a day. Indeed, his alcoholism in later life can in part be blamed on the midge.

There's a historical mystery over the midge. Dr Johnson, touring just 27 years later, didn't notice the midge at all. The poet Samuel Taylor Coleridge, walking the Great Glen in 1803, found them mildly annoying, but the bed-bugs were much worse. By 1872 the midges were bad enough to completely ruin one of Queen Victoria's picnics. This increase in the midge may be down to the Highland Clearances. Glens formerly farmed

Overleaf: The shores of Loch Shieldaig (Walk 94)

became their bog breeding grounds. But the worst midge story of all is said to have happened at Gairloch. A replacement minister, the Revd John Morrison, was sent to the Presbyterian church there in 1711, and the congregation so disapproved of his sermon that they stripped him naked, tied him to a tree and left him overnight for the midges!

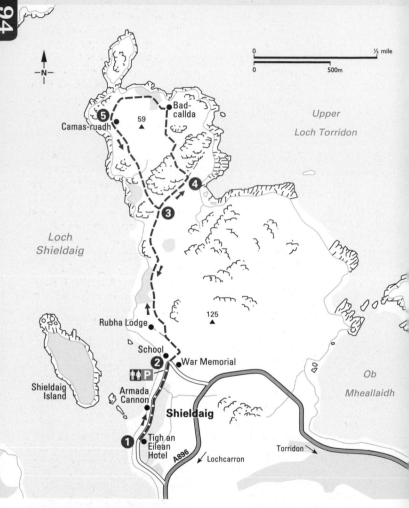

WALK 94 DIRECTIONS

❶ Follow the street along the shoreline past a cannon salvaged from the Spanish Armada of 1588. At the village end it rises slightly, with another parking area, and a war memorial above on the right.

❷ In front of the village school, turn right up a rough track. The

track passes a couple of houses to turn left. In another 100yds (91m) it divides; here the main track for Rubha Lodge forks off left, but your route bears right, passing to the right of a glacier-smoothed rock knoll. The terraced path runs through birch woods at first, with Loch Shieldaig below on the left. It passes above two rocky bays, then strikes across a peat bog, bright in mid-summer with bell heather and the fluffy white tops of cotton grass. In the middle of this flat area it divides at a cairn.

❸ The right-hand path runs along the edge of the peaty area, with rocky ground above on its left, then next to birch trees for 50yds (46m). Look out for the point where its pink gravel surface becomes peaty, with a rock formation like a low ruin on the right, because here is an easily missed path junction.

WHILE YOU'RE THERE

The natural tree cover of the Highlands is pine, oak or birch, depending on the local climate. Ancient ashwood is a surprise. Rassal ashwood grows on a small outcrop of limestone, and pollen in peat sediments suggests that it's 6,000 years old. Now fenced as a National Nature Reserve, it is regrowing its original limestone-loving wild flowers. The reserve's small car park is on the single-track A896 at grid ref NG 840432.

---

❹ What seems like the main footpath, ahead and slightly downhill, peters out eventually. The correct path forks off to the left, slanting up to the higher ground just above. The path is now clear, crossing slabby ground in the direction of the peninsula's trig point, 0.25 mile (400m) away. After 220yds (201m) it rises slightly to a gateway in a former fence. Aiming right of the trig point, it crosses a small heather moor. At a broken wall, the path turns down right through a gap to the top of a grassy meadow. The first of the two shoreline cottages, Bad-callda, is just below. Rough paths lead to the left across the boggy top of the meadow and above a birchwood, with the trig point just above on the left. Keep going forward at the same level to a heather knoll, with a pole on it. Just below you is a second cottage, Camas-ruadh.

❺ The footpath zig-zags down to the right between rocks. White paint spots lead round to the right of the cottage and its shed. Turn left behind the shed to join a clear path coming from the cottage. The return path is easy to follow, mostly along the top of the slope dropping to the right to Loch Shieldaig. After 0.5 mile (800m) it rejoins the outward route at the cairn, Point ❸.

WHERE TO EAT AND DRINK

In Shieldaig, the restaurant and Shieldaig Bar at Tigh an Eilean Hotel serve fresh local seafood (April–October). In high summer, the small, friendly bar is often very busy with visitors.

WHAT TO LOOK OUT FOR

Look and listen for eider ducks and divers. The male eider is black-and-white, the female an inconspicuous brown; their call is a sort coo-ing murmur. On a still evening, a flock of eider out on the loch is the softest sound ever. If you hear a wild, haunting cry that could be a lamenting mermaid, it's probably a black-throated diver (though it could, of course, be a lamenting mermaid: they have been recorded on Loch Torridon).

Coire Lair and the Coulin Forest

Deer stalkers' paths lead into the heart of the South Torridon mountains

---

DISTANCE 9 miles (14.5km)   **MINIMUM TIME** 5hrs

ASCENT/GRADIENT 1,700ft (518m) ▲▲▲   **LEVEL OF DIFFICULTY** +++

PATHS Well-made path, then track, no stiles

LANDSCAPE Boulder-scattered moorland between high hills

SUGGESTED MAP OS Explorer 429 Glen Carron & West Monar

START/FINISH Grid reference: NH 005484

DOG FRIENDLINESS Keep under control in deer forest

PARKING On A890 below Achnashellach Station

PUBLIC TOILETS None on route

NOTE During stalking season on Achnashellach Estate (15 September–20 October, not Sundays), keep strictly to route, which is right of way

---

The path winds up from Strath Carron into Coire Lair. The corrie is a fine one, with scattered pines, waterfalls and craggy mountains. The path that takes you there is terraced at the steep places, drained at the level places and avoids the boggy places altogether. Over a century old, it was built not for walkers but stalkers – or rather for their sturdy Highland ponies bringing down a deer corpse weighing 2cwt (100kg) or more. Recent resurfacing has been done sympathetically in the traditional style.

Deer stalking calls on the legs and the intelligence in equal measure, appealing to man's ancient hunting urges. 'The beautiful motions of the deer, his sagacity and the skilful generalship that can alone ensure success in the pursuit of him, keep the mind in a pleasurable state of constant excitement.' Thus said William Scrope Esq, in the book *Days of Deerstalking*, which presented this sport to the leisured and affluent of 1845.

Red Bedrock

As the path rises above the tree line, you'll notice slabs of Torridonian sandstone underfoot – the ghillies have deliberately routed it over this maintenance-free surface. On the left, Fuar Tholl ('cold hole') is of the same red rock, but ahead on the right, Beinn Liath Mhor is composed of pale Cambrian quartzite. As you top the pass and look east, the hills ahead are rounded, grey and slightly less exciting all the way to the North Sea. As you come to know Scotland you realise that all the way along its north-western edge there's a zone of rather special hills. Applecross, Torridon, the Great Wilderness, Coigach, Inverpolly: these names mean sandstone and quartzite to the geologist, and pure magic to the mountaineer.

The rest of the Northern Highlands is made of a speckly grey rock – Moinian schist. The boundary line is the Moine Thrust. It's called a 'thrust' because these grey mountains have been pushed in over the top of the Torridonian red and the Cambrian white. It marks the western limit of the crumple zone from when England crashed into Scotland 400 million years ago. On the face of Beinn Liath Mhor, the arrival of the Moinian has crumpled the quartzite, like a boot landing on a carelessly placed cheese sandwich. A short wander from Point ❸ further into the corrie will show this more clearly, and you'll also see the famous Mainreachan Buttress on the north side of Fuar Tholl.

WALK 95 DIRECTIONS

❶ The track to the station runs up behind a red phone box, then turns right to reach the platform end. Cross the line through two gates and head up the stony track opposite, past a waymarker arrow.

After 100yds (91m) you reach a junction under low-voltage power lines. Turn left here on a smooth gravel road to a gate through a deer fence. After 0.25 mile (400m), look out for a signpost where a new path turns back to the left.

2 This path goes back through the deer fence at a pot-hole type, then runs up alongside the River Lair. As the slope steepens above the tree-line, a short side path on the left gives a view of a waterfall. The well-maintained stalkers' path runs over slabs of bare sandstone. A cairn marks the point where it arrives in the upper valley, Coire Lair, with a view to the high pass at its head, 2 miles (3.2km) away.

WHERE TO EAT AND DRINK

The Strathcarron Hotel at Strathcarron Station serves home cooking and real ales in its restaurant, bar (dogs and children welcome) and coffee shop. Loch Carron Hotel at Lochcarron village does good bar meals and also welcomes children and dogs.

3 About 200yds (183m) after this first cairn, another marks a junction of paths. Bear right here, between two pools. In 110yds (100m) there is a second junction with a tall, well-built cairn. Bear right, on a path that leaves the corrie through a wide, shallow col just 350yds (320m) above. An elegant conical cairn marks a final path junction. Bear right; in a few steps you're heading downhill above the path. The path runs downhill among drumlins and sandstone boulders, slanting down to the right to join the wooded Allt nan Dearcag. The path now runs down alongside this stream; you may notice pale grey quartzite. The path drops to reach a footbridge. This bridge crosses a side stream, the Allt Coire Beinne Leithe, with the Easan Geal, White Waterfalls, just above.

4 At an open bothy shelter hut, a track continues downhill, with the gorge of the Easan Dorcha

WHILE YOU'RE THERE

Strome Castle stands on a romantic headland overlooking the narrows of Loch Carron. It was besieged by the Mackenzies in 1602, and surrendered after some 'silly women' poured drinking water into the gunpowder. The Mackenzies blew it up, but left enough of the walls to make a fine foreground for views along the loch.

(Dark Waterfalls) on its right. After a mile (1.6km) there's a stone bridge on the right. Turn across this, on to a track that runs up the wide, open valley to the Coulin Pass at its head. Coulin, pronounced Cowlinn, is the name of the deer forest, the river and the loch at its foot. Gaelic 'Cuilion' means holly tree.

5 After the pass, the track goes through a gate into plantations, then bends right to slant down the side of Strath Carron. At a Scottish Rights of Way Society signpost, follow the main track ahead towards Achnashellach. A clear-felled area gives views to the left, then the trees are bigger until just before you cross a bridge to a mobile phone mast. Fork left, just before a second mast, and descend gently to reach the junction above Achnashellach Station.

WHAT TO LOOK OUT FOR

The hill on the left as you enter Coire Lair is Fuar Tholl. A rocky projection seen from Glen Carron is known as Wellington's Nose, in commemoration of the duke who defeated Napoleon in 1815. From Coire Lair, it reveals itself as the top of the steep Mainreachan Buttress. The first climbers in the 1960s found classic routes of middling difficulty. Today, it's climbed even when covered in winter ice.

Following the Diabaig Coast Path

A walk above Loch Torridon in the footsteps of the fairy folk – the legendary Duine Sithe.

DISTANCE 9.5 miles (15.3km)   **MINIMUM TIME** 6hrs

ASCENT/GRADIENT 1,805ft (550m) ▲▲▲   **LEVEL OF DIFFICULTY** +++

PATHS Narrow, rough and wet in places, no stiles

LANDSCAPE Rocky knolls and small lochans

SUGGESTED MAP OS Explorer 433 Torridon – Beinn Eighe & Liathach

START/FINISH Grid reference: NG 842073

DOG FRIENDLINESS Keep on lead passing Alligin Shuas and near sheep

PARKING Wester Alligin, pull-off on side road near Alligin River

PUBLIC TOILETS Torridon village

New Year's Eve in Wester Ross is a time when old songs are sung, whisky is drunk (not all of it approved by the exciseman either) and tales are told in both English and Gaelic. Over the years these stories mature and grow, and also change location, so that the tailor who lost his hump to the fairies lived not only in Scotland, but in Ireland and even Italy. Today it is categorised as 'folktale type 503'.

Fairy Tales and Ghosts

Many of the tales told in Alligin take place in the knolly, magical ground on the way to Diabaig. One story concerns two villagers who were bringing whisky for the New Year from Gairloch by way of the coast path. They heard wonderful music and came upon a cave in the hill where the fairy people had started their Hogmanay celebrations a few hours early. Fascinated, the man with the keg crept closer and closer until he was actually inside, whereupon the cave closed up and disappeared. A year later the other man came back, found the cave open and dragged his friend out across the threshold. The friend thought he'd been in there only a few minutes, but of the whisky he carried there was no trace.

At the top of the hill road is tiny Lochan Dearg, and here there is a ghost that appears only to people bearing his own name, Murdo Mackenzie. The kilted spirit, one of the Mackenzies of Gairloch, was slain by a Torridon MacDonald and buried somewhere near by.

Horse Tales and Fairy Folk

Loch Diabaigas Airde (Point ③) is haunted by the water spirit called the kelpie. This appears as a magnificent white horse, but if you mount it, the horse gallops rapidly into the loch and you're never seen again. That is, unless you just happen to have a bridle that's made of pure silver to tame it. Another kelpie lives in the Lochan Toll nam Biast, the Lochan of the Beast Hole, at the back of Beinn Alligin.

Fairy music has been heard above the gorge of the Alligin burn. So, to protect yourself from the Duine Sithe, be polite, but don't accept food

LOCH TORRIDON

from them. At best it'll be cow dung, at worst it'll enslave you for ever. Carry iron, oatmeal or a groundsel root for protection, and a cry of 'am monadh oirbh, a' bheistein' ('back to the hill, you wee beastie') is effective. Approaching Alligin Shuas, walk carefully past Cnoc nan Sithe, the Fairy Knoll, so as not to disturb them.

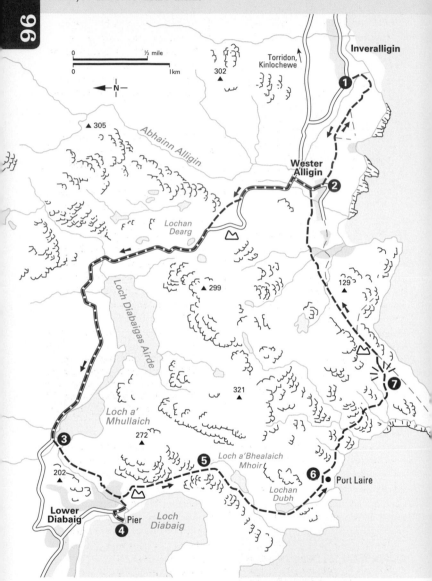

WALK 96 DIRECTIONS

❶ From the parking place, follow the road over the Abhainn Alligin river. A path leads along the shoreline for 100yds (91m) and then makes its way up right among sandstone outcrops. Bear left underneath a power line to join the corner of a tarmac driveway. Keep ahead to reach Wester Alligin.

2 Turn up the road and then left, on the road for Diabaig. As the road steepens, you can take a path to the right of power lines, rejoining the road across a high pass and then down past two lochs – Loch Diabaigas Airde and Loch a'Mhullaich – which are linked.

WHILE YOU'RE THERE

The National Trust for Scotland has a countryside centre at Torridon village, right below the frowning sandstone wall of Liathach (open April–September). It has audio-visual displays on the scenery and wildlife, with an unstaffed deer museum close by.

3 Turn off left, crossing the outflow of Loch a'Mhullaich on a footbridge. A clear path leads out along the high wall of a stream valley, then zig-zags down to a grey gate. Go down through woods to a white house, No 1 Diabaig. Turn right to reach the old stone pier.

4 Return up the path you just came down to pass a stone shed. Here a sign indicates a turn to the right, under an outcrop and between boulders. The path heads up to a small rock step with an arrow mark and a convenient tree root which you can use to hold on to. It then leads up to a gate in a fence and zig-zags into an open gully with a large crag on the right. At the top of this, it turns

WHAT TO LOOK OUT FOR

You'll pass grey Lewisian gneiss, worn into knolly shapes by glaciers. Look closely and you'll see it has coloured zig-zag stripes, like tweed. It is the oldest rock in Britain and is made of other, even older, rocks, bashed about through half the history of the planet.

right along a shelf, with still more crag above. The path slants gently down along the foot of another crag, then up to a col, with a last view of Diabaig.

5 From here the path is small but clear. It bends right to Loch a' Bhealaich Mhoir and then turns left below it to Lochan Dubh. Cross its outbound slant down left towards the cottage of Port Laire.

6 Pass above the house, then slant gradually up away from the sea. The path crosses the head of a bracken valley with a ruined croft house into a bleak knolly area out of sight of the sea. Cross two branches of a stream and go up to a cairn which marks where the path bears left up the spur. It now contours across a heathery meadow among the knolls, at the end of which it climbs pink rocks over a final spur. Just ahead is a gate in the deer fence.

WHERE TO EAT AND DRINK

Mrs Ross at Ben Bhraggie in Diabaig sometimes offers teas. Look for the notice outside the house. But carry food, as the next shop is at Torridon village.

7 The path leads along a level shelf with views to Liathach and the head of Loch Torridon, then it crosses a high, steep slope of heather. Near the end of this slope, the path forks. Take the upper branch, to go through a wide col. The rather boggy path heads down towards Wester Alligin. From a gate above the village, a faint path runs down in the direction of a distant green shed. It descends through a wood, then contours just above the village to reach the road above Point **2**. Retrace your steps to the start of the walk.

Flowerdale Falls

*Porpoise-watching along the Gairloch shore,
then up a rocky valley.*

DISTANCE 5.25 miles (8.4km)   **MINIMUM TIME** 2hrs 45min

ASCENT/GRADIENT 800ft (244m) ▲▲▲   **LEVEL OF DIFFICULTY** ✦✦✦

PATHS Tracks and smooth paths, mostly waymarked, no stiles

LANDSCAPE Gentle river valley and rocky coast

SUGGESTED MAP OS Explorer 433 Torridon – Beinn Eighe & Liathach
or 434 Gairloch & Loch Ewet

START/FINISH Grid reference: NG 807756 on OS Explorer 433

DOG FRIENDLINESS Keep on lead past Flowerdale House (as signs indicate)

PARKING Beach car park, southern end of Gairloch

PUBLIC TOILETS Walk start and Charlestown pier

On a calm day in 1809, three fisherman drowned in Loch Ewe when their small boat was attacked and sunk by a whale. These waters are among the best in Europe for cetaceans (whales, dolphins and porpoises). The Gulf Stream brings warm, plankton-rich water and the swirling currents around the islands bring nutrients to the surface. The plankton flourish; the fish eat the plankton; the whales and dolphins eat the fish.

Porpoise or Dolphin?

The strongest currents are at headlands and narrow sea passages, so these are good places to look for marine wildlife. Calm days are best, and early morning best of all when looking west, as the low sunlight shines off their wet backs. On most summer days, either the harbour porpoise or common dolphin – or possibly both – can be seen, given a little patience, in Loch Gairloch. But which is which? At 6ft (2m) or less, the porpoise is smaller. It has a short, stubby fin compared with the dolphin's more elegant one. Harbour porpoises are normally shy, but the ones at Gairloch are untypically friendly, often approaching boats. Endangered in the world as a whole, the ones at Gairloch are doing well and a Special Area of Conservation has been proposed for them here.

What the Future Holds

The whaling industry in Scotland ended in 1951, but serious threats remain. Dolphins and porpoises are accidentally caught in fishing nets and floating plastic rope and old nets are another danger. Pollution from agriculture and forestry releases heavy metals and pesticides into the ocean. Fish farming is also probably damaging the dolphins. More fish sewage than human sewage goes into the Hebridean seas, all of it untreated, and anti-fouling paint on fish farms contributes more chemicals, pesticides and antibiotics.

Cetaceans use sound signals for finding fish, as well as for communication. Interference comes from ships, dredging nets, seismic oil exploration and seal scammers – underwater beepers fitted to fish farms.

GAIRLOCH

We don't know how well the dolphins and porpoises are doing. The growth of the whale-spotting industry means that we are just starting to discover how the populations are growing or declining. Marine tourism is now a £9 million concern with 400 jobs. By going on one of these trips, you'll contribute to crucial research. A responsible boatman will not pursue the animals or steer into the middle of a group, but move quietly and wait for the dolphins to approach the boat.

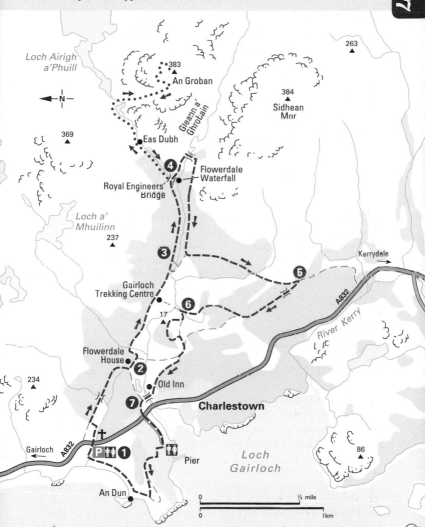

WALK 97 DIRECTIONS

1 Cross the road and head up to the right of the newer cemetery. Turn left at its corner, going into trees to a path above. Turn right until a footbridge leads on to a wide path that soon runs downhill. The main path bends right (green-top waymarker) and runs down to a tarred driveway.

2 Turn left along a tarred track to pass Flowerdale House. The track passes to the left of a lovely old barn and turns right at a sign for the waterfall to pass Gairloch Trekking Centre. In about 0.25 mile (400m) you pass a timber-surfaced bridge on the right.

3 Follow the main path ahead, still to the left of the stream to reach a footbridge built by the Royal Engineers, just before you get to Flowerdale Waterfall.

4 The path leads up past the waterfall to cross a footbridge above. It runs up into a wind-blown pine clump, then turns back down the valley. After another footbridge it joins a rough track. You pass a memorial to the blind piper of Gairloch, just before a forest road beside Point **3**. Turn left, away from the timber-surfaced bridge, through felled forest that's regenerating naturally (with birch, alder, pine, willow and rowan).

5 A blue-topped pole marks a path to the right with a footbridge. It leads through scrub birch and bracken with blue waymarker poles. The path bends right at an old fence cornerpost and goes down through bracken and birch to pass above and to the left of an enclosed field. Turn right underneath two large oak trees and cross a small stream to an earth track.

WHILE YOU'RE THERE

The Gairloch Marine Life Centre has a display on cetaceans, seals and seabirds. It runs two-hour cruises on the *Starquest*, where you'll see porpoises and seals, and possibly dolphins and minke whales. Every trip contributes to scientific knowledge of the wildlife populations. Cruises depend on the weather and are often fully booked.

---

6 Turn left for a few steps, until a small bracken path runs up to the right past a waymarked power pole. The path bends left under oaks, then drops to rejoin the earth track. This soon meets a larger track, which is the old road from Loch Maree to Gairloch. Turn right along this, through a couple of gates, to reach the Old Inn at Charlestown.

WHERE TO EAT AND DRINK

The Old Inn, beside the former bridge over the Abhainn Ghlas in Charlestown, offers live music, fresh local seafood (including a cook-what-you-catch service), a barbecue grill and outdoor tables. Dogs are allowed outdoors. The one thing it lacks is a sea view.

---

7 Cross the old bridge, and the main road, towards the pier. Turn right at the signpost for the beach, to a stepped path to the left of Gairloch Chandlery. The tarred path passes to the left of a pinewood, then turns right into the trees. It bends left and emerges to run along the spine of a small headland. Just before being carried out to sea it turns sharp right, and crosses above a rocky bay to the fort (An Dun). A duckboard path runs along the back of the beach, then turns right to the car park.

EXTENDING THE WALK

An Groban is a tough little hill of Lewisian gneiss. It makes a good extension to this walk, though the going can be surprisingly hard. Leave the main route just before the Royal Engineers' Bridge and take a rough path to the left to a rush-choked lochan. Cross the stream and zig-zag up grassy shelves to the summit. Return the same way to continue the walk.

Into Scotland's Great Wilderness

A pleasant walk around Loch Kernsary and down the Ewe — the country's shortest river.

DISTANCE 6.5 miles (10.4km) **MINIMUM TIME** 2hrs 45min

ASCENT/GRADIENT 250ft (76m) ▲▲▲ **LEVEL OF DIFFICULTY** ✦✦✦

PATHS Mostly good, but one short rough, wet section, 3 stiles

LANDSCAPE Moorland and loch side

SUGGESTED MAP OS Explorer 434 Gairloch & Loch Ewe

START/FINISH Grid reference: NG 857808

DOG FRIENDLINESS Close control on moorland and tracks carrying estate traffic

PARKING In Poolewe, just up B8057 side street

PUBLIC TOILETS At start

As you walk inland from Poolewe, you're entering one of the largest empty areas in Britain. Turn left instead of right at Kernsary Farm, and you can walk for two full days before you reach any road.

Great Wilderness

On the slight rise before Loch Kernsary, you get a surprise view right into the heart of this mountain wonderland. At the back of the view is A'Mhaighdean, the Maiden, Scotland's most remote mountain. It takes half a day's walk to get to this hill from anywhere. That walk will be along the edges of long dark lochs and under some very large crags. Beinn Lair has a quartzite cliff with an evil north-face gleam that's 3 miles (4.8km) wide, as big as the north face of Ben Nevis, but a whole lot less visited.

Behind A'Mhaighdean is An Teallach, called the Forge because of the cloudy vapours that stream across its semicircular ridge. That ridge has great lumpy towers to scramble round, 3ft-wide (1m) ridges to walk along and an edge that if you fall off it will take about four seconds before you land on anything at all.

All this belongs to a gentleman from Holland called Paul van Vlissingen. In 1993 he signed an agreement with the Mountaineering Council of Scotland that first set out the principle of responsible access for all. Deer stalking restrictions would be only on days when deer stalking was actually taking place — a step forward when walkers were sometimes threatened with high-velocity rifle fire from August to February. The estate also undertook not to build any new landrover tracks. As a result, business here is carried out on foot, by boat and by pony. This Letterewe Accord became the foundation of the new century's access legislation.

Rights of Way

The paths used on this walk are, as it happens, on established rights of way. Even so, you'll notice a sudden change near the head of Loch Kernsary. The first part of the path has been rebuilt by the National Trust for Scotland, using their members' annual subscriptions. One new member pays for about 2ft (60cm) of path. At the edge of National Trust land the path repairs stop abruptly, mid-bog.

In Scotland, no one is obliged to build or maintain footpaths. The surprising thing, if you walk all of these walks, is how many people are doing it anyway. Paths in this book are looked after by charities such as the John Muir Trust, by Scottish Natural Heritage and Forest Enterprise, by private landowners in Argyll and Atholl, by regional and community councils and groups of ordinary walkers.

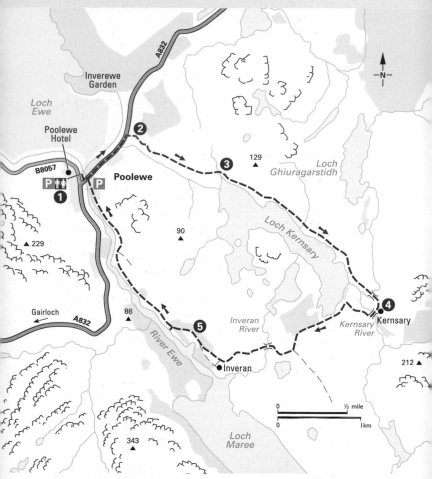

WALK 98 DIRECTIONS

1 A kissing gate beside the public toilets leads to a path that crosses the Marie Curie Field of Hope to the main road. Turn left to cross the bridge over the River Ewe and then head all the way through the village. At the 40mph

derestriction sign, there's a white cottage on the right. Beside it, a tarred trackway has a Scottish Rights of Way Society signpost for Kernsary.

2 Follow the track over a cattle grid to a new track that forks off to the left. After 50yds (46m), keep ahead on a path with a wall on its left. It passes through a kissing gate into Cnoc na Lise, the Garden Hill. This has been replanted as a community wood with oak and birch trees. Another kissing gate leads out of the young wood. The good, reconstructed path runs through gorse and then under a low-voltage power line. It crosses a low spur to a fine view of Loch Kernsary and the remote, steep-sided hills of the Great Wilderness, then goes over a stream to the loch side.

> ### WHAT TO LOOK OUT FOR
>
> The River Ewe may be short, but it's very full of salmon. As well as stony piers for anglers, you'll see artificial rapids where partial dams force the water into a central channel. Salmon will lie up in the pools below, waiting for rain to fill up the river, instead of proceeding immediately into Loch Maree.

3 The path follows the left-hand shore of the loch, passing through patches of birch scrub. After a stile, near the loch head, it suddenly deteriorates, becoming a braided trod of boulder and bog. Once past the loch head, slant to the left down a meadow to find a footbridge under an oak tree. Head up, with a fence on your right, to join a track beside Kernsary farm.

> ### WHERE TO EAT AND DRINK
>
> The Poolewe Hotel was the original village inn. It has a restaurant, with fine sunset views (across the car park) and offers lighter meals in the bar/bistro (children are welcome, but not dogs). Opposite the car park is the Bridge House Coffee Shop and Gallery.

4 Turn right, through a gate. Follow the track past the farm, to a culvert crossing of the Kernsary River. This becomes a ford only after heavy rain. If needed, you will find a footbridge 70yds (64m) upstream. After crossing, turn right on a smooth track. The new track bears left, away from Loch Kernsary towards the hollow containing Loch Maree. After the bridge over the Inveran River is a gate with a ladder stile. Signs welcoming responsible walkers (and even cyclists) reflect the principles of the Letterewe Accord. Soon come the first views of Loch Maree. The driveway of Inveran house joins from the left and the track starts being tarred.

5 At a sign, 'Blind Corners', a green track on the left leads down to the point where the narrow loch imperceptibly becomes a wide river. Return to the main track and follow it above and then beside the River Ewe. It reaches Poolewe just beside the bridge.

> ### WHILE YOU'RE THERE
>
> One of Scotland's greatest gardens lies beside the Great Wilderness. In 1862, the Gairloch Mackenzies found themselves free of feuding Macleods and MacDonalds and turned their attention to gardening. Osgood Mackenzie planted trees to create shelter belts against the salt winds, improved (or rather, created) the soil using vast quantities of seaweed hauled up from the beach by basket, and found that the mild western climate would grow exotic plants from Chile and South Africa. Now managed by the National Trust for Scotland, Inverewe Garden is one of Ross-shire's most surprising and popular attractions.

Strathpeffer and the Rogie Falls

From a Victorian spa to a salmon-leaping waterfall.

DISTANCE 10 miles (16.1km)	MINIMUM TIME 5hrs

ASCENT/GRADIENT 1,200ft (365m) ▲▲▲   LEVEL OF DIFFICULTY +++

PATHS Waymarked paths and track, no stiles

LANDSCAPE Plantation, wild forest and riverside

SUGGESTED MAP OS Explorer 437 Ben Wyvis & Strathpeffer

START/FINISH Grid reference: NH 483582

DOG FRIENDLINESS Keep on lead for section past Loch Kinellan

PARKING Main square, Strathpeffer

PUBLIC TOILETS At start, Contin (Point ❹) and Rogie Falls car parks

Stand on the suspension bridge at Rogie Falls between July and September, at a time when the river's fairly full, and you might catch a glimpse of the silver flash of a leaping salmon. It's a thrilling sight to see a 3ft (1m) long fish attempting to swim up against the force of the water. Eventually it'll make it, or else discover the easy way round – the fish ladder carved out of the rock on the right-hand side. But if you'd been here 200 years ago, that single salmon would have been a dozen or even a hundred. During the autumn run, the falls must have appeared almost to flow in reverse, an upstream current of flashing fish.

The Rise and Fall of the Salmon

Salmon was once food for the taking, like blackberries today. You went down to the river and took as many as you thought you could eat. Smoked above the peat fire of the black houses, it was a staple food through the winter. Farm workers even used their industrial muscle to demand that they shouldn't be obliged to eat salmon more than three times a week.

Today, however, this majestic fish is steadily heading towards extinction. In the last ten years, the catch in Scotland's rivers has shrunk from 1,200 tons to 200 tons. The main reason for this has been netting in the estuaries, and in their feeding grounds around the Arctic pack ice. Angling clubs have bought up and discontinued estuary netting rights. The international community still squabbles on about the Arctic drift nets, and now a new danger to wild fish is posed by parasites and disease leaking out of the sea cages of Scotland's 340 fish farms.

Seven Ages of a Trout

Egg, fry, alevin, parr, smolt, salmon, kelt – these are the seven ages of the salmon's extraordinary life. For one or two years it behaves like a trout, hanging in the still water behind a boulder and waiting for food to float by. But then in one of nature's changes, as striking in its way as a caterpillar becoming a butterfly or a tadpole becoming a frog, its scales become silver and it turns downstream, totally altering its body chemistry to enable it to

Overleaf: Hillside scenery above Strathpeffer (Walk 99)

live in salt water. Its new name of 'smolt' is probably a reference to silver poured from the furnace.

Return of the Salmon

Four or five years later, now called a salmon, it returns. We don't know how it navigates from Greenland back to the Cromarty Firth. Once back in Scotland, it identifies the outflow of the Conon by the taste of the water and works its way upstream, taking all the correct turnings to return to the patch of gravel where it was once an egg and an alevin.

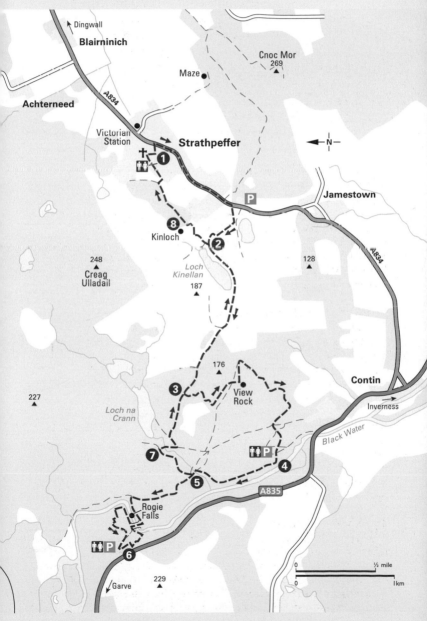

WALK 99 DIRECTIONS

❶ Head along the main road towards Contin. When you reach the edge of the town, turn right at a metal signpost for Garve then, at a bend in the lane, turn left, following another signpost.

❷ Follow track to the left of Loch Kinellan. As it bends right, keep ahead up a path beside tall broom bushes to the corner of a plantation. Here you join a larger track leading into the forest. Continue for 0.5 mile (800m) until it reaches a signpost.

❸ Turn left for View Rock on a good path with green waymarkers. At View Rock, a side-path diverts to the right for the viewpoint, then rejoins. After a long descent, ignore a green path turning off to the left and follow green waymarkers downhill. At a forest road go straight over beside a signpost. The path crosses two more forest roads to Contin Forest car park.

❹ At the end of the car park you'll pick up a wide path signed 'River Walk'. Where red waymarkers turn back right, keep ahead on a rougher path with deer head markers. It bends up right beside a stream to a forest road. Turn left, signposted 'Garve', and in another 80yds (73m) bear left, heading slightly downhill.

❺ Go on for 600yds (549m), when a small track on the left is signed 'Rogie Falls Bridge'.

At its foot, cross a spectacular footbridge below the falls and turn right, upstream. The path has green waymarkers and after 0.25 mile (400m) bends left away from the river. It crosses rocky ground to a junction. Turn up right, to Rogie Falls car park.

❻ Leave the car park through a wooden arch and follow green waymarkers back to the bridge. Retrace the outward route to Point **❺** and turn sharp left up another forest road. It leads uphill to where a much fainter track crosses.

❼ Turn right down the smaller track to pass between obstructing boulders, to a signpost. Turn left , signed 'Strathpeffer'. After 600yds (549m) it reaches the signpost at Point **❸**. Keep ahead and retrace the outward route to Point **❷**. Turn left on the tarred lane, which becomes a track. At Kinloch house bear right, then turn left through a kissing gate, with a second one beyond leading into a plantation with a signpost for Strathpeffer.

❽ Follow the main path ahead until you see Strathpeffer down on the right. At the next junction bear right down the wood edge and turn right into the town. The street on the left leads past a church with a square steeple, where you turn down right to the main square.

The Gloup Loop

*An easy circular walk around Mull Head,
a Local Nature Reserve.*

DISTANCE 4 miles (6.4km)	**MINIMUM TIME** 2hrs 30min

ASCENT/GRADIENT 93ft (28m) ▲▲▲   **LEVEL OF DIFFICULTY** +++

PATHS Continuous, 6 kissing gates

LANDSCAPE Moorland, cliff edge

SUGGESTED MAP OS Explorer 461 Orkney – East Mainland

START/FINISH Grid reference: HY 590079

DOG FRIENDLINESS Dogs must be kept under control due to wildlife

PARKING Mull Head car park

PUBLIC TOILETS Nearest is 4 miles (6.4km) at Sandi Sand

This walk follows the story of the landscape. The Gloup for a start – from the Old Norse word 'gluppa' meaning 'chasm' – is not the only collapsed cave in Orkney, but at 100ft (30m) deep, it is the most visited and a remarkable feature formed entirely by the force of the North Sea. The parish of Deerness where it lies is a peninsula joined to Orkney's Mainland only by a very narrow spit and the land has been affected constantly by people and the climate.

The *Orkneyinga Saga* mentions Deerness several times and nearby excavations by archaeologists have turned up an Iron Age settlement, a Pictish farm, obvious Norse remains and a hog-back gravestone in the kirkyard dating from AD 1100. The first people to have an impact on Mull Head were neolithic. The ancient scrubland was grazed by animals, then Norsemen played their part, followed in their turn by folk 'paring' – stripping off the top soil for use elsewhere – during the 18th century. Thus Mull Head has been continuously grazed, creating a mature heather heath and very impoverished soil.

Nature's Influence

Mull Head was declared a Local Nature Reserve by Orkney Islands Council in 1993, the ninth in Scotland, and because it has been spared modern agricultural 'improvement' it is now very rich. The rocks themselves, which you will see as you walk the headland, are 350 million years old. There are two types: Eday flags, which are coarse red sandstone, and Rousay flags at the south end of the reserve, both formed from conditions when Lake Orcadie covered this land. Visible ripples in the stone are characteristic of formation in shallow flowing water.

The plants which survive here are determined by the location too – how close to the sea they are, how fertile the soil is where they grow, how marshy it is and how influenced by humans. Plants that have to withstand the salt spray at the cliff edge, such as sea pink or thrift, will hug the ground. As well as salt tolerators and salt haters, plants which prefer marshy conditions, such as grass of Parnassus, grow here.

Mull Head has never been ploughed, although Clu Ber, the first range of cliffs you will see, has been burned, cultivated and fertilised to allow grazing for stock, and even though this was done generations ago, the heather's destruction means that grass and different herb species thrive. The final influence on the plants are the activities of some of the birds. Islands of lush grass found on the heath are where great black-backed gulls roost each night, the grasses benefiting because they fertilise the soil.

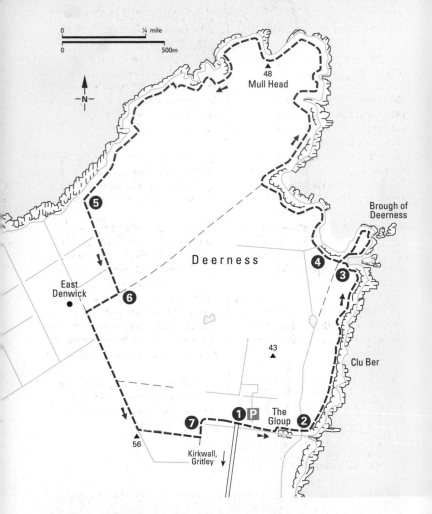

WALK 100 DIRECTIONS

① Leave the car park at the right-hand corner, where there is an information plaque. Follow the direction sign along the gravel path to The Gloup, where you will find two viewing platforms.

② Past The Gloup you will see a red-painted kissing gate and a directional sign pointing left; this will lead you along a grassy footpath to the Brough of Deerness (pronounced broch), but a more interesting route, perhaps, is straight ahead and